The Supreme Court on Church and State

The Supreme Court on Church and State

edited by
ROBERT S. ALLEY
University of Richmond

New York Oxford
OXFORD UNIVERSITY PRESS
1988

Oxford University Press
Oxford New York Toronto
Delhi Bombay Calcutta Madras Karachi
Petaling Jaya Singapore Hong Kong Tokyo
Nairobi Dar es Salaam Cape Town
Melbourne Auckland

and associated companies in
Berlin Ibadan

Published by Oxford University Press, Inc.,
200 Madison Avenue, New York, New York 10016

Library of Congress Cataloging-in-Publication Data
The Supreme Court on church and state / edited by Robert S. Alley.
p. cm.
Updated ed. of: The Supreme Court on church & state / edited by
Joseph Tussman. 1962.
ISBN 0-19-505028-2. ISBN 0-19-505029-0 (pbk.)
1. Freedom of religion—United States—Cases.
I. Alley, Robert S., 1932- . II. United States. Supreme Court. III. Supreme Court on
church & state.
KF4783.A52S87 1988
342.73′0852—dc19
[347.302852]
87-23294
CIP

3 5 7 9 8 6 4

Printed in the United States of America
on acid-free paper

This volume is dedicated
to the memory of

Richard Levinson,

my liberating friend, who, with his partner William Link,
through a distinguished succession of
television dramas,
translated the principles of the Bill of Rights
into the form of popular art.

Preface

This edition of the volume edited by Joseph Tussman has much the same rationale as the original. I share the conviction that the work of the Supreme Court should be available to the general public. As Tussman noted in his preface, the Court may be more important as an educational institution than as a governing tribunal. Certainly, the wide range of political philosophy contained in the decisions is a national treasure. In no area is this more clearly the case than on the subject of the religion clauses of the First Amendment.

I am in debt to Professor Tussman, who made available a 1962 book, now tattered, that contributed in important ways to both my teaching and my writing. Admiration for the mind and work of James Madison was given birth through the life and practice of my father, Reuben E. Alley. Respect for the Supreme Court grew from the influence of *Brown v. Board of Education,* Martin Luther King, Jr., and civil rights attorney Oliver Hill. Devotion to the study of the Court's decisions on the religion clauses emerged from my own distressing public school experiences involving "released time" on school property and, later, the impact of the writings of Leo Pfeffer, Henry Steele Commager, and Justice Hugo Black. My wife, Norma, master teacher of young children, our sons Bob and John, and our daughter-in-law Vickie have encouraged me and contributed a sense of understanding of those citizens most directly affected by the Court decisions, American youth.

In this current endeavor, the addition of twenty-five years of Supreme Court thinking to the 1962 volume, I am grateful to a number of generous friends for their time and criticism. Particular words of appreciation are due to Professors A. E. Dick Howard of the University of Virginia Law School, William Lee Miller of the University of Virginia, J. Martin Ryle of the University of Richmond, and Robert

E. Shepherd of the University of Richmond Law School. A special thanks is due my friend and associate in many things academic, Professor Irby B. Brown, whose humor and style are ever invigorating.

Richmond, Va.
December 1987

R.S.A.

Preface to 1962 Edition

"Preoccupation by our people with the constitutionality, instead of with the wisdom, of legislation or executive action is preoccupation with a false value."

These words of Justice Frankfurter, emerging, as they do, from a lifetime of involvement with the theory and practice of government in America pose something of a challenge to anyone who sets about to increase that preoccupation. No one, I suppose, would argue that we should not be concerned with the wisdom of our actions, and perhaps the warning is only against excess. But when all allowances are made the suggestion still remains that constitutional-mindedness is something of a spiritual disorder.

This, of course, raises some questions about the place of the Supreme Court in American life, and I think it would not be unfair to Justice Frankfurther's position to see in it the suggestion that if, indeed, all were well with us the Supreme Court would be a far less interesting and significant institution than it is.

But questions of wisdom and of constitutionality are not so easily separated, and it is because he is aware of this that Justice Frankfurter is also a leading advocate of judicial "self-restraint." The relation of constitutionality to wisdom is a complex problem. Some degree of folly is "legitimate" and the remedy is not the court but the "political" process. But it is also the case that, on occasion, what we think wise may be unconstitutional; and there we chafe at the restraint of rule and principle, robe and parchment. Here is all our twentieth-century electronic equipment, there the encumbering legacy of the eighteenth century. Are we then, where we are concerned with constitutionality, preoccupied with a false value?

In the end the answer to this question takes us to the heart of the theory of the state and the theory of moral behavior. And it is because it takes us there that the study of the Supreme Court is especially rewarding.

Foreign observers, Tocqueville among them, have been struck with our constitutional preoccupation. It is a fact of American life. But its significance has not always been grasped. Some countries seem old countries even when their governments are new. But ours seems young even as it ages. Put shortly, they have traditions; we have a charter. We are a people of the Text and the Gloss.

It is not through perversity or accident that constitutionality looms large in our lives. It is a reflection of the fact that our political life has not floated easily on a stable, homogeneous cultural foundation. We have not had the deep-rooted moral consensus based in centuries of a common history; we have not had an established church. The result is that we have had to pay more explicit attention to the moral basis of political life.

The constitution, the idea of constitutionality, has thus come to occupy a crucial position. It stands somewhere between the daily products of political machinery and the moral sense of a culture; it is a peculiar merging of the political and the moral, and it gives to our politics a moral flavor and to our moral controversies a political form. On the one hand it keeps politics always subject to moral demands and prevents it from moving off on its own into a condition in which it would need to rest more heavily on sanction or coercion. On the other hand, providing the common ground on which our political life is played, it makes less urgent the drives for religious and moral orthodoxy and sustains such separation as is possible of church and state.

The constitution is thus both a political and a moral charter and, seen in this light, our preoccupation with it is hardly an addiction to a false value. There are, to be sure, diseases into which it is all too easy to fall. We can worship the letter at the expense of the spirit or presume too much in the name of the spirit. We can disguise our self-serving as law-mindedness or can develop casuistry to the point of shamelessness and hypocrisy. These are tendencies to which moral life is always prone, and it is just at this point that the Supreme Court has a special, guiding role.

We look to the court as the arbiter of constitutionality. Whether intended or not, it has established this position and holds it against recurrent challenge and even, at times, its own misgivings. Day in, day out it faces the question of whether the actions of government are within the bounds of constitutional propriety. The particular problem may be about the meaning of free speech, or double jeopardy, or equal protection or due process, and this is interesting enough. But as it deals with these problems it must also deal with questions about the nature of rules and principles, the proper art of interpretation, and the role of a constitution in a democratic society. Thus the court deals not only with the principles of the constitution but also with the principles of constitutionalism; and I know of no better way of coming to grips with the fundamental problems of political life than by sharing in these preoccupations of the court.

I am not sure that the Supreme Court is not more important as an educational institution than as a governing tribunal. It is, of course, important for what it does. But it is even more important for what it thinks and says as it does it. Decade after decade some of our most powerful minds have grappled with the most urgent and perplexing issues of American life. Its judicial character—although it is far from being simply a "court"—brings it within the tradition of adversary proceedings and requires that it support its decisions with carefully stated opinions. These are subjected to a powerful barrage of criticism and analysis, professional and amateur, from many points of view. The court must give reasons for what it does. It must display its wisdom. It must demonstrate capacity to grasp the baffling details of a concrete situation, give meaning to principles which seem applicable, make difficult consequential decisions—and do all this with the awareness of the implications of its activity for the theory of the state and for democratic political life. Moreover, the tradition of dissenting opinions makes publicly apparent the conflicting strains within the court, develops counterargument of great power, and pushes the court into greater depth of analysis—to everyone's profit.

In the course of its way of life the Supreme Court produces a body of literature quite unique in quality and significance. It welds fact and theory in a context of action. The study of this literature is exciting and rewarding. Unfortunately, however, several things contribute to the fact that it remains, for most people, an unexplored domain.

First, because it is a court its activity brings it within the purview of the legal profession which, to some extent, guards it as a mystery which only the elect can approach. It is of special concern to lawyers, and they study it in a special way. But it is not entirely *their* oracle, although the habit of seeing it this way tends to warn others off.

Political scientists also deal with the court, generally in the form of the study of "constitutional law"; and it is in this form that most nonlawyers who read or have read opinions come to do so. In spite of the variety of approaches, it is a testimony to the intrinsic quality of Supreme Court opinions that such courses almost invariably stand as a high-point in college education. But even here, the dominance of a professional attitude does little to dispel the technical and professional aura which shrouds the court. So that it is generally assumed, incorrectly I believe, that only after hard technical training can one understand what the court is talking about or profitably read its opinions.

Second, not unrelated to what has just been said, is the astonishing unavailability of Supreme Court opinions. There are, of course, complete sets of Supreme Court reports—in three different editions—available in law libraries and even general libraries. But these are forbidding to the nonexpert and are not really available for convenient and leisurely perusal. In addition, there are various collections of opinions or of selections from opinions, volumes of "great" or "leading" decisions or the collected opinions of some Justice of unusual stature or interest. These are all useful, especially for the particular purpose for which they have been created. But they do not serve the general purpose at which this series aims.

Suppose, for example, that one would want to read the great controversy over the Smith Act as it bears on the communication activities of communists; or the great case involving the use of public funds to pay transportation costs for parochial school children. These are generally available only in fragments in extant collections. One is driven to the sets of complete reports, and these, as I said, are generally inaccessible and forbidding. The Dennis and Everson cases do not deserve this fate and we cannot afford this form of burial.

JOSEPH TUSSMAN

Contents

The Supreme Court on Church and State

Introduction

The opening sixteen words of the Constitution's First Amendment, "Congress shall make no law respecting an establishment of religion, or prohibiting the free exercise thereof," are the subject of this volume.

The reader quickly perceives that two clauses in the amendment refer to religion. The Supreme Court has been particularly careful in distinguishing between two types of cases—establishment and free exercise—and the arrangement of cases in this volume follows that pattern.

In supplying the massive literature on church and state matters in this century, the Court has relied heavily on the founders James Madison and Thomas Jefferson. Not only have the justices focused upon the role of these men in the evolution of the First Amendment, they have also regularly related their decisions and dissents to Jefferson's 1802 letter to the Danbury Baptist Association, in which he created a phrase to define the Amendment as "building a wall of separation between church and state." Often since 1947 the Court has focused upon the meaning of Jefferson's descriptive phrase and its appropriate application to the amendment itself. In truth, the Court's words on the Religion Clauses since 1947 are hardly comprehensible apart from that particular historical perspective.

Ratification of the Bill of Rights was accomplished in 1791. The amendments did not apply to the states, and in *Barron v. Baltimore* (1833) the Supreme Court ruled that the Religion Clauses were not enforceable against the states. (Coincidentally, it was in that same year that Massachusetts, the last state to retain vestiges of church establishment in its constitution, saw fit to remove that condition in the commonwealth.) In 1845 the Court decided in *Permoli v. New Orleans* that a priest convicted by the state of Louisiana for conducting a funeral at an unlicensed chapel had no recourse to the First Amendment. It was only after the ratification of the Fourteenth Amendment in 1868 that the Court was enabled to apply the Bill of Rights to the states, although it did not do so immediately. In specific language it was *Cantwell v. Connecticut* (1940) that nationalized the Religion Clauses. Quoting the First Amendment prohibitions, Justice Roberts wrote concerning a Connecticut law that denied free exercise of religion: "The Fourteenth Amendment has rendered the legislatures of the states as incompetent as Congress to enact such laws."

While there have been justices and constitutional scholars who have debated that conclusion and continue so to do, the weight of Supreme Court decisions in all Bill of Rights cases in the past half century is so overwhelming as to make alternative readings unlikely in the future.

Respecting an Establishment

As Joseph Tussman wrote, "Everyone agrees that under the First Amendment there can be no official church nor even, short of that, a specially favored church." The problem lies with areas of cooperation and aid in the "public interest."

In the first major establishment case, *Everson,* the focus was on public support for parochial schools. Writing for the majority, Justice Black noted: "The 'establishment of religion' clause of the First Amendment means at least this: Neither a state nor the Federal Government can set up a church. Neither can pass laws which aid one religion, aid all religions, or prefer one religion over another. . . . In the words of Jefferson, the clause against establishment of religion by law was intended to erect 'a wall of separation between church and state.'" In this sentiment the four dissenting justices agreed. But the five-member majority was able to uphold New Jersey's use of public transportation for parochial schoolchildren as in the public interest. The minority felt the wall had been breached.

As more and more cases have emerged that revolve around parochial schools, the Court has wrestled with means to accommodate them. In 1970 Chief Justice Burger argued for what he termed "benevolent neutrality." Nevertheless, while a vocal Court minority sees merit in greater flexibility in such cases, the Court majority has remained reasonably consistent in denying tax funds for any but the most limited of child benefits. In the process the justices have developed a three-part test for establishment—secular legislative purpose, primary effect, and excessive entanglement. Justice Harlan added a fourth, political divisiveness, in his concurring opinion in *Walz*. In 1977 Justice Stevens suggested, in *Wolmer v. Walter*, scrapping all the tests and returning to the *Everson* principle, thereby discouraging states that would "search for new ways of achieving forbidden ends."

The Court has been far more lenient in the several church-related college cases that have commanded its attention. The pragmatic dimension of this attitude may be found in *Tilton v. Richardson* and *Roemer v. Board of Public Works of Maryland.*

Establishment also entered the picture with respect to public education in the form of prayer and Bible reading. No cases besides *Brown v. Board of Education* have engendered such heated public debate as *Engel* and *Schempp*. The Court has remained consistent in asserting the unconstitutional nature of religious observances sanctioned by public schools. In recent years a new strategy has surfaced among those anxious to place prayer in the schools. It is now being argued that religious establishment has occurred in the form of "secularism." Further, it is contended that freedom of conscience has been jeopardized for Christians attending such schools. This tactic may move future cases into the free exercise arena.

Within the past year the nation has been witness to two critically important lower court decisions, one in Church Hill, Tennessee and the other in Mobile, Alabama. Both had to do with education and in each instance the issue was the definition of "secular." In Tennessee the judge found for the plaintiffs who argued that the curriculum of the public schools established secularism as a religion and denied their children free exercise thereof. He did not require the schools to alter their offering, but rather ordered the school board to pay for alternative schooling for the affected children. In Alabama, the parents involved on the losing side in *Wallace v. Jaffree* were persuaded to argue that the textbooks of the public schools taught secular humanism, thereby violating the First Amendment. Judge Brevard Hand found for the plaintiffs and ordered a select group of texts removed from the schools. Pending an appeal, the order was temporarily stayed. In the week of August 23, 1987, both Hull and Hand were reversed by U.S. Courts of Appeals. The Sixth Circuit Court ruled that the Tennessee parents' claim that their children might be led to conclusions contrary to their religious beliefs was "not sufficient to establish an unconstitutional burden." A three-judge panel of the Eleventh Circuit ruled two days later that Judge Hand should dissolve his ruling and dismiss the suit. The Circuit judges wrote that Hand's order had turned the neutrality toward religion required by the First Amendment "into an affirmative obligation to speak about religion."

Anticipated appeals in both cases will rely heavily on a growing and formidable school of "nonpreferentialists." Its advocates argue that the First Amendment merely forbids any single religion from being established and in no way denies the right to create a general or plural establishment. This position was espoused in Justice Rehnquist's *Wallace v. Jaffree* dissent. Constitutional authority Leonard Levy describes nonpreferentialism as "a plausible but fundamentally defective interpretation of the establishment clause to prove that its framers had no intention of prohibiting government aid to all denominations or to religion on a nonpreferential basis."[1] (See page 13 for a further examination of this matter.)

Prohibiting the Free Exercise

As the record indicates, free exercise cases, until now, have been less common. The earliest was *Reynolds v. United States,* in which Jefferson's "separation" was first employed by the Court. Early decisions concerning the Mormons, later cases involving Jehovah's Witnesses, and, more recently, considerations of the Amish community in *Yoder,* have generally been outside the mainstream of public interest. To be sure, from time to time, justices have identified free exercise implications in a variety of the establishment cases. But by nature the free exercise clause most often has been invoked to protect a minority. It remains to be seen whether the new wave of challenges directed at prevailing values in the public education sector as well as religious objections to laws on subjects such as abortion will ignite a new series of free exercise cases.

In nearly every case involving free exercise, the Court has been required to weigh the conflicting interests of the state on the one hand, and the petitioning minority on the other. In a recent case, see, for instance, *Yoder v. Wisconsin.*

First Amendment Origins

Joseph Tussman's comments in his introduction remain remarkable fresh twenty-five years later. He wrote:

> It is, I hope, hardly necessary to add, as we try to understand and deal wisely with the problems of religious freedom, that the freedom and dignity of the nonbeliever—the agnostic or the atheist—is as precious and as much to be protected as that of the believer. Earlier, we would have called ourselves a "Christian nation." More recently the phrase is a "religious nation." Someday, we may come to think of ourselves as a spiritual nation, deeply involved in the quest for truth about the nature of the universe and man's [and woman's] place in it.

These comments put in mind the early history of colonial efforts to deal with religious establishment and free exercise, beginning with the remarkable career of Roger Williams of Rhode Island. The Supreme Court has been so consistently conscious of that heritage that a survey of the events surrounding the writing of the First Amendment provides an appropriate prologue to the justices' words.

History binds James Madison inextricably to the First Amendment and its "Religion Clauses." The classic statement of his position on religion and the state is to be found in "Memorial and Remonstrance," written in the spring of 1785. Madison's later correspondence makes it clear that he considered the "Memorial" to be his definitive argument for freedom of conscience. As such it is an unequaled source for understanding the intention of the First Amendment. The principles that guided Madison were evident, however, in his earliest political thought. And the entire debate over religious liberty, in turn, had its roots in a clash of ideas and wills that began to emerge in Virginia in the 1740's.

The Virginia Commonwealth, like most other seventeenth-century colonial experiments, accepted the concept of an established religion inherited from English practice. But because the various colonizing efforts were undertaken by Puritans and Separatists, as well as Anglicans, no common pattern of establishment emerged. Massachusetts created a theocratic model with the rule of the "saints." Other colonies tended to adopt systems that subordinated religious institutions to temporal power. With the striking exceptions of Roger Williams' tenure in Rhode Island, along with the colonies of New Jersey and Delaware, the universal practice was that of establishment. To be sure, there were degrees of rigor in implementation, but this cannot obscure the single pattern. By 1700 a sufficient variety of Protestant expression was present to require, even in the most restrictive colonies, a degree of toleration. The concept of toleration was quite compatible with a liberalized definition of establishment because neither presumed freedom of conscience as a natural right. Even the enlightened policies of Pennsylvania suffered from a common flaw ("All persons who profess to believe in Jesus Christ . . . shall be capable to serve this government in any capacity. . . .") described by Madison in the "Memorial." "Who does not see that the same authority which can establish Christianity, in exclusion of all other Religions, may establish with the same ease any particular sect of Christians, in exclusion of all other Sects?"

In the case of Virginia, the Church of England was the established religion. Dissenting Protestants were resisted, and laws requiring Anglican observances were commonplace. The Act of Toleration of 1689, passed by Parliament in London, had little effect upon Virginia practice. As late as 1740 there was scant evidence of Protestant activity outside the Anglican communion. However, in 1748 a Presbyterian minister, Samuel Davies, became the leader of a small band of dissenters just north of

Richmond. Davies insisted that the restrictions imposed by the colonial government on his activities violated the Act of Toleration. By the time Davies left Virginia in 1759, he had prevailed, and Presbyterians were tolerated according to English law. Davies' success was in large measure dependent upon his strong support of the war against the French and Indians. Further, the heavy population of Presbyterians in the western mountain areas that separated the more settled towns and villages from the "hostiles" was calculated to cause officials to develop a more accepting policy toward that denomination.

By the 1760s Baptists had moved into the colony; many of them refused to live under the restrictions of "toleration," insisting instead upon total religious freedom. Refusing to obtain licenses from colonial authorities to preach, many Baptist clergy were beaten and jailed. It was this practice in a neighboring county that prompted the young Madison, only recently returned from his studies at Princeton, to write to his classmate, William Bradford of Philadelphia, in December 1773. Madison inquired about the "extent of your [Pennsylvania's] religious Toleration" and asked: "Is an ecclesiastical establishment absolutely necessary to support civil society in a supreme government? and how far is it hurtful to a dependent state?" Bradford was given little time for reflection because, in January 1774, Madison, providing his own answer to his inquiry, wrote to his friend: "Ecclesiastical establishments tend to great ignorance and corruption all of which facilitate the execution of mischievous projects." He spoke of "that diabolical hell conceived principle of persecution," noting "there are at this [time] in the adjacent County not less than 5 or 6 well meaning men in close Goal [jail] for publishing their religious Sentiment." Madison observed that he was "without common patience" on the subject and begged his friend "to pity me and pray for Liberty of Conscience." In the month separating the two letters, Madison moved from the use of the term "toleration" to employ the phrase "liberty of conscience."

Within a short time Madison was in a position to act on his concerns. In 1776 he served on a committee with George Mason to develop a Virginia declaration of rights. The final document was largely the work of Mason, but one critical change was accomplished by Madison when he convinced Mason to replace the term "toleration in the exercise of religion" with the now-familiar phrase "the free exercise of religion." While Madison later wrote a generous interpretation of that incident, stating that Mason "had inadvertently adopted the word 'toleration,'" in fact Madison was advancing a radical departure from tradition, anticipating the Jeffersonian notion of religious freedom as a "natural right of mankind."

The practical cause of Madison's writing of the "Memorial" was the introduction of an act in the Virginia General Assembly in 1784, an act entitled The General Assessment Bill, meant to raise funds "for the support of Christian teachers" in order "to correct the morals of men, restrain their vices, and preserve the peace of society." This measure had the strong endorsement of Patrick Henry. Those delegates pushing the bill saw it as a "support of religion in general" necessitated by the need for the state "to be the guardian of morals." Some of Henry's biographers contend that he "feared a decline in virtue if church services were not held regularly with enforced public support." From Madison's notes it is evident that Henry used a historical argument, noting the fall of states where morality was lacking.

In the notes for his debate with Henry on the Assessment Bill in the House of Delegates, Madison affirmed that religion is "not within [the] purview of civil authority" and reminded Henry that all the ancient nations that had collapsed had religious establishments. In July 1784 Madison wrote to Jefferson, then in Paris, that Henry was not only supporting assessment and incorporation but was also obstructing plans for a constitutional convention. In December Jefferson replied, "what we have to do I think is devoutly to pray for his [Henry's] death." A few weeks earlier Madison had chosen a secular alternative, having Henry selected governor, thereby removing him from the House—"a circumstance," Madison wrote, "very inauspicious to his offspring [the Assessment Bill]."Nevertheless, the decision in December of 1784 to delay passage was the result of further adroit political action by Madison who "assented . . . with reluctance" to incorporating the Episcopal Church, for "I consider the passage of this Act however as having been so far useful as to have parried for the present the General Assessment which would otherwise have certainly been saddled upon us." And he was convinced that incorporation would prove "unpopular among the laity" and "will soon be repealed." Writing to Jefferson the next month, Madison affirmed that, "A negative of the bill (incorporation) too would have doubled the eagerness and the pretexts for a much greater evil, a General Assessment."[2]

When the Assessment Bill was made available to the public in the spring of 1785, there was a severe reaction from Baptist and Presbyterian groups, which flooded the Assembly with petitions and memorials, signed by thousands of citizens, opposing the measure. George Nicholas and George Mason, seeing the swell of public opinion, urged Madison to write a memorial on the subject and "commit it to paper." Madison agreed, putting his thoughts into the brilliant "Memorial and Remonstrance." It is probable that Madison considered his authorship a potential liability in the debate he anticipated in the House of Delegates later in the year. So when his document was distributed for signatures, it appeared anonymously, leading some to conclude that Mason might have penned it. Madison's letter to Jefferson in August 1785 identified the source of the "Memorial": "I drew up the remonstrance herewith enclosed," a fact that became common knowledge by 1786.

When the Assembly returned to work in the fall, a great number of memorials and petitions from dissenting religious groups awaited the body. So dramatic was the change of mood resulting from the "Memorial" and the other petitions that the Assessment Bill never reached the House floor. George Washington inadvertently wrote its epitaph in an October letter to Mason: "I wish an assessment had never been agitated, and as it has gone so far, that the Bill could die an easy death." So complete was the reversal that Madison was made bold to introduce Jefferson's Revised Code for Virginia that included a Bill for Establishing Religious Freedom. That bill was reported to the House on December 14, 1785. On January 16, 1786, the House passed the Jefferson statute in a form slightly altered from the original. Upon agreement from the Senate, the speaker of the house signed the bill into law on January 19. Jefferson wrote Madison in December of that year that the bill had been received with "infinite approbation in Europe," noting "it is comfortable to see the standard of reason at length prevail."

The "Memorial and Remonstrance" was both the affirmation

of the principle of religious freedom and the practical means by which the Assessment Bill was defeated. It memorialized the General Assembly, offering fifteen "remonstrances" against the proposed bill.

From the vantage point of the historian, it is reasonable to conclude that the events in Virginia, coupled with a growing number of Protestant sects in most colonies and a variety of types of colonial religious establishments, probably made inevitable the practical solution set forth in the First Amendment. But if that were the sum of it, then an emerging majority in a later generation could easily justify a "practical" return to toleration under new circumstances. It was the genius of Madison and Jefferson that they laid down a political solution, a "wall of separation," in the context of a principle best described by Jefferson in his "Bill for Establishing Religious Freedom." Of the freedom of conscience, he wrote:"[The] rights hereby asserted are of the natural rights of mankind, and that if any act shall be hereafter passed to repeal the present, or narrow its operation, such act will be an infringement of natural rights."

In 1789 Madison, as a member of the First Congress under the new Constitution was appointed to the Select Committee on Constitutional Amendments. A chief function was to provide a Bill of Rights for consideration by the House of Representatives. In floor debate on August 15, Madison remarked to his colleagues that he understood the meaning of the proposed first clause of the Bill of Rights: "No religion shall be established by Law, nor shall the equal rights of conscience be infringed," to be "that Congress should not establish a religion, and enforce the legal observation of it by law, nor compel men to worship God in any manner contrary to their conscience." After debate the wording of the phrase was altered to read: "Congress shall make no laws touching religion, or infringing the rights of conscience," Shortly thereafter it was changed to its final form: "Congress shall make no law respecting an establishment of religion, or prohibiting the free exercise thereof," employing the Madison phrase "free exercise" that he supplied to the Virginia Declaration of Rights in 1776. Madison would have preferred to extend the guarantees of free conscience, free speech, free press, and trial by jury to the states. He reasoned that "it was equally necessary that they [rights] be secured against the state governments." His failure to achieve extension of protection of these rights to the states had no effect upon Madison's full and vigorous support of the First Amendment as adopted. Until his death in 1836, he consistently interpreted the work of that First Congress, and the resulting ratification by the states, as in full accord with his commitment to total and complete separation of church and state.

This assertion would be challenged by the nonpreferentialists, who agree with Justice Rehnquist's dissent in the *Jaffree* case. Contrasted with the analysis set forth above, Rehnquist insisted that Madison's "original language 'nor shall any national religion be established' obviously does not conform to the 'wall of separation' between church and state which latter day commentators have ascribed to him." Rehnquist believes Madison was seeking merely to restrict Congress from establishing a particular national church. There are three problems with this contention. First, nothing in Madison's acts or words support such a proposition. Indeed, his opposition to the General Assessment Bill in Virginia, detailed in the "Memorial and Remonstrance," contradicts Rehnquist directly. Second, all of Madison's writings after 1789 support the Court's twentieth-century understanding of the term "wall of separation." Third, the reference to Madison's use of "national" simply misses his definition of the word. Madison had an expansive intention when he used the term national. He believed that "religious proclamations by the Executive recommending thanksgivings and fasts . . . imply and certainly nourish the erroneous idea of a national religion."[3] He commented in a similar way about chaplains for the House and Senate. Historical evidence lends no support to the Rehnquist thesis. And clearly Jefferson, even though absent from the First Congress, seems a far more secure source of "original intent" than Justice Rehnquist.

The richness of America's philosophical heritage includes profound religious thinkers, brilliant humanists, and dedicated rationalists. As the eighteenth century drew to a close, a fortuitous coalition of events and ideas resulted in a free church and a secular republic. It offered an exciting environment in which religious leaders were proffered the unhindered opportunity, all too often ignored, to exercise voluntarily a prophetic voice on matters of justice, peace, and freedom. By the same token, the politician was encouraged to seek rational justification for policies, rather than retreat into pious pronouncements and national messianism.

Americans today are in the midst of a shouting match about the Founders. Some say Madison was unconcerned about establishment of religion in the states. Others seek to uncover flaws of inconsistency in the historical records related to Madison and Jefferson. Some distort the records to suit their interpretations. All miss the point. When the framers are discussed it should not be as heroes created as ideological models. One should not embrace religious freedom in 1988 merely because two prominent Virginians did so two centuries ago. Rather, we develop respect for those individuals and their associates because they espoused principles considered essential to representative democracy. This is no game in which each side seeks to uncover old quotes favorable to its cause; it is a confrontation over basic presuppositions.

Writing just as the Supreme Court began its post–World-War II series of cases focused on the Religion Clauses of the First Amendment, Joseph L. Blau offered an effective definition of the task set before those who would seek to reinforce the principles enunciated by Madison and Jefferson:

> The true history of the struggle for religious freedom is to be found after the principle of the wall of separation had been formulated. The struggle of the past century and three quarters to give substance to the formula of religious freedom is the true history of religious freedom. It is an unending struggle; it has not been finally determined by the McCollum decision, nor will any future decision determine the meaning of the principle once and for all. Each generation must fight the battles of freedom anew in terms of the problems and powers of its time. To use unchanged the arms of tradition is to invite defeat; to see in the past a guide and instrument in the development of unfolding values and meanings is to be on the road to victory.[4]

Those who espouse unconditioned religious liberty, with its broad implications, are inclined to understand the nation in terms of human rights, freedom, and social justice rather than in dogmatic phrases. A historical sense allows one to identify past political leadership that exhibited those same concerns, albeit affected by time and circumstance. Hence certain eighteenth-century figures become important because they share a common experience with us.

Our pride in them is a reflection of our pride in our national character. Voices of other patriots reflected a different spirit in the colonial period, committed to oligarchy and theocracy, church establishment, and religious intolerance. We are a nation with a diverse quilt of political and religious traditions: Some of those traditions do not translate well or inspire emulation today. None of the Founders had the wisdom or courage to include Native Americans, slaves, and women as participants in our democracy. They gave us an infinished Constitution. One does not need to invoke Madison or any person in order to justify an unswerving dedication to the principles of justice and liberty; *but* the nation will always require women and men to champion those rights and freedoms if they are to be secured for posterity. To such citizens we owe a debt that can be paid only in the currency of continued vigilance regarding the first experiment on our liberties. Daniel Boorstin caught the spirit of that heritage:

> The courage to doubt, on which American pluralism, federalism, and religious liberty are founded, is a special brand of courage, a more selfless brand of courage, than the courage of orthodoxy. A brand that has been far rarer and more precious in the history of the West than the courage of the crusaders or the true believer who has so little respect for his fellow man and for his thoughts and feelings that he makes himself the court of last resort on the most difficult matters on which wise men have disagreed for millennia.[5]

While the public debate continues over the ligitimacy of the Madison-Jefferson primacy, all modern interpretations of the First Amendment must come to terms with Madison's eloquent presentation of his principles regarding a free conscience in a secular state. This is so not only because of Madison's leading role in Congress in 1789, but also because his insights have a remarkable authenticity for the continuing discussion of this constitutional question.

Editorial Observations

When Professor Tussman published *The Supreme Court on Church and State* twenty-five years ago he had no way to ascertain that a Court which had remained relatively silent on church/state issues for a decade would shortly issue a string of decisions in the sixties, touching off major national debates. As 1962 began the cases related to the "Religion Clauses" were numerous, but easily contained in a moderate size book. Fifteen years later when Robert Miller and Ronald Flowers published *Toward Benevolent Neutrality: Church, State, and the Supreme Court,* a complete offering of all significant Supreme Court church/state decisions filled six hundred closely set pages. In their impressive third edition the size of the work nearly doubled. While indispensible to scholars, it is "not really available for convenient and leisurely perusal." Indeed, the past ten years of activity in the field made a manageable single volume including all the decisions, along with every opinion and dissent, a practical impossibility. The task has become one of selectivity. Out of the vast store of those opinions and dissents the problem has been to identify the writing that will prove enduring and meet the criteria set by Tussman in his preface. In the process of making those choices omissions have been necessary. Every effort has been made to include a representative sample of the various types of issues that have been considered by the Supreme Court justices. All of the "landmark" decisions are offered in full. Summary reference is made to eight cases not included because they were deemed less critical. For a historian the most painful omissions are the concurring opinions of Justices Frankfurter and Brennan in *McCollum* and *Schempp* respectively.

The full text of each Court opinion chosen for inclusion has been reproduced. In a limited number of instances, concurring opinions, where not considered fundamental to the continuing debate, have been deleted or edited. The scholar seeking specific references or nuances in such concurring remarks can readily search the Supreme Court cases either in the *United States Reports* or the *Supreme Court Reporter*, and by using the chart of voting by each twentieth-century justice to be found on page 28. Since I am convinced that many of the dissents reveal much of the spirit of the Court in split decisions, I have included a substantial number of them. In every instance where deletions from the full text of either opinions or dissents have seemed prudent, a notation is inserted. In order to make the book work for the general reader, to highlight the "powerful minds" of those justices who "have grappled with the most urgent and perplexing issues of American life," footnotes and case citations have been uniformly omitted, along with a few lengthy quotations from earlier cases.

Notes

[1]Leonard W. Levy, *The Establishment Clause* (New York: Macmillan, 1986), 91.

[2]*The Papers of James Madison,* Robert Rutland and William Rachal, eds. (Chicago: University of Chicago Press, 1973), vol. 8, 217, 229. This is a critically important point to understand about Madison's position. Why would he have viewed assessment as "a much greater evil" than incorporation of a church? His fear was that if the Assessment Bill were to pass, there would be put in place a principle of plural establishment far more difficult to dislodge. He saw clearly that in maintaining religious factions in Virginia, he could more easily accomplish his goal—complete separation. Madison, in a letter to Jefferson, commented that the "mutual hatred of these sects [Presbyterians and Episcopalians] has been much inflamed by the late act incorporating the latter. I am far from being sorry for it as a coalition between them could alone endanger our religious rights and a tendency to such an event had been suspected." Madison knew that much of the dissenters' opposition to laws concerning religion was "soft," a result of their disenfranchisment. Appeals for an ecumenical Christian establishment might easily erode support for his radical separationist principle. The result could well be a tyranny of the majority respecting conscience. Thus plural establishment was a far more dangerous threat than single establishment to the free exercise of religion, since it effectively eliminated tensions between the most powerful religious sects. It would set them on a course calculated to establish a general Christianity.

[3]Elizabeth Fleet, ed., "Madison's Detached Memoranda," *The William and Mary Quarterly* 3 no. 4 (October 1946): 534–568.

[4]Joseph L. Blau, ed., *Cornerstone of Religious Freedom in America* (Boston: Beacon Press, 1950), 30.

[5]Daniel Boorstin, "The Founding Fathers and the Courage to Doubt," in Robert S. Alley, ed., *James Madison on Religious Liberty* (Buffalo: Prometheus Books, 1985), 214.

James Madison's "Memorial and Remonstrance Against Religious Assessments"

To The Honorable The General Assembly of
The Commonwealth Of Virigina.
A Memorial and Remonstrance.

We, the subscribers, citizens of the said Commonwealth, having taken into serious consideration, a Bill printed by order of the last Session of General Assembly, entitled "A Bill establishing a provision for Teachers of the Christian Religion," and conceiving that the same, if finally armed with the sanctions of a law, will be a dangerous abuse of power, are bound as faithful members of a free State, to remonstrate against it, and to declare the reasons by which we are determined. We remonstrate against the said Bill,

1. Because we hold it for a fundamental and undeniable truth, "that Religion or the duty which we owe to our Creator and the Manner of discharging it, can be directed only by reason and conviction, not by force or violence." The Religion then of every man must be left to the conviction and conscience of every man; and it is the right of every man to exercise it as these may dictate. This right is in its nature an unalienable right. It is unalienable; because the opinions of men, depending only on the evidence contemplated by their own minds, cannot follow the dictates of other men: It is unalienable also; because what is here a right towards men, is a duty towards the Creator. It is the duty of every man to render to the Creator such homage, and such only, as he believes to be acceptable to him. This duty is precedent

both in order of time and degree of obligation, to the claims of Civil Society. Before any man can be considered as a member of Civil Society, he must be considered as a subject of the Governor of the Universe: And if a member of Civil Society, who enters into any subordinate Association, must always do it with a reservation of his duty to the general authority; much more must every man who becomes a member of any particular Civil Society, do it with a saving of his allegiance to the Universal Sovereign. We maintain therefore that in matters of Religion, no man's right is abridged by the institution of Civil Society, and that Religion is wholly exempt from its cognizance. True it is, that no other rule exists, by which any question which may divide a Society, can be ultimately determined, but the will of the majority; but it is also true, that the majority may trespass on the rights of the minority.

2. Because if religion be exempt from the authority of the Society at large, still less can it be subject to that of the Legislative Body. The latter are but the creatures and vicegerents of the former. Their jurisdiction is both derivative and limited: it is limited with regard to the co-ordinate departments, more necessarily is it limited with regard to the constituents. The preservation of a free government requires not merely, that the metes and bounds which separate each department of power may be invariably maintained; but more especially, that neither of them be suffered to overleap the great Barrier which defends the rights of the people. The Rulers who are guilty of such an encroachment, exceed the commission from which they derive their authority, and are Tyrants. The People who submit to it are governed by laws made neither by themselves, nor by an authority derived from them, and are slaves.

3. Because, it is proper to take alarm at the first experiment on our liberties. We hold this prudent jealousy to be the first duty of citizens, and one of [the] noblest characteristics of the late Revolution. The freemen of America did not wait till usurped power had strengthened itself by exercise, and entangled the question in precedents. They saw all the consequences in the principle, and they avoided the consequences by denying the principle. We revere this lesson too much, soon to forget it. Who does not see that the same authority which can establish Christianity, in exclusion of all other Religions, may establish with the same ease any particular sect of Christians, in exlcusion of all other Sects? That the same authority which can force a citizen

to contribute three pence only of his property for the support of any one establishment, may force him to conform to any other establishment in all cases whatsoever?

4. Because, the bill violates that equality which ought to be the basis of every law, and which is more indispensible, in proportion as the validity or expediency of any law is more liable to be impeached. If "all men are by nature equally free and independent," all men are to be considered as entering into Society on equal conditions; as relinquishing no more, and therefore retaining no less, one than another, of their natural rights. Above all are they to be considered as retaining an *"equal* title to the free exercise of Religion according to the dictates of conscience.*"* Whilst we assert for ourselves a freedom to embrace, to profess and to observe the Religion which we believe to be of divine origin, we cannot deny an equal freedom to those whose minds have not yet yielded to the evidence which has convinced us. If this freedom be abused, it is an offence against god, not against man: To God, therefore, not to men, must an account of it be rendered. As the Bill violates equality by subjecting some to peculiar burdens; so it violates the same principle, by granting to others peculiar exemptions. Are the Quakers and Menonists the only sects who think a compulsive support of their religions unnecessary and unwarrantable? Can their piety alone be intrusted with the care of public worship? Ought their Religions to be endowed above all others, with extraordinary privileges, by which proselytes may be enticed from all others? We think too favorably of the justice and good sense of these denominations, to believe that they either covet pre-eminencies over their fellow citizens, or that they will be seduced by them, from the common opposition to the measure.

5. Because the bill implies either that the Civil Magistrate is a competent Judge of Religious truth; or that he may employ Religion as an engine of Civil policy. The first is an arrogant pretension falsified by the contradictory opinions of Rulers in all ages, and throughout the world: The second an unhallowed perversion of the means of salvation.

6. Because the establishment proposed by the Bill is not requisite for the support of the Christian Religion. To say that it is, is a contradiction to the Christian Religion itself; for every page of it disavows a dependence on the powers of this world: it is a contradiction to fact; for it is known that this Religion both existed and flourished, not only

without the support of human laws, but in spite of every opposition from them; and not only during the period of miraculous aid, but long after it had been left to its own evidence, and the ordinary care of Providence: Nay, it is a contradiction in terms; for a Religion not invented by human policy, must have pre-existed and been supported, before it was established by human policy. It is moreover to weaken in those who profess this Religion a pious confidence in its innate excellence, and the patronage of its Author; and to foster in those who still reject it, a suspicion that its friends are too conscious of its fallacies, to trust it to its own merits.

7. Because experience witnesseth that ecclesiastical establishments, instead of maintaining the purity and efficacy of Religion, have had a contrary operation. During almost fifteen centuries, has the legal establishment of Christianity been on trial. What have been its fruits? More or less in all places, pride and indolence in the Clergy; ignorance and servility in the laity; in both, superstition, bigotry, and persecution. Enquire of the Teachers of Christianity for the ages in which it appeared in its greatest lustre; those of every sect, point to the ages prior to its incorporation with Civil policy. Propose a restoration of this primitive state in which its Teachers depended on the voluntary rewards of their flocks; many of them predict its downfall. On which side ought their testimony to have greatest weight, when for or when against their interest?

8. Because the establishment in question is not necessary for the Support of Civil Government. If it be urged as necessary for the support of Civil Government only as it is a means of supporting Religion, and it be not necessary for the latter purpose, it cannot be necessary for the former. If Religion be not within [the] cognizance of Civil Government, how can its legal establishment be said to be necessary to Civil Government? What influence in fact have ecclesiastical establishments had on Civil Society? In some instances they have been seen to erect a spiritual tyranny on the ruins of Civil authority; in many instances they have been seen upholding the thrones of political tyranny; in no instance have they been seen the guardians of the liberties of the people. Rulers who wished to subvert the public liberty, may have found an established clergy convenient auxiliaries. A just government, instituted to secure & perpetuate it, needs them not. Such a government will be best supported by protecting every citizen in the enjoyment of his Religion with the same equal hand which protects

his person and his property; by neither invading the equal rights of any Sect, nor suffering any Sect to invade those of another.

9. Because the proposed establishment is a departure from that generous policy, which, offering an asylum to the persecuted and oppressed of every Nation and Religion, promised a lustre to our country, and an accession to the number of its citizens. What a melancholy mark is the Bill of sudden degeneracy? Instead of holding forth an asylum to the persecuted, it is itself a signal of persecution. It degrades from the equal rank of Citizens all those whose opinions in Religion do not bend to those of the Legislative authority. Distant as it may be, in its present form, from the Inquisition it differs from it only in degree. The one is the first step, the other the last in the career of intolerance. The magnanimous sufferer under this cruel scourge in foreign Regions, must view the Bill as a Beacon on our Coast, warning him to seek some other haven, where liberty and philanthrophy in their due extent may offer a more certain repose from his troubles.

10. Because, it will have a like tendency to banish our Citizens. The allurements presented by other situations are every day thinning their number. To superadd a fresh motive to emigration, by revoking the liberty which they now enjoy, would be the same species of folly which has dishonoured and depopulated flourishing kingdoms.

11. Because, it will destroy that moderation and harmony which the forbearance of our laws to intermeddle with Religion, has produced amongst its several sects. Torrents of blood have been spilt in the old world, by vain attempts of the secular arm to extinguish Religious discord, by proscribing all difference in Relgious opinions. Time has at length revealed the true remedy. Every relaxation of narrow and rigorous policy, wherever it has been tried, has been found to assuage the disease. The American Theatre has exhibited proofs, that equal and compleat liberty, if it does not wholly eradicate it, sufficiently destroys its malignant influence on the health and prosperity of the State. If with the salutary effects of this system under our own eyes, we begin to contract the bonds of Religious freedom, we know no name that will too severely reproach our folly. At least let warning be taken at the first fruits of the threatened innovation. The very appearance of the Bill has transformed that "Christian forbearance, love and charity," which of late mutually prevailed, into animosities and jealousies, which may not soon be appeased. What mischiefs may not be dreaded should this enemy to the public quiet be armed with the force of a law?

12. Because, the policy of the bill is adverse to the diffusion of the light of Christianity. The first wish of those who enjoy this precious gift, ought to be that it may be imparted to the whole race of mankind. Compare the number of those who have as yet received it with the number still remaining under the dominion of false Religions; and how small is the former! Does the policy of the Bill tend to lessen the disproportion? No; it at once discourages those who are strangers to the light of [revelation] from coming into the Region of it; and countenances, by example the nations who continue in darkness, in shutting out those who might convey it to them. Instead of levelling as far as possible, every obstacle to the victorious progress of truth, the Bill with an ignoble and unchristian timidity would circumscribe it, with a wall of defence, against the encroachments of error.

13. Because attempts to enforce by legal sanctions, acts obnoxious to so great a proportion of Citizens, tend to enervate the laws in general, and to slacken the bands of Society. If it be difficult to execute any law which is not generally deemed necessary or salutary, what must be the case where it is deemed invalid and dangerous? and what may be the effect of so striking an example of impotency in the Government, on its general authority.

14. Because a measure of such singular magnitude and delicacy ought not to be imposed, without the clearest evidence that it is called for by a majority of citizens: and no satisfactory method is yet proposed by which the voice of the majority in this case may be determined, or its influence secured. "The people of the respective counties are indeed requested to signify their opinion respecting the adoption of the Bill to the next Session of Assembly." But the representation must be made equal, before the voice either of the Representatives or of the Counties, will be that of the people. Our hope is that neither of the former will, after due consideration, espouse the dangerous principle of the Bill. Should the event disappoint us, it will still leave us in full confidence, that a fair appeal to the latter will reverse the sentence against our liberties.

15. Because, finally, "the equal right of every citizen to the free exercise of his Religion according to the dictates of conscience" is held by the same tenure with all our other rights. If we recur to its origin, it is equally the gift of nature; if we weigh its importance, it cannot be less dear to us; if we consult the Declaration of those rights which pertain to the good people of Virginia, as the "basis and foundation of gov-

ernment," it is enumerated with equal solemnity, or rather studied emphasis.

Either then, we must say, that the will of the Legislature is the only measure of their authority; and that in the plenitude of this authority, they may sweep away all our fundamental rights; or, that they are bound to leave this particular right untouched and sacred: Either we must say, that they may controul the freedom of the press, may abolish the trial by jury, may swallow up the Executive and Judiciary Powers of the State; nay that they may despoil us of our very right of suffrage, and erect themselves into an independent and hereditary assembly: or we may say, that they have no authority to enact into law the Bill under consideration. We the subscribers say, that the General Assembly of this Commonwealth have no such authority: And that no effort may be omitted on our part against so dangerous an usurpation, we oppose to it, this remonstrance; earnestly praying, as we are in duty bound, that the Supreme Lawgiver of the Universe, by illuminating those to whom it is addressed, may on the one hand, turn their councils from every act which would affront his holy prerogative, or violate the trust committed to them: and on the other, guide them into every measure which may be worthy of his [blessing, may re]dound to their own praise, and may establish more firmly the liberties, the prosperity, and the Happiness of the Commonwealth.

Thomas Jefferson's "Bill for Establishing Religious Freedom"

I. Whereas Almighty God hath created the mind free; that all attempts to influence it by temporal punishments or burthens, or by civil incapacitations, tend only to beget habits of hypocrisy and meanness, and are a departure from the plan of the Holy author of our religion, who being Lord both of body and mind, yet chose not to propagate it by coercions on either, as was in his Almighty power to do; that the impious presumption of legislators and rulers, civil as well as ecclesiastical, who being themselves but fallible and uninspired men, have assumed dominion over the faith of others, setting up their own opinions and modes of thinking as the only true and infallible, and as such endeavouring to impose them on others, hath established and maintained false religions over the greatest part of the world, and through all time; that to compel a man to furnish contributions of money for the propagation of opinions which he disbelieves, is sinful and tyrannical; that even the forcing him to support this or that teacher of his own religious persuasion, is depriving him of the comfortable liberty of giving his contributions to the particular pastor, whose morals he would make his pattern, and whose powers he feels most persuasive to righteousness, and is withdrawing from the ministry those temporary rewards, which proceeding from an approbation of their personal conduct, are an additional incitement to earnest and unremitting labours for the instruction of mankind; that our civil rights have no dependence on our religious opinions, any more than our opinions in physics or geometry; that therefore the proscribing any citizen as unworthy the public confidence by laying upon him an incapacity of being called to offices of trust and emolument, unless he profess or renounce this or that religious opinion, is depriving him injuriously of those privileges and advantages to which in common with his fellow-citizens he has a natural right; that it tends only to corrupt the principles of that religion it is meant to encourage, by bribing with a monopoly of worldly honours and emoluments, those who will externally profess and conform to it; that though indeed these are criminal who do not withstand such temptation, yet neither are those innocent who lay the bait in their way; that to suffer the civil magistrate to intrude his powers into the field of opinion, and to restrain the profession or propagation of principles on supposition of their ill tendency, is a dangerous fallacy, which at once destroys all religious liberty, because he being of course judge of that tendency will make his opinions the rule of judgment, and approve or condemn the sentiments of others only as they shall square with or differ from his own; that it is time enough for the rightful purposes of civil government, for its officers to interfere when principles break out into overt acts against peace and good order; and finally, that truth is great and will prevail if left to herself, that she is the proper and sufficient antagonist to error, and has nothing to fear from the conflict, unless by human interposition disarmed of her natural weapons, free argument and debate, errors ceasing to be dangerous when it is permitted freely to contradict them:

II. *Be it enacted by the General Assembly,* That no man shall be compelled to frequent or support any religious worship, place or ministry whatsoever, nor shall be enforced, restrained, molested, or burthened in his body or goods, nor shall otherwise suffer on account of his religious opinions or belief; but that all men shall be free to profess, and by argument to maintain, their opinions in matters of religion, and that the same shall in no wise diminish, enlarge, or affect their civil capacities.

III. And though we well know that this Assembly, elected by the people for the ordinary purposes of legislation only, have no power to restrain the acts of succeeding Assemblies, constituted with powers equal to our own, and that therefore to declare this act to be irrevocable would be of no effect in law; yet we are free to declare, and do declare, that the rights hereby asserted are of the natural rights of mankind, and that if any act shall be hereafter passed to repeal the present, or to narrow its operation, such act will be an infringement of natural right.

Fifty Years of Court Decisions on Church and State

A = Wrote majority opinion
M = Voted with majority
D/M = Concurred in part; dissented in part
D = Dissented
X = Took no part in decision

Supreme Court Justices		'40 CANTWELL	'40 GOBITIS	'43 BARNETTE	'47 EVERSON	'48 McCOLLUM	'52 ZORACH	'61 McGOWAN	'61 BRAUNFELD	'61 TORCASO	'62 ENGEL	'63 SCHEMPP	'63 MURRAY	'63 VERNER	'68 ALLEN	'68 EPPERSON	'68 FLAST	'70 WALZ	'71 LEMON-I	'71 TILTON	'72 YODER	'73 LEMON-II	'73 HUNT	'73 NYQUIST	'73 LEVITT	'75 MEEK	'76 ROEMER	'77 WOLMAN	'83 MUELLER	'83 MARSH	'84 LYNCH	'85 BALL	'85 AGUILAR	'85 WALLACE	'85 CALDOR	'87 EDWARDS
James C. McReynolds [Wilson]	1914-1941	M	M																																	
Charles E. Hughes [Hoover] {CJ}	1930-1941	M	M																																	
Owen Roberts [Hoover]	1930-1945	A	M	D																																
Hugo Black [Roosevelt]	1937-1971	M	M	M	A	A	D	M	M	A	A	M	M	M	D	M	M	M	M	D																
Stanley Reed [Roosevelt]	1938-1957	M	M	D	M	D	M																													
Felix Frankfurter [Roosevelt]	1939-1962	M	A	D	D	M	D	M	M	M	X																									
William Douglas [Roosevelt]	1939-1975	M	M	M	M	M	A	D	D	M	M	M	M	M	D	M	M	D	M	D	D	M	D	M	M	D										
Frank Murphy [Roosevelt]	1940-1949	M	M	M	M	M																														
Harlan Fiske Stone [Roosevelt] {CJ}	1941-1946		D	M																																
James Byrnes [Roosevelt]	1941-1942			M																																
Robert Jackson [Roosevelt]	1941-1954			A	D	M	D																													
Wiley Rutledge [Roosevelt]	1943-1949				D	M																														
Harold Burton [Truman]	1945-1958				D	M	M																													
Fred Vinson [Truman] {CJ}	1946-1953				M	M	M																													
Thomas Clark [Truman]	1949-1967						M	M	M	M	M	A	A	M																						
Sherman Minton [Truman]	1949-1956						M																													
Earl Warren [Eisenhower] {CJ}	1953-1969							A	A	M	M	M	M	M	M	M	A																			
John Harlan [Eisenhower]	1955-1971							M	M	M	M	M	M	D	M	M	D	M	M	M																
William Brennan [Eisenhower]	1956-							M	D	M	M	M	M	A	M	M	M	M	M	D	M	M	D	M	M	D	D	D/M	D	D	D	A	A	M	M	A
Charles Whitaker [Eisenhower]	1957-1962							M	M	M																										
Potter Stewart [Eisenhower]	1958-1982							M	D	M	D	D	D	M	M	M	M	M	M	M	M	M	M	M	M	A	D	M	M							
Byron White [Kennedy]	1962-										X	X	X	D	A	M	M	M	D/M	M	M	D	M	D	D	M	M	D/M	M	M	M	D	D	D	M	M
Arthur Goldberg [Kennedy]	1962-1965											M	M	M																						
Abe Fortas [Johnson]	1965-1969														D	A	M																			
Thurgood Marshall [Johnson]	1967-														M	M	M	M	X	D	M	M	D	M	M	D	D	D/M	D	D	D	M	M	M	M	M
Warren Burger [Nixon] {CJ}	1969-1986																	A	A	A	A	D	M	D	A	D	M	D/M	M	A	A	D	D	D	A	
Harry Blackmun [Nixon]	1970-																	X	M	M	M	M	M	M	M	M	A	A	D	M	D	M	M	M	M	M
Lewis Powell [Nixon]	1971-1987																				X	A	A	A	M	M	M	D/M	M	M	M	M	M	M	M	M
William Rehnquist [Nixon] {CJ-'86}	1971-																				X	D	M	D	M	M	M	D/M	A	M	M	D	D	D	D	D
John Paul Stevens [Ford]	1975-																										D	D/M	D	D	D	M	M	A	M	M
Sandra Day O'Connor [Reagan]	1932-																													M	M	D/M	D	M	M	M
Antonin Scalia [Reagan]	1936-																																			D

THE ESTABLISHMENT CLAUSE

Church Schools

Pierce v. Society of Sisters, 268 U.S. 510 (1925)

Often described as the "Magna Carta" of American parochial schools, the *Pierce* case struck down an Oregon law mandating that all children attend public schools through high school. The Court established that the parent has the right to send his or her child to a nonpublic school. Justice McReynolds spoke for the Court: "The child is not the mere creature of the State; those who nurture him and direct his destiny have the right, coupled with the high duty, to recognize and prepare him for additional obligations." While *Pierce* was not a "Religious Clause" case, Chief Justice Burger in *Wisconsin v. Yoder* (1972) affirmed that the basic right of parents to guide the religious future and education of children "is now established beyond doubt as an enduring American tradition." *Pierce* has not been interpreted by the Court to allow public funds to finance children attendance at parochial schools. The 1986 Tennessee lower court decision providing reimbursement by the public school system of parochial tuition for children whose parents found the teachings of those schools religiously offensive raises this question in another form.

MR. JUSTICE MC REYNOLDS DELIVERED THE OPINION OF THE COURT.

These appeals are from decrees, based upon undenied allegations, which granted preliminary orders restraining appellants from threatening or attempting to enforce the Compulsory Education Act adopted November 7, 1922, under the initiative provision of her Constitution by the voters of Oregon. They present the same points of law: there are no controverted questions of fact. Rights said to be guaranteed by the Federal Constitution were specially set up, and appropriate prayers asked for their protection.

The challenged act, effective September 1, 1926, requires every parent, guardian, or other person having control or charge or custody of a child between eight and sixteen years to send him "to a public school for the period of time a public school shall be held during the current year" in the district where the child resides; and failure so to do is declared a misdemeanor. There are exemptions—not specially important here—for children who are not normal, or who have completed the eighth grade, or whose parents or private teachers reside at considerable distances from any public school, or who hold special permits from the county superintendent. The manifest purpose is to compel general attendance at public schools by normal children, between eight and sixteen, who have not completed the eighth grade. And without doubt enforcement of the statute would seriously impair, perhaps destroy, the profitable features of appellees' business, and greatly diminish the value of their property.

Appellee the Society of Sisters is an Oregon corporation, organized in 1880, with power to care for orphans, educate and instruct the youth, establish and maintain academies or schools, and acquire necessary real and personal property. It has long devoted its property and effort to the secular and religious education and care of children, and has acquired the valuable good will of many parents and guardians. It conducts interdependent primary and high schools and junior colleges, and maintains orphanages for the custody and control of children between eight and sixteen. In its primary schools many children between those ages are taught the subjects usually pursued in Oregon public schools during the first eight years. Systematic religious instruction and moral training according to the tenets of the Roman Catholic Church are also regularly provided. All courses of study, both temporal and religious, contemplate continuity of training under appellee's charge; the primary schools are essential to the system and the most profitable. It owns valuable buildings, especially constructed and equipped for school purposes. The business is remunerative—the annual income from primary schools exceeds $30,000—and the successful conduct of this requires long-time contracts with teachers and parents. The Compulsory Education Act of 1922 has already caused the withdrawal from its schools of children who would otherwise continue, and their income has steadily declined. The appellants, public officers, have proclaimed their purpose strictly to enforce the statute.

After setting out the above facts, the Society's bill alleges that the enactment conflicts with the right of parents to choose schools where their children will receive appropriate mental and religious training, the right of the child to influence the parents' choice of a school, the right of schools and teachers therein to engage in a useful business or profession, and is accordingly repugnant to the Constitution and void. And, further, that unless enforcement of the measure is enjoined, the corporation's business and property will suffer irreparable injury.

Appellee Hill Military Academy is a private corporation organized in 1908 under the laws of Oregon, engaged in owning, operating, and conducting for profit an elementary, college preparatory, and military training school for boys between the ages of five and twenty-one years. The average attendance is one hundred, and the annual fees received for each student amount to some $800. The elementary department is divided into eight grades, as in the public schools; the college preparatory department has four grades, similar to those of the public high schools; the courses of study conform to the requirements of the state board of education. Military instruction and training are also given, under the supervision of an Army officer. It owns considerable real and personal property, some useful only for school purposes. The business and incident good will are very valuable. In order to conduct its affairs long-time contracts must be made for supplies, equipment, teachers, and pupils. Appellants, law officers of the state and county, have publicly announced that the Act of November 7, 1922, is valid, and have declared their intention to enforce it. By reason of the statute and threat of enforcement, appellee's business is being destroyed and its property depreciated; parents and guardians are refusing to make contracts for the future instruction of their sons, and some are being withdrawn.

The Academy's bill states the foregoing facts and then alleges that the challenged act contravenes the corporation's rights guaranteed by the 14th Amendment, and that unless appellants are restrained from proclaiming its validity and threatening to enforce it, irreparable injury will result. The prayer is for an appropriate injunction.

No answer was interposed in either cause, and after proper notices they were heard by three judges on motions for preliminary injunctions upon the specifically alleged facts. The court ruled that the 14th Amendment guaranteed appellees against the deprivation of their property without due process of law consequent upon the unlawful interference by appellants with the free choice of patrons, present and prospective. It declared the right to conduct schools was property, and that parents and guardians, as a part of their liberty, might direct the education of children by selecting reputable teachers and places. Also, that appellees' schools were not unfit or harmful to the public, and that enforcement of the challenged statute would unlawfully deprive them of patronage, and thereby destroy appellee's business and property. Finally, that the threats to enforce the act would continue to cause irreparable injury; and the suits were not premature.

No question is raised concerning the power of the state reasonably to regulate all schools, to inspect, supervise, and examine them, their teachers and pupils; to require that all children of proper age attend some school, that teachers shall be of good moral character and patriotic disposition, that certain studies plainly essential to good citizenship must be taught, and that nothing be taught which is manifestly inimical to the public welfare.

The inevitable practical result of enforcing the act under consideration would be destruction of appellees' primary schools, and perhaps all other private primary schools for normal children within the state of Oregon. Appellees are engaged in a kind of undertaking not inherently harmful, but long regarded as useful and meritorious. Certainly there is nothing in the present records to indicate that they have failed to discharge their obligations to patrons, students, or the state. And there are no peculiar circumstances or present emergencies which demand extraordinary measures relative to primary education.

Under the doctrine of *Meyer v. Nebraska*, we think it entirely plain that the Act of 1922 unreasonably interferes with the liberty of parents and guardians to direct the upbringing and education of children under their control. As often heretofore pointed out, rights guaranteed by the Constitution may not be abridged by legislation which has no reasonable relation to some purposes within the competency of the state. The fundamental theory of liberty upon which all governments in this Union repose excludes any general power of the state to standardize its children by forcing them to accept instruction from public teachers only. The child is not the mere creature of the state; those who nurture him and direct his destiny have the right, coupled with the high duty, to recognize and prepare him for additional obligations.

Appellees are corporations, and therefore, it is said, they cannot claim for themselves the liberty which the 14th Amendment guarantees. Accepted in the proper sense, this is true. But they have business and property for which they claim protection. These are threatened with destruction through the unwarranted compulsion which appellants are exercising over present and prospective patrons of their schools. And this court has gone very far to protect against loss threatened by such action.

The courts of the state have not construed the act, and we must determine its meaning for ourselves. Evidently it was expected to have general application, and cannot be construed as though merely intended to amend the charters of certain private corporations, as in *Berea College v. Kentucky.* No argument in favor of such view has been advanced.

Generally it is entirely true, as urged by counsel, that no person in any business has such an interest in possible customers as to enable him to restrain exercise of proper power of the state upon the ground that he will be deprived of patronage. But the injunctions here sought are not against the exercise of any proper power. Appellees asked protection against arbitrary, unreasonable, and unlawful interference with their patrons, and the consequent destruction of their business and property. Their interest is clear and immediate, within the rule approved in *Truax v. Raich, Truax v. Corrigan, and Terrace v. Thompson,* and many other cases where injunctions have issued to protect business enterprises against interference with the freedom of patrons or customers.

The suits were not premature. The injury to appellees was present and very real,—not a mere possibility in the remote future. If no relief had been possible prior to the effective date of the act, the injury would have become irreparable. Prevention of impending injury by unlawful action is a well-recognized function of courts of equity.

The decrees below are affirmed.

Cochran v. Board of Education, 281 U.S. 370 (1930)

The Court upheld a Louisiana law that provided for the purchase of textbooks dealing with secular subjects for use by children enrolled in parochial schools in the state. In this decision the Court reflected what has come to be known as the "child-benefit" theory. Justice Black, writing for the majority, used a similar argument in the landmark case *Everson v. Board of Education* (1947).

MR. CHIEF JUSTICE HUGHES DELIVERED THE OPINION OF THE COURT.

The appellants, as citizens and taxpayers of the State of Louisiana, brought this suit to restrain the State Board of Education and other state officials from expending any part of the severance tax fund in purchasing school books and in supplying them free of cost to the school children of the State, under Acts No. 100 and No. 143 of 1928, upon the ground that the legislation violated specified provisions of the constitution of the State and also section 4 of Article IV and the Fourteenth Amendment of the Federal Constitution. The Supreme Court of the State affirmed the judgment of the trial court, which refused to issue an injunction.

Act No. 100 of 1928 provided that the severance tax fund of the State after allowing funds and appropriations as required by the state constitution, should be devoted "first, to supplying school books to the school children of the State." The Board of Education was directed to provide "school books for school children free of cost to such children." Act No. 143 of 1928 made appropriations in accordance with the above provisions.

The Supreme Court of the State, following its decision in *Borden v. Louisiana State Board of Education*, held that these acts were not repugnant to either the state or the Federal Constitution.

No substantial Federal question is presented under section 4 of Article IV of the Federal Constitution guaranteeing to every State a republican form of government, as questions arising under this provision are political, not judicial, in character.

The contention of the appellant under the Fourteenth Amendment is that taxation for the purchase of school books constituted a taking of private property for a private purpose. Thie purpose is said to be to aid private, religious, sectarian, and other schools not embraced in the public educational system of the State by furnishing text-books free to the children attending such private schools. The operation and effect of the legislation in question were described by the Supreme Court of the State as follows:

> One may scan the acts in vain to ascertain where any money is appropriated for the purchase of school books for the use of any church, private, sectarian or even public school. The appropri-

> ations were made for the specific purpose of purchasing school books for the use of the school children of the state, free of cost to them. It was for their benefit and the resulting benefit to the state that the appropriations were made. True, these children attend some school, public or private, the latter, sectarian or non-sectarian, and that the books are to be furnished them for their use, free of cost, whichever they attend. The schools, however, are not the beneficiaries of these appropriations. They obtain nothing from them, nor are they relieved of a single obligation, because of them. The school children and the state alone are the beneficiaries. It is also true that the sectarian schools, which some of the children attend, instruct their pupils in religion, and books are used for that purpose, but one may search diligently the acts, though without result, in an effort to find anything to the effect that it is the purpose of the state to furnish religious books for the use of such children. . . . What the statutes contemplate is that the same books that are furnished children attending public schools shall be furnished children attending private schools. This is the only practical way of interpreting and executing the statutes, and this is what the state board of education is doing. Among these books, naturally, none is to be expected, adapted to religious instruction.

The Court also stated, although the point is not of importance in relation to the Federal question, that it was "only the use of the books that is granted to the children, or, in other words, the books are lent to them."

Viewing the statute and having the effect thus attributed to it, we can not doubt that the taxing of the State is exerted for a public purpose. The legislation does not segregate private schools, or their pupils, as its beneficiaries or attempt to interfere with any matters of exclusively private concern. Its interest is education, broadly; its method, comprehensive. Individual interests are aided only as the common interest is safeguarded.

Judgment affirmed.

Everson v. Board of Education, 330 U.S. 1 (1947)

Constitutional law authority A. E. Dick Howard has written that, concerning establishment of religion, "The seminal case in the modern Court is *Everson*." In a split decision Justice Black wrote for the majority (Justices Reed, Douglas, Murphy, Vinson) that New Jersey, in providing public school bus transportation to parochial school students, had not violated the Establishment Clause, a clause that "means at least this: Neither a state nor the Federal Government . . . can pass laws which aid one religion, aid all religions, or prefer one religion over another." Relying upon the Jeffersonian "wall of separation" phrase, Black then employed child benefit as the reason to uphold the state practice, a practice that "requires the state to be neutral" but not an adversary. Justice Rutledge, writing for Justices Frankfurter, Jackson, and Burton, used almost identical references to Madison and Jefferson in arriving at an opposite position.

Yet even as the Justices were divided over the New Jersey issue, they made common cause in identifying, for future decision, Madison and Jefferson as the appropriate interpreters of the meaning of the Religion Clauses of the First Amendment. An appendix to the decision quoting in full Madison's "Memorial and Remonstrance" left no doubt on that score. Equally significant, *Everson* settled that the Establishment Clause applies to the states.

MR. JUSTICE BLACK DELIVERED THE OPINION OF THE COURT.

A New Jersey statute authorizes its local school districts to make rules and contracts for the transportation of children to and from schools. The appellee, a township board of education, acting pursuant to this statute authorized reimbursement to parents of money expended by them for the bus transportation of their children on regular busses operated by the public transportation system. Part of this money was for the payment of transportation of some children in the community to Catholic parochial schools. These church schools give their students, in addition to secular education, regular religious instruction conforming to the religious tenets and modes of worship of the Catholic Faith. The superintendent of these schools is a Catholic priest.

The appellant, in his capacity as a direct taxpayer, filed suit in a State court challenging the right of the Board to reimburse parents of parochial school students. He contended that the statute and the resolution passed pursuant to it violated both the State and the Federal

Constitutions. That court held that the legislature was without power to authorize such payment under the State constitution. The New Jersey Court of Errors and Appeals reversed, holding that neither the statute nor the resolution passed pursuant to it was in conflict with the State constitution or the provisions of the Federal Constitution in issue.

Since there has been no attack on the statute on the ground that a part of its language excludes children attending private schools operated for profit from enjoying state payment for their transportation, we need not consider this exclusionary language; it has no relevancy to any constitutional question here presented. Furthermore, if the exclusion clause had been properly challenged, we do not know whether New Jersey's highest court would construe its statutes as precluding payment of the school transportation of any group of pupils, even those of a private school run for profit. Consequently, we put to one side the question as to the validity of the statute against the claim that it does not authorize payment for the transportation generally of school children in New Jersey.

The only contention here is that the State statute and the resolution, in so far as they authorized reimbursement to parents of children attending parochial schools, violate the Federal Constitution in these two respects, which to some extent, overlap. First. They authorize the State to take by taxation the private property of some and bestow it upon others, to be used for their own private purposes. This, it is alleged, violates the due process clause of the Fourteenth Amendment. Second. The statute and the resolution forced inhabitants to pay taxes to help support and maintain schools which are dedicated to, and which regularly teach, the Catholic Faith. This is alleged to be a use of State power to support church schools contrary to the prohibition of the First Amendment which the Fourteenth Amendment made applicable to the states.

First. The due process argument that the State law taxes some people to help others carry out their private purposes is framed in two phases. The first phase is that a state cannot tax A to reimburse B for the cost of transporting his children to church schools. This is said to violate the due process clause because the children are sent to these church schools to satisfy the personal desires of their parents, rather than the public's interest in the general education of all children. This argument, if valid, would apply equally to prohibit state payment for the transportation of children to any non-public school, whether operated by a church, or any other non-government individual or group. But, the New Jersey legislature has decided that a public purpose will be served by using tax-raised funds to pay the bus fares of all school children, including those who attend parochial schools. The New Jersey Court of Errors and Appeals has reached the same conclusion. The fact that a state law, passed to satisfy a public need, coincides with the personal desires of the individuals most directly affected is certainly an inadequate reason for us to say that a legislature has erroneously appraised the public need.

It is true that this Court has, in rare instances, struck down state statutes on the ground that the purpose for which tax-raised funds were to be expended was not a public one. But the Court has also pointed out that this far-reaching authority must be exercised with the most extreme caution. Otherwise, a state's power to legislate for the public welfare might be seriously curtailed, a power which is a primary reason for the existence of states. Changing local conditions create new local problems which may lead a state's people and its local authorities to believe that laws authorizing new types of public services are necessary to promote the general well-being of the people. The Fourteenth Amendment did not strip the states of their power to meet problems previously left for individual solution.

It is much too late to argue that legislation intended to facilitate the opportunity of children to get a secular education serves no public purpose. The same thing is no less true of legislation to reimburse needy parents, or all parents, for payment of the fares of their children so that they can ride in public busses to and from schools, rather than run the risk of traffic and other hazards incident to walking or "hitchhiking." Nor does it follow that a law has a private rather than a public purpose because it provides that tax-raised funds will be paid to reimburse individuals on account of money spent by them in a way which furthers a public program. Subsidies and loans to individuals such as farmers and home owners, and to privately owned transportation systems, as well as many other kinds of businesses, have been commonplace practices in our state and national history.

Insofar as the second phase of the due process argument may differ from the first, it is by suggesting that taxation for transportation of children to church schools constitutes support of a religion by the State. But if the law is invalid for this reason, it is because it violates the First Amendment's prohibition against the establishment of religion by law. This is the exact question raised by appellant's second contention, to consideration of which we now turn.

Second. The New Jersey statute is challenged as a "law respecting an establishment of religion." The First Amendment, as made applicable to the states by the Fourteenth, commands that a state "shall make no law respecting an establishment of religion, or prohibiting the free exercise thereof." These words of the First Amendment reflected in the minds of early Americans a vivid mental picture of conditions and practices which they fervently wished to stamp out in order to preserve liberty for themselves and for their posterity. Doubtless their goal has not been entirely reached; but so far has the Nation moved toward it that the expression "law respecting an establishment of religion," probably does not so vividly remind present-day Americans of the evils, fears, and political problems that caused that expression to be written into our Bill of Rights. Whether this New Jersey law is one respecting the "establishment of religion" requires an understanding of the meaning of that language, particularly with respect to the imposition of taxes. Once again, therefore, it is not inappropriate briefly to review the background and environment of the period in which that constitutional language was fashioned and adopted.

A large proportion of the early settlers of this country came here from Europe to escape the bondage of laws which compelled them to support and attend government favored churches. The centuries immediately before and contemporaneous with the colonization of America had been filled with turmoil, civil strife, and persecution, generated in large part by established sects determined to maintain their absolute political and religious supremacy. With the power of government supporting them, at various times and places, Catholics had persecuted Protestants, Protestants had persecuted Catholics, Protestant sects had persecuted other Protestant sects, Catholics of one shade of belief had persecuted Catholics of another shade of belief, and all of these had from time to time persecuted Jews. In efforts to force loyalty to whatever religious group happened to be on top and in league with the government of a particular time and place, men and women had been fined, cast in jail, cruelly tortured, and killed. Among the offenses for which these punishments had been inflicted were such things as speaking disrespectfully of the views of ministers of government-established churches, non-attendance at those churches, expressions of non-belief in their doctrines, and failure to pay taxes and tithes to support them.

These practices of the old world were transplanted to and began to thrive in the soil of the new America. The very charters granted by the English Crown to the individuals and companies designated to make the laws which would control the destinies of the colonials authorized these individuals and companies to erect religious establishments which all, whether believers or non-believers, would be required to support and attend. An exercise of this authority was accompained by a repetition of many of the old-world practices and persecutions. Catholics found themselves hounded and proscribed because of their faith; Quakers who followed their conscience went to jail; Baptists were peculiarly obnoxious to certain dominant Protestant sects; men and women of varied faiths who happened to be in a minority in a particular locality were persecuted because they steadfastly persisted in worshipping God only as their own consciences dictated. And all of these dissenters were compelled to pay tithes and taxes to support government-sponsored churches whose ministers preached inflammatory sermons designed to strengthen and consolidate the established faith by generating a burning hatred against dissenters.

These practices became so commonplace as to shock the freedom-loving colonials into a feeling of abhorrence. The imposition of taxes to pay ministers' salaries and to build and maintain churches and church property aroused their indignation. It was these feelings which found expression in the First Amendment. No one locality and no one group throughout the Colonies can rightly be given entire credit for having aroused the sentiment that culminated in adoption of the Bill of Rights' provisions embracing religious liberty. But Virginia, where the established church had achieved a dominant influence in political affairs and where many excesses attracted wide public attention, provided a great stimulus and able leadership for the movement. The people there, as elsewhere, reached the conviction that individual religious liberty could be achieved best under a government which was stripped of all power to tax, to support, or otherwise to assist any or all religions, or to interfere with the beliefs of any religious individual or group.

The movement toward this end reached its dramatic climax in Virginia's tax levy for the support of the established church. Thomas Jefferson and James Madison led the fight against this tax. Madison wrote his great Memorial and Remonstrance against the law. In it, he eloquently argued that a true religion did not need the support of law; that no person, either believer or non-believer, should be taxed to support a religious institution of any kind; that the best interest of a society required that the minds of men always be wholly free; and that cruel persecutions were the inevitable result of government-established religions. Madison's Remonstrance received strong support throughout Virginia, and the Assembly postponed consideration of the proposed tax measure until its next session. When the proposal came up for consideration at that session, it not only died in committee, but the Assembly enacted the famous "Virginia Bill for Religious Liberty" originally written by Thomas Jefferson. The preamble to the Bill stated among other things that

> Almighty God hath created the mind free; that all attempts to influence it by temporal punishment, or burthens, or by civil incapacitations, tend only to beget habits of hypocrisy and meanness, and are a departure from the plan of the Holy author of our religion who being Lord both of body and mind, yet chose not to propagate it by coercions on either . . . ; that to compel a man to furnish contributions of money for the propagation of opinions which he disbelieves, is sinful and tyrannical; that even the forcing him to support this or that teacher of his own religious persuasion, is depriving him of the comfortable liberty of giving his contributions to the particular pastor, whose morals he would make his pattern.

And the statute itself enacted

> That no man shall be compelled to frequent or support any religious worship, place, or ministry whatsoever, nor shall be enforced, restrained, molested, or burthened, in his body or goods, nor shall otherwise suffer on account of his religious opinions or belief. . . .

This Court has previously recognized that the provisions of the First Amendment, in the drafting and adoption of which Madison and Jefferson played such leading roles, had the same objective and were intended to provide the same protection against governmental intrusion on religious liberty as the Virginia statute. Prior to the adoption of the Fourteenth Amendment, the First Amendment did not apply as a restraint against the states. Most of them did soon provide similar constitutional protections for religious liberty. But some states persisted for about half a century in imposing restraints upon the free exercise of religion and in discriminating against particular religious groups. In recent years, so far as the provision against the establishment of a religion is concerned, the question has most frequently arisen in connection with proposed state aid to church schools and efforts to carry on religious teachings in the public schools in accordance with the tenets of a particular sect. Some churches have either sought or accepted state financial support for their schools. Here again the efforts to obtain state aid or acceptance of it have not been limited to any one particular faith. The state courts, in the main, have remained faithful to the language of their own constitutional provisions designated to protect religious freedom and to separate religions and governments. Their decisions, however, show the difficulty in drawing the line between tax legislation which provides funds for the welfare of the general public and that which is designed to support institutions which teach religion.

The meaning and scope of the First Amendment, preventing establishment of religion or prohibiting the free exercise thereof, in the light of its history and the evils it was designed forever to suppress, have been several times elaborated by the decisions of this Court prior to the application of the First Amendment to the states by the Fourteenth. The broad meaning given the Amendment by these earlier cases has been accepted by this Court in its decisions concerning an individual's religious freedom rendered since the Fourteenth Amendment was interpreted to make the prohibitions of the First applicable to state action abridging religious freedom. There is every reason to give the same application and broad interpretation to the "establishment of religion" clause. The interrelation of these complementary clauses was well summarized in a statement of the Court of Appeals of South Carolina, quoted with approval by this Court, in *Watson v. Jones*, "The structure of our government has, for the preservation of civil liberty, rescued the temporal institutions from religious interference. On the other hand, it has secured religious liberty from the invasions of the civil authority."

The "establishment of religion" clause of the First Amendment means at least this: Neither a state nor the Federal Government can set up a church. Neither can pass laws which aid one religion, aid all religions, or prefer one religion over another. Neither can force nor influence a person to go to or to remain away from church against his will or force him to profess a belief or disbelief in any religion. No person can be punished for entertaining or professing religious beliefs or disbeliefs, for church attendance or non-attendance. No tax in any amount, large or small, can be levied to support any religious activities or institutions, whatever they may be called, or whatever form they may adopt to teach or practice religion. Neither a state nor the Federal Government can, openly or secretly, participate in the affairs of any religious organizations or groups and vice versa. In the words of Jefferson, the clause against establishment of religion by law was intended to erect "a wall of separation between Church and State."

We must consider the New Jersey statute in accordance with the foregoing limitations imposed by the First Amendment. But we must not strike that state statute down if it is within the state's constitutional power even though it approaches the verge of that power. New Jersey cannot consistently with the "establishment of religion" clause of the First Amendment contribute tax-raised funds to the support of an institution which teaches the tenets and faith of any church. On the other hand, other language of the amendment commands that New Jersey cannot exclude individual Catholics, Lutherans, Mohammedans, Baptists, Jews, Methodists, Non-belivers, Presbyterians, or the members of any other faith, because of their faith, or lack of it, from receiving the benefits of public welfare legislation. While we do not mean to intimate that a state could not provide transportation only to children attending public schools, we must be careful, in protecting the citizens of New Jersey against state-established churches, to be sure that we do not inadvertently prohibit New Jersey from extending its general State law benefits to all its citizens without regard to their religious belief.

Measured by these standards, we cannot say that the First Amendment prohibits New Jersey from spending tax-raised funds to pay the bus fares of parochial school pupils as a part of a general program under which it pays the fares of pupils attending public and other schools. It is undoubtedly true that children are helped to get to church schools. There is even a possibility that some of the children might not be sent to the church schools if the parents were compelled to pay their children's bus fares out of their own pockets when transportation to a public school would have been paid for by the State. The same possibility exists where the state requires a local transit company to provide reduced fares to school children including those attending parochial schools, or where a municipally owned transportation system undertakes to carry all school children free of charge. Moreover, state-paid policemen, detailed to protect children going to and from church schools from the very real hazards of traffic, would serve much the same purpose and accomplish much the same result as state provisions intended to guarantee free transportation of a kind which the state deems to be best for the school children's welfare. And parents might refuse to risk their children to the serious danger of traffic accidents going to and from parochial schools, the approaches to which were not protected by policemen. Similarly, parents might be reluctant to permit their children to attend schools which the state had cut off from such general government services as ordinary police and fire protection, connections for sewage disposal, public highways and sidewalks. Of course, cutting off church schools from these services, so separate and so indisputably marked off from the religious function, would make it far more difficult for the schools to operate. But such is obviously not the purpose of the First Amendment. That Amendment requires the state to be a neutral in its relations with groups of religious believers and non-believers; it does not require the state to be their adversary. State power is no more to be used so as to handicap religions, than it is to favor them.

This Court has said that parents may, in the discharge of their duty under state compulsory education laws, send their children to a religious rather than a public school if the school meets the secular educational requirements which the state has power to impose. It appears that these parochial schools meet New Jersey's requirements. The State contributes no money to the schools. It does not support them. Its legislation, as applied, does no more than provide a general program to help parents get their children, regardless of their religion, safely and expeditiously to and from accredited schools.

The First Amendment has erected a wall between church and state. That wall must be kept high and impregnable. We could not approve the slightest breach. New Jersey has not breached it here.

Affirmed.

MR. JUSTICE JACKSON, DISSENTING.

I find myself, contrary to first impressions, unable to join in this decision. I have a sympathy, though it is not ideological, with Catholic citizens who are compelled by law to pay taxes for public schools, and also feel constrained by conscience and discipline to support other schools for their own children. Such relief to them as this case involves is not in itself a serious burden to taxpayers and I have assumed it to be as little serious in principle. Study of this case convinces me otherwise. The Court's opinion marshals every argument in favor of state aid and puts the case in its most favorable light, but much of its reasoning confirms my conclusions that there are no good grounds upon which to support the present legislation. In fact, the undertones of the opinion, advocating complete and uncompromising separation of Church from State, seem utterly discordant with its conclusion yielding support to their commingling in educational matters. The case which irresistibly comes to mind as the most fitting precedent is that of Julia who according to Byron's reports, "whispering 'I will ne'er consent,'—consented."

I

The Court sustains this legislation by assuming two deviations from the facts of this particular case; first, it assumes a state of facts the record does not support, and secondly, it refuses to consider facts which are inescapable on the record.

The Court concludes that this "legislation, as applied, does no more than provide a general program to help parents get their children, regardless of their religion, safely and expeditiously to and from accredited schools," and it draws a comparision between "state provisions intended to guarantee free transportation" for school children with services such as police and fire protection, and implies that we are here dealing with "laws authorizing new types of public services . . . " This hypothesis permeates the opinion. The facts will not bear that construction.

The Township of Ewing is not furnishing transportation to the children in any form; it is not operating school busses itself or contracting for their operation; and it is not performing any public service of any kind with this taxpayer's money. All school children are left to ride as ordinary paying passengers on the regular busses operated by the public transportation system. What the Township does, and what the taxpayer complains of, is at stated intervals to reimburse parents for the fares paid, provided the children attend either public schools or Catholic Church schools. This expenditure of tax funds has no possible effect on the child's safety or expedition in transit. As passengers on the public busses they travel as fast and no faster, and are safe and no safer, since their parents are reimbursed as before.

In addition to this assuming a type of service that does not exist, the Court also insists that we must close our eyes to a discrimination which does exist. The resolution which authorizes disbursement of this taxpayer's money limits reimbursement to those who attend public schools and Catholic schools. That is the way the Act is applied to this taxpayer.

The New Jersey Act in question makes the character of the school, not the needs of the children determine the eligibility of parents to reimbursement. The Act permits payment for transportation to parochial schools or public schools but prohibits it to private schools operated in whole or in part for profit. Children often are sent to private schools because their parents feel that they require more individual instruction than public schools can provide, or because they are backward or defective and need special attention. If all children of the state were objects of impartial solicitude, no reason is obvious for denying transportation reimbursement to students of this class, for these often are as needy and as worthy as those who go to public or parochial schools. Refusal to reimburse those who attend such schools is understandable only in the light of a purpose to aid the schools, because the state might well abstain from aiding a profit-making private enterprise. Thus, under the Act and resolution brought to us by this case children are classified according to the schools they attend and are to be aided if they attend the public schools or private Catholic schools, and they are not allowed to be aided if they attend private secular schools or private religious schools of other faiths.

Of course, this case is not one of a Baptist or a Jew or an Episcopalian or a pupil of a private school complaining of discrimination. It is one of a taxpayer urging that he is being taxed for an unconstitutional purpose. I think he is entitled to have us consider the Act just as it is written. The statement by the New Jersey court that it holds the Legislature may authorize use of local funds "for the transportation of pupils to any school," in view of the other constitutional views expressed, is not a holding that this Act authorizes transportation for all pupils to all schools. As applied to this taxpayer by the action he complains of, certainly the Act does not authorize reimbursement to those who choose any alternative to the public school except Catholic Church schools.

If we are to decide this case on the facts before us, our question is simply this: Is it constitutional to tax this complainant to pay the cost of carrying pupils to Church schools of one specified denomination?

II

Whether the taxpayer constitutionally can be made to contribute aid to parents of students because of their attendance at parochial schools depends upon the nature of those schools and their relation to the Church. The Constitution says nothing of education. It lays no obligation on the states to provide schools and does not undertake to regulate state systems of education if they see fit to maintain them. But they cannot, through school policy any more than through other means, invade rights secured to citizens by the Constitution of the United States. One of our basic rights is to be free of taxation to support a transgression of the constitutional command that the authorities "shall make no law respecting an establishment of religion, or prohibiting the free exercise thereof."

The function of the Church school is a subject on which this record is meager. It shows only that the schools are under superintendence of a priest and that "religion is taught as part of the curriculum." But we know that such schools are parochial only in name—they, in fact, represent a world-wide and age-old policy of the Roman Catholic Church. Under the rubric "Catholic Schools," the Canon Law of the Church by which all Catholics are bound, provides:

"1216. In every elementary school the children must, according to their age, be instructed in Christian doctrine."

"The young people who attend the higher schools are to receive a deeper religious knowledge, and the bishops shall appoint priests qualified for such work by their learning and piety. (Canon 1373.)"

"1217. Catholic children shall not attend non-Catholic, indifferent, schools that are mixed, that is to say schools open to Catholic and non-Catholics alike. The bishop of the diocese only has the right, in harmony with the instructions of the Holy See, to decide under what circumstances, and with what safeguards to prevent loss of faith, it may be tolerated that Catholic children go to such schools. (Canon 1374.)"

"1224. The religious teaching of youth in any schools is subject to the authority and inspection of the Church."

"The local Ordinaries have the right and duty to watch that nothing is taught contrary to faith or good morals, in any of the schools of their territory."

"They, moreover, have the right to approve the books of Christian doctrine and the teachers of religion, and to demand, for the sake of safeguarding religion and morals, the removal of teachers and books. (Canon 1381.)" (Woywod, Rev. Stanislaus, The New Canon Law, under imprimatur of Most Rev. Francis J. Spellman, Archbishop of New York and others, 1940.)

It is no exaggeration to say that the whole historic conflict in temporal policy between the Catholic Church and non-Catholics comes to a focus in their respective school policies. The Roman Catholic Church, counseled by experience in many ages and many lands and with all sorts and conditions of men, takes what, from the viewpoint of its own progress and the success of its mission, is a wise estimate of the importance of education to religion. It does not leave the individual to pick up religion by chance. It relies on early and indelible indoctrination in the faith and order of the Church by the word and example of persons consecrated to the task.

Our public school, if not a product of Protestantism, at least is more consistent with it than with the Catholic culture and scheme of values. It is a relatively recent development dating from about 1840. It is organized on the premise that secular education can be isolated from all religious teaching so that the school can inculcate all needed temporal knowledge and also maintain a strict and lofty neutrality as to religion. The assumption is that after the individual has been instructed in worldly wisdom he will be better fitted to choose his religion. Whether such a disjunction is possible, and if possible whether it is wise, are questions I need not to try to answer.

I should be surprised if any Catholic would deny that the parochial school is a vital, if not the most vital, part of the Roman Catholic Church. If put to the choice, that venerable institution, I should expect, would forego its whole service for mature persons before it would give up education of the young, and it would be a wise choice. Its growth and cohesion, discipline and loyalty, spring from its schools. Catholic education is the rock on which the whole structure rests, and to render tax aid to its Church school is indistinguishable to me from rendering the same aid to the Church itself.

III

It is of no importance in this situation whether the beneficiary of this expenditure of tax-raised funds is primarily the parochial school and incidentally the pupil, or whether the aid is directly bestowed on the pupil with indirect benefits to the school. The state cannot maintain a Church and it can no more tax its citizens to furnish free carriage to those who attend a Church. The prohibition against establishment of religion cannot be circumvented by a subsidy, bonus or reimbursement of expense to individuals for receiving religious instruction and indoctrination.

The Court, however, compares this to other subsidies and loans to individuals and says, "Nor does it follow that a law has a private rather than a public purpose because it provides that tax-raised funds will be paid to reimburse individuals on account of money spent by them in a way which furthers a public program." Of course, the state may pay out tax-raised funds to relieve pauperism, but it may not spend funds to secure religion against skepticism. It may compensate individuals for loss of employment, but it cannot compensate them for adherence to a creed.

It seems to me that the basic fallacy in the Court's reasoning, which accounts for its failure to apply the principles it avows, is in ignoring the essentially religious test by which beneficiaries of this expenditure are selected. A policeman protects a Catholic, of course—but not because he is a Catholic, it is because he is a man and a member of our society. The fireman protects the Church school—but not because it is a Church school; it is because it is property, part of the assets of our society. Neither the fireman nor the policeman has to ask before he renders aid "Is this man or building identified with the Catholic Church?" But before these school authorities draw a check to reimburse for a student's fare they must ask just that question, and if the school is a Catholic one they may render aid because it is such, while if it is of any other faith or is run for profit, the help must be withheld. To consider the converse of the Court's reasoning will best disclose its fallacy. That there is no parallel between police and fire protection and this plan of reimbursement is apparent from the incongruity of the limitation of this Act if applied to police and fire service. Could we sustain an Act that said police shall protect pupils on the way to or from public schools and Catholic schools but not while going to and coming from other schools, and firemen shall extinguish a blaze in public or Catholic school buildings but shall not put out a blaze in Protestant Church schools or private schools operated for profit? That is the true analogy to the case we have before us and I should think it pretty plain that such a scheme would not be valid.

The Court's holding is that this taxpayer has no grievance because the state has decided to make the reimbursement a public purpose and therefore we are bound to regard it as such. I agree that this Court has left, and always should leave to each state, great latitude in deciding for itself, in the light of its own conditions, what shall be public purposes in its scheme of things. It may socialize utilities and economic enterprises and make taxpayers' business out of what conventionally had been private business. It may make public business of individual welfare, health, education, entertainment or security. But it cannot make public business of religious worship or instruction, or of attendance at religious institutions of any character. There is no answer to the proposition more fully expounded by Mr. Justice Rutledge that the effect of the religious freedom Amendment to our Constitution was to take every form of propagation of religion out of the realm of things which could directly or indirectly be made public business and thereby be supported in whole or in part at taxpayers' expense. That is a difference which the Constitution sets up between religion and almost every other subject matter of legislation, a difference which goes to the very root of religious freedom and which the Court is overlooking today. This freedom was first in the Bill of Rights because it was first in the forefathers' minds; it was set forth in absolute terms, and its strength is its rigidity. It was intended not only to keep the states' hands out of religion, but to keep religions' hands off the state, and above all, to keep bitter religious controversy out of public life by denying to every denomination any advantage from getting control of public policy or the public purse. Those great ends I cannot but think are immeasurably compromised by today's decision.

This policy of our Federal Constitution has never been wholly pleasing to most religious groups. They all are quick to invoke its protections; they all are irked when they feel its restraints. This Court has gone a long way, if not an unreasonable way, to hold that public business of such paramount importance as maintenance of public order, protection of the privacy of the home, and taxation may not be pursued by a state in a way that even indirectly will interfere with religious proselyting.

But we cannot have it both ways. Religious teaching cannot be a private affair when the state seeks to impose regulations which infringe on it indirectly, and a public affair when it comes to taxing citizens of one faith to aid another, or those of no faith to aid all. If these principles seem harsh in prohibiting aid to Catholic education, it must not be forgotten that it is the same Constitution that alone assures Catholics the right to maintain these schools at all when predominant local sentiment would forbid them. Nor should I think that those who have done so well without this aid would want to see this separation between Church and State broken down. If the state may aid these religious schools, it may therefore regulate them. Many groups have sought aid from tax funds only to find that it carried political controls with it. Indeed this Court has declared that "It is hardly lack of due process for the Government to regulate that which it subsidizes."

But in any event, the great purposes of the Constitution do not depend on the approval or convenience of those they restrain. I cannot read the history of the struggle to separate political from ecclesiastical affairs, well summarized in the opinion of Mr. Justice Rutledge in which I generally concur, without a conviction that the Court today is unconsciously giving the clock's hands a backward turn.

Mr. Justice Frankfurter joins in this opinion.

MR. JUSTICE RUTLEDGE, WITH WHOM MR. JUSTICE FRANKFURTER, MR. JUSTICE JACKSON AND MR. JUSTICE BURTON AGREE, DISSENTING.

> Congress shall make no law respecting an establishment of religion, or prohibiting the free exercise thereof. . . . " U.S. Const. Am. Art. I. . . .
>
> Well aware that Almighty God hath created the mind free; . . . that to compel a man to furnish contributions of money for the propagation of opinions which he disbelieves, is sinful and tyrannical; . . .
>
> We, the General Assembly, do enact, that no man shall be compelled to frequent or support any religious worship, place, or ministry whatsoever, nor shall be enforced, restrained,

> molested, or burthened in his body or goods, nor shall otherwise suffer on account of his religious opinions or belief. . . .

I cannot believe that the great author of those words, or the men who made them law, could have joined in this decision. Neither so high nor so impregnable today as yesterday is the wall raised between church and state by Virginia's great statute of religious freedom and the First Amendment, now made applicable to all the states by the Fourteenth. New Jersey's statute sustained is the first, if indeed it is not the second breach to be made by this Court's action. That a third, and a fourth, and still others will be attempted, we may be sure. For just as *Cochran v. Louisiana State Board of Education*, has opened the way by oblique ruling for this decision, so will the two make wider the breach for a third. Thus with time the most solid freedom steadily gives way before continuing corrosive decision.

This case forces us to determine squarely for the first time what was "an establishment of religion" in the First Amendment's conception; and by that measure to decide whether New Jersey's action violates its command. The facts may be stated shortly, to give setting and color to the constitutional problem.

By statute New Jersey has authorized local boards of education to provide for the transportation of children "to and from school other than a public school" except one operated for profit wholly or in part over established public school routes, or by other means when the child lives "remote from any school." The school board of Ewing Township has provided by resolution for "the transportation of pupils of Ewing to the Trenton and Pennington High Schools and Catholic Schools by way of public carrier. . . . "

Named parents have paid the cost of public conveyance of their children from their homes in Ewing to three public high schools and four parochial schools outside the district. Semiannually the Board has reimbursed the parents from public school funds raised by general taxation. Religion is taught as part of the curriculum in each of the four private schools, as appears affirmatively by the testimony of the superintendent of parochial schools in the Diocese of Trenton.

The Court of Errors and Appeals of New Jersey, reversing the Supreme Court's decision, has held the Ewing board's action not in contravention of the state constitution or statutes or of the Federal Constitution. We have to consider only whether this ruling accords with the prohibition of the First Amendment implied in the due process clause of the Fourteenth.

I

Not simply an established church, but any law respecting an establishment of religion is forbidden. The Amendment was broadly but not loosely phrased. It is the compact and exact summation of its author's views formed during his long struggle for religious freedom. In Madison's own words characterizing Jefferson's Bill for Establishing Religious Freedom, the guaranty he put in our national charter, like the bill he piloted through the Virginia Assembly, was "a Model of technical precision, and perspicuous brevity." Madison could not have confused "church" and "an establishment of religion."

The Amendment's purpose was not to strike merely at the official establishment of a single sect, creed or religion, outlawing only a formal relation such as had prevailed in England and some of the colonies. Necessarily it was to uproot all such relationships. But the object was broader than separating church and state in this narrow sense. It was to create a complete and permanent separation of the spheres of religious activity and civil authority by comprehensively forbidding every form of public aid or support for religion. In proof the Amendment's wording and history unite with this Court's consistent utterances whenever attention has been fixed directly upon the question.

"Religion" appears only once in the Amendment. But the word governs two prohibitions and governs them alike. It does not have two meanings, one narrow to forbid "an establishment" and another, much broader, for securing "the free exercise thereof." "Thereof" brings down "religion" with its entire and exact content, no more and no less, from the first into the second guaranty, so that Congress and now the states are as broadly restricted concerning the one as they are regarding the other.

No one would claim today that the Amendment is constricted, in "prohibiting the free exercise" of religion, to securing the free exercise of some formal or creedal observance of one sect or of many. It secures all forms of religious expression, creedal, sectarian or nonsectarian wherever and however taking place, except conduct which trenches upon the like freedoms of others or clearly and presently endangers the community's good order and security. For the protective purposes of this phase of the basic freedom street preaching, oral or by distribution of literature, has been given "the same high estate under the First Amendment as . . . worship in the churches and preaching from the pulpits." And on this basis parents have been held entitled to send their children to private, religious schools. Accordingly, daily religious education commingled with secular is "religion" within the guaranty's comprehensive scope. So are religious training and teaching in whatever form. The word connotes the broadest content, determined not by the form or formality of the teaching, or where it occurs, but by its essential nature regardless of those details.

"Religion" has the same broad significance in the twin prohibition concerning "an establishment." The Amendment was not duplicitous. "Religion" and "establishment" were not used in any formal or technical sense. The prohibition broadly forbids state support, financial or other, of religion in any guise, form or degree. It outlaws all use of public funds for religious purposes.

II

No provision of the Constitution is more closely tied to or given consent by its generating history than the religious clause of the First Amendment. It is at once the refined product and the terse summation of that history. The history includes not only Madison's authorship and the proceedings before the First Congress, but also the long and intensive struggle for religious freedom in America, more especially in Virginia, of which the Amendment was the direct culmination. In the documents of the times, particularly of Madison, who was leader in the Virginia struggle before he became the Amendment's sponsor, but also in the writings of Jefferson and others and in the issues which engendered them is to be found irrefutable confirmation of the Amendment's sweeping content.

For Madison, as also for Jefferson, religious freedom was the crux of the struggle for freedom in general. Madison was coauthor with George Mason of the religious clause in Virginia's great Declaration of Rights of 1776. He is credited with changing it from a mere statement of the principle of tolerance to the first official legislative pronouncement that freedom of conscience and religion are inherent rights of the individual. He sought also to have the Declaration expressly condemn the existing Virginia establishment. But the forces supporting it were then too strong.

Accordingly Madison yielded on this phase but not for long. At once he resumed the fight, continuing it before succeeding legislative sessions. As a member of the General Assembly in 1779 he threw his full weight behind Jefferson's historic Bill for Establishing Religious Freedom. That bill was a prime phase of Jefferson's broad program of democratic reform undertaken on his return from the Continental Congress in 1776 and submitted for the General Assembly's consideration in 1779 as his proposed revised Virginia code. With Jefferson's departure for Europe in 1784, Madison became the Bill's prime sponsor. Enactment failed in successive legislatures from its introduction in June 1779, until its adoption in January, 1786. But during all this time the fight for religious freedom moved forward in Virginia on various fronts with growing intensity. Madison led throughout, against Patrick Henry's powerful opposing leadership until Henry was elected governor in November, 1784.

The climax came in the legislative struggle of 1784–1785 over the Assessment Bill (pertinent portions below*). This was nothing more nor less than a taxing measure for the support of religion, designed to revive the payment of tithes suspended since 1777. So long as it singled out a particular sect for preference it incurred the active and general hostility of dissentient groups. It was broadened to include them, with the result that some subsided temporarily in their opposition. As altered, the bill gave to each taxpayer the privilege of designating which church should receive his share of the tax. In default of desig-

*The operative portions of that Bill "Establishing a Provision for Teachers of the Christian Religion" were:

> Be it therefore enacted by the General Assembly, That for the support of Christian teachers, per centum on the amount, or in the pound on the amount, or in the pound on the sum payable for tax on the property within this Commonwealth, is hereby assessed, and shall be paid by every person chargeable with the said tax at the time the same shall become due; and the Sheriffs of the several Counties shall have power to levy and collect the same in the same manner and under the like restrictions and limitations, as are or may be prescribed by the laws for raising the revenues of this State.
>
> And be it further enacted, That the money to be raised by virtue of this act, shall be by the Vestries, Elders, or Directors of each religious society, appropriated to a provision for a Minister or Teacher of the Gospel of their denomination, or the providing places of divine worship, and to none other use whatsoever; except in the denominations of Quakers and Menonists, who may receive what is collected from their members, and place it in their general fund, to be disposed of in a manner which they shall think best calculated to promote their particular mode of worship.

nation the legislature applied it to pious uses. But what is of the utmost significance here, "in its final form the bill left the taxpayer the option of giving his tax to education."

Madison was unyielding at all times, opposing with all his vigor the general and nondiscriminatory assessments proposed. The modified Assessment Bill passed second reading in December, 1784, and was all but enacted. Madison and his followers, however, maneuvered deferment of final consideration until November, 1785. And before the Assembly reconvened in the fall he issued his historic Memorial and Remonstrance.

This is Madison's complete, though not his only, interpretation of religious liberty. It is a broadside attack upon all forms of "establishment" of religion, both general and particular, nondiscriminatory or selective. Reflecting not only the many legislative conflicts over the Assessment Bill and the Bill for Establishing Religious Freedom but also, for example, the struggles for religious incorporations and the continued maintenance of the glebes, the Remonstrance is at once the most concise and the most accurate statement of the views of the First Amendment's author concerning what is "an establishment of religion." Because it behooves us in the dimming distance of time not to lose sight of what he and his coworkers had in mind when, by a single sweeping stroke of the pen, they forbade an establishment of religion and secured its free exercise, the text of the Remonstrance is appended at the end of this opinion for its wider current reference, . . .

The Remonstrance, stirring up a storm of popular protest, killed the Assessment Bill. It collapsed in committee shortly before Christmas, 1785. With this, the way was cleared at last for enactment of Jefferson's Bill for Establishing Religious Freedom. Madison promptly drove it through in January of 1786, seven years from the time it was first introduced. This dual victory substantially ended the fight over establishments, settling the issue against them.

The next year Madison became a member of the Constitutional Convention. Its work done, he fought valiantly to secure the ratification of its great product in Virginia as elsewhere, and nowhere else more effectively. Madison was certain in his own mind that under the Constitution "there is not a shadow of right in the general government to intermeddle with religion" and that "this subject is, for the honor of America, perfectly free and unshackled. The Government has no jurisdiction over it. . . ." Nevertheless he pledged that he would work for a Bill of Rights, including a specific guaranty of religious freedom, and Virginia, with other states, ratified the Constitution on this assurance.

Ratification thus accomplished, Madison was sent to the first Congress. There he went at once about performing his pledge to establish freedom for the nation as he had done in Virginia. Within a little more than three years from his legislative victory at home he had proposed and secured the submission and ratification of the First Amendment as the first article of our Bill of Rights.

All the great instruments of the Virginia struggle for religious liberty thus became warp and woof of our constitutional tradition, not simply by the course of history, but by the common unifying force of Madison's life, thought and sponsorship. He epitomized the whole of that tradition in the Amendment's compact, but nonetheless comprehensive, phrasing.

As the Remonstrance discloses throughout, Madison opposed every form and degree of official relation between religion and civil authority. For him religion was a wholly private matter beyond the scope of civil power either to restrain or to support. Denial or abridgment of religious freedom was a violation of rights both of conscience and of natural equality. State aid was no less obnoxious or destructive to freedom and to religion itself than other forms of state interference. "Establishment" and "free exercise" were correlative and coextensive ideas, representing only different facets of the single great and fundamental freedom. The Remonstrance, following the Virginia statute's example, referred to the history of religious conflicts and the effects of all sorts of establishment, current and historical, to suppress religion's free exercise. With Jefferson, Madison believed that to tolerate any fragment of establishment would be by so much to perpetuate restraint upon that freedom. Hence he sought to tear out the institution not partially but root and branch, and to bar its return forever.

In no phase was he more unrelentingly absolute than in opposing state support or aid by taxation. Not even "three pence" contribution was thus to be exacted from any citizen for such a purpose. Tithes had been the life blood of establishment before and after other compulsions disappeared. Madison and his coworkers made no exceptions or abridgments to the complete separation they created. Their objection was not to small tithes. It was to any tithes whatsoever. "If it were lawful to impose a small tax for religion the admission would pave the way for oppressive levies." Not the amount but "the principle of assessment was wrong." And the principle was as much to prevent "the interference of law in religion" as to restrain religious intervention in political matters. In this field the authors of our freedom would not tolerate "the first experiment on our liberties" or "wait till usurped power had strengthened itself by exercise, and entangled the question in precedents." Nor should we.

In view of this history no further proof is needed that the Amendment forbids any appropriation, large or small, from public funds to aid or support any and all religious exercises. But if more were called for, the debates in the First Congress and this Court's consistent expressions, whenever it has touched on the matter directly, supply it.

By contrast with the Virginia history, the congressional debates on consideration of the Amendment reveal only sparse discussion, reflecting the fact that the essential issues had been settled. Indeed the matter had become so well understood as to have been taken for granted in all but formal phrasing. Hence, the only enlightening reference shows concern, not to preserve any power to use public funds in aid of religion, but to prevent the Amendment from outlawing private gifts inadvertently by virtue of the breadth of its wording.

III

Compulsory attendance upon religious exercise went out early in the process of separating church and state, together with forced observance of religious forms and ceremonies. Test oaths and religious qualification for office followed later. These things none devoted to our great tradition of religious liberty would think of bringing back. Hence today, apart from efforts to inject religious training or exercises and sectarian issues into the public schools, the only serious surviving threat to maintaining the complete and permanent separation of religion and civil power which the First Amendment commands is through use of the taxing power to support religion, religious establishment, or establishments having a religious foundation whatever their form or special religious function.

Does New Jersey's action furnish support for religion by use of the taxing power? Certainly it does, if the test remains undiluted as Jefferson and Madison made it, that money taken by taxation from one is not to be used or given to support another's religious training or belief, or indeed one's own. Today as then the furnishing of "contributions of money for the propagation of opinions which he disbelieves" is the forbidden exaction; and the prohibition is absolute for whatever measure brings that consequence and whatever amount may be sought or given to that end.

The funds used here were raised by taxation. The Court does not dispute nor could it that their use does in fact give aid and encouragement to religious instruction. It only concludes that this aid is not "support" in law. But Madison and Jefferson were concerned with aid and support in fact not as a legal conclusion "entangled in precedents." Here parents pay money to send their children to parochial schools and funds raised by taxation are used to reimburse them. This not only helps the children to get to school and the parents to send them. It aids them in a substantial way to get the very thing which they are sent to the particular school to secure, namely, religious training and teaching.

Believers of all faiths, and others who do not express their feeling toward ultimate issues of existence in any creedal form, pay the New Jersey tax. When the money so raised is used to pay for transportation to religious schools, the Catholic taxpayer to the extent of his proportionate share pays for the transportation of Lutheran, Jewish and otherwise religiously affiliated children to receive their non-Catholic religious instruction. Their parents likewise pay proportionately for the transportation of Catholic children to receive Catholic instruction. Each thus contributes to "the propagation of opinions which he disbelieves" in so far as their religions differ, as do others who accept no creed without regard to those differences. Each thus pays taxes also to support the teaching of his own religion, an exaction equally forbidden since it denies "the comfortable liberty" of giving one's contribution to the particular agency of instruction he approves.

New Jersey's action therefore exactly fits the type of exaction and the kind of evil at which Madison and Jefferson struck. Under the test they framed it cannot be said that the cost of transportation is no part of the cost of education or of the religious instruction given. That it is a substantial and a necessary element is shown most plainly by the continuing and increasing demand for the state to assume it. Nor is there pretense that it relates only to the secular instruction given in religious schools or that any attempt is or could be made toward allocating proportional shares as between the secular and the religious instruction. It is precisely because the instruction is religious and relates to a particular faith, whether one or another, that parents send their children to religious schools under the Pierce doctrine. And the very purpose of the state's contribution is to defray the cost of conveying the pupil to the place where he will receive not simply secular, but also and primarily religious, teaching and guidance.

Indeed the view is sincerely avowed by many of various faiths, that the basic purpose of all education is or should be religious, that the secular cannot be and should not be separated from the religious phase and emphasis. Hence, the inadequacy of public or secular education and the necessity for sending the child to a school where religion is taught. But whatever may be the philosophy or its justification, there is undeniably an admixture of religious with secular teaching in all such institutions. That is the very reason for their being. Certainly for purposes of constitutionality we cannot contradict the whole basis of the ethical and educational convictions of people who believe in religious schooling.

Yet this very admixture is what was disestablished when the First Amendment forbade "an establishment of religion." Commingling the religious with the secular teaching does not divest the whole of its religious permeation and emphasis or make them of minor part, if proportion were material. Indeed, on any other view, the Constitutional prohibition always could be brought to naught by adding a modicum of the secular.

An appropriation from the public treasury to pay the cost of transportation to Sunday school, to weekday special classes at the church or parish house, or to the meeting of various young people's religious societies, such as the Y.M.C.A., the Y.W.C.A., the Y.M.H.A., the Epworth League, could not withstand the constitutional attack. This would be true, whether or not secular activities were mixed with the religious. If such an appropriation could not stand, then it is hard to see how one becomes valid for the same thing upon the more extended scale of daily instruction. Surely constitutionality does not turn on where or how often the mixed teaching occurs.

Finally transportation, where it is needed, is as essential to education as any other element. Its cost is as much a part of the total expense, except at times in amount, as the cost of textbooks, of school lunches, of athletic equipment, of writing and other materials; indeed of all other items composing the total burden. Now as always the core of the educational process is the teacher-pupil relationship. Without this the richest equipment and facilities would go for naught. But the proverbial Mark Hopkins conception no longer suffices for the country's requirements. Without buildings, without equipment, without library, textbooks and other materials, and without transportation to bring teacher and pupil together in such an effective teaching environment, there can be not even the skeleton of what our times require. Hardly can it be maintained that transportation is the least essential of these items, or that it does not in fact aid, encourage, sustain and support, just as they do, the very process which is its purpose to accomplish. No less essential is it or the payment of its cost, than the very teaching in the classroom or the payment of the teacher's sustenance. Many types of equipment, now considered essential, better could be done without.

For me, therefore, the feat is impossible to select so indispensable an item from the composite of total costs, and characterize it as not aiding, contributing to, promoting or sustaining the propagation of beliefs which it is the very end of all to bring about. Unless this can be maintained, and the Court does not maintain it, the aid thus given is outlawed. Payment of transportation is no more, nor is it any the less essential to education, whether religious or secular, than payment for tuitions, for teachers' salaries, for buildings, equipment and necessary materials. Nor is it any the less directly related, in a school giving religious instruction, to the primary religious objective all those essential items of cost are intended to achieve. No rational line can be drawn between payment for such larger, but not more necessary, items and payment for transportation. The only line that can be so drawn is one between more dollars and less. Certainly in this realm such a line can be no valid constitutional measure.

Now as in Madison's time, not the amount but the principle of assessment is wrong.

IV

But we are told that the New Jersey statute is valid in its present application because the appropriation is for a public, not a private purpose, namely, the promotion of education, and the majority accept this idea in the conclusion that all we have here is "public welfare legislation." If that is true and the Amendment's force can be thus destroyed, what has been said becomes all the more pertinent. For then there could be no possible objection to more extensive support of religious education by New Jersey.

If the fact alone be determinative that religious schools are engaged in education, thus promoting the general and individual welfare, together with the legislature's decision that the payment of public moneys for their aid makes their work a public function, then I can see no possible basis, except one of dubious legislative policy, for the state's refusal to make full appropriation for support of private, religious schools, just as is done for public instruction. There could not be, on that basis, valid constitutional objection.

Of course paying the cost of transportation promotes the general cause of education and the welfare of the individual. So does paying all other items of educational expense. And obviously, as the majority say, it is much too late to urge that legislation designed to facilitate the opportunities of children to secure a secular education serves no public purpose. Our nation-wide system of public education rests on the contrary view, as do all grants-in-aid of education, public or private, which is not religious in character.

These things are beside the real question. They have no possible materiality except to obscure the all-pervading inescapable issue. Stripped of its religious phase, the case presents no substantial federal question. The public function argument, by casting the issue in terms of promoting the general cause of education and the welfare of the individual, ignores the religious factor and its essential connection with the transportation, thereby leaving out the only vital element in the case. So of course do the "public welfare" and "social legislation" ideas, for they come to the same thing.

We have here then one substantial issue, not two. To say that New Jersey's appropriation and her use of the power of taxation for raising the funds appropriated are not for public purposes but are for private ends, is to say that they are for the support of religion and religious teaching. Conversely, to say that they are for public purposes is to say that they are not for religious ones.

This is precisely for the reason that education which includes religious training and teaching, and its support, have been made matters of private right and function not public, by the very terms of the First Amendment. That is the effect not only in its guaranty of religion's free exercise, but also in the prohibition of establishments. It was on this basis of the private character of the function of religious education that this Court held parents entitled to send their children to private, religious schools. Now it declares in effect that the appropriation of public funds to defray part of the cost of attending those schools is for a public purpose. If so, I do not understand why the state cannot go farther or why this case approaches the verge of its power.

In truth this view contradicts the whole purpose and effect of the First Amendment as heretofore conceived. The "public function"—"public welfare"—"social legislation" argument seeks in Madison's words, to "employ Religion (that is, here, religious education) as an engine of Civil policy." It is of one piece with the Assessment Bill's preamble, although with the vital difference that it wholly ignores what that preamble explicitly states.

Our constitutional policy is exactly the opposite. It does not deny the value or the necessity for religious training, teaching or observance. Rather it secures their free exercise. But to that end it does deny that the state can undertake or sustain them in any form or degree. For this reason the sphere of religious activity, as distinguished from the secular intellectual liberties, has been given the twofold protection and, as the state cannot forbid, neither can it perform or aid in performing the religious function. The dual prohibition makes that function altogether private. It cannot be made a public one by legislative act. This was the very heart of Madison's Remonstrance, as it is of the Amendment itself.

It is not because religious teaching does not promote the public or the individual's welfare, but because neither is furthered when the state promotes religious education, that the Constitution forbids it to do so. Both legislatures and courts are bound by that distinction. In failure to observe it lies the fallacy of the "public function"—"social legislation" argument, a fallacy facilitated by easy transference of the argument's basing from due process unrelated to any religious aspect to the First Amendment.

By no declaration that a gift of public money to religious uses will promote the general or individual welfare, or the cause of education generally, can legislative bodies overcome the Amendment's bar. Nor may the courts sustain their attempts to do so by finding such consequences for appropriations which in fact give aid to or promote religious uses. Legislatures are free to make, and courts to sustain, appropriations only when it can be found that in fact they do not aid, promote, encourage or sustain religious teaching or observances, be the amount large or small. No such finding has been or could be made in this case. The Amendment has removed this form of promoting the public welfare from legislative and judicial competence to make a public function. It is exclusively a private affair.

The reasons underlying the Amendment's policy have not vanished with time or diminished in force. Now as when it was adopted the price of religious freedom is double. It is that the church and religion shall live both within and upon that freedom. There cannot be freedom of religion, safeguarded by the state, and intervention by the church or its agencies in the state's domain or dependency on its largesse. The great condition of religious liberty is that it be free from sustenance, as also from other interferences, by the state. For when it comes to rest upon that secular foundation it vanishes with the resting. Public money devoted to payment of religious costs, educational or other, brings the quest for more. It brings too the struggle of sect against sect for the larger share or for any. Here one by numbers alone will benefit the most, there another. That is precisely the history of societies which have had an established religion and dissident groups. It is the very thing Jefferson and Madison experienced and sought to guard against, whether in its blunt or in its more screened forms. The end of such strife cannot be other than to destroy the cherished liberty. The dominating group will achieve the dominant benefit; or all will embroil the state in their dissensions.

Exactly such conflicts have centered of late around providing transportation to religious schools from public funds. The issue and the dissension work typically, in Madison's phrase, to "destroy that moderation and harmony which the forbearance of our laws to intermeddle with Religion, has produced amongst its several sects." This occurs, as he well knew, over measures at the very threshold of departure from the principle.

In these conflicts wherever success has been obtained it has been upon the contention that by providing the transportation the general cause of education, the general welfare of the individual will be forwarded; hence that the matter lies within the realm of public function, for legislative determination. State courts have divided upon the issue, some taking the view that only the individual, others that the institution receives the benefit. A few have recognized that this dichotomy is false, that both in fact are aided.

The majority here does not accept in terms any of those views. But neither does it deny that the individual or the school, or indeed both, are benefited directly and substantially. To do so would cut the ground from under the public function-social legislation thesis. On the contrary, the opinion conceded that the children are aided by being helped to get to the religious schooling. By converse necessary implication as well as by the absence of express denial, it must be taken to concede also that the school is helped to reach the child with its religious teaching. The religious enterprise is common to both, as is the interest in having transporation for its religious purposes provided.

Notwithstanding the recognition that this two-way aid is given and the absence of any denial that religious teaching is thus furthered, the Court concludes that the aid so given is not "support" of religion. It is rather only support of education as such, without reference to its religious content, and thus becomes public welfare legislation. To this elision of the religious element from the case is added gloss in two respects, one that the aid extended partakes of the nature of a safety measure, the other that failure to provide it would make the state unneutral in religious matters, discriminating against or hampering such children concerning public benefits all others receive.

As will be noted, the one gloss is contradicted by the facts of record and the other is of whole cloth with the "public function" argument's excision of the religious factor. But most important is that this approach, if valid, supplies a ready method for nullifying the Amendment's guaranty, not only for this case and others involving small grants in aid for religious education, but equally for larger ones. The only thing needed will be for the Court again to transplant the "public welfare—public function" view from its proper nonreligious due process bearing to First Amendment application, holding that religious education is not "supported" though it may be aided by the appropriation, and that the cause of education generally is furthered by helping the pupil to secure that type of training.

This is not therefore just a little case over bus fares. In paraphrase of Madison, distant as it may be in its present form from a complete establishment of religion, it differs from it only in degree; and is the first step in that direction. Today as in his time "the same authority which can force a citizen to contribute three pence only . . . for the support of any one religious establishment, may force him" to pay more; or "to conform to any other establishment in all cases whatsoever." And now, as then, "either . . . We must say, that the will of the

Legislature is the only measure of their authority; and that in the plenitude of this authority, they may sweep away all our fundamental right; or, that they are bound to leave this particular right untouched and sacred."

The realm of religious training and belief remains, as the Amendment made it, the kindgom of the individual man and his God. It should be kept inviolately private, not "entangled . . . in precedents" or confounded with what legislatures legitimately may take over into the public domain.

V

No one conscious of religious values can be unsympathetic toward the burden which our constitutional separation puts on parents who desire religious instruction mixed with secular for their children. They pay taxes for others' children's education, at the same time the added cost of instruction for their own. Nor can one happily see benefits denied to children which others receive, because in conscience they or their parents for them desire a different kind of training others do not demand.

But if those feelings should prevail, there would be an end to our historic constitutional policy and command. No more unjust or discriminatory in fact is it to deny atttendants at religious schools the cost of their transportation than it is to deny them tuitions, sustenance for their teachers, or any other educational expense which others receive at public cost. Hardship in fact there is which none can blink. But, for assuring to those who undergo it the greater, the most comprehensive freedom, it is one written by design and firm intent into our basic law.

Of course discrimination in the legal sense does not exist. The child attending the religious school has the same right as any other to attend the public school. But he foregoes exercising it because the same guaranty which assures this freedom forbids the public school or any agency of the state to give or aid him in securing the religious instruction he seeks.

Were he to accept the common school, he would be the first to protest the teaching there of any creed or faith not his own. And it is precisely for the reason that their atmosphere is wholly secular that children are not sent to public schools under the Pierce doctrine. But that is a constitutional necessity, because we have staked the very existence of our country on the faith that complete separation between the state and religion is best for the state and best for religion.

That policy necessarily entails hardship upon persons who forego the right to educational advantages the state can supply in order to secure others it is precluded from giving. Indeed this may hamper the parent and the child forced by conscience to that choice. But it does not make the state unneutral to withhold what the Constitution forbids it to give. On the contrary it is only by observing the prohibition rigidly that the state can maintain its neutrality and avoid partisanship in the dissensions inevitable when sect opposes sect over demands for public moneys to further religious education, teaching or training in any form or degree, directly or indirectly. Like St. Paul's freedom, religious liberty with a great price must be bought. And for those who exercise it most fully, by insisting upon religious education for their children mixed with secular, by the terms of our Constitution the price is greater than for others.

The problem then cannot be cast in terms of legal discrimination or its absence. This would be true, even though the state in giving aid should treat all religious instruction alike. Thus, if the present statute and its application were shown to apply equally to all religious schools of whatever faith, yet in the light of our tradition it could not stand. For then the adherent of one creed still would pay for the support of another, the childless taxpayer with others more fortunate. Then too there would seem to be no bar to making appropriations for transportation and other expenses of children attending public or other secular schools, after hours in separate places and classes for their exclusively religious instruction. The person who embraces no creed also would be forced to pay for teaching what he does not believe. Again, it was the furnishing of "contributions of money for the propagation of opinions which he disbelieves" that the fathers outlawed. That consequence and effect are not removed by multiplying to all-inclusiveness the sects for which support is exacted. The Constitution requires, not comprehensive identification of state with religion, but complete separation.

VI

Short treatment will dispose of what remains. Whatever might be said of some other application of New Jersey's statute, the one made here has no semblance of bearing as a safety measure or, indeed, for securing expeditious conveyance. The transportation supplied is by public conveyance, subject to all the hazards and delays of the highway and the streets incurred by the public generally in going about its multifarious business.

Nor is the case comparable to one of furnishing fire or police protection, or access to public highways. These things are matters of common right, part of the general need for safety. Certainly the fire department must not stand idly by while the church burns. Nor is this reason why the state should pay the expense of transportation or other items of the cost of religious education.

Needless to add, we have no such case as *Green v. Frazier*, which dealt with matters wholly unrelated to the First Amendment, involving only situations where the "public function" issue was determinative.

I have chosen to place my dissent upon the broad ground I think decisive, though strictly speaking the case might be decided on narrower issues. The New Jersey statute might be held invalid on its face for the exclusion of children who attend private, profit-making schools. I cannot assume, as does the majority, that the New Jersey courts would write off this explicit limitation from the statute. Moreover, the resolution by which the statute was applied expressly limits its benefits to students of public and Catholic schools. There is no showing that there are no other private or religious schools in this populous district. I do not think it can be assumed there were none. But in the view I have taken, it is unnecessary to limit grounding to these matters.

Two great drives are constantly in motion to abridge, in the name of education, the complete division of religion and civil authority which our forefathers made. One is to introduce religious education and observances into the public schools. The other, to obtain public funds for the aid and support of various private religious schools. In my opinion both avenues were closed by the Constitution. Neither should be opened by this Court. The matter is not one of quantity, to be measured by the amount of money expended. Now as in Madison's day it is one of principle, to keep separate the separate spheres as the First Amendment drew them; to prevent the first experiment upon our liberties; and to keep the question from becoming entangled in corrosive precedents. We should not be less strict to keep strong and untarnished the one side of the shield of religious freedom than we have been of the other.

The judgment should be reversed.

Board of Education v. Allen, 392 U.S. 236 (1968)

Justice White, writing for the majority, affirmed that a New York program of lending state-approved texts free of charge to all students in grades seven to twelve, including those in private schools, was constitutional. The Court applied the *Schempp* test and concluded that the law had a "secular legislative purpose and a primary effect that neither advances nor inhibits religion." The principle adopted was the same as that identified in *Everson*—child benefit. Justice Black, in a vigorous dissent, challenged this connection, insisting that public bus transportation for parochial schoolchildren was of a different order than using tax funds "to buy school books for a religious school." Justices Douglas and Fortas also dissented, the latter arguing, "This case is not within the principle of *Everson*."

MR. JUSTICE WHITE DELIVERED THE OPINION OF THE COURT.

A law of the State of New York requires local public school authorities to lend textbooks free of charge to all students in grades seven through 12; students attending private schools are included. This case presents the question whether this statute is a "law respecting an establishment of religion, or prohibiting the free exercise thereof," and so in conflict with the First and Fourteenth Amendments to the Constitution, because it authorizes the loan of textbooks to students attending parochial schools. We hold that the law is not in violation of the Constitution.

Until 1965, § 701 of the Education Law of the State of New York authorized public school boards to designate textbooks for use in the public schools, to purchase such books with public funds, and to rent or sell the books to public school students. In 1965 the Legislature amended § 701, basing the amendments on findings that the "public welfare and safety require that the state and local communities give assistance to educational programs which are important to our national defense and the general welfare of the state." Beginning with the 1966–1967 school year, local school boards were required to purchase textbooks and lend them without charge "to all children residing in such district who are enrolled in grades seven to twelve of a public or private school which complies with the compulsory education law." The books now loaned are "text-books which are designated for use in any public, elementary or secondary schools of the state or are approved by any boards of education," and which—according to a 1966 amendment—"a pupil is required to use as a text for a semester or more in a particular class in the school he legally attends."

Appellant Board of Education of Central School District No. 1 in Rensselaer and Columbia Counties, brought suit in New York courts against appellee James Allen. The complaint alleged that § 701 violated both the State and Federal Constitutions; that if appellants, in reliance on their interpretation of the Constitution, failed to lend books to parochial school students within their counties appellee Allen would remove appellants from office; and that to prevent this, appellants were complying with the law and submitting to their constituents a school budget including funds for books to be lent to parochial school pupils. Appellants therefore sought a declaration that § 701 was invalid, an order barring appellee Allen from removing appellants from office for failing to comply with it, and another order restraining him from apportioning state funds to school districts for the purchase of textbooks to be lent to parochial students. After answer, and upon cross-motions for summary judgment, the trial court held the law unconstitutional under the First and Fourteenth Amendments and entered judgment for appellants. The Appellate Division reversed, ordering the complaint dismissed on the ground that appellant school boards had no standing to attack the validity of a state statute. On appeal, the New York Court of Appeals concluded by a 4–3 vote that appellants did have standing but by a different 4–3 vote held that § 701 was not in violation of either the State or the Federal Constitution. The Court of Appeals said that the law's purpose was to benefit all school children, regardless of the type of school they attended, and that only textbooks approved by public school authorities could be loaned. It therefore considered § 701 "completely neutral with respect to religion, merely making available secular textbooks at the request of the individual student and asking no question about what school he attends." Section 701, the Court of Appeals concluded, is not a law which "establishes a religion or constitutes the use of public funds to aid religious schools." We noted probable jurisdiction.

Everson is the case decided by this Court that is most nearly in point for today's problem. New Jersey reimbursed parents for expenses incurred in busing their children to parochial schools. The Court stated that the Establishment Clause bars a State from passing "laws which aid one religion, aid all religions, or prefer one religion over another," and bars too any "tax in any amount, large or small . . . levied to support any religious activities or institutions, whatever they may be called, or whatever form they may adopt to teach or practice religion." Nevertheless, said the Court, the Establishment Clause does not prevent a State from extending the benefits of state laws to all citizens without regard for their religious affiliation and does not prohibit "New Jersey from spending tax-raised funds to pay the bus fares of parochial school pupils as a part of a general program under which it pays the fares of pupils attending public and other schools." The statute was held to be valid even though one of its results was that "children are helped to get to church schools" and "some of the children might not be sent to the church schools if the parents were compelled to pay their children's bus fares out of their own pockets." As with public provision of police and fire protection, sewage facilities, and streets and sidewalks, payment of bus fares was of some value to the religious school, but was nevertheless not such support of a religious institution as to be a prohibited establishment of religion within the meaning of the First Amendment.

Everson and later cases have shown that the line between state neutrality to religion and state support of religion is not easy to locate. "The constitutional standard is the separation of Church and State. The problem, like many problems in constitutional law, is one of degree." Based on *Everson, Zorach, McGowan,* and other cases, *Abington School District* v. *Schempp* fashioned a test subscribed to by eight Justices for distinguishing between forbidden involvements of the State with religion and those contacts which the Establishment Clause permits:

> The test may be stated as follows: what are the purpose and the primary effect of the enactment? If either is the advancement or inhibition of religion then the enactment exceeds the scope of legislative power as circumscribed by the Constitution. That is to say that to withstand the strictures of the Establishment

> Clause there must be a secular legislative purpose and a primary effect that neither advances nor inhibits religion.

This test is not easy to apply, but the citation of *Everson* by the *Schempp* Court to support its general standard made clear how the *Schempp* rule would be applied to the facts of *Everson*. The statute upheld in *Everson* would be considered a law having "a secular legislative purpose and a primary effect that neither advances nor inhibits religion." We reach the same result with respect to the New York law requiring school books to be loaned free of charge to all students in specified grades. The express purpose of § 701 was stated by the New York Legislature to be furtherance of the educational opportunities available to the young. Appellants have shown us nothing about the necessary effects of the statute that is contrary to its stated purpose. The law merely makes available to all children the benefits of a general program to lend school books free of charge. Books are furnished at the request of the pupil and ownership remains, at least technically, in the State. Thus no funds or books are furnished to parochial schools, and the financial benefit is to parents and children, not to schools. Perhaps free books make it more likely that some children choose to attend a sectarian school, but that was true of the state-paid bus fares in *Everson* and does not alone demonstrate an unconstitutional degree of support for a religious institution.

Of course books are different from buses. Most bus rides have no inherent religious significance, while religious books are common. However, the language of § 701 does not authorize the loan of religious books, and the State claims no right to distribute religious literature. Although the books loaned are those required by the parochial school for use in specific courses, each book loaned must be approved by the public school authorities; only secular books may receive approval. The law was construed by the Court of Appeals of New York as "merely making available secular textbooks at the request of the individual student," and the record contains no suggestion that religious books have been loaned. Absent evidence, we cannot assume that school authorities, who constantly face the same problem in selecting textbooks for use in the public schools, are unable to distinguish between secular and religious books or that they will not honestly discharge their duties under the law. In judging the validity of the statute on this record we must proceed on the assumption that books loaned to students are books that are not unsuitable for use in the public schools because of religious content.

The major reason offered by appellants for distinguishing free textbooks from free bus fares is that books, but not buses, are critical to the teaching process, and in a sectarian school that process is employed to teach religion. However this Court has long recognized that religious schools pursue two goals, religious instruction and secular education. In the leading case of *Pierce,* the Court held that although it would not question Oregon's power to compel school attendance or require that attendance be at an institution meeting State-imposed requirements as to quality and nature of curriculum, Oregon had not shown that its interest in secular education required that all children attend publicly operated schools. A premise of this holding was the view that the State's interest in education would be served sufficiently by reliance on the secular teaching that accompanied religious training in the schools maintained by the Society of Sisters. Since *Pierce,* a substantial body of case law has confirmed the power of the States to insist that attendance at private schools, if it is to satisfy state compulsory-attendance laws, be at institutions which provide minimum hours of instruction, employ teachers of specified training, and cover prescribed subjects of instruction. Indeed, the State's interest in assuring that these standards are being met has been considered a sufficient reason for refusing to accept instruction at home as compliance with compulsory education statutes. These cases were a sensible corollary of *Pierce:* if the State must satisfy its interest in secular education through the instrument of private schools, it has a proper interest in the manner in which those schools perform their secular educational function. Another corollary was *Cochran* v. *Louisiana State Board of Education,* where appellants said that a statute requiring school books to be furnished without charge to all students, whether they attended public or private schools, did not serve a "public purpose," and so offended the Fourteenth Amendment. Speaking through Chief Justice Hughes, the Court summarized as follows its conclusion that Louisiana's interest in the secular education being provided by private schools made provision of textbooks to students in those schools a properly public concern: "[The State's] interest is education, broadly; its method, comprehensive. Individual interests are aided only as the common interest is safeguarded."

Underlying these cases, and underlying also the legislative judgments that have preceded the court decisions, has been a recognition that private education has played and is playing a significant and valuable role in raising national levels of knowledge, competence, and experience. Americans care about the quality of the secular education available to their children. They have considered high quality education to be an indispensable ingredient for achieving the kind of nation, and the kind of citizenry, that they have desired to create. Considering this attitude, the continued willingness to rely on private school systems, including parochial systems, strongly suggests that a wide segment of informed opinion, legislative and otherwise, has found that those schools do an acceptable job of providing secular education to their students. This judgment is further evidence that parochial schools are performing, in addition to their sectarian function, the task of secular education.

Against this background of judgment and experience, unchallenged in the meager record before us in this case, we cannot agree with appellants either that all teaching in a sectarian school is religious or that the processes of secular and religious training are so intertwined that secular textbooks furnished to students by the public are in fact instrumental in the teaching of religion. This case comes to us after summary judgment entered on the pleadings. Nothing in this record supports the proposition that all textbooks, whether they deal with mathematics, physics, foreign languages, history, or literature, are used by the parochial schools to teach religion. No evidence has been offered about particular schools, particular courses, particular teachers, or particular books. We are unable to hold, based solely on judicial notice, that this statute results in unconstitutional involvement of the State with religious instruction or that § 701, for this or the other reasons urged, is a law respecting the establishment of religion within the meaning of the First Amendment.

Appellants also contend that § 701 offends the Free Exercise Clause of the First Amendment. However, "it is necessary in a free exercise case for one to show the coercive effect of the enactment as it operates against him in the practice of his religion," and appellants have not contended that the New York law in any way coerces them as individuals in the practice of their religion.

The judgment is affirmed.

MR. JUSTICE BLACK, DISSENTING.

The Court here confirms a judgment of the New York Court of Appeals which sustained the constitutionality of a New York law providing state tax-raised funds to supply school books for use by pupils in schools owned and operated by religious sects. I believe the New York law held valid is a flat, flagrant, open violation of the First and Fourteenth Amendments which together forbid Congress or state legislatures to enact any law "respecting an establishment of religion." For that reason, I would reverse the New York Court of Appeals' judgment. This, I am confident, would be in keeping with the deliberate statement we made in *Everson* and repeated in *McCollum*. . . .

* * * * *

The *Everson* and *McCollum* cases plainly interpret the First and Fourteenth Amendments as protecting the taxpayers of a State from being compelled to pay taxes to their government to support the agencies of private religious organizations the taxpayers oppose. To authorize a State to tax its residents for such church purposes is to put the State squarely in the religious activities of certain religious groups that happen to be strong enough politically to write their own religious preferences and prejudices into the laws. This links state and churches together in controlling the lives and destinies of our citizenship—a citizenship composed of people of myriad religious faiths, some of them bitterly hostile to and completely intolerant of the others. It was to escape laws precisely like this that a large part of the Nation's early immigrants fled to this country. It was also to escape such laws and consequences that the First Amendment was written in language strong and clear barring passage of any law "respecting an establishment of religion."

It is true, of course, that the New York law does not as yet formally adopt or establish a state religion. But it takes a great stride in that direction and coming events cast their shadows before them. The same powerful sectarian religious propagandists who have succeeded in securing passage of the present law to help religious schools carry on their sectarian religious purposes can and doubtless will continue their propaganda, looking toward complete domination and supremacy of their particular brand of religion. And it nearly always is by insidious approaches that the citadels of liberty are most successfully attacked.

I know of no prior opinion of this Court upon which the majority here can rightfully rely to support its holding this New York law constitutional. . . .

As my Brother Douglas so forcefully shows, in an argument with which I fully agree, upholding a State's power to pay bus or streetcar fares for school children cannot provide support for the validity of a state law using tax-raised funds to buy school books for a religious school. The First Amendment's bar to establishment of religion must preclude a State from using funds levied from all of its citizens to purchase books for use by sectarian schools, which, although "secular," realistically will in some way inevitably tend to propagate the religious views of the favored sect. Books are the most essential tool of education since they contain the resources of knowledge which the educational process is designed to exploit. In this sense it is not difficult to distinguish books, which are the heart of any school, from bus fares, which provide a convenient and helpful general public transportation service. With respect to the former, state financial support actively and directly assists the teaching and propagation of sectarian religious viewpoints in clear conflict with the First Amendment's establishment bar; with respect to the latter, the State merely provides a general and nondiscriminatory transportation service in no way related to substantive religious views and beliefs.

This New York law, it may be said by some, makes but a small inroad and does not amount to complete state establishment of religion. But that is no excuse for upholding it. It requires no prophet to foresee that on the argument used to support this law others could be upheld providing for state or federal government funds to buy property on which to erect religious school buildings or to erect the buildings themselves, to pay the salaries of the religious school teachers, and finally to have the sectarian religious groups cease to rely on voluntary contributions of members of their sects while waiting for the Government to pick up all the bills for the religious schools. Arguments made in favor of this New York law point squarely in this direction, namely, that the fact that government has not heretofore aided religious schools with tax-raised funds amounts to a discrimination against those schools and against religion. And that there are already efforts to have government supply the money to erect buildings for sectarian religious schools is shown by a recent Act of Congress which apparently allows for precisely that.

I still subscribe to the belief that the tax-raised funds cannot constitutionally be used to support religious schools, buy their school books, erect their buildings, pay their teachers, or pay any other of their maintenance expenses, even to the extent of one penny. The First Amendment's prohibition against governmental establishment of religion was written on the assumption that state aid to religion and religious schools generates discord, disharmony, hatred, and strife among our people, and that any government that supplies such aids is to that extent a tyranny. And I still believe that the only way to protect minority religious groups from majority groups in this country is to keep the wall of separation between church and state high and impregnable as the First and Fourteenth Amendments provide. The Court's affirmance here bodes nothing but evil to religious peace in this country.

MR. JUSTICE FORTAS, DISSENTING.

The majority opinion of the Court upholds the New York statute by ignoring a vital aspect of it. Public funds are used to buy, for students in sectarian schools, textbooks which are selected and prescribed by the sectarian schools themselves. As my Brother Douglas points out, despite the transparent camouflage that the books are furnished to students, the reality is that they are selected and their use is prescribed by the sectarian authorities. The child must use the prescribed book. He cannot use a different book prescribed for use in the public schools. The State cannot choose the book to be used. It is true that the public school boards must "approve" the book selected by the sectarian authorities; but this has no real significance. The purpose of these provisions is to hold out promise that the books will be "secular" but the fact remains that the books are chosen by and for the sectarian schools.

It is misleading to say, as the majority opinion does, that the New York "law merely makes available to all children the benefits of a general program to lend school books free of charge." This is not a "general" program. It is a specific program to use state funds to buy books prescribed by sectarian schools which, in New York, are primarily Catholic, Jewish, and Lutheran sponsored schools. It could be called a "general" program only if the school books made available to all children were precisely the same—the books selected for and used in the public schools. But this program is not one in which all children are treated alike, regardless of where they go to school. This program, in its unconstitutional features, is hand-tailored to satisfy the specific needs of sectarian schools. Children attending such schools are given *special* books—books selected by the sectarian authorities. How can this be other than the use of public money to aid those sectarian establishments?

It is also beside the point, in my opinion, to "assume," as the majority opinion does, that "books loaned to students are books that are not unsuitable for use in the public schools because of religious content." The point is that the books furnished to students of sectarian schools are selected by the religious authorities and are prescribed by them.

This case is not within the principle of *Everson*. Apart from the differences between textbooks and bus rides, the present statute does not call for extending to children attending sectarian schools the same service or facility extended to children in public schools. This statute calls for furnishing special, separate, and particular books, specially, separately, and particularly chosen by religious sects or their representatives for use in their sectarian schools. This is the infirmity, in my opinion. This is the feature that makes it impossible, in my view, to reach any conclusion other than that this statute is an unconstitutional use of public funds to support an establishment of religion.

This is the feature of the present statute that makes it totally inaccurate to suggest, as the majority does here, that furnishing these specially selected books for use in sectarian schools is like "public provision of police and fire protection, sewage facilities, and streets and sidewalks." These are furnished to all alike. They are not selected on the basis of specification by a religious sect. And patrons of any one sect do not receive services or facilities different from those accorded members of other religions or agnostics or even atheists.

I would reverse the judgment below.

Walz v. Tax Commission, 397 U.S. 664 (1970)

Observers of the Court's decisions regarding parochial schools perceived, in the *Allen* case, a shift toward a more lenient attitude respecting general aid to those church-related institutions. Chief Justice Burger's opinion in *Walz*, two years later, appeared to confirm that perception. While the case concerned tax exemptions for religious property, Justice Burger set forth a "benevolent neutrality" concept that might have much broader application. He asserted that laws could be fashioned on grounds of such neutrality toward religion "so long as none was favored over others and none suffered interference." Sensing the direction of the Court, Justice Douglas, the sole dissenter, wrote, "But subsidies either through direct grant or tax exemption for sectarian causes, whether carried on by church *qua* church or by church *qua* welfare agency, must be treated differently, lest we in time allow the church *qua* church to be on the public payroll, which, I fear, is imminent."

Another aspect of the Burger decision was the addition of a third test of establishment to the two employed in the 1963 Bible and prayer cases. The chief justice affirmed that any program must not result in an "excessive governmental entanglement with religion." It was this test that would prove fatal to Rhode Island and Pennsylvania laws in the *Lemon* decision in 1971.

MR. CHIEF JUSTICE BURGER DELIVERED THE OPINION OF THE COURT.

Appellant, owner of real estate in Richmond County, New York, sought an injunction in the New York courts to prevent the New York City Tax Commission from granting property tax exemptions to religious organizations for religious properties used solely for religious worship. The exemption from state taxes is authorized by Art. 16, § 1, of the New York Constitution, which provides in relevant part:

> Exemptions from taxation may be granted only by general laws. Exemptions may be altered or repealed except those exempting real or personal property used exclusively for religious, educational or charitable purposes as defined by law and owned by any corporation or association organized or conducted exclusively for one or more of such purposes and not operating for profit.

The essence of appellant's contention was that the New York City Tax Commission's grant of an exemption to church property indirectly requires the appellant to make a contribution to religious bodies and thereby violates provisions prohibiting establishment of religion under the First Amendment which under the Fourteenth Amendment is binding on the States.

Appellee's motion for summary judgment was granted and the Appellate Division of the New York Supreme Court, and the New York Court of Appeals affirmed. We noted probable jurisdiction and affirm.

I

Prior opinions of this Court have discussed the development and historical background of the First Amendment in detail. It would therefore serve no useful purpose to review in detail the background of the Establishment and Free Exercise Clauses of the First Amendment or to restate what the Court's opinions have reflected over the years.

It is sufficient to note that for the men who wrote the Religion Clauses of the First Amendment the "establishment" of a religion connoted sponsorship, financial support, and active involvement of the sovereign in religious activity. In England, and in some Colonies at the time of the separation in 1776, the Church of England was sponsored and supported by the Crown as a state, or established, church; in other countries "establishment" meant sponsorship by the sovereign of the Lutheran or Catholic Church. . . .

The Establishment and Free Exercise Clauses of the First Amendment are not the most precisely drawn portions of the Constitution. The sweep of the absolute prohibitions in the Religion Clauses may have been calculated; but the purpose was to state an objective, not to write a statute. In attempting to articulate the scope of the two Religion Clauses, the Court's opinions reflect the limitations inherent in formulating general principles on a case-by-case basis. The considerable internal inconsistency in the opinions of the Court derives from what, in retrospect, may have been too sweeping utterances on aspects of these clauses that seemed clear in relation to the particular cases but have limited meaning as general principles.

The Court has struggled to find a neutral course between the two Religion Clauses, both of which are cast in absolute terms, and either of which, if expanded to a logical extreme, would tend to clash with the other. For example, in *Zorach* Mr. Justice Douglas, writing for the Court, noted:

> The First Amendment, however, does not say that in every and all respects there shall be a separation of Church and State.
>
> We sponsor an attitude on the part of government that shows no partiality to any one group and that lets each flourish according to the zeal of its adherents and the appeal of its dogma.

Mr. Justice Harlan expressed something of this in his dissent in *Sherbert* v. *Verner,* saying that the constitutional neutrality imposed on us

> is not so narrow a channel that the slightest deviation from an absolutely straight course leads to condemnation.

The course of constitutional neutrality in this area cannot be an absolutely straight line; rigidity could well defeat the basic purpose of these provisions, which is to insure that no religion be sponsored or favored, none commanded, and none inhibited. The general principle deducible from the First Amendment and all that has been said by the Court is this: that we will not tolerate either governmentally established religion or governmental interference with religion. Short of those expressly proscribed governmental acts there is room for play in the joints productive of a benevolent neutrality which will permit religious exercise to exist without sponsorship and without interference.

Each value judgment under the Religion Clauses must therefore turn on whether particular acts in question are intended to establish or interfere with religious beliefs and practices or have the effect of doing so. Adhcrence to the policy of neutrality that derives from an accommodation of the Establishment and Free Exercise Clauses has prevented the kind of involvement that would tip the balance toward government control of churches or governmental restraint on religious practice.

Adherents of particular faiths and individual churches frequently take strong positions on public issues including, as this case reveals in the several briefs *amici,* vigorous advocacy of legal or constitutional positions. Of course, churches as much as secular bodies and private citizens have that right. No perfect or absolute separation is really possible; the very existence of the Religion Clauses is an involvement of sorts—one that seeks to mark boundaries to avoid excessive entanglement.

The hazards of placing too much weight on a few words or phrases of the Court is abundantly illustrated within the pages of the Court's opinion in *Everson.*

* * * * *

With all the risks inherent in programs that bring about administrative relationships between public education bodies and church-sponsored schools, we have been able to chart a course that preserved the autonomy and freedom of religious bodies while avoiding any semblance of established religion. This is a "tight rope" and one we have successfully traversed.

II

The legislative purpose of the property tax exemption is neither the advancement nor the inhibition of religion; it is neither sponsorship nor hostility. New York, in common with the other States, has determined that certain entities that exist in a harmonious relationship to the community at large, and that foster its "moral or mental improvement," should not be inhibited in their activities by property taxation or the hazard of loss of those properties for nonpayment of taxes. It has not singled out one particular church or religious group or even churches as such; rather, it has granted exemption to all houses of religious worship within a broad class of property owned by nonprofit, quasi-public corporations which include hospitals, libraries, playgrounds, scientific, professional, historical, and patriotic groups. The State has an affirmative policy that considers these groups as beneficial and stabilizing influences in community life and finds this classification useful, desirable, and in the public interest. Qualification for tax exemption is not perpetual or immutable; some tax-exempt groups lose that status when their activities take them outside the classification and new entities can come into being and qualify for exemption.

Governments have not always been tolerant of religious activity, and hostility toward religion has taken many shapes and forms—economic, political, and sometimes harshly oppressive. Grants of exemption historically reflect the concern of authors of constitutions and statutes as to the latent dangers inherent in the imposition of property taxes; exemption constitutes a reasonable and balanced attempt to guard against those dangers. The limits of permissible state accommodation to religion are by no means co-extensive with the noninterference mandated by the Free Exercise Clause. To equate the two would be to deny a national heritage with roots in the Revolution itself. We cannot read New York's statute as attempting to establish religion; it is simply sparing the exercise of religion from the burden of property taxation levied on private profit institutions.

We find it unnecessary to justify the tax exemption on the social welfare services or "good works" that some churches perform for parishioners and others—family counselling, aid to the elderly and the infirm, and to children. Churches vary substantially in the scope of such services; programs expand or contract according to resources and need. As public-sponsored programs enlarge, private aid from the church sector may diminish. The extent of social services may vary, depending on whether the church serves an urban or rural, a rich or poor constituency. To give emphasis to so variable an aspect of the work of religious bodies would introduce an element of governmental evaluation and standards as to the worth of particular social welfare programs, thus producing a kind of continuing day-to-day relationship which the policy of neutrality seeks to minimize. Hence, the use of a social welfare yardstick as a significant element to qualify for tax exemption could conceivably give rise to confrontations that could escalate to constitutional dimensions.

Determining that the legislative purpose of tax exemption is not aimed at establishing, sponsoring, or supporting religion does not end the inquiry, however. We must also be sure that the end result—the effect—is not an excessive government entanglement with religion. The test is inescapably one of degree. Either course, taxation of churches or exemption, occasions some degree of involvement with religion. Elimination of exemption would tend to expand the involvement of government by giving rise to tax valuation of church property, tax liens, tax foreclosures, and the direct confrontations and conflicts that follow in the train of those legal processes.

Granting tax exemptions to churches necessarily operates to afford an indirect economic benefit and also gives rise to some, but yet a lesser, involvement than taxing them. In analyzing either alternative the questions are whether the involvement is excessive, and whether it is a continuing one calling for official and continuing surveillance leading to an impermissible degree of entanglement. Obviously a direct money subsidy would be a relationship pregnant with involvement and, as with most governmental grant programs, could encompass sustained and detailed administrative relationships for enforcement of statutory or administrative standards, but that is not this case. The hazards of churches supporting government are hardly less in their potential than the hazards of government supporting churches; each relationship carries some involvement rather than the desired insulation and separation. We cannot ignore the instances in history when church support of government led to the kind of involvement we seek to avoid.

The grant of a tax exemption is not sponsorship since the government does not transfer part of its revenue to churches but simply abstains from demanding that the church support the state. No one has ever suggested that tax exemption has converted libraries, art galleries, or hospitals into arms of the state or put employees "on the public payroll." There is no genuine nexus between tax exemption and establishment of religion. As Mr. Justice Holmes commented in a related context "a page of history is worth a volume of logic." The exemption creates only a minimal and remote involvement between church and state and far less than taxation of churches. It restricts the fiscal relationship between church and state, and tends to complement and reinforce the desired separation insulating each from the other.

Separation in this context cannot mean absence of all contact; the complexities of modern life inevitably produce some contact and the fire and police protection received by houses of religious worship are no more than incidental benefits accorded all persons or institutions within a State's boundaries, along with many other exempt organizations. The appellant has not established even an arguable quantitative correlation between the payment of an ad valorem property tax and the receipt of these municipal benefits.

All of the 50 States provide for tax exemption of places of worship, most of them doing so by constitutional guarantees. For so long as federal income taxes have had any potential impact on churches—over 75 years—religious organizations have been expressly exempt from the tax. Such treatment is an "aid" to churches no more and no less in principle than the real estate tax exemption granted by States. Few concepts are more deeply embedded in the fabric of our national life, beginning with pre-Revolutionary colonial times, than for the government to exercise at the very least this kind of benevolent neutrality toward churches and religious exercise generally so long as none was favored over others and none suffered interference.

It is significant that Congress, from its earliest days, has viewed the Religion Clauses of the Constitution as authorizing statutory real estate tax exemption to religious bodies. In 1802 the 7th Congress enacted a taxing statute for the County of Alexandria, adopting the 1800 Virginia statutory pattern which provided tax exemptions for churches. As early as 1813 the 12th Congress refunded import duties paid by religious societies on the importation of religious articles. During this period the City Council of Washington, D.C., acting under congressional authority, enacted a series of real and personal property assessments that uniformly exempted church property. In 1870 the Congress specifically exempted all churches in the District of Columbia and appurtenant grounds and property "from any and all taxes or assessments, national, municipal, or county."

It is obviously correct that no one acquires a vested or protected right in violation of the Constitution by long use, even when that span of time covers our entire national existence and indeed predates it. Yet an unbroken practice of according the exemption to churches, openly and by affirmative state action, not covertly or by state inaction, is not something to be lightly cast aside. Nearly 50 years ago Mr. Justice Holmes stated: "If a thing has been practiced for two hundred years by common consent, it will need a strong case for the Fourteenth Amendment to affect it. . . . "

Nothing in this national attitude toward religious tolerance and two centuries of uninterrupted freedom from taxation has given the remotest sign of leading to an established church or religion and on the contrary it has operated affirmatively to help guarantee the free exercise of all forms of religious belief. Thus, it is hardly useful to suggest that tax exemption is but the "foot in the door" or the "nose of the camel in the tent" leading to an established church. If tax exemption can be seen as this first step toward "establishment" of religion, as Mr. Justice Douglas fears, the second step has been long in coming. Any move that realistically "establishes" a church or tends to do so can be dealt with "while this Court sits."

Mr. Justice Cardozo commented on the "tendency of a principle to expand itself to the limit of its logic"; such expansion must always be contained by the historical frame of reference of the principle's purpose and there is no lack of vigilance on this score by those who fear religious entanglement in government.

The argument that making "fine distinctions" between what is and what is not absolute under the Constitution is to render us a government of men, not laws, gives too little weight to the fact that it is an essential part of adjudication to draw distinctions, including fine ones, in the process of interpreting the Constitution. We must frequently decide, for example, what are "reasonable" searches and seizures under the Fourth Amendment. Determining what acts of government tend to establish or interfere with religion falls well within what courts have long been called upon to do in sensitive areas.

It is interesting to note that while the precise question we now decide has not been directly before the Court previously, the broad question was discussed by the Court in relation to real estate taxes assessed nearly a century ago on land owned by and adjacent to a church in Washington, D.C. At that time Congress granted real estate tax exemptions to buildings devoted to art, to institutions of public charity, libraries, cemeteries, and "church buildings, and grounds actually occupied by such buildings." In denying tax exemption as to land owned by but not used for the church, but rather to produce income, the Court concluded:

> In the exercise of this [taxing] power, Congress, like any State legislature unrestricted by constitutional provisions, may at its discretion wholly exempt certain classes of property from taxation, or may tax them at a lower rate than other property.

It appears that at least up to 1885 this Court, reflecting more than a century of our history and uninterrupted practice, accepted without discussion the proposition that federal or state grants of tax exemption to churches were not a violation of the Religion Clauses of the First Amendment. As to the New York statute, we now confirm that view.

Affirmed.

MR. JUSTICE DOUGLAS, DISSENTING.

Petitioner is the owner of real property in New York and is a Christian. But he is not a member of any of the religious organizations, "rejecting them as hostile." The New York statute exempts from taxation real property "owned by a corporation or association organized exclusively for . . . religious . . . purposes" and used "exclusively for carrying out" such purposes. Yet nonbelievers who own realty are taxed at the usual rate. The question in the case therefore is whether believers—organized in church groups—can be made exempt from real estate taxes, merely because they are believers, while nonbelievers, whether organized or not, must pay the real estate taxes.

My Brother Harlan says he "would suppose" that the tax exemption extends to "groups whose avowed tenets may be antitheological, atheistic, or agnostic." If it does, then the line between believers and nonbelievers has not been drawn. But, with all respect, there is not even a suggestion in the present record that the statute covers property used exclusively by organizations for "antitheological purposes," "atheistic purposes," or "agnostic purposes."

In *Torcaso v. Watkins* we held that a State could not bar an atheist from public office in light of the freedom of belief and religion guaranteed by the First and Fourteenth Amendments. Neither the State nor the Federal Government, we said, "can constitutionally pass laws or impose requirements which aid all religions as against non-believers, and neither can aid those religions based on a belief in the existence of God as against those religions founded on different beliefs."

That principle should govern this case.

There is a line between what a State may do in encouraging "religious" activities and what a State may not do by using its resources to promote "religious" activities or bestowing benefits because of them. Yet that line may not always be clear. Closing public schools on Sunday is in the former category; subsidizing churches, in my view, is in the latter. Indeed I would suppose that in common understanding one of the best ways to "establish" one or more religions is to subsidize them, which a tax exemption does. The State may not do that any more than it may prefer "those who believe in no religion over those who do believe."

In affirming this judgment the Court largely overlooks the revolution initiated by the adoption of the Fourteenth Amendment. That revolution involved the imposition of new and far-reaching constitutional restraints on the States. Nationalization of many civil liberties has been the consequence of the Fourteenth Amendment, reversing the historic position that the foundations of those liberties rested largely in state law.

The process of the "selective incorporation" of various provisions of the Bill of Rights into the Fourteenth Amendment, although often provoking lively disagreement at large as well as among the members of this Court, has been a steady one. . . . The Establishment Clause was not incorporated in the Fourteenth Amendment until *Everson* was decided in 1947.

Those developments in the last 30 years have had unsettling effects. It was, for example, not until 1962 that state-sponsored, sectarian prayers were held to violate the Establishment Clause. That decision brought many protests, for the habit of putting one sect's prayer in public schools had long been practiced. Yet if the Catholics, controlling one school board, could put their prayer into one group of public schools, the Mormons, Baptists, Moslems, Presbyterians, and others could do the same, once they got control. And so the seeds of Establishment would grow and a secular institution would be used to serve a sectarian end.

Engel was as disruptive of traditional state practices as was *Stromberg*. Prior to *Stromberg*, a State could arrest an unpopular person who made a rousing speech on the charge of disorderly conduct. Since *Stromberg,* that has been unconstitutional. And so the revolution occasioned by the Fourteenth Amendment has progressed as Article after Article in the Bill of Rights has been incorporated in it and made applicable to the States.

Hence the question in the present case makes irrelevant the "two centuries of uninterrupted freedom from taxation," referred to by the Court. If history be our guide, then tax exemption of church property in this country is indeed highly suspect, as it arose in the early days when the church was an agency of the state. The question here, though, concerns the meaning of the Establishment Clause and the Free Exercise Clause made applicable to the States for only a few decades at best.

With all due respect the governing principle is not controlled by *Everson. Everson* involved the use of public funds to bus children to parochial as well as to public schools. Parochial schools teach religion; yet they are also educational institutions offering courses competitive with public schools. They prepare students for the professions and for activities in all walks of life. Education in the secular sense was combined with religious indoctrination at the parochial schools involved in *Everson.* Even so, the *Everson* decision was five to four and, though one of the five, I have since had grave doubts about it, because I have become convinced that grants to institutions teaching a sectarian creed violate the Establishment Clause.

This case, however, is quite different. Education is not involved. The financial support rendered here is to the church, the place of worship. A tax exemption is a subsidy. Is my Brother Brennan correct in saying that we would hold that state or federal grants to churches, say, to construct the edifice itself would be unconstitutional? What is the difference between that kind of subsidy and the present subsidy?

* * * * *

State aid to places of worship, whether in the form of direct grants or tax exemption, takes us back to the Assessment Bill and the Remonstrance. The church *qua* church would not be entitled to that support from believers and from nonbelievers alike. Yet the church *qua* nonprofit, charitable institution is one of many that receive a form of subsidy through tax exemption. To be sure, the New York statute does not single out the church for grant or favor. It includes churches in a long list of nonprofit organizations: for the moral or mental improvement of men and women; for charitable, hospital, or educational purposes; for playgrounds; for scientific or literary objects; for bar associations, medical societies, or libraries; for patriotic and historical purposes; for cemeteries; for the enforcement of laws relating to children or animals; for opera houses; for fraternal organizations; for academies of music; for veterans' organizations; for pharmaceutical societies; and for dental societies. While the beneficiaries cover a wide range, "atheistic," "agnostic," or "antitheological" groups do not seem to be included.

Churches perform some functions that a State would constitutionally be empowered to perform. I refer to nonsectarian social welfare operations such as the care of orphaned children and the destitute and people who are sick. A tax exemption to agencies performing those functions would therefore be as constitutionally proper as the grant of direct subsidies to them. Under the First Amendment a State may not, however, provide worship if private groups fail to do so.

* * * * *

That is a major difference between churches on the one hand and the rest of the nonprofit organizations on the other. Government could provide or finance operas, hospitals, historical societies, and all the rest because they represent social welfare programs within the reach of the police power. In contrast, government may not provide or finance worship because of the Establishment Clause any more than it may single out "atheistic" or "agnostic" centers or groups and create or finance them.

* * * * *

Since 1947, when the Establishment Clause was made applicable to the States, that report would have to state that the exemption would be justified only where "the legislative body *could make*" an appropriation for the cause.

On the record of this case, the church *qua* nonprofit, charitable organization is intertwined with the church *qua* church. A church may use the same facilities, resources, and personnel in carrying out both its secular and its sectarian activities. The two are unitary and on the present record have not been separated one from the other. The state has a public policy of encouraging private public welfare organizations, which it desires to encourage through tax exemption. Why may it not do so and include churches *qua* welfare organizations on a nondiscriminatory basis? That avoids, it is argued, a discrimination against churches and in a real sense maintains neutrality toward religion which the First Amendment was designed to foster. Welfare services, whether performed by churches or by nonreligious groups, may well serve the public welfare.

Whether a particular church seeking an exemption for its welfare work could constitutionally pass muster would depend on the special facts. The assumption is that the church is a purely private institution, promoting a sectarian cause. The creed, teaching, and beliefs of one may be undesirable or even repulsive to others. Its sectarian faith sets it apart from all others and makes it difficult to equate its constituency with the general public. The extent that its facilities are open to all may only indicate the nature of its proselytism. Yet though a church covers up its religious symbols in welfare work, its welfare activities may merely be a phase of sectarian activity. I have said enough to indicate the nature of this tax exemption problem.

Direct financial aid to churches or tax exemptions to the church *qua* church is not, in my view, even arguably permitted. Sectarian causes are certainly not antipublic and many would rate their own church or perhaps all churches as the highest form of welfare. The difficulty is that sectarian causes must remain in the private domain not subject to public control or subsidy. That seems to me to be the requirement of the Establishment Clause.

* * * * *

The exemptions provided here insofar as welfare projects are concerned may have the ring of neutrality. But subsidies either through direct grant or tax exemption for sectarian causes, whether carried on by church *qua* church or by church *qua* welfare agency, must be treated differently, lest we in time allow the church *qua* church to be on the public payroll, which, I fear, is imminent.

As stated by my Brother Brennan in *Schempp,* "It is not only the nonbeliever who fears the injection of sectarian doctrines and controversies into the civil polity, but in as high degree it is the devout believer who fears the secularization of a creed which becomes too deeply involved with and dependent upon the government."

Madison as President vetoed a bill incorporating the Protestant Episcopal Church in Alexandria, Virginia, as being a violation of the Establishment Clause. He said,

> [T]he bill vests in the said incorporated church an authority to provide for the support of the poor and the education of poor children of the same, an authority which, being altogether superfluous if the provision is to be the result of pious charity, would be a precedent for giving to religious societies as such a legal agency in carrying into effect a public and civil duty.

He also vetoed a bill that reserved a parcel of federal land "for the use" of the Baptist Church, as violating the Establishment Clause.

What Madison would have thought of the present state subsidy to churches—a tax exemption as distinguished from an outright grant—no one can say with certainty. The fact that Virginia early granted church tax exemptions cannot be credited to Madison. Certainly he seems to have been opposed. In his paper Monopolies, Perpetuities, Corporations, Ecclesiastical Endowments he wrote: "Strongly guarded as is the separation between Religion & Govt in the Constitution of the United States the danger of encroachment by Ecclesiastical Bodies, may be illustrated by precedents already furnished in their short history." And he referred to the "attempt in Kentucky for example, where it was proposed to exempt Houses of Worship from taxes." From these three statements, Madison, it seems, opposed all state subsidies to churches.

We should adhere to what we said in *Torcaso,* that neither a State nor the Federal Government "can constitutionally pass laws or impose requirements *which aid all religions as against nonbelievers,* and neither can aid those religions based on a belief in the existence of God as against those religions founded on different beliefs."

Unless we adhere to that principle, we do not give full support either to the Free Exercise Clause or to the Establishment Clause.

If a church can be exempted from paying real estate taxes, why may not it be made exempt from paying special assessments? The benefits in the two cases differ only in degree; and the burden on non-believers is likewise no different in kind.

The religiously used real estate of the churches today constitutes a vast domain. Their assets total over $141 billion and their annual income at least $22 billion. And the extent to which they are feeding from the public trough in a variety of forms is alarming.

We are advised that since 1968 at least five States have undertaken to give subsidies to parochial and other private schools—Pennsylvania, Ohio, New York, Connecticut, and Rhode Island. And it is reported that under two federal Acts, the Elementary and Secondary Education Act of 1965 and the Higher Education Act of 1965, *billions of dollars* have been granted to parochial and other private schools.

* * * * *

If believers are entitled to public financial support, so are nonbelievers. A believer and nonbeliever under the present law are treated differently because of the articles of their faith. Believers are doubtless comforted that the cause of religion is being fostered by this legislation. Yet one of the mandates of the First Amendment is to promote a viable, pluralistic society and to keep government neutral, not only between sects, but also between believers and nonbelievers. The present involvement of government in religion may seem *de minimis.* But it is, I fear, a long step down the Establishment path. Perhaps I have been misinformed. But as I have read the Constitution and its philosophy, I gathered that independence was the price of liberty.

I conclude that this tax exemption is unconstitutional.

Lemon v. Kurtzman, 403 U.S. 602 (1971)

This case involved parochial school aid programs in Pennsylvania and Rhode Island. Both states had sought to protect their statutes by including numerous restrictions and protections against First Amendment violations. It was these safeguards that ultimately undermined both programs. Justice Burger, writing for the eight-member majority, used the *Walz* test of excessive governmental entanglement to deny "parochaid" to the two states. Justices Douglas and Brennan offered lengthy concurring opinions. Justice White, the lone dissenter on the Rhode Island case, concurred in the Pennsylvania part of the majority opinion. Included in his opinion is Justice White's concurring argument in the *Tilton* case. This case is often referred to as *Lemon I* to distinguish it from the 1973 decision allowing the two states to fulfill the remainder of their contracts with the schools.

MR. CHIEF JUSTICE BURGER DELIVERED THE OPINION OF THE COURT.

These two appeals raise questions as to Pennsylvania and Rhode Island statutes providing state aid to church-related elementary and secondary schools. Both statutes are challenged as violative of the Establishment and Free Exercise Clauses of the First Amendment and the Due Process Clause of the Fourteenth Amendment.

Pennsylvania has adopted a statutory program that provides financial support to nonpublic elementary and secondary schools by way of reimbursement for the cost of teachers' salaries, textbooks, and instructional materials in specified secular subjects. Rhode Island has adopted a statute under which the State pays directly to teachers in nonpublic elementary schools a supplement of 15% of their annual salary. Under each statute state aid has been given to church-related educational institutions. We hold that both statutes are unconstitutional.

I

The Rhode Island Statute

The Rhode Island Salary Supplement Act was enacted in 1969. It rests on the legislative finding that the quality of education available in nonpublic elementary schools has been jeopardized by the rapidly rising salaries needed to attract competent and dedicated teachers. The Act authorizes state officials to supplement the salaries of teachers of secular subjects in nonpublic elementary schools by paying directly to a teacher an amount not in excess of 15% of his current annual salary. As supplemented, however, a nonpublic school teacher's salary cannot exceed the maximum paid to teachers in the State's public schools, and the recipient must be certified by the state board of education in substantially the same manner as public school teachers.

In order to be eligible for the Rhode Island salary supplement, the recipient must teach in a nonpublic school at which the average per-pupil expenditure on secular education is less than the average in the State's public schools during a specified period. Appellant State Commissioner of Education also requires eligible schools to submit financial data. If this information indicates a per-pupil expenditure in excess of the statutory limitation, the records of the school in question must be examined in order to assess how much of the expenditure is attributable to secular education and how much to religious activity.

The Act also requires that teachers eligible for salary supplements must teach only those subjects that are offered in the State's public schools. They must use "only teaching materials which are used in the public schools." Finally, any teacher applying for a salary supplement must first agree in writing "not to teach a course in religion for so long as or during such time as he or she receives any salary supplements" under the Act.

Appellees are citizens and taxpayers of Rhode Island. They brought this suit to have the Rhode Island Salary Supplement Act declared unconstitutional and its operation enjoined on the ground that it violates the Establishment and Free Exercise Clauses of the First Amendment. Appellants are state officials charged with administration of the Act, teachers eligible for salary supplements under the Act, and parents of children in church-related elementary schools whose teachers would receive state salary assistance.

A three-judge federal court was convened. It found that Rhode Island's nonpublic elementary schools accommodated approximately 25% of the State's pupils. About 95% of these pupils attended schools affiliated with the Roman Catholic church. To date some 250 teachers have applied for benefits under the Act. All of them are employed by Roman Catholic schools.

The court held a hearing at which extensive evidence was introduced concerning the nature of the secular instruction offered in the Roman Catholic schools whose teachers would be eligible for salary assistance under the Act. Although the court found that concern for religious values does not necessarily affect the content of secular subjects, it also found that the parochial school system was "an integral part of the religious mission of the Catholic Church."

The District Court concluded that the Act violated the Establishment Clause, holding that it fostered "excessive entanglement" between government and religion. In addition two judges thought that the Act had the impermissible effect of giving "significant aid to a religious enterprise." We affirm.

The Pennsylvania Statute

Pennsylvania has adopted a program that has some but not all of the features of the Rhode Island program. The Pennsylvania Nonpublic Elementary and Secondary Education Act was passed in 1968 in response to a crisis that the Pennsylvania Legislature found existed in the State's nonpublic schools due to rapidly rising costs. The statute affirmatively reflects the legislative conclusion that the State's educational goals could appropriately be fulfilled by government support of "those purely secular educational objectives achieved through nonpublic education. . . ."

The statute authorizes appellee state Superintendent of Public Instruction to "purchase" specified "secular educational services" from nonpublic schools. Under the "contracts" authorized by the statute, the State directly reimburses nonpublic schools solely for their actual expenditures for teachers' salaries, textbooks, and instructional materials. A school seeking reimbursement must maintain prescribed accounting procedures that identify the "separate" cost of the "secular educational service." These accounts are subject to state audit. The funds for this program were originally derived from a new tax on horse and harness racing, but the Act is now financed by a portion of the state tax on cigarettes.

There are several significant statutory restrictions on state aid. Reimbursement is limited to courses "presented in the curricula of the public schools." It is further limited "solely" to courses in the following "secular" subjects: mathematics, modern foreign languages, physical science, and physical education. Textbooks and instructional materials included in the program must be approved by the state Superintendent of Public Instruction. Finally, the statute prohibits reimbursement for any course that contains "any subject matter expressing religious teaching, or the morals or forms of worship of any sect."

The Act went into effect on July 1, 1968, and the first reimbursement payments to schools were made on September 2, 1969. It appears that some $5 million has been expended annually under the Act. The State has now entered into contracts with some 1,181 nonpublic elementary and secondary schools with a student population of some 535,215 pupils—more than 20% of the total number of students in the State. More than 96% of these pupils attend church-related schools, and most of these schools are affiliated with the Roman Catholic church.

Appellants brought this action in the District Court to challenge the constitutionality of the Pennsylvania statute. The organizational plaintiffs-appellants are associations of persons resident in Pennsylvania declaring belief in the separation of church and state; individual plaintiffs-appellants are citizens and taxpayers of Pennsylvania. Appellant Lemon, in addition to being a citizen and a taxpayer, is a parent of a child attending public school in Pennsylvania. Lemon also alleges that he purchased a ticket at a race track and thus had paid the specific tax that supports the expenditures under the Act. Appellees are state officials who have the responsibility for administering the Act. In addition seven church-related schools are defendants-appellees.

A three-judge federal court was convened. The District Court held that the individual plaintiffs-appellants had standing to challenge the Act. The organizational plaintiffs-appellants were denied standing under *Flast v. Cohen.*

The court granted appellees' motion to dismiss the complaint for failure to state a claim for relief. It held that the Act violated neither the Establishment nor the Free Exercise Clause, Chief Judge Hastie dissenting. We reverse.

II

In *Everson* this Court upheld a state statute that reimbursed the parents of parochial school children for bus transportation expenses. There Mr. Justice Black, writing for the majority, suggested that the decision carried to "the verge" of forbidden territory under the Religion Clauses. Candor compels acknowledgment, moreover, that we can only dimly perceive the lines of demarcation in this extraordinarily sensitive area of constitutional law.

The language of the Religion Clauses of the First Amendment is at best opaque, particularly when compared with other portions of the Amendment. Its authors did not simply prohibit the establishment of a state church or a state religion, an area history shows they regarded as very important and fraught with great dangers. Instead they commanded that there should be "no law *respecting* an establishment of religion." A law may be one "respecting" the forbidden objective while falling short of its total realization. A law "respecting" the proscribed result, that is, the establishment of religion, is not always easily identifiable as one violative of the Clause. A given law might not *establish* a state religion but nevertheless be one "respecting" that end in the sense of being a step that could lead to such establishment and hence offend the First Amendment.

In the absence of precisely stated constitutional prohibitions, we must draw lines with reference to the three main evils against which the Establishment Clause was intended to afford protection: "sponsorship, financial support, and active involvement of the sovereign in religious activity."

Every analysis in this area must begin with consideration of the cumulative criteria developed by the Court over many years. Three such tests may be gleaned from our cases. First, the statute must have a secular legislative purpose; second, its principal or primary effect must be one that neither advances nor inhibits religion; finally, the statute must not foster "an excessive government entanglement with religion."

Inquiry into the legislative purposes of the Pennsylvania and Rhode Island statutes affords no basis for a conclusion that the legislative intent was to advance religion. On the contrary, the statutes themselves clearly state that they are intended to enhance the quality of the secular education in all schools covered by the compulsory attendance laws. There is no reason to believe the legislatures meant anything else. A State always has a legitimate concern for maintaining minimum standards in all schools it allows to operate. As in *Allen,* we find nothing here that undermines the stated legislative intent; it must therefore be accorded appropriate deference.

In *Allen* the Court acknowledged that secular and religious teachings were not necessarily so intertwined that secular textbooks furnished to students by the State were in fact instrumental in the teaching of religion. The legislatures of Rhode Island and Pennsylvania have concluded that secular and religious education are identifiable and separable. In the abstract we have no quarrel with this conclusion.

The two legislatures, however, have also recognized that church-related elementary and secondary schools have a significant religious mission and that a substantial portion of their activities is religiously oriented. They have therefore sought to create statutory restrictions designed to guarantee the separation between secular and religious educational functions and to ensure that State financial aid supports only the former. All these provisions are precautions taken in candid recognition that these programs approached, even if they did not intrude upon, the forbidden areas under the Religion Clauses. We need not decide whether these legislative precautions restrict the principal or primary effect of the programs to the point where they do not offend the Religion Clauses, for we conclude that the cumulative impact of the entire relationship arising under the statutes in each

State involves excessive entanglement between government and religion.

III

In *Walz* the Court upheld state tax exemptions for real property owned by religious organizations and used for religious worship. That holding, however, tended to confine rather than enlarge the area of permissible state involvement with religious institutions by calling for close scrutiny of the degree of entanglement involved in the relationship. The objective is to prevent, as far as possible, the intrusion of either into the precincts of the other.

Our prior holdings do not call for total separation between church and state; total separation is not possible in an absolute sense. Some relationship between government and religious organizations is inevitable. Fire inspections, building and zoning regulations, and state requirements under compulsory school-attendance laws are examples of necessary and permissible contacts. Indeed, under the statutory exemption before us in *Walz,* the State had a continuing burden to ascertain that the exempt property was in fact being used for religious worship. Judicial caveats against entanglement must recognize that the line of separation, far from being a "wall," is a blurred, indistinct, and variable barrier depending on all the circumstances of a particular relationship.

This is not to suggest, however, that we are to engage in a legalistic minuet in which precise rules and forms must govern. A true minuet is a matter of pure form and style, the observance of which is itself the substantive end. Here we examine the form of the relationship for the light that it casts on the substance.

In order to determine whether the government entanglement with religion is excessive, we must examine the character and purposes of the institutions that are benefited, the nature of the aid that the State provides, and the resulting relationship between the government and the religious authority. Mr. Justice Harlan, in a separate opinion in *Walz,* echoed the classic warning as to "programs, whose very nature is apt to entangle the state in details of administration. . . ." Here we find that both statutes foster an impermissible degree of entanglement.

(a) *Rhode Island Program*

The District Court made extensive findings on the grave potential for excessive entanglement that inheres in the religious character and purpose of the Roman Catholic elementary schools of Rhode Island, to date the sole beneficiaries of the Rhode Island Salary Supplement Act.

The church schools involved in the program are located close to parish churches. This understandably permits convenient access for religious exercises since instruction in faith and morals is part of the total educational process. The school buildings contain identifying religious symbols such as crosses on the exterior and crucifixes, and religious paintings and statues either in the classrooms or hallways. Although only approximately 30 minutes a day are devoted to direct religious instruction, there are religiously oriented extracurricular activities. Approximately two-thirds of the teachers in these schools are nuns of various religious orders. Their dedicated efforts provide an atmosphere in which religious instruction and religious vocations are natural and proper parts of life in such schools. Indeed, as the District Court found, the role of teaching nuns in enhancing the religious atmosphere has led the parochial school authorities to attempt to maintain a one-to-one ratio between nuns and lay teachers in all schools rather than to permit some to be staffed almost entirely by lay teachers.

On the basis of these findings the District Court concluded that the parochial schools constituted "an integral part of the religious mission of the Catholic Church." The various characteristics of the schools make them "a powerful vehicle for transmitting the Catholic faith to the next generation." This process of inculcating religious doctrine is, of course, enhanced by the impressionable age of the pupils, in primary schools particularly. In short, parochial schools involve substantial religious activity and purpose.

The substantial religious character of these church-related schools gives rise to entangling church-state relationships of the kind the Religion Clauses sought to avoid. Although the District Court found that concern for religious values did not inevitably or necessarily intrude into the content of secular subjects, the considerable religious activities of these schools led the legislature to provide for careful governmental controls and surveillance by state authorities in order to ensure that state aid supports only secular education.

The dangers and corresponding entanglements are enhanced by the particular form of aid that the Rhode Island Act provides. Our decisions from *Everson* to *Allen* have permitted the States to provide church-related schools with secular, neutral, or nonideological services, facilities, or materials. Bus transportation, school lunches, public health services, and secular textbooks supplied in common to all students were not thought to offend the Establishment Clause. We note that the dissenters in *Allen* seemed chiefly concerned with the pragmatic difficulties involved in ensuring the truly secular content of the textbooks provided at state expense.

In *Allen* the Court refused to make assumptions, on a meager record, about the religious content of the textbooks that the State would be asked to provide. We cannot, however, refuse here to recognize that teachers have a substantially different ideological character from books. In terms of potential for involving some aspect of faith or morals in secular subjects, a textbook's content is ascertainable, but a teacher's handling of a subject is not. We cannot ignore the danger that a teacher under religious control and discipline poses to the separation of the religious from the purely secular aspects of precollege education. The conflict of functions inheres in the situation.

In our view the record shows these dangers are present to a substantial degree. The Rhode Island Roman Catholic elementary schools are under the general supervision of the Bishop of Providence and his appointed representative, the Diocesan Superintendent of Schools. In most cases, each individual parish, however, assumes the ultimate financial responsibility for the school, with the parish priest authorizing the allocation of parish funds. With only two exceptions, school principals are nuns appointed either by the Superintendent or the Mother Provincial of the order whose members staff the school. By 1969 lay teachers constituted more than a third of all teachers in the parochial elementary schools, and their number is growing. They are first interviewed by the superintendent's office and then by the school principal. The contracts are signed by the parish priest, and he retains some discretion in negotiating salary levels. Religious authority necessarily pervades the school system.

The schools are governed by the standards set forth in a "Handbook of School Regulations," which has the force of synodal law in the diocese. It emphasizes the role and importance of the teacher in parochial schools: "The prime factor for the success or the failure of the school is the spirit and personality, as well as the professional competency, of the teacher. . . ." The Handbook also states that: "Religious formation is not confined to formal courses; nor is it restricted to a single subject area." Finally, the Handbook advises teachers to stimulate interest in religious vocations and missionary work. Given the mission of the church school, these instructions are consistent and logical.

Several teachers testified, however, that they did not inject religion into their secular classes. And the District Court found that religious values did not necessarily affect the content of the secular instruction. But what has been recounted suggests the potential if not actual hazards of this form of state aid. The teacher is employed by a religious organization, subject to the direction and discipline of religious authorities, and works in a system dedicated to rearing children in a particular faith. These controls are not lessened by the fact that most of the lay teachers are of the Catholic faith. Inevitably some of a teacher's responsibilities hover on the border between secular and religious orientation.

We need not and do not assume that teachers in parochial schools will be guilty of bad faith or any conscious design to evade the limitations imposed by the statute and the First Amendment. We simply recognize that a dedicated religious person, teaching in a school affiliated with his or her faith and operated to inculcate its tenets, will inevitably experience great difficulty in remaining religiously neutral. Doctrines and faith are not inculcated or advanced by neutrals. With the best of intentions such a teacher would find it hard to make a total separation between secular teaching and religious doctrine. What would appear to some to be essential to good citizenship might well for others border on or constitute instruction in religion. Further difficulties are inherent in the combination of religious discipline and the possibility of disagreement between teacher and religious authorities over the meaning of the statutory restrictions.

We do not assume, however, that parochial school teachers will be unsuccessful in their attempts to segregate their religious beliefs from their secular educational responsibilities. But the potential for impermissible fostering of religion is present. The Rhode Island Legislature has not, and could not, provide state aid on the basis of a mere assumption that secular teachers under religious discipline can avoid conflicts. The State must be certain, given the Religion Clauses, that subsidized teachers do not inculcate religion—indeed the State here has undertaken to do so. To ensure that no trespass occurs, the State has therefore carefully conditioned its aid with pervasive restrictions. An eligible recipient must teach only those courses that are offered in the public schools and use only those texts and materials that are found in the public schools. In addition the teacher must not engage in teaching any course in religion.

A comprehensive, discriminating, and continuing state surveillance will inevitably be required to ensure that these restrictions are obeyed and the First Amendment otherwise respected. Unlike a book, a teacher cannot be inspected once so as to determine the extent and intent of his or her personal beliefs and subjective acceptance of the limitations imposed by the First Amendment. These prophylactic contacts will involve excessive and enduring entanglement between state and church.

There is another area of entanglement in the Rhode Island program that gives concern. The statute excludes teachers employed by non-public schools whose average per-pupil expenditures on secular education equal or exceed the comparable figures for public schools. In the event that the total expenditures of an otherwise eligible school exceed this norm, the program requires the government to examine the school's records in order to determine how much of the total expenditures is attributable to secular education and how much to religious activity. This kind of state inspection and evaluation of the religious content of a religious organization is fraught with the sort of entanglement that the Constitution forbids. It is a relationship pregnant with dangers of excessive government direction of church schools and hence of churches. The Court noted "the hazards of government supporting churches" in *Walz,* and we cannot ignore here the danger that pervasive modern governmental power will ultimately intrude on religion and thus conflict with the Religion Clauses.

(b) *Pennsylvania Program*

The Pennsylvania statute also provides state aid to church-related schools for teachers' salaries. The complaint describes an educational system that is very similar to the one existing in Rhode Island. According to the allegations, the church-related elementary and secondary schools are controlled by religious organizations, have the purpose of propagating and promoting a particular religious faith, and conduct their operations to fulfill that purpose. Since this complaint was dismissed for failure to state a claim for relief, we must accept these allegations as true for purposes of our review.

As we noted earlier, the very restrictions and surveillance necessary to ensure that teachers play a strictly nonideological role give rise to entanglements between church and state. The Pennsylvania statute, like that of Rhode Island, fosters this kind of relationship. Reimbursement is not only limited to courses offered in the public schools and materials approved by state officials, but the statute excludes "any subject matter expressing religious teaching, or the morals or forms of worship of any sect." In addition, schools seeking reimbursement must maintain accounting procedures that require the State to establish the cost of the secular as distinguished from the religious instruction.

The Pennsylvania statute, moreover, has the further defect of providing state financial aid directly to the church-related school. This factor distinguishes both *Everson* and *Allen,* for in both those cases the Court was careful to point out that state aid was provided to the student and his parents—not to the church-related school. In *Walz* the Court warned of the dangers of direct payments to religious organizations:

> Obviously a direct money subsidy would be a relationship pregnant with involvement and, as with most governmental grant programs, could encompass sustained and detailed administrative relationships for enforcement of statutory or administrative standards. . . .

The history of government grants of a continuing cash subsidy indicates that such programs have almost always been accompanied by varying measures of control and surveillance. The government cash grants before us now provide no basis for predicting that comprehensive measures of surveillance and controls will not follow. In particular the government's post-audit power to inspect and evaluate a church-related school's financial records and to determine which expenditures are religious and which are secular creates an intimate and continuing relationship between church and state.

IV

A broader base of entanglement of yet a different character is presented by the divisive political potential of these state programs. In a community where such a large number of pupils are served by church-related schools, it can be assumed that state assistance will entail considerable political activity. Partisans of parochial schools, understandably concerned with rising costs and sincerely dedicated to both the religious and secular educational missions of their schools, will inevitably champion this cause and promote political action to achieve their goals. Those who oppose state aid, whether for constitutional, religious, or fiscal reasons, will inevitably respond and employ all of the usual political campaign techniques to prevail. Candidates will be forced to declare and voters to choose. It would be unrealistic to ignore the fact that many people confronted with issues of this kind will find their votes aligned with their faith.

Ordinarily political debate and division, however vigorous or even partisan, are normal and healthy manifestations of our democratic system of government, but political division along religious lines was one of the principal evils against which the First Amendment was intended to protect. The potential divisiveness of such conflict is a threat to the normal political process. To have States or communities divide on the issues presented by state aid to parochial schools would tend to confuse and obscure other issues of great urgency. We have an expanding array of vexing issues, local and national, domestic and international, to debate and divide on. It conflicts with our whole history and tradition to permit questions of the Religion Clauses to assume such importance in our legislatures and in our elections that they could divert attention from the myriad issues and problems that confront every level of government. The highways of church and state relationships are not likely to be one-way streets, and the Constitution's authors sought to protect religious worship from the pervasive power of government. The history of many countries attests to the hazards of religions' intruding into the political arena or of political power intruding into the legitimate and free exercise of religious belief.

Of course, as the Court noted in *Walz,* "[a]dherents of particular faiths and individual churches frequently take strong positions on public issues." We could not expect otherwise, for religious values pervade the fabric of our national life. But in *Walz* we dealt with a status under state tax laws for the benefit of all religious groups. Here we are confronted with successive and very likely permanent annual appropriations that benefit relatively few religious groups. Political fragmentation and divisiveness on religious lines are thus likely to be intensified.

The potential for political divisiveness related to religious belief and practice is aggravated in these two statutory programs by the need for continuing annual appropriations and the likelihood of larger and larger demands as costs and populations grow. The Rhode Island District Court found that the parochial school system's "monumental and deepening financial crisis" would "inescapably" require larger annual appropriations subsidizing greater percentages of the salaries of lay teachers. Although no facts have been developed in this respect in the Pennsylvania case, it appears that such pressures for expanding aid have already required the state legislature to include a portion of the state revenues from cigarette taxes in the program.

V

In *Walz* it was argued that a tax exemption for places of religious worship would prove to be the first step in an inevitable progression leading to the establishment of state churches and state religion. That claim could not stand up against more than 200 years of virtually universal practice imbedded in our colonial experience and continuing into the present.

The progression argument, however, is more persuasive here. We have no long history of state aid to church-related educational institutions comparable to 200 years of tax exemption for churches. Indeed, the state programs before us today represent something of an innovation. We have already noted that modern governmental programs have self-perpetuating and self-expanding propensities. These internal pressures are only enhanced when the schemes involve institutions whose legitimate needs are growing and whose interests have substantial political support. Nor can we fail to see that in constitutional adjudication some steps, which when taken were thought to approach "the verge," have become the platform for yet further steps. A certain momentum develops in constitutional theory and it can be a "downhill thrust" easily set in motion but difficult to retard or stop. Development by momentum is not invariably bad; indeed, it is the way the common law has grown, but it is a force to be recognized and reckoned with. The dangers are increased by the difficulty of perceiving in advance exactly where the "verge" of the precipice lies. As well as constituting an independent evil against which the Religion Clauses were intended to protect, involvement or entanglement between government and religion serves as a warning signal.

Finally, nothing we have said can be construed to disparage the role of church-related elementary and secondary schools in our national life. Their contribution has been and is enormous. Nor do we ignore their economic plight in a period of rising costs and expanding need. Taxpayers generally have been spared vast sums by the maintenance of these educational institutions by religious organizations, largely by the gifts of faithful adherents.

The merit and benefits of these schools, however, are not the issue before us in these cases. The sole question is whether state aid to these schools can be squared with the dictates of the Religion Clauses. Under our system the choice has been made that government is to be entirely excluded from the area of religious instruction and churches excluded from the affairs of government. The Constitution decrees that religion must be a private matter for the individual, the family, and the institutions of private choice, and that while some involvement and entanglement are inevitable, lines must be drawn.

The judgment of the Rhode Island District Court in No. 569 and No. 570 is affirmed. The judgment of the Pennsylvania District Court in No. 89 is reversed, and the case is remanded for further proceedings consistent with this opinion.

MR. JUSTICE WHITE, CONCURRING IN THE JUDGMENTS IN TILTON AND NO. 89 AND DISSENTING IN NOS. 569 AND 570.

It is our good fortune that the States of this country long ago recognized that instruction of the young and old ranks high on the scale of proper governmental functions and not only undertook secular education as a public responsibility but also required compulsory attendance at school by their young. Having recognized the value of educated citizens and assumed the task of educating them, the States now before us assert a right to provide for the secular education of children whether they attend public schools or choose to enter private institutions, even when those institutions are church-related. The Federal Government also asserts that it is entitled, where requested, to contribute to the cost of secular education by furnishing buildings and facilities to all institutions of higher learning, public and private alike. Both the United States and the States urge that if parents choose to have their children receive instruction in the required secular subjects in a school where religion is also taught and a religious atmosphere may prevail, part or all of the cost of such secular instruction may be paid for by governmental grants to the religious institution conducting the school and seeking the grant. Those who challenge this position would bar official contributions to secular education where the family prefers the parochial to both the public and nonsectarian private school.

The issue is fairly joined. It is precisely the kind of issue the Constitution contemplates this Court must ultimately decide. This is true although neither affirmance nor reversal of any of these cases follows automatically from the spare language of the First Amendment, from its history, or from the cases of this Court construing it and even though reasonable men can very easily and sensibly differ over the import of that language.

But, while the decision of the Court is legitimate, it is surely quite wrong in overturning the Pennsylvania and Rhode Island statutes on the ground that they amount to an establishment of religion forbidden by the First Amendment.

No one in these cases questions the constitutional right of parents to satisfy their state-imposed obligation to educate their children by sending them to private schools, sectarian or otherwise, as long as those schools meet minimum standards established for secular instruction. The States are not only permitted, but required by the Constitution, to free students attending private schools from any public school attendance obligation. The States may also furnish transportation for students, and books for teaching secular subjects to students attending parochial and other private as well as public schools; we have also upheld arrangements whereby students are released from public school classes so that they may attend religious instruction. Outside the field of education, we have upheld Sunday closing laws, state and federal laws exempting church property and church activity from taxation, and governmental grants to religious organizations for the purpose of financing improvements in the facilities of hospitals managed and controlled by religious orders.

Our prior cases have recognized the dual role of parochial schools in American society: they perform both religious and secular functions. Our cases also recognize that legislation having a secular purpose and extending governmental assistance to sectarian schools in the performance of their secular functions does not constitute "law[s] respecting an establishment of religion" forbidden by the First Amendment merely because a secular program may incidentally benefit a church in fulfilling its religious mission. That religion may indirectly benefit from governmental aid to the secular activities of churches does not convert that aid into an impermissible establishment of religion.

This much the Court squarely holds in the *Tilton* case, where it also expressly rejects the notion that payments made directly to a religious institution are, without more, forbidden by the First Amendment. In *Tilton,* the Court decides that the Federal Government may finance the separate function of secular education carried on in a parochial setting. It reaches this result although sectarian institutions undeniably will obtain substantial benefit from federal aid; without federal funding to provide adequate facilities for secular education, the student bodies of those institutions might remain stationary or even decrease in size and the institutions might ultimately have to close their doors.

It is enough for me that the States and the Federal Government are financing a separable secular function of overriding importance in order to sustain the legislation here challenged. That religion and private interests other than education may substantially benefit does not convert these laws into impermissible establishments of religion.

It is unnecessary, therefore, to urge that the Free Exercise Clause of the First Amendment at least permits government in some respects to modify and mold its secular programs out of express concern for free-exercise values. The Establishment Clause, however, coexists in the First Amendment with the Free Exercise Clause and the latter is surely relevant in cases such as these. Where a state program seeks to ensure the proper education of its young, in private as well as public schools, free exercise considerations at least counsel against refusing support for students attending parochial schools simply because in that setting they are also being instructed in the tenets of the faith they are constitutionally free to practice.

I would sustain both the federal and the Rhode Island programs at issue in these cases, and I therefore concur in the judgment in *Tilton* (153) and dissent from the judgments in Nos. 569 and 570. Although I would also reject the facial challenge to the Pennsylvania statute, I concur in the judgment in No. 89 for the reasons given below.

The Court strikes down the Rhode Island statute on its face. No fault is found with the secular purpose of the program; there is no suggestion that the purpose of the program was aid to religion disguised in secular attire. Nor does the Court find that the primary effect of the program is to aid religion rather than to implement secular goals. The Court nevertheless finds that impermissible "entanglement" will result from administration of the program. The reasoning is a curious and mystifying blend, but a critical factor appears to be an unwillingness to accept the District Court's express findings that on the evidence before it none of the teachers here involved mixed religious and secular instruction. Rather, the District Court struck down the Rhode Island statute because it concluded that activities outside the secular classroom would probably have a religious content and that support for religious education therefore necessarily resulted from the financial aid to the secular programs, since that aid generally strengthened the parochial schools and increased the number of their students.

In view of the decision in *Tilton,* however, where these same factors were found insufficient to invalidate the federal plan, the Court is forced to other considerations. Accepting the District Court's observation in *DiCenso* that education is an integral part of the religious mission of the Catholic church—an observation that should neither surprise nor alarm anyone, especially judges who have already approved substantial aid to parochial schools in various forms—the majority then interposes findings and conclusions that the District Court expressly abjured, namely, that nuns, clerics, and dedicated Catholic laymen unavoidably pose a grave risk in that they might not be able to put aside their religion in the secular classroom. Although stopping short of considering them untrustworthy, the Court concludes that for them the difficulties of avoiding teaching religion along with secular subjects would pose intolerable risks and would in any event entail an unacceptable enforcement regime. Thus, the potential for impermissible fostering of religion in secular classrooms—an untested assumption of the Court—paradoxically renders unacceptable the State's efforts at insuring that secular teachers under religious discipline successfully avoid conflicts between the religious mission of the school and the secular purpose of the State's education program.

* * * * *

The Court thus creates an insoluble paradox for the State and the parochial schools. The State cannot finance secular instruction if it permits religion to be taught in the same classroom; but if it exacts a promise that religion not be so taught—a promise the school and its teachers are quite willing and on this record able to give—and enforces it, it is then entangled in the "no entanglement" aspect of the Court's Establishment Clause jurisprudence.

Why the federal program in the *Tilton* case is not embroiled in the same difficulties is never adequately explained. Surely the notion that college students are more mature and resistant to indoctrination is a make weight, for in *Tilton* there is careful note of the federal condition on funding and the enforcement mechanism available. If religious teaching in federally financed buildings was permitted, the powers of resistance of college students would in no way save the federal scheme. Nor can I imagine the basis for finding college clerics more reliable in keeping promises than their counterparts in elementary and secondary schools—particularly those in the Rhode Island case, since within five years the majority of teachers in Rhode Island parochial schools will be lay persons, many of them non-Catholic.

Both the District Court and this Court in *DiCenso* have seized on the Rhode Island formula for supplementing teachers' salaries since it requires the State to verify the amount of school money spent for secular as distinguished from religious purposes. Only teachers in those schools having per-pupil expenditures for secular subjects below the state average qualify under the system, an aspect of the state scheme which is said to provoke serious "entanglement." But this is also a slender reed on which to strike down this law, for as the District Court found, only once since the inception of the program has it been necessary to segregate expenditures in this manner.

* * * * *

With respect to Pennsylvania, the Court, accepting as true the factual allegations of the complaint, as it must for purposes of a motion to dismiss, would reverse the dismissal of the complaint and invalidate the legislation. The critical allegations, as paraphrased by the Court, are that "the church-related elementary and secondary schools are controlled by religious organizations, have the purpose of propagating and promoting a particular religious faith, and conduct their operations to fulfill that purpose." From these allegations the Court concludes that forbidden entanglements would follow from enforcing compliance with the secular purpose for which the state money is being paid.

I disagree. There is no specific allegation in the complaint that sectarian teaching does or would invade secular classes supported by state funds. That the schools are operated to promote a particular religion is quite consistent with the view that secular teaching devoid of religious instruction can successfully be maintained, for good secular instruction is, as Judge Coffin wrote for the District Court in the Rhode Island case, essential to the success of the religious mission of the parochial school. I would no more here than in the Rhode Island case substitute presumption for proof that religion is or would be taught in state-financed secular courses or assume that enforcement measures would be so extensive as to border on a free exercise violation. We should not forget that the Pennsylvania statute does not compel church schools to accept state funds. I cannot hold that the First Amendment forbids an agreement between the school and the State that the state funds would be used only to teach secular subjects.

I do agree, however, that the complaint should not have been dismissed for failure to state a cause of action. Although it did not specifically allege that the schools involved mixed religious teaching with secular subjects, the complaint did allege that the schools were operated to fulfill religious purposes and one of the legal theories stated in the complaint was that the Pennsylvania Act "finances and participates in the blending of sectarian and secular instruction." At trial under this complaint, evidence showing such a blend in a course supported by state funds would appear to be admissible and, if credited, would establish financing of religious instruction by the State. Hence, I would reverse the judgment of the District Court and remand the case for trial, thereby holding the Pennsylvania legislation valid on its face but leaving open the question of its validity as applied to the particular facts of this case.

I find it very difficult to follow the distinction between the federal and state programs in terms of their First Amendment acceptability. My difficulty is not surprising, since there is frank acknowledgment that "we can only dimly perceive the boundaries of permissible government activity in this sensitive area of constitutional adjudication." I find it even more difficult, with these acknowledgments in mind, to understand how the Court can accept the considered judgment of Congress that its program is constitutional and yet reject the equally considered decisions of the Rhode Island and Pennsylvania legislatures that their programs represent a constitutionally acceptable accommodation between church and state.

Committee for Public Education and Religious Liberty v. Nyquist, 413 U.S. 756 (1973)

On June 25, 1973, several decisions were handed down that had direct bearing upon "parochaid." The major case was *Nyquist*, in which Justice Powell, writing for the majority, struck down three New York programs, all of which were found to have the "effect" of advancing religion: "Because we have found that the challenged sections have the impermissible effect of advancing religion, we need not consider whether such aid would result in entanglement of the State with religion."

The Court now found itself divided, with Justices Burger, White, and Rehnquist all writing strong opinions dissenting in whole or in part.

On the same day the Court struck down a Pennsylvania tuition reimbursement plan that was brought as *Sloan v. Lemon* and a New York law authorizing payment to religious schools for testing and record keeping *(Levitt v. Committee for Public Education and Religious Liberty).*

MR. JUSTICE POWELL DELIVERED THE OPINION OF THE COURT.

These cases raise a challenge under the Establishment Clause of the First Amendment to the constitutionality of a recently enacted New York law which provides financial assistance, in several ways, to nonpublic elementary and secondary schools in that State. The cases involve an intertwining of societal and constitutional issues of the greatest importance.

James Madison, in his Memorial and Remonstrance Against Religious Assessments, admonished that a "prudent jealousy" for religious freedoms required that they never become "entangled . . . in precedents." His strongly held convictions, coupled with those of Thomas Jefferson and others among the Founders, are reflected in the first Clauses of the First Amendment of the Bill of Rights, which state that "Congress shall make no law respecting an establishment of religion, or prohibiting the free exercise thereof." Yet, despite Madison's admonition and the "sweep of the absolute prohibitions" of the Clauses, this Nation's history has not been one of entirely sanitized separation between Church and State. It has never been thought either possible or desirable to enforce a regime of total separation, and as a consequence cases arising under these Clauses have presented some of the most perplexing questions to come before this Court. Those cases have occasioned thorough and thoughtful scholarship by several of this Court's most respected former Justices, including Justices Black, Frankfurter, Harlan, Jackson, Rutledge, and Chief Justice Warren.

As a result of these decisions and opinions, it may no longer be said that the Religion Clauses are free of "entangling" precedents. Neither, however, may it be said that Jefferson's metaphoric "wall of separation" between Church and State has become "as winding as the famous serpentine wall" he designed for the University of Virginia. Indeed, the controlling constitutional standards have become firmly rooted and the broad contours of our inquiry are now well defined. Our task, therefore, is to assess New York's several forms of aid in the light of principles already delineated.

I

In May 1972, the Governor of New York signed into law several amendments to the State's Education and Tax Laws. The first five sections of these amendments established three distinct financial aid programs for non-public elementary and secondary schools. Almost immediately after the signing of these measures a complaint was filed in the United States District Court for the Southern District of New York challenging each of the three forms of aid as violative of the Establishment Clause. The plaintiffs were an unincorporated association, known as the Committee for Public Education and Religious Liberty (PEARL), and several individuals who were residents and taxpayers in New York, some of whom had children attending public schools. Named as defendants were the State Commissioner of Education, the Comptroller, and the Commissioner of Taxation and Finance. Motions to intervene on behalf of defendants were granted to a group of parents with children enrolled in nonpublic schools, and to the Majority Leader and President pro tem of the New York State Senate. By consent of the parties, a three-judge court was convened and the case was decided without an evidentiary hearing. Because the questions before the District Court were resolved on the basis of the pleadings, that court's decision turned on the constitutionality of each provision on its face.

The first section of the challenged enactment, entitled "Health and Safety Grants for Nonpublic School Children," provides for direct money grants from the State to "qualifying" nonpublic schools to be used for the "maintenance and repair of . . . school facilities and equipment to ensure the health, welfare and safety of enrolled pupils." A "qualifying" school is any nonpublic, nonprofit elementary or secondary school which "has been designated during the [immediately preceding] year as serving a high concentration of pupils from low-income families for purposes of Title IV of the Federal Higher Education Act of nineteen hundred sixty-five." Such schools are entitled to receive a grant of $30 per pupil per year, or $40 per pupil per year if the facilities are more than 25 years old. Each school is required to submit to the Commissioner of Education an audited statement of its expenditures for maintenance and repair during the preceding year, and its grant may not exceed the total of such expenses. The Commissioner is also required to ascertain the average per-pupil cost for equivalent maintenance and repair services in the public schools, and in no event may the grant to nonpublic qualifying schools exceed 50% of that figure.

"Maintenance and repair" is defined by the statute to include "the provision of heat, light, water, ventilation and sanitary facilities; cleaning, janitorial and custodial services; snow removal; necessary upkeep and renovation of buildings, grounds and equipment; fire and accident protection; and such other items as the commissioner may deem necessary to ensure the health, welfare and safety of enrolled pupils." This section is prefaced by a series of legislative findings which shed light on the State's purpose in enacting the law. These findings conclude that the State "has a primary responsibility to ensure the health, welfare and safety of children attending . . . nonpublic schools"; that the "fiscal crisis in nonpublic education . . . has caused a diminution of proper maintenance and repair programs, threatening the health, welfare and safety of nonpublic school children" in low-income urban areas; and that "a healthy and safe school environment" contributes "to the stability of urban neighborhoods." For these reasons, the statute declares that "the state has the right to make grants for maintenance and repair expenditures which are clearly secular, neutral and non-ideological in nature."

The remainder of the challenged legislation—§§ 2 through 5—is a single package captioned the "Elementary and Secondary Education Opportunity Program." It is composed, essentially, of two parts, a tuition grant program and a tax benefit program. Section 2 establishes a limited plan providing tuition reimbursements to parents of children attending elementary or secondary nonpublic schools. To qualify under this section a parent must have an annual taxable income of less than $5,000. The amount of reimbursement is limited to $50 for each grade school child and $100 for each high school child. Each parent is required, however, to submit to the Commissioner of Education a verified statement containing a receipted tuition bill, and the amount of state reimbursement may not exceed 50% of that figure. No restrictions are imposed on the use of the funds by the reimbursed parents.

This section, like § 1, is prefaced by a series of legislative findings designed to explain the impetus for the State's action. Expressing a dedication to the "vitality of our pluralistic society," the findings state that a "healthy competitive and diverse alternative to public education is not only desirable but indeed vital to a state and nation that have continually reaffirmed the value of individual differences." The findings further emphasize that the right to select among alternative educational systems "is diminished or even denied to children of lower-income families, whose parents, of all groups, have the least options in determining where their children are to be educated." Turning to the public schools, the findings state that any "precipitous decline in the number of nonpublic school pupils would cause a massive increase in public school enrollment and costs," an increase that would "aggravate an already serious fiscal crisis in public education" and would "seriously jeopardize quality education for all children." Based on these premises, the statute asserts the State's right to relieve the financial burden of parents who send their children to nonpublic schools through this tuition reimbursement program. Repeating the declaration contained in § 1, the findings conclude that "[s]uch assistance is clearly secular, neutral and nonideological."

The remainder of the "Elementary and Secondary Education Opportunity Program," contained in §§ 3, 4, and 5 of the challenged law, is designed to provide a form of tax relief to those who fail to qualify for tuition reimbursement. Under these sections parents may subtract from their adjusted gross income for state income tax purposes a designated amount for each dependent for whom they have paid at least $50 in nonpublic school tuition. If the taxpayer's adjusted gross income is less than $9,000 he may subtract $1,000 for each of as many as three dependents. As the taxpayer's income rises, the amount he may subtract diminishes. Thus, if a taxpayer has adjusted gross income of $15,000, he may subtract only $400 per dependent, and if his adjusted gross income is $25,000 or more, no deduction is allowed. The amount of the deduction is not dependent upon how much the taxpayer actually paid for nonpublic school tuition, and is given in addition to any deductions to which the taxpayer may be entitled for other religious or charitable contributions. As indicated in the memorandum from the Majority Leader and President pro tem of the Senate, submitted to each New York legislator during consideration of the bill, the actual tax benefits under these provisions were carefully calculated in advance. Thus, comparable tax benefits pick up at approximately the point at which tuition reimbursement benefits leave off.

While the scheme of the enactment indicates that the purposes underlying the promulgation of the tuition reimbursement program should be regarded as pertinent as well to these tax law sections, § 3 does contain an additional series of legislative findings. Those findings may be summarized as follows: (i) contributions to religious, charitable and educational institutions are already deductible from gross income; (ii) nonpublic educational institutions are accorded tax exempt status; (iii) such institutions provide education for children attending them and also serve to relieve the public school systems of the burden of providing for their education; and, therefore, (iv) the "legislature . . . finds and determines that similar modifications . . . should also be provided to parents for tuition paid to nonpublic elementary and secondary schools on behalf of their dependents."

Although no record was developed in these cases, a number of pertinent generalizations may be made about the nonpublic schools which would benefit from these enactments. The District Court, relying on findings in a similar case recently decided by the same court, adopted a profile of these sectarian, nonpublic schools similar to the one suggested in the plaintiffs' complaint. Qualifying institutions, under all three segments of the enactment, could be ones that

> (a) impose religious restrictions on admissions; (b) require attendance of pupils at religious activities; (c) require obedience by students to the doctrines and dogmas of a particular faith; (d) require pupils to attend instruction in the theology or doctrine of a particular faith; (e) are an integral part of the religious mission of the church sponsoring it; (f) have as a substantial purpose the inculcation of religious values; (g) impose religious restrictions on faculty appointments; and (h) impose religious restrictions on what or how the faculty may teach.

Of course, the characteristics of individual schools may vary widely from that profile. Some 700,000 to 800,000 students, constituting almost 20% of the State's entire elementary and secondary school population, attend over 2,000 nonpublic schools, approximately 85% of which are church affiliated. And while "all or practically all" of the 280 schools entitled to receive "maintenance and repair" grants "are related to the Roman Catholic Church and teach Catholic religious doctrine to some degree," institutions qualifying under the remainder of the statute include a substantial number of Jewish, Lutheran, Episcopal, Seventh Day Adventist, and other church-affiliated schools.

Plaintiffs argued below that because of the substantially religious character of the intended beneficiaries, each of the State's three enactments offended the Establishment Clause. The District Court, in an opinion carefully canvassing this Court's recent precedents, held unanimously that § 1 (maintenance and repair grants) and § 2 (tuition reimbursement grants) were invalid. As to the income tax provisions of §§ 3, 4, and 5, however, a majority of the District Court, over the dissent of Circuit Judge Hays, held that the Establishment Clause had not been violated. Finding the provisions of the law severable, it enjoined permanently any further implementation of §§ 1 and 2 but declared the remainder of the law independently enforceable. The plaintiffs (hereinafter appellants) appealed directly to this Court, challenging the District Court's adverse decision as to the third segment of the statute. The defendant state officials (hereinafter appellees) have appealed so much of the court's decision as invalidates the first and second portions of the 1972 law, the intervenor Majority Leader and President pro tem of the Senate (hereinafter appellee or intervenor) has also appealed from those aspects of the lower court's opinion, and the intervening parents of nonpublic schoolchildren (hereinafter appellee or intervenor) have appealed only from the decision as to § 2. This Court noted probable jurisdiction over each appeal and ordered the cases consolidated for oral argument. Thus, the constitutionality of each of New York's recently promulgated aid provisions is squarely before us. We affirm the District Court insofar as it struck down §§ 1 and 2 and reverse its determination regarding §§ 3, 4, and 5.

II

The history of the Establishment Clause has been recounted frequently and need not be repeated here. It is enough to note that it is now firmly established that a law may be one "respecting an establishment of religion" even though its consequence is not to promote a "state religion," and even though it does not aid one religion more than another but merely benefits all religions alike. It is equally well established, however, that not every law that confers an "indirect," "remote," or "incidental" benefit upon religious institutions is, for that reason alone, constitutionally invalid. What our cases require is careful examination of any law challenged on establishment grounds with a view to ascertaining whether it furthers any of the evils against which that Clause protects. Primarily among those evils have been "sponsorship, financial support, and active involvement of the sovereign in religious activity."

Most of the cases coming to this Court raising Establishment Clause questions have involved the relationship between religion and education. Among these religion-education precedents, two general categories of cases may be identified: those dealing with religious activities within the public schools, and those involving public aid in varying forms to sectarian educational institutions. While the New York legislation places this case in the latter category, its resolution requires consideration not only of the several aid-to-sectarian-education cases, but also of our other education precedents and of several important noneducation cases. For the now well-defined three-part test that has emerged from our decisions is a product of considerations derived from the full sweep of the Establishment Clause cases. Taken together, these decisions dictate that to pass muster under the Establishment Clause the law in question, first, must reflect a clearly secular legislative purpose *(Epperson),* second, must have a primary effect that neither advances nor inhibits religion *(McGowan), (Schempp),* and third, must avoid excessive government entanglement with religion *(Walz).*

In applying these criteria to the three distinct forms of aid involved in this case, we need touch only briefly on the requirement of a "secular legislative purpose." As the recitation of legislative purposes appended to New York's law indicates, each measure is adequately supported by legitimate, nonsectarian state interests. We do not question the propriety, and fully secular content, of New York's interest in preserving a healthy and safe educational environment for all of its schoolchildren. And we do not doubt—indeed, we fully recognize—the validity of the State's interests in promoting pluralism and diversity among its public and nonpublic schools. Nor do we hesitate to acknowledge the reality of its concern for an already overburdened public school system that might suffer in the event that a significant percentage of children presently attending nonpublic schools should abandon those schools in favor of the public schools.

But the propriety of a legislature's purposes may not immunize from further scrutiny a law which either has a primary effect that advances religion, or which fosters excessive entanglements between Church and State. Accordingly, we must weigh each of the three aid provisions challenged here against these criteria of effect and entanglement.

A

The "maintenance and repair" provisions of § 1 authorize direct payments to nonpublic schools, virtually all of which are Roman Catholic schools in low-income areas. The grants, totaling $30 or $40 per pupil depending on the age of the institution, are given largely without restriction on usage. So long as expenditures do not exceed 50% of comparable expenses in the public school system, it is possible for a sectarian elementary or secondary school to finance its entire "maintenance and repair" budget from state tax-raised funds. No attempt is made to restrict payments to those expenditures related to the upkeep of facilities used exclusively for secular purposes, nor do we think it possible within the context of these religion-oriented institutions to impose such restrictions. Nothing in the statute, for instance, bars a qualifying school from paying out of state funds the salaries of employees who maintain the school chapel, or the cost of renovating classrooms in which religion is taught, or the cost of heating and lighting those same facilities. Absent appropriate restrictions on expenditures for these and similar purposes, it simply cannot be denied that this section has a primary effect that advances religion in that it subsidizes directly the religious activities of sectarian elementary and secondary schools.

The state officials nevertheless argue that these expenditures for "maintenance and repair" are similar to other financial expenditures approved by this Court.

Primarily they rely on *Everson* and *Tilton.* In each of those cases it is true that the Court approved a form of financial assistance which conferred undeniable benefits upon private, sectarian schools. But a close examination of those cases illuminates their distinguishing characteristics. In *Everson,* the Court, in a five-to-four decision, approved a program of reimbursements to parents of public as well as parochial schoolchildren for bus fares paid in connection with transportation to and from school, a program which the Court characterized as approaching the "verge" of impermissible state aid. In *Allen,* decided some 20 years later, the Court upheld a New York law authorizing the provision of *secular* textbooks for all children in grades seven through 12 attending public and nonpublic schools. Finally, in *Tilton,* the Court upheld federal grants of funds for the construction of facilities to be used for clearly *secular* purposes by public and nonpublic institutions of higher learning.

These cases simply recognize that sectarian schools perform secular, educational functions as well as religious functions, and that some forms of aid may be channeled to the secular without providing direct aid to the sectarian. But the channel is a narrow one, as the above cases illustrate. Of course, it is true in each case that the provision of such neutral, nonideological aid, assisting only the secular functions of sectarian schools, served indirectly and incidentally to promote the religious function by rendering it more likely that children would attend sectarian schools and by freeing the budgets of those schools for use in other nonsecular areas. But an indirect and incidental effect beneficial to religious institutions has never been thought a sufficient defect to warrant the invalidation of a state law. In *McGowan,* Sunday Closing Laws were sustained even though one of their undeniable effects was to render it somewhat more likely that citizens would respect religious institutions and even attend religious services. Also, in *Walz,* property tax exemptions for church property were held not violative of the Establishment Clause despite the fact that such exemptions relieved churches of a financial burden.

Tilton draws the line most clearly. While a bare majority was there persuaded, for the reasons stated in the plurality opinion and in Mr. Justice White's concurrence, that carefully limited construction grants to colleges and universities could be sustained, the Court was unanimous in its rejection of one clause of the federal statute in question. Under that clause, the Government was entitled to recover a portion of its grant to a sectarian institution in the event that the constructed facility was used to advance religion by, for instance, converting the building to a chapel or otherwise allowing it to be "used to promote religious interests." But because the statute provided that the condition would expire at the end of 20 years, the facilities would thereafter be available for use by the institution for any sectarian purpose. In striking down this provision, the plurality opinion emphasized that "[l]imiting the prohibition for religious use of the structure to 20 years obviously opens the facility to use for any purpose at the end of that period." And in that event, "the original federal grant will in part have the effect of advancing religion." If tax-raised funds may not be granted to institutions of higher learning where the possibility exists that those funds will be used to construct a facility utilized for sectarian activities 20 years hence, *a fortiori* they may not be distributed to elementary and secondary sectarian schools for the maintenance and repair of facilities without any limitations on their use. If the State may not erect buildings in which religious activities are to take place, it may not maintain such buildings or renovate them when they fall into disrepair.

It might be argued, however, that while the New York "maintenance and repair" grants lack specifically articulated secular restrictions, the statute does provide a sort of statistical guarantee of separation by limiting grants to 50% of the amount expended for comparable services in the public schools. The legislature's supposition might have been that at least 50% of the ordinary public school maintenance and repair budget would be devoted to purely secular facility upkeep in sectarian schools. The shortest answer to this argument is that the statute itself allows, as a ceiling, grants satisfying the entire "amount of expenditures for maintenance and repair of such school" providing only that it is neither more than $30 or $40 per pupil nor more than 50% of the comparable public school expenditures. Quite apart from the language of the statute, our cases make clear that a mere statistical judgment will not suffice as a guarantee that state funds will not be used to finance religious education. In *DiCenso,* a companion case to *Kurtzman,* the Court struck down a Rhode Island law authorizing salary supplements to teachers of secular subjects. The grants were not to exceed 15% of any teacher's annual salary. Although the law was invalidated on entanglement grounds, the Court made clear that the State could not have avoided violating the Establishment Clause by merely assuming that its teachers would succeed in segregating "their religious beliefs from their secular educational responsibilities."

* * * * *

... Nor could the State of Rhode Island have prevailed by simply relying on the assumption that, whatever a secular teacher's inabilities to refrain from mixing the religious with the secular, he would surely devote at least 15% of his efforts to purely secular education, thus exhausting the state grant. It takes little imagination to perceive the extent to which States might openly subsidize parochial schools under such a loose standard of scrutiny.

What we have said demonstrates that New York's maintenance and repair provisions violate the Establishment Clause because their effect, inevitably, is to subsidize and advance the religious mission of sectarian schools. We have no occasion, therefore, to consider the further question whether those provisions as presently written would also fail to survive scrutiny under the administrative entanglement aspect of the three-part test because assuring the secular use of all funds requires too intrusive and continuing a relationship between Church and State.

B

New York's tuition reimbursement program also fails the "effect" test, for much the same reasons that govern its maintenance and repair grants. The state program is designed to allow direct, unrestricted grants of $50 to $100 per child (but no more than 50% of tuition actually paid) as reimbursement to parents in low-income brackets who send their children to nonpublic schools, the bulk of which is concededly sectarian in orientation. To qualify, a parent must have earned less than $5,000 in taxable income and must present a receipted tuition bill from a nonpublic school.

There can be no question that these grants could not, consistently with the Establishment Clause, be given directly to sectarian schools, since they would suffer from the same deficiency that renders invalid the grants for maintenance and repair. In the absence of an effective means of guaranteeing that the state aid derived from public funds will be used exclusively for secular, neutral, and nonideological purposes, it is clear from our cases that direct aid in whatever form is invalid. . . . The controlling question here, then, is whether the fact that the grants are delivered to parents rather than schools is of such significance as to compel a contrary result. The State and intervenor-appellees rely on *Everson* and *Allen* for their claim that grants to parents, unlike grants to institutions, respect the "wall of separation" required by the Constitution. It is true that in those cases the Court upheld laws that provided benefits to children attending religious schools and to their parents: As noted above, in *Everson* parents were reimbursed for bus fares paid to send children to parochial schools, and in *Allen* textbooks were loaned directly to the children. But those decisions make clear that, far from providing a *per se* immunity from examination of the substance of the State's program, the fact that aid is disbursed to parents rather than to the schools is only one among many factors to be considered.

In *Everson,* the Court found the bus fare program analogous to the provision of services such as police and fire protection, sewage disposal, highways and sidewalks for parochial schools. Such services, provided in common to all citizens, are "so separate and so indisputably marked off from the religious function," that they may fairly be viewed as reflections of a neutral posture toward religious institutions. *Allen* is founded upon a similar principle. The Court there repeatedly emphasized that upon the record in that case there was no indication that textbooks would be provided for anything other than purely secular courses. "Of course books are different from buses. Most bus rides have no inherent religious significance, while religious books are common. However, the language of [the law under consideration] does not authorize the loan of religious books, and the State claims no right to distribute religious literature. . . . Absent evidence, we cannot assume that school authorities . . . are unable to distinguish between secular and religious books or that they will not honestly discharge their duties under the law."

The tuition grants here are subject to no such restrictions. There has been no endeavor "to guarantee the separation between secular and religious educational functions and to ensure that State financial aid supports only the former." Indeed, it is precisely the function of New York's law to provide assistance to private schools, the great majority of which are sectarian. By reimbursing parents for a portion of their tuition bill, the State seeks to relieve their financial burdens sufficiently to assure that they continue to have the option to send their children to religion-oriented schools. And while the other purposes for that aid—to perpetuate a pluralistic educational environment and to protect the fiscal integrity of overburdened public schools—are certainly unexceptionable, the effect of the aid is unmistakably to provide desired financial support for nonpublic, sectarian institutions.

* * * * *

Although we think it clear, for the reasons above stated, that New York's tuition grant program fares no better under the "effect" test than its maintenance and repair program, in view of the novelty of the question we will address briefly the subsidiary arguments made by the state officials and intervenors in its defense.

First, it has been suggested that it is of controlling significance that New York's program calls for *reimbursement* for tuition already paid rather than for direct contributions which are merely routed through the parents to the schools, in advance of or in lieu of payment by the parents. The parent is not a mere conduit, we are told, but is absolutely free to spend the money he receives in any manner he wishes. There is no element of coercion attached to the reimbursement, and no assurance that the money will eventually end up in the hands of religious schools. The absence of any element of coercion, however, is irrelevant to questions arising under the Establishment Clause. In *Schempp* it was contended that Bible recitations in public schools did not violate the Establishment Clause because participation in such exercises was not coerced. The Court rejected that argument, noting that while proof of coercion might provide a basis for a claim under the Free Exercise Clause, it was not a necessary element of any claim under the Establishment Clause. Mr. Justice Brennan's concurring views reiterated the Court's conclusion:

> Thus the short, and to me sufficient, answer is that the availability of excusal or exemption simply has no relevance to the establishment question, if it is once found that these practices are essentially religious exercises designed at least in part to achieve religious aims. . . .

A similar inquiry governs here: if the grants are offered as an incentive to parents to send their children to sectarian schools by making unrestricted cash payments to them, the Establishment Clause is violated whether or not the actual dollars given eventually find their way into the sectarian institutions. Whether the grant is labeled a reimbursement, a reward, or a subsidy, its substantive impact is still the same. In sum, we agree with the conclusion of the District Court that "[w]hether he gets it during the current year, or as reimbursement for the past year, is of no constitutional importance."

Second, the Majority Leader and President pro tem of the State Senate argues that it is significant here that the tuition reimbursement grants pay only a portion of the tuition bill, and an even smaller portion of the religious school's total expenses. The New York statute limits reimbursement to 50% of any parent's actual outlay. Additionally, intervenor estimates that only 30% of the total cost of nonpublic education is covered by tuition payments, with the remaining coming from "voluntary contribution, endowments and the like." On the basis of these two statistics, appellees reason that the "maximum tuition reimbursement by the State is thus only 15% of educational costs in the nonpublic schools." And, "since the compulsory education laws of the State, by necessity require significantly more than 15% of school time to be devoted to teaching secular courses," the New York statute provides "a statistical guarantee of neutrality." It should readily be seen that this is simply another variant of the argument we have rejected as to maintenance and repair costs, and it can fare no better here. Obviously, if accepted, this argument would provide the foundation for massive, direct subsidization of sectarian elementary and secondary schools. Our cases, however, have long since foreclosed the notion that mere statistical assurances will suffice to sail between the Scylla and Charybdis of "effect" and "entanglement."

Finally, the State argues that its program of tuition grants should survive scrutiny because it is designed to promote the free exercise of religion. The State notes that only "low-income parents" are aided by this law, and without state assistance their right to have their children educated in a religious environment "is diminished or even denied." It is true, of course, that this Court has long recognized and maintained the right to choose nonpublic over public education. It is also true that a state law interfering with a parent's right to have his child educated in a sectarian school would run afoul of the Free Exercise Clause. But this Court repeatedly has recognized that tension inevitably exists between the Free Exercise and the Establishment Clauses, *e.g., Everson* and *Walz,* and that it may often not be possible to promote the former without offending the latter. As a result of this tension, our cases require the State to maintain an attitude of "neutrality," neither "advancing" nor "inhibiting" religion. In its attempt to enhance the opportunities of the poor to choose between public and nonpublic education, the State has taken a step which can only be regarded as one "advancing" religion. However great our sympathy for the burdens experienced by those who must pay public school taxes at the same time that they support other schools because of the constraints of "conscience and discipline," and notwithstanding the "high social importance" of the State's purposes, neither may justify an eroding of the limitations of the Establishment Clause now firmly emplanted.

C

Sections 3, 4, and 5 establish a system for providing income tax benefits to parents of children attending New York's nonpublic schools. In this Court, the parties have engaged in a considerable debate over what label best fits the New York law. Appellants insist that the law is, in effect, one establishing a system of tax "credits." The State and the intervenors reject that characterization and would label it, instead, a system of income tax "modifications." The Solicitor General, in an *amicus curiae* brief filed in this Court, has referred throughout to the New York law as one authorizing tax "deductions." The District Court majority found that the aid was "in effect a tax *credit.*" Because of the peculiar nature of the benefit allowed, it is difficult to adopt any single traditional label lifted from the law of income taxation. It is, at least in its form, a tax deduction since it is an amount subtracted from adjusted gross income, prior to computation of the tax due. Its effect, as the District Court concluded, is more like that of a tax credit since the deduction is not related to the amount actually spent for tuition and is apparently designed to yield a predetermined amount of tax "forgiveness" in exchange for performing a specific act which the State desires to encourage—the usual attribute of a tax credit. We see no reason to select one label over another, as the constitutionality of this hybrid benefit does not turn in any event on the label we accord it. As Mr. Chief Justice Burger's opinion for the Court in *Lemon* v. *Kurtzman* notes, constitutional analysis is not a "legalistic minuet in which precise rules and forms must govern." Instead we must "examine the form of the relationship for the light that it casts on the substance."

These sections allow parents of children attending nonpublic elementary and secondary schools to subtract from adjusted gross income a specified amount if they do not receive a tuition reimbursement under § 2, and if they have an adjusted gross income of less than $25,000. The amount of the deduction is unrelated to the amount of money actually expended by any parent on tuition, but is calculated on the basis of a formula contained in the statute. The formula is apparently the product of a legislative attempt to assure that each family would receive a carefully estimated net benefit, and that the tax benefit would be comparable to, and compatible with, the tuition grant for lower income families. Thus, a parent who earns less than $5,000 is entitled to a tuition reimbursement of $50 if he has one child attending an elementary, nonpublic school, while a parent who earns more (but less than $9,000) is entitled to have a precisely equal amount taken off his tax bill. Additionally, a taxpayer's benefit under these sections is unrelated to, and not reduced by, any deductions to which he may be entitled for charitable contributions to religious institutions.

In practical terms there would appear to be little difference, for purposes of determining whether such aid has the effect of advancing religion, between the tax benefit allowed here and the tuition grant allowed under § 2. The qualifying parent under either program receives the same form of encouragement and reward for sending his children to nonpublic schools. The only difference is that one parent receives an actual cash payment while the other is allowed to reduce by an arbitrary amount the sum he would otherwise be obliged to pay over to the State. We see no answer to Judge Hays' dissenting statement below that "[i]n both instances the money involved represents a charge made upon the state for the purpose of religious education."

Appellees defend the tax portion of New York's legislative package on two grounds. First, they contend that it is of controlling significance that the grants or credits are directed to the parents rather than to the schools. This is the same argument made in support of the tuition reimbursements and rests on the same reading of the same precedents of this Court, primarily *Everson* and *Allen.* Our treatment of this issue in Part II-B is applicable here and requires rejection of this claim. Second, appellees place their strongest reliance on *Walz*, in which New York's property tax exemption for religious organizations was upheld. We think that *Walz* provides no support for appellees' position. Indeed, its rationale plainly compels the conclusion that New York's tax package violates the Establishment Clause.

Tax exemptions for church property enjoyed an apparently universal approval in this country both before and after the adoption of the First Amendment. The Court in *Walz* surveyed the history of tax exemptions and found that each of the 50 States has long provided for tax exemptions for places of worship, that Congress has exempted religious organizations from taxation for over three-quarters of a century, and that congressional enactments in 1802, 1813, and 1870 specifically exempted church property from taxation. In sum, the Court concluded that "[f]ew concepts are more deeply embedded in the fabric of our national life, beginning with pre-Revolutionary colonial times, than for the government to exercise at the very least this kind of benevolent neutrality toward churches and religious exercise generally." We know of no historical precedent for New York's recently promulgated tax relief program. Indeed, it seems clear that tax benefits for parents whose children attend parochial schools are a recent innovation, occasioned by the growing financial plight of such nonpublic institutions and designed, albeit unsuccessfully, to tailor state aid in a manner not incompatible with the recent decisions of this Court

But historical acceptance without more would not alone have sufficed, as "no one acquires a vested or protected right in violation of the Constitution by long use." It was the reason underlying that long history of tolerance of tax exemptions for religion that proved controlling. A proper respect for both the Free Exercise and the Establishment Clauses compels the State to pursue a course of "neutrality" toward religion. Yet governments have not always pursued such a course, and oppression has taken many forms, one of which has been taxation of religion. Thus, if taxation was regarded as a form of "hostility" toward religion, "exemption constitute[d] a reasonable and balanced attempt to guard against those dangers." Special tax benefits, however, cannot be squared with the principle of neutrality established by the decisions of this Court. To the contrary, insofar as such benefits render assistance to parents who send their children to sectarian schools, their purpose and inevitable effect are to aid and advance those religious institutions.

Apart from its historical foundations, *Walz* is a product of the same dilemma and inherent tension found in most government-aid-to-religion controversies. To be sure, the exemption of church property from taxation conferred a benefit, albeit an indirect and incidental one. Yet that "aid" was a product not of any purpose to support or to subsidize, but of a fiscal relationship designed to minimize involvement and entanglement between Church and State. "The exemption," the Court emphasized, "tends to complement and reinforce the desired separation insulating each from the other." Furthermore, "[e]limination of the exemption would tend to expand the involvement of government by giving rise to tax valuation of church property, tax liens, tax foreclosures, and the direct confrontations and conflicts that follow in the train of those legal processes." The granting of the tax benefits under the New York statute, unlike the extension of an exemption, would tend to increase rather than limit the involvement between Church and State.

One further difference between tax exemptions for church property and tax benefits for parents should be noted. The exemption challenged in *Walz* was not restricted to a class composed exclusively or even predominantly of religious institutions. Instead, the exemption covered all property devoted to religious, educational, or charitable purposes. As the parties here must concede, tax reductions authorized by this law flow primarily to the parents of children attending sectarian, nonpublic schools. Without intimating whether this factor alone might have controlling significance in another context in some future case, it should be apparent that in terms of the potential divisiveness of any legislative measure the narrowness of the benefited class would be an important factor.

In conclusion, we find the *Walz* analogy unpersuasive, and in light of the practical similarity between New York's tax and tuition reimbursement programs, we hold that neither form of aid is sufficiently restricted to assure that it will not have the impermissible effect of advancing the sectarian activities of religious schools.

III

Because we have found that the challenged sections have the impermissible effect of advancing religion, we need not consider whether such aid would result in entanglement of the State with religion in the sense of "[a] comprehensive, discriminating, and continuing state surveillance." But the importance of the competing societal interests implicated here prompts us to make the further observation that, apart from any specific entanglement of the State in particular religious programs, assistance of the sort here involved carries grave potential for entanglement in the broader sense of continuing political strife over aid to religion.

Few would question most of the legislative findings supporting this statute. We recognized in *Board of Education* v. *Allen* that "private education has played and is playing a significant and valuable role in raising national levels of knowledge, competence, and experience," and certainly private parochial schools have contributed importantly to this role. Moreover, the tailoring of the New York statute to channel the aid provided primarily to afford low-income families the option of determining where their children are to be educated is most appealing. There is no doubt that the private schools are confronted with increasingly grave fiscal problems, that resolving these problems by increasing tuition charges forces parents to turn to the public schools, and that this in turn—as the present legislation recognizes—exacerbates the problems of public education at the same time that it weakens support for the parochial schools.

These, in briefest summary, are the underlying reasons for the New York legislation and for similar legislation in other States. They are substantial reasons. Yet they must be weighed against the relevant provisions and purposes of the First Amendment, which safeguard the separation of Church from State and which have been regarded from the beginning as among the most cherished features of our constitutional system.

One factor of recurring significance in this weighing process is the potentially divisive political effect of an aid program. As Mr. Justice Black's opinion in *Everson* emphasizes, competition among religious sects for political and religious supremacy has occasioned considerable civil strife, "generated in large part" by competing efforts to gain or maintain the support of government. As Mr. Justice Harlan put it, "[w]hat is at stake as a matter of policy [in Establishment Clause cases] is preventing that kind and degree of government involvement in religious life that, as history teaches us, is apt to lead to strife and frequently strain a political system to the breaking point."

The Court recently addressed this issue specifically and fully in *Lemon* v. *Kurtzman*. . . .

. . . In this situation, where the underlying issue is the deeply emotional one of Church-State relationships, the potential for seriously divisive political consequences needs no elaboration. And while the prospect of such divisiveness may not alone warrant the invalidation of state laws that otherwise survive the careful scrutiny required by the decisions of this Court, it is certainly a "warning signal" not to be ignored.

Our examination of New York's aid provisions, in light of all relevant considerations, compels the judgment that each, as written, has a "primary effect that advances religion" and offends the constitutional prohibition against laws "respecting an establishment of religion." We therefore affirm the three-judge court's holding as to §§ 1 and 2, and reverse as to §§ 3, 4, and 5.

It is so ordered.

MR. CHIEF JUSTICE BURGER, JOINED IN PART BY MR. JUSTICE WHITE, AND JOINED BY MR. JUSTICE REHNQUIST, CONCURRING IN PART AND DISSENTING IN PART.

I join in that part of the Court's opinion in *Committee for Public Education & Religious Liberty* v. *Nyquist* which holds the New York "maintenance and repair" provision unconstitutional under the Establishment Clause because it is a direct aid to religion. I disagree, however, with the Court's decisions in *Nyquist* and in *Sloan* v. *Lemon* to strike down the New York and Pennsylvania tuition grant programs and the New York tax relief provisions. I believe the Court's decisions on those statutory provisions ignore the teachings of *Everson* and fail to observe what I thought the Court had held in *Walz.* I therefore dissent as to those aspects of the two holdings.*

While there is no straight line running through our decisions interpreting the Establishment and Free Exercise Clauses of the First Amendment, our cases do, it seems to me, lay down one solid, basic principle: that the Establishment Clause does not forbid governments, state or federal, to enact a program of general welfare under which benefits are distributed to private individuals, even though many of those individuals may elect to use those benefits in ways that "aid" religious instruction or worship. Thus, in *Everson* the Court held that a New Jersey township could reimburse *all* parents of school-age children for bus fares paid in transporting their children to school. Mr. Justice Black's opinion for the Court stated that the New Jersey "legislation, as applied, does no more than provide a general program to *help parents* get their children, regardless of their religion, safely and expeditiously to and from accredited schools."

Twenty-one years later, in *Board of Education* v. *Allen,* the Court again upheld a state program that provided for direct aid to the parents of all schoolchildren including those in private schools. The statute there required "local public school authorities to lend textbooks free of charge to all students in grades seven through 12; students attending private schools [were] included." Recognizing that *Everson*

*Mr. Justice Rehnquist's dissent, which I join, states the reasons why I believe the Court has gravely misrepresented the Court's opinion in *Walz.* In this opinion, I state additional reasons why I dissent from Parts II-B and II-C of the Court's opinion.

was the case "most nearly in point," the *Allen* Court interpreted *Everson* as holding that "the Establishment Clause does not prevent a State from extending the benefits of state laws to all citizens without regard for their religious affiliation. . . . "

* * * * *

The Court's opinions in both *Everson* and *Allen* recognized that the statutory programs at issue there may well have facilitated the decision of many parents to send their children to religious schools. Indeed, the Court in both cases specifically acknowledged that some children might not obtain religious instruction but for the benefits provided by the State. Notwithstanding, the Court held that such an indirect or incidental "benefit" to the religious institutions that sponsored parochial schools was not a conclusive indicium of a "law respecting an establishment of religion."

* * * * *

The essence of all these decisions, I suggest, is that government aid to individuals generally stands on an entirely different footing from direct aid to religious institutions. I say "generally" because it is obviously possible to conjure hypothetical statutes that constitute either a subterfuge for direct aid to religious institutions or a discriminatory enactment favoring religious over nonreligious activities. Thus, a State could not enact a statute providing for a $10 gratuity to everyone who attended religious services weekly. Such a law would plainly be governmental sponsorship of religious activities; no statutory preamble expressing purely secular legislative motives would be persuasive. But, at least where the state law is genuinely directed at enhancing a recognized freedom of individuals, even one involving both secular and religious consequences, such as the right of parents to send their children to private schools, the Establishment Clause no longer has a prohibitive effect.

This fundamental principle which I see running through our prior decisions in this difficult and sensitive field of law, and which I believe governs the present cases, is premised more on experience and history than on logic. It is admittedly difficult to articulate the reasons why a State should be permitted to reimburse parents of private school children—partially at least—to take into account the State's enormous savings in not having to provide schools for those children, when a State is not allowed to pay the same benefit directly to sectarian schools on a per-pupil basis. In either case, the private individual makes the ultimate decision that may indirectly benefit church-sponsored schools; to that extent the state involvement with religion is substantially attenuated. The answer, I believe, lies in the experienced judgment of various members of this Court over the years that the balance between the policies of free exercise and establishment of religion tips in favor of the former when the legislation moves away from direct aid to religious institutions and takes on the character of general aid to individual families. This judgment reflects the caution with which we scrutinize any effort to give official support to religion and the tolerance with which we treat general welfare legislation. . . .

The tuition grant and tax relief programs now before us are, in my view, indistinguishable in principle, purpose, and effect from the statutes in *Everson* and *Allen*. In the instant cases as in *Everson* and *Allen*, the States have merely attempted to equalize the costs incurred by parents in obtaining an education for their children. The only discernible difference between the programs in *Everson* and *Allen* and these cases is in the method of the distribution of benefits: here the particular benefits of the Pennsylvania and New York statutes are given only to parents of private school children, while in *Everson* and *Allen* the statutory benefits were made available to parents of both public and private school children. But to regard that difference as constitutionally meaningful is to exalt form over substance. It is beyond dispute that the parents of public school children in New York and Pennsylvania presently receive the "benefit" of having their children educated totally at state expense; the statutes enacted in those States and at issue here merely attempt to equalize that "benefit" by giving to parents of private school children, in the form of dollars or tax deductions, what the parents of public school children receive in kind. It is no more than simple equity to grant partial relief to parents who support the public schools they do not use.

The Court appears to distinguish the Pennsylvania and New York statutes from *Everson* and *Allen* on the ground that here the state aid is not apportioned between the religious and secular activities of the sectarian schools attended by some recipients, while in *Everson* and *Allen* the state aid was purely secular in nature. But that distinction has not been followed in the past, and is not likely to be considered controlling in the future. There are at present many forms of government assistance to individuals that can be used to serve religious ends, such as social security benefits or "G. I. Bill" payments, which are not subject to nonreligious-use restrictions. Yet, I certainly doubt that today's majority would hold those statutes unconstitutional under the Establishment Clause.

Since I am unable to discern in the Court's analysis of *Everson* and *Allen* any neutral principle to explain the result reached in these cases, I fear that the Court has in reality followed the unsupportable approach of measuring the "effect" of a law by the percentage of the recipients who choose to use the money for religious, rather than secular, education. Indeed, in discussing the New York tax credit provisions, the Court's opinion argues that the "tax reductions authorized by this law flow primarily to the parents of children attending sectarian, nonpublic schools." While the opinion refrains from "intimating whether this factor alone might have controlling significance in another context in some future case," similar references to this factor elsewhere in the Court's opinion suggest that it has been given considerable weight. Thus, the Court observes as to the New York tuition grant program: "Indeed, it is precisely the function of New York's law to provide assistance to private schools, *the great majority of which are sectarian.*" (Emphasis added.)

With all due respect, I submit that such a consideration is irrelevant to a constitutional determination of the "effect" of a statute. For purposes of constitutional adjudication of that issue, it should make no difference whether 5%, 20%, or 80% of the beneficiaries of an educational program of general application elect to utilize their benefits for religious purposes. The "primary effect" branch of our three-pronged test was never, at least to my understanding, intended to vary with the *number* of churches benefited by a statute under which state aid is distributed to private citizens.

Such a consideration, it is true, might be relevant in ascertaining whether the *primary legislative purpose* was to advance the cause of religion. But the Court has, and I think correctly, summarily dismissed the contention that either New York or Pennsylvania had an improper purpose in enacting these laws. The Court fully recognizes that the legislatures of New York and Pennsylvania have a legitimate interest in "promoting pluralism and diversity among . . . public and nonpublic schools," in assisting those who reduce the State's expenses in providing public education, and in protecting the already overburdened public school system against a massive influx of private school children. And in light of this Court's recognition of these secular legislative purposes, I fail to see any acceptable resolution to these cases except one favoring constitutionality.

I would therefore uphold these New York and Pennsylvania statutes. However sincere our collective protestations of the debt owed by the public generally to the parochial school systems, the wholesome diversity they engender will not survive on expressions of good will.

MR. JUSTICE WHITE JOINS THIS OPINION INSOFAR AS IT RELATES TO THE NEW YORK AND PENNSYLVANIA TUITION GRANT STATUTES AND THE NEW YORK TAX RELIEF STATUTE. (JUSTICE WHITE ALSO WROTE A PARTIAL DISSENT.)

* * * * *

MR. JUSTICE REHNQUIST, WITH WHOM THE CHIEF JUSTICE AND MR. JUSTICE WHITE CONCUR, DISSENTING IN PART.

Differences of opinion are undoubtedly to be expected when the Court turns to the task of interpreting the meaning of the Religion Clauses of the First Amendment, since our previous cases arising under these Clauses, as the Court notes, "have presented some of the most perplexing questions to come before this Court."

I dissent from those portions of the Court's opinion which strike down §§ 2 through 5, N.Y. Laws 1972, c. 414. Section 2 grants limited state aid to low-income parents sending their children to nonpublic schools and §§ 3 through 5 make roughly comparable benefits available to middle-income parents through the use of tax deductions. I find both the Court's reasoning and result all but impossible to reconcile with *Walz,* decided only three years ago, and with *Allen* and *Everson.*

I

The opinions in *Walz* make it clear that tax deductions and exemptions, even when directed to religious institutions, occupy quite a different constitutional status under the Religion Clauses of the First Amendment than do outright grants to such institutions. Chief Justice Burger, speaking for the Court in *Walz,* said:

> The grant of a tax exemption is not sponsorship since the government does not transfer part of its revenue to churches but simply abstains from demanding that the church support the state. No one has ever suggested that tax exemption has converted libraries, art galleries, or hospitals into arms of the state

> or put employees "on the public payroll." *There is no genuine nexus between tax exemption and establishment of religion.* (Emphasis added.)

Mr. Justice Brennan in his concurring opinion amplified the distinction between tax benefits and direct payments in these words:

> Tax exemptions and general subsidies, however, are qualitatively different. Though both provide economic assistance, they do so in fundamentally different ways. A subsidy involves the direct transfer of public monies to the subsidized enterprise and uses resources exacted from taxpayers as a whole. An exemption, on the other hand, involves no such transfer. . . . Tax exemptions, accordingly, constitute mere passive state involvement with religion and not the affirmative involvement characteristic of outright governmental subsidy.

Here the effect of the tax benefit is trebly attenuated as compared with the outright exemption considered in *Walz*. There the result was a complete forgiveness of taxes, while here the result is merely a reduction in taxes. There the ultimate benefit was available to an actual house of worship, while here even the ultimate benefit redounds only to a religiously sponsored school. There the churches themselves received the direct reduction in the tax bill, while here it is only the parents of the children who are sent to religiously sponsored schools who receive the direct benefit.

The Court seeks to avoid the controlling effect of *Walz* by comparing its historical background to the relative recency of the challenged deduction plan; by noting that in its historical context, a property tax exemption is religiously neutral, whereas the educational cost deduction here is not; and by finding no substantive difference between a direct reimbursement from the State to parents and the State's abstention from collecting the full tax bill which the parents would otherwise have had to pay.

While it is true that the Court reached its result in *Walz* in part by examining the unbroken history of property tax exemptions for religious organizations in this country, there is no suggestion in the opinion that only those particular tax exemption schemes that have roots in pre-Revolutionary days are sustainable against an Establishment Clause challenge. As the Court notes in its opinion, historical acceptance alone would not have served to validate the tax exemption upheld in *Walz* because "'no one acquires a vested or protected right in violation of the Constitution by long use.'"

But what the Court gives in the form of *dicta* with one hand, it takes away in the form of its holding with the other. For if long-established use of a particular tax exemption scheme leads to a holding that the scheme is constitutional, that holding should extend equally to newly devised tax benefit plans which are indistinguishable in principle from those long established.

The Court's statements that "[s]pecial tax benefits, however, cannot be squared with the principle of neutrality established by the decisions of this Court," and that "insofar as such benefits render assistance to parents who send their children to sectarian schools, their purpose and inevitable effect are to aid and advance those religious institutions," are impossible to reconcile with *Walz*. Who can doubt that the tax exemptions which that case upheld were every bit as much of a "special tax benefit" as the New York tax deduction plan here, or that the benefits resulting from the exemption in *Walz* had every bit as much tendency to "aid and advance . . . religious institutions" as did New York's plan here?

The Court nonetheless declares that what has been authorized by the legislature is not a true deduction and in substance provides an incentive for parents to send their children to sectarian schools because the amount deductible from adjusted gross income bears no relationship to amounts actually expended for nonpublic education. Support for its notion that the authorization is essentially the same as a tax credit or a reimbursement is drawn from the fact that the net benefit under the reimbursement plan established in § 2 of c. 414 is equal to the net tax savings for those at the lower-income end of the tax deduction plan. But the deduction here allowed is analytically no different from any other flat-rate exemptions or deductions currently in use in both federal and state tax systems. Surely neither the standard deduction, usable by those taxpayers who do not itemize their deductions, nor personal or dependency exemptions, for example, bear any relationship whatsoever to the actual expenses accrued in earning any of them. Yet none of these could properly be called a reimbursement from the State. And it would take more of a record than is present in this case to prove that the possibility of a slightly lower aggregate tax bill accorded New York taxpayers who send their dependents to nonpublic schools provides any more incentive to send children to such schools than personal exemptions provide for getting married or having children. That parents might incidentally find it easier to send children to nonpublic schools has not heretofore been held to require invalidation of a state statute.

The sole difference between the flat-rate exemptions currently in widespread use and the deduction established in §§ 4 and 5 is that the latter provides a regressive benefit. This legislative judgment, however, as to the appropriate spread of the expense of public and nonpublic education is consonant with the State's concern that those at the lower end of the income brackets are less able to exercise freely their consciences by sending their children to nonpublic schools, and is surely consistent with the "benevolent neutrality" we try to uphold in reconciling the tension between the Free Exercise and Establishment Clauses. Regardless of what the Court chooses to call the New York plan, it is still abstention from taxation, and that abstention stands on no different theoretical footing, in terms of running afoul of the Establishment Clause, from any other deduction or exemption currently allowable for religious contributions or activities. The invalidation of the New York plan is directly contrary to this Court's pronouncements in *Walz*.

II

In striking down both plans, the Court places controlling weight on the fact that the State has not purported to restrict to secular purposes either the reimbursements or the money which it has not taxed. This factor assertedly serves to distinguish *Allen* and *Everson* and compels the result that inevitably the primary effect of the plans is to provide financial support for sectarian schools.

* * * * *

The reimbursement and tax benefit plans today struck down, no less than the plans in *Everson* and *Allen,* are consistent with the principle of neutrality. New York has recognized that parents who are sending their children to nonpublic schools are rendering the State a service by decreasing the costs of public education and by physically relieving an already overburdened public school system. Such parents are nonetheless compelled to support public school services unused by them and to pay for their children's education. Rather than offering "an incentive to parents to send their children to sectarian schools," as the majority suggests, New York is effectuating the secular purpose of the equalization of the cost of educating New York children that are borne by parents who send their children to nonpublic schools. As in *Everson* and *Allen,* the impact, if any, on religious education from the aid granted is significantly diminished by the fact that the benefits go to the parents rather than to the institutions.

The increasing difficulties faced by private schools in our country are no reason at all for this Court to readjust the admittedly rough-hewn limits on governmental involvement with religion which are found in the First and Fourteenth Amendments. But, quite understandably, these difficulties can be expected to lead to efforts on the part of those who wish to keep alive pluralism in education to obtain through legislative channels forms of permissible public assistance which were not thought necessary a generation ago. Within the limits permitted by the Constitution, these decisions are quite rightly hammered out on the legislative anvil. If the Constitution does indeed allow for play in the legislative joints, the Court must distinguish between a new exercise of power within constitutional limits and an exercise of legislative power which transgresses those limits. I believe the Court has failed to make that distinction here, and I therefore dissent.

Meek v. Pittenger, 421 U.S. 349 (1975)
(Summary)

Justice Stewart wrote for the majority of six in this case, which simply extended the position already set forth in *Nyquist.* In *Meek* three tests were failed—effect, entanglement, divisive political potential—by Pennsylvania programs that were designed to lend textbooks to private school students, lend instructional material to the schools directly, and provide auxiliary services and speech therapy to private schoolchildren.

In dissent, Justice Burger wrote concerning the disallowed counseling and therapy services: "[I]t penalizes *children*—children who have the misfortune to have to cope with the learning process under extraordinarily heavy physical and psychological burdens, for the most part congenital." He continued: "The melancholy consequence of what the Court does today is to force the parent to choose between the 'free exercise' of a religious belief . . . or to forego the opportunity for his child to learn to cope with

. . . handicaps, through remedial assistance financed by his taxes."

We have not included the text of the case here because the course of the Court had been rather clearly charted in *Lemon* and *Nyquist.*

Mueller v. Allen, 436 U.S. (1983)
(Summary)

Justice Rehnquist's opinion in this case, which validated a Minnesota program of tax deductions for tuition and other parental expenses of an educational nature, appeared at the time to advance the cause of accommodation.

The decision was split, with Justice Rehnquist arguing that the Minnesota law passed the *Lemon* tests. He wrote: "Where, as here, aid to parochial schools is available only as a result of decisions of individual parents no 'imprimatur of state approval' can be deemed to have been conferred on any particular religion, or on religion generally."

The four dissenters contended that "the Court has upheld financial support for religious schools without any reason at all to assume that the support will be restricted to the secular functions of those schools and will not be used to support religious instruction."

In 1985 the *Grand Rapids* and *Aguilar* cases left the *Mueller* decision quite isolated, related, as it was, only to educational expenses across the board for all categories of parents. While, for that reason, the text is omitted here, altered personnel on the Court in the future could redirect attention to this Rehnquist opinion.

Grand Rapids School District v. Ball, 105 S.Ct. 3216 (1985)

The Court's decisions in *Lynch* and *Marsh* caused many observers to speculate that in succeeding cases more accommodationist positions would be adopted. In June 1985 the Court reported decisions on four cases that confounded the experts. In *Grand*

Rapids and *Aguilar,* one sees a reaffirmation of the separationist position espoused in the seventies.

The issue here revolved around whether shared time and community education programs violated the Establishment Clause. Justice Brennan wrote for the majority: "This effect—the symbolic union of government and religion in one sectarian enterprise—is an impermissible effect under the Establishment Clause."

Justice O'Connor, dissenting in part, argued that the shared time program did not advance religion.

JUSTICE BRENNAN DELIVERED THE OPINION OF THE COURT.

The School District of Grand Rapids, Michigan, adopted two programs in which classes for nonpublic school students are financed by the public school system, taught by teachers hired by the public school system, and conducted in "leased" classrooms in the nonpublic schools. Most of the nonpublic schools involved in the programs are sectarian religious schools. This case raises the question whether these programs impermissibly involve the government in the support of sectarian religious activities and thus violate the Establishment Clause of the First Amendment.

I

A

At issue in this case are the Community Education and Shared Time programs offered in the nonpublic schools of Grand Rapids, Michigan. These programs, first instituted in the 1976–1977 school year, provide classes to nonpublic school students at public expense in classrooms located in and leased from the local nonpublic schools.

The Shared Time program offers classes during the regular school day that are intended to be supplementary to the "core curriculum" courses that the State of Michigan requires as a part of an accredited school program. Among the subjects offered are "remedial" and "enrichment" mathematics, "remedial" and "enrichment" reading, art, music, and physical education. A typical nonpublic school student attends these classes for one or two class periods per week; approximately "ten percent of any given nonpublic school student's time during the academic year would consist of Shared Time instruction." Although Shared Time itself is a program offered only in the nonpublic schools, there was testimony that the courses included in that program are offered, albeit perhaps in a somewhat different form, in the public schools as well. All of the classes that are the subject of this case are taught in elementary schools, with the exception of Math Topics, a remedial math course taught in the secondary schools.

The Shared Time teachers are full-time employees of the public schools, who often move from classroom to classroom during the course of the school day. A "significant portion" of the teachers (approximately 10%) "previously taught in nonpublic schools, and many of those had been assigned to the same nonpublic school where they were previously employed." The School District of Grand Rapids hires Shared Time teachers in accordance with its ordinary hiring procedures. The public school system apparently provides all of the supplies, materials, and equipment used in connection with Shared Time instruction.

The Community Education Program is offered throughout the Grand Rapids community in schools and on other sites, for children as well as adults. The classes at issue here are taught in the nonpublic elementary schools and commence at the conclusion of the regular school day. Among the courses offered are Arts and Crafts, Home Economics, Spanish, Gymnastics, Yearbook Production, Christmas Arts and Crafts, Drama, Newspaper, Humanities, Chess, Model Building, and Nature Appreciation. The District Court found that "[a]lthough certain Community Education courses offered at nonpublic school sites are not offered at the public schools on a Community Education basis, all Community Education programs are otherwise available at the public schools, usually as a part of their more extensive regular curriculum."

Community Education teachers are part-time public school employees. Community Education courses are completely voluntary and are offered only if 12 or more students enroll. Because a well-known teacher is necessary to attract the requisite number of students, the School District accords a preference in hiring to instructors already teaching within the school. Thus, "virtually every Community Education course conducted on facilities leased from nonpublic schools has an instructor otherwise employed full time by the same nonpublic school."

Both programs are administered similarly. The Director of the program, a public school employee, sends packets of course listings to the participating nonpublic schools before the school year begins. The nonpublic school administrators then decide which courses they want to offer. The Director works out an academic schedule for each school, taking into account the varying religious holidays celebrated by the schools of different denominations.

Nonpublic school administrators decide which classrooms will be used for the programs, and the Director then inspects the facilities and consults with Shared Time teachers to make sure the facilities are satisfactory. The public school system pays the nonpublic schools for the use of the necessary classroom space by entering into "leases" at the rate of $6 per classroom per week. The "leases," however, contain no mention of the particular room, space, or facility leased and teachers' rooms, libraries, lavatories, and similar facilities are made available at no additional charge. Each room used in the programs has to be free of any crucifix, religious symbol, or artifact, although such religious symbols can be present in the adjoining hallways, corridors, and other facilities used in connection with the program. During the time that a given classroom is being used in the programs, the teacher is required to post a sign stating that it is a "public school classroom." However, there are no signs posted outside the school buildings indicating that public school courses are conducted inside or that the facilities are being used as a public school annex.

Although petitioners label the Shared Time and Community Education students as "part-time public school students," the students attending Shared Time and Community Education courses in facilities leased from a nonpublic school are the same students who attend that particular school otherwise. There is no evidence that any public school student has ever attended a Shared Time or Community Education class in a nonpublic school. The District Court found that "[t]hough Defendants claim the Shared Time program is available to all students, the record is abundantly clear that only nonpublic school students wearing the cloak of a 'public school student' can enroll in it." The District Court noted that "[w]hereas public school students are assembled at the public facility nearest to their residence, students in religious schools are assembled on the basis of religion without any consideration of residence or school district boundaries." Thus, "beneficiaries are wholly designated on the basis of religion," and these "public school" classes, in contrast to ordinary public school classes which are largely neighborhood-based, are as segregated by religion as are the schools at which they are offered.

Forty of the forty-one schools at which the programs operate are sectarian in character. The schools of course vary from one another, but substantial evidence suggests that they share deep religious purposes. For instance, the Parent Handbook of one Catholic school states the goals of Catholic education as "[a] God oriented environment which *permeates* the total educational program," "[a] Christian atmosphere which guides and encourages participation in the church's commitment to social justice," and "[a] continuous development of knowledge of the Catholic faith, its traditions, teachings and theology." A policy statement of the Christian schools similarly proclaims that "it is not sufficient that the teachings of Christianity be a separate subject in the curriculum, but *the Word of God must be an all-pervading force in the educational program."* These Christian schools require all parents seeking to enroll their children either to subscribe to a particular doctrinal statement or to agree to have their children taught according to the doctrinal statement. The District Court found that the schools are "pervasively sectarian," and concluded "without hesitation that the purposes of these schools is to advance their particular religions," and that "a substantial portion of their functions are subsumed in the religious mission."

B

[1] Respondents are six taxpayers who filed suit against the School District of Grand Rapids and a number of state officials. They charged that the Shared Time and Community Education programs violated the Establishment Clause of the First Amendment of the Constitution, made applicable to the States through the Fourteenth Amendment. After an 8-day bench trial, the District Court entered a judgment on the merits on behalf of respondents and enjoined further operation of the programs.

Applying the familiar three-part purpose, effect, and entanglement test set out in *Lemon v. Kurtzman,* the court held that, although the purpose of the programs was secular, their effect was "distinctly impermissible." The court relied in particular on the fact that the programs at issue involved publicly provided instructional services that served nonpublic school students segregated largely by religion on nonpublic school premises. The court also noted that the programs conferred "direct benefits, both financial and otherwise, to the sectarian institutions." Finally, the court found that the programs necessarily entailed an unacceptable level of entanglement, both political and administrative, between the public school systems and the sectarian schools. Petitioners appealed the judgment of the District Court to the Court of Appeals for the Sixth Circuit. A divided panel of the Court of Appeals affirmed. We granted certiorari, and now affirm.

II

A

[2] The First Amendment's guarantee that "Congress shall make no law respecting an establishment of religion," as our cases demonstrate, is more than a pledge that no single religion will be designated as a state religion. It is also more than a mere injunction that governmental programs discriminating among religions are unconstitutional. The Establishment Clause instead primarily proscribes "sponsorship, financial support, and active involvement of the sovereign in religious activity." As Justice Black, writing for the Court in *Everson* stated: "Neither [a State nor the Federal Government] can pass laws which aid one religion, aid all religions, or prefer one religion over another. . . . No tax in any amount, large or small, can be levied to support any religious activities or institutions, whatever they may be called, or whatever form they may adopt to teach or practice religion."

Since *Everson* made clear that the guarantees of the Establishment Clause apply to the States, we have often grappled with the problem of state aid to nonpublic, religious schools. In all of these cases, our goal has been to give meaning to the sparse language and broad purposes of the Clause, while not unduly infringing on the ability of the States to provide for the welfare of their people in accordance with their own particular circumstances. Providing for the education of schoolchildren is surely a praiseworthy purpose. But our cases have consistently recognized that even such a praiseworthy, secular purpose cannot validate government aid to parochial schools when the aid has the effect of promoting a single religion or religion generally or when the aid unduly entangles the government in matters religious. For just as religion throughout history has provided spiritual comfort, guidance, and inspiration to many, it can also serve powerfully to divide societies and to exclude those whose beliefs are not in accord with particular religions or sects that have from time to time achieved dominance. The solution to this problem adopted by the Framers and consistently recognized by this Court is jealously to guard the right of every individual to worship according to the dictates of conscience while requiring the government to maintain a course of neutrality among religions, and between religion and nonreligion. Only in this way can we "make room for as wide a variety of beliefs and creeds as the spiritual needs of man deem necessary" and "sponsor an attitude on the part of government that shows no partiality to any one group and lets each flourish according to the zeal of its adherents and the appeal of its dogma."

[3] We have noted that the three-part test first articulated in *Lemon* guides "[t]he general nature of our inquiry in this area."

> Every analysis in this area must begin with consideration of the cumulative criteria developed by the Court over many years. Three such tests may be gleaned from our cases. First, the statute must have a secular legislative purpose; second, its principal or primary effect must be one that neither advances nor inhibits religion; finally, the statute must not foster "an excessive government entanglement with religion."

These tests "must not be viewed as setting the precise limits to the necessary constitutional inquiry, but serve only as guidelines with which to identify instances in which the objectives of the Establishment Clause have been impaired." We have particularly relied on *Lemon* in every case involving the sensitive relationship between government and religion in the education of our children. The government's activities in this area can have a magnified impact on impressionable young minds, and the occasional rivalry of parallel public and private school systems offers an all-too-ready opportunity for divisive rifts along religious lines in the body politic. The *Lemon* test concentrates attention on the issues—purposes, effect, entanglement—that determine whether a particular state action is an improper "law respecting an establishment of religion." We therefore reaffirm that state action alleged to violate the Establishment Clause should be measured against the *Lemon* criteria.

As has often been true in school aid cases, there is no dispute as to the first test. Both the District Court and the Court of Appeals found that the purpose of the Community Education and Shared Time programs was "manifestly secular." We find no reason to disagree with this holding, and therefore go on to consider whether the primary or principal effect of the challenged programs is to advance or inhibit religion.

B

Our inquiry must begin with a consideration of the nature of the institutions in which the programs operate. Of the 41 private schools where these "part-time public schools" have operated, 40 are identifiably religious schools. It is true that each school may not share all of the characteristics of religious schools as articulated, for example, in the complaint in *Meek.* The District Court found, however, that "[b]ased upon the massive testimony and exhibits, the conclusion is inescapable that the religious institutions receiving instructional services from the public schools are sectarian in the sense that a substantial portion of their functions are subsumed in the religious mission.". . . . At the religious schools here—as at the sectarian schools that have been the subject of our past cases—"the secular education those schools provide goes hand in hand with the religious mission that is the only reason for the schools' existence. Within that institution, the two are inextricably intertwined."

Given that 40 of the 41 schools in this case are thus "pervasively sectarian," the challenged public-school programs operating in the religious schools may impermissibly advance religion in three different ways. First, the teachers participating in the programs may become involved in intentionally or inadvertently inculcating particular religious tenets or beliefs. Second, the programs may provide a crucial symbolic link between government and religion, thereby enlisting—at least in the eyes of impressionable youngsters—the powers of government to the support of the religious denomination operating the school. Third, the programs may have the effect of directly promoting religion by impermissibly providing a subsidy to the primary religious mission of the institutions affected.

(1)

[4] Although Establishment Clause jurisprudence is characterized by few absolutes, the Clause does absolutely prohibit government-financed or government-sponsored indoctrination into the beliefs of a particular religious faith. . . . Such indoctrination, if permitted to occur, would have devastating effects on the right of each individual voluntarily to determine what to believe (and what not to believe) free of any coercive pressures from the State, while at the same time tainting the resulting religious beliefs with a corrosive secularism.

In *Meek* the Court invalidated a statute providing for the loan of state-paid professional staff—including teachers—to nonpublic schools to provide remedial and accelerated instruction, guidance counseling and testing, and other services on the premises of the nonpublic schools. Such a program, if not subjected to a "comprehensive, discriminating, and continuing state surveillance," would entail an unacceptable risk that the state-sponsored instructional personnel would "advance the religious mission of the church-related schools in which they serve." Even though the teachers were paid by the State, "[t]he potential for impermissible fostering of religion under these circumstances, although somewhat reduced, is nonetheless present." The program in *Meek,* if not sufficiently monitored, would simply have entailed too great a risk of state-sponsored indoctrination.

The programs before us today share the defect that we identified in *Meek.* With respect to the Community Education Program, the District Court found that "virtually every Community Education course conducted on facilities leased from nonpublic schools has an instructor otherwise employed full time by the same nonpublic school." These instructors, many of whom no doubt teach in the religious schools precisely because they are adherents of the controlling denomination and want to serve their religious community zealously, are expected during the regular school day to inculcate their students with the tenets and beliefs of their particular religious faiths. Yet the premise of the program is that those instructors can put aside their religious convictions and engage in entirely secular Community Education instruction as soon as the school day is over. Moreover, they are expected to do so before the same religious-school students and in the same religious-school classrooms that they employed to advance religious purposes during the "official" school day. Nonetheless, as petitioners themselves asserted, Community Education classes are not specifically monitored for religious content.

We do not question that the dedicated and professional religious school teachers employed by the Community Education program will attempt in good faith to perform their secular mission conscientiously. Nonetheless, there is a substantial risk that, overtly or subtly, the religious message they are expected to convey during the regular school day will infuse the supposedly secular classes they teach after school. The danger arises "not because the public employee [is] likely deliberately to subvert his task to the service of religion, but rather because the pressures of the environment might alter his behavior from its normal course." "The conflict of functions inheres in the situation."

The Shared Time program, though structured somewhat differently, nonetheless also poses a substantial risk of state-sponsored indoctrination. The most important difference between the programs is that most of the instructors in the Shared Time program are full-time teachers hired by the public schools. Moreover, although "virtually every" Community Education instructor is a full-time religious school teacher, only "[a] significant portion" of the Shared Time instructors previously worked in the religious schools. Nonetheless, as with the Community Education program, no attempt is made to monitor the Shared Time courses for religious content.

Thus, despite these differences between the two programs, our holding in *Meek* controls the inquiry with respect to Shared Time, as well as Community Education. Shared Time instructors are teaching academic subjects in religious schools in courses virtually indistinguishable from the other courses offered during the regular religious-school day. The teachers in this program, even more than their Community Education colleagues, are "performing important educational services in schools in which education is an integral part of the dominant sectarian mission and in which an atmosphere dedicated to the advancement of religious belief is constantly maintained." Teachers in such an atmosphere may well subtly (or overtly) conform their instruction to the environment in which they teach, while students will perceive the instruction provided in the context of the dominantly religious message of the institution, thus reinforcing the indoctrinating effect. As we stated in *Meek,* "[w]hether the subject is 'remedial reading,' 'advanced reading,' or simply 'reading' a teacher remains a teacher, and the danger that religious doctrine will become intertwined with secular instruction persists." Unlike types of aid that the Court has upheld, such as state-created standardized tests or diagnostic services, there is a "substantial risk" that programs operating in this environment would "be used for religious educational purposes."

The Court of Appeals of course recognized that respondents adduced no evidence of specific incidents of religious indoctrination in this case. But the absence of proof of specific incidents is not dispositive. When conducting a supposedly secular class in the pervasively sectarian environment of a religious school, a teacher may knowingly or unwillingly tailor the content of the course to fit the school's announced goals. If so, there is no reason to believe that this kind of ideological influence would be detected or reported by students, by their parents, or by the school system itself. The students are presumably attending religious schools precisely in order to receive religious instruction. After spending the balance of their school day in classes heavily influenced by a religious perspective, they would have little motivation or ability to discern improper ideological content that may creep into a Shared Time or Community Education course. Neither their parents nor the parochial schools would have cause to complain if the effect of the publicly-supported instruction were to advance the schools' sectarian mission. And the public school system itself has no incentive to detect or report any specific incidents of improper state-sponsored indoctrination. Thus, the lack of evidence of specific incidents of indoctrination is of little significance.

(2)

Our cases have recognized that the Establishment Clause guards against more than direct, state-funded efforts to indoctrinate youngsters in specific religious beliefs. Government promotes religion as effectively when it fosters a close identification of its powers and responsibilities with those of any—or all—religious denominations as when it attempts to inculcate specific religious doctrines. If this identification conveys a message of government endorsement or disapproval of religion, a core purpose of the Establishment Clause is violated. . . . As we stated in *Grendel's Den, Inc.*, "[T]he mere appearance of a joint exercise of legislative authority by Church and State provides a significant symbolic benefit to religion in the minds of some by reason of the power conferred."

It follows that an important concern of the effects test is whether the symbolic union of church and state effected by the challenged governmental action is sufficiently likely to be perceived by adherents of the controlling denominations as an endorsement, and by the nonadherents as a disapproval, of their individual religious choices. The inquiry into this kind of effect must be conducted with particular care when many of the citizens perceiving the governmental message are children in their formative years. The symbolism of a union between church and state is most likely to influence children of tender years, whose experience is limited and whose beliefs consequently are the function of environment as much as of free and voluntary choice.

Our school-aid cases have recognized a sensitivity to the symbolic impact of the union of church and state. Grappling with problems in many ways parallel to those we face today, *McCollum* held that a public school may not permit part-time religious instruction on its premises as a part of the school program, even if participation in that instruction is entirely voluntary and even if the instruction itself is conducted only by nonpublic-school personnel. Yet in *Zorach* the Court held that a similar program conducted off the premises of the public school passed constitutional muster. The difference in symbolic impact helps to explain the difference between the cases. The symbolic connection of church and state in the *McCollum* program presented the students with a graphic symbol of the "concert or union or dependency" of chuch and state. This very symbolic union was conspicuously absent in the *Zorach* program.

In the programs challenged in this case, the religious school students spend their typical school day moving between religious-school and "public-school" classes. Both types of classes take place in the same religious-school building and both are largely composed of students who are adherents of the same denomination. In this environment, the students would be unlikely to discern the crucial difference between the religious-school classes and the "public-school" classes, even if the latter were successfully kept free of religious indoctrination. As one commentator has written:

> This pervasive [religious] atmosphere makes on the young student's mind a lasting imprint that the holy and transcendental should be central to all facets of life. It increases respect for the church as an institution to guide one's total life adjustments and undoubtedly helps stimulate interest in religious vocations. . . . In short, the parochial school's total operation serves to fulfill both secular and religious functions concurrently, and the two cannot be completely separated. Support of any part of its activity entails some support of the disqualifying religious function of molding the religious personality of the young student.

Consequently, even the student who notices the "public school" sign temporarily posted would have before him a powerful symbol of state endorsement and encouragement of the religious beliefs taught in the same class at some other time during the day.

As Judge Friendly, writing for the Second Circuit in the companion case to the case at bar, stated:

> Under the City's plan public school teachers are, so far as appearance is concerned, a regular adjunct of the religious

> school. They pace the same halls, use classrooms in the same building, teach the same students, and confer with the teachers hired by the religious schools, many of them members of religious orders. The religious school appears to the public as a joint enterprise staffed with some teachers paid by its religious sponsor and others by the public.

This effect—the symbolic union of government and religion in one sectarian enterprise—is an impermissible effect under the Establishment Clause.

(3)

In *Everson* the Court stated that "[n]o tax in any amount, large or small, can be levied to support any religious activities or institutions, whatever they may be called, or whatever form they may adopt to teach or practice religion." With but one exception, our subsequent cases have struck down attempts by States to make payments out of public tax dollars directly to primary or secondary religious educational institutions.

Aside from cash payments, the Court has distinguished between two categories of programs in which public funds are used to finance secular activities that religious schools would otherwise fund from their own resources. In the first category, the Court has noted that it is "well established . . . that not every law that confers an 'indirect,' 'remote,' or 'incidental' benefit upon religious institutions is, for that reason alone, constitutionally invalid." In such "indirect" aid cases, the government has used primarily secular means to accomplish a primarily secular end, and no "primary effect" of advancing religion has thus been found. On this rationale, the Court has upheld programs providing for loans of secular textbooks to nonpublic school students and programs providing bus transportation for nonpublic school children.

In the second category of cases, the Court has relied on the Establishment Clause prohibition of forms of aid that provide "direct and substantial advancement of the sectarian enterprise." In such "direct aid" cases, the government, although acting for a secular purpose, has done so by directly supporting a religious institution. Under this rationale, the Court has struck down state schemes providing for tuition grants and tax benefits for parents whose children attend religious school and programs providing for "loan" of instructional materials to be used in religious schools. In *Sloan* and *Nyquist,* the aid was formally given to parents and not directly to the religious schools, while in *Wolman* and *Meek,* the aid was in-kind assistance rather than the direct contribution of public funds. Nonetheless, these differences in form were insufficient to save programs whose effect was indistinguishable from that of a direct subsidy to the religious school.

Thus, the Court has never accepted the mere possibility of subsidization, as the above cases demonstrate, as sufficient to invalidate an aid program. On the other hand, this effect is not wholly unimportant for Establishment Clause purposes. If it were, the public schools could gradually take on themselves the entire responsibility for teaching secular subjects on religious school premises. The question in each case must be whether the effect of the proffered aid is "direct and substantial" or indirect and incidental. "The problem, like many problems in consitutional law, is one of degree."

We have noted in the past that the religious school has dual functions, providing its students with a secular education while it promotes a particular religious perspective. In *Meek* and *Wolman,* we held unconstitutional state programs providing for loans of instructional equipment and materials to religious schools, on the ground that the programs advanced the "primary, religion-oriented educational function of the sectarian school." The programs challenged here, which provide teachers in addition to the instructional equipment and materials, have a similar—and forbidden—effect of advancing religion. This kind of direct aid to the educational function of the religious school is indistinguishable from the provision of a direct cash subsidy to the religious school that is most clearly prohibited under the Establishment Clause.

Petitioners claim that the aid here, like the textbooks in *Allen,* flows primarily to the students, not to the religious schools. Of course, all aid to religious schools ultimately "flows to" the students, and petitioners' argument if accepted would validate all forms of nonideological aid to religious schools, including those explicitly rejected in our prior cases. Yet in *Meek,* we held unconstitutional the loan of instructional materials to religious schools and in *Wolman,* we rejected the fiction that a similar program could be saved by masking it as aid to individual students. It follows *a fortiori* that the aid here, which includes not only instructional materials but also the provision of instructional services by teachers in the parochial school building, "inescapably [has] the primary effect of providing a direct and substantial advancement of the sectarian enterprise." Where, as here, no meaningful distinction can be made between aid to the student and aid to the school, "the concept of a loan to individuals is a transparent fiction."

Petitioners also argue that this "subsidy" effect is not significant in this case, because the Community Education and Shared Time programs supplemented the curriculum with courses not previously offered in the religious schools and not required by school rule or state regulation. Of course, this fails to distinguish the programs here from those found unconstitutional in *Meek*. As in *Meek*, we do not find that this feature of the program is controlling. First, there is no way of knowing whether the religious schools would have offered some or all of these courses if the public school system had not offered them first. The distinction between courses that "supplement" and those that "supplant" the regular curriculum is therefore not nearly as clear as petitioners allege. Second, although the precise courses offered in these programs may have been new to the participating religious schools, their general subject matter—reading, math, etc.—was surely a part of the curriculum in the past, and the concerns of the Establishment Clause may thus be triggered despite the "supplemental" nature of the courses. Third, and most important, petitioners' argument would permit the public schools gradually to take over the entire secular curriculum of the religious school, for the latter could surely discontinue existing courses so that they might be replaced a year or two later by a Community Education or Shared Time course with the same content. The average religious school student, for instance, now spends 10 percent of the school day in Shared Time classes. But there is no principled basis on which this Court can impose a limit on the percentage of the religious-school day that can be subsidized by the public school. To let the genie out of the bottle in this case would be to permit ever larger segments of the religious school curriculum to be turned over to the public school system, thus violating the cardinal principle that the State may not in effect become the prime supporter of the religious school system.

III

[5] We conclude that the challenged programs have the effect of promoting religion in three ways. The state-paid instructors, influenced

by the pervasively sectarian nature of the religious schools in which they work, may subtly or overtly indoctrinate the students in particular religious tenets at public expense. The symbolic union of church and state inherent in the provision of secular, state-provided instruction in the religious school buildings threatens to convey a message of state support for religion to students and to the general public. Finally, the programs in effect subsidize the religious functions of the parochial schools by taking over a substantial portion of their responsibility for teaching secular subjects. For these reasons, the conclusion is inescapable that the Community Education and Shared Time programs have the "primary or principal" effect of advancing religion, and therefore violate the dictates of the Establishment Clause of the First Amendment.

Nonpublic schools have played an important role in the development of American education, and we have long recognized that parents and their children have the right to choose between public schools and available sectarian alternatives. As the Chief Justice noted in *Lemon v. Kurtzman,* "nothing we have said can be construed to disparage the role of church-related elementary and secondary schools in our national life. Their contribution has been and is enormous." But the Establishment Clause "rest[s] on the belief that a union of government and religion tends to destroy government and to degrade religion." Therefore, "[t]he Constitution decrees that religion must be a private matter for the individual, the family, and the institutions of private choice, and that while some involvement and entanglement are inevitable, lines must be drawn." Because "the controlling constitutional standards have become firmly rooted and the broad contours of our inquiry are now well defined," the position of those lines has by now become quite clear and requires affirmance of the Court of Appeals.

It is so ordered.

JUSTICE O'CONNOR, CONCURRING IN THE JUDGMENT IN PART AND DISSENTING IN PART.

For the reasons stated in my dissenting opinion in *Aguilar v. Felton,* I dissent from the Court's holding that the Grand Rapids Shared Time program impermissibly advances religion. Like the New York Title I program, the Grand Rapids Shared Time program employs full-time public school teachers who offer supplemental instruction to parochial school children on the premises of religious schools. Nothing in the record indicates that Shared Time instructors have attempted to proselytize their students. I see no reason why public school teachers in Grand Rapids are any more likely than their counterparts in New York to disobey their instructions.

The Court relies on the District Court's finding that a "significant portion of the Shared Time instructors previously taught in nonpublic schools, and many of these had been assigned to the same nonpublic school where they were previously employed." In fact, only 13 Shared Time instructors have ever been employed by any parochial school, and only a fraction of those 13 now work in a parochial school where they were previously employed. The experience of these few teachers does not significantly increase the risk that the perceived or actual effect of the Shared Time program will be to inculcate religion at public expense. I would uphold the Shared Time program.

I agree with the Court, however, that the Community Education program violates the Establishment Clause. The record indicates that Community Education courses in the parochial schools are overwhelmingly taught by instructors who are current full-time employees of the parochial school. The teachers offer secular subjects to the same parochial school students who attend their regular parochial school classes. In addition, the supervisors of the Community Education program in the parochial schools are by and large the principals of the very schools where the classes are offered. When full-time parochial school teachers receive public funds to teach secular courses to their parochial school students under parochial school supervision, I agree that the program has the perceived and actual effect of advancing the religious aims of the church-related schools. This is particularly the case where, as here, religion pervades the curriculum and the teachers are accustomed to bring religion to play in everything they teach. I concur in the judgment of the Court that the Community Education program violates the Establishment Clause.

JUSTICE REHNQUIST, DISSENTING.

I dissent for the reasons stated in my dissenting opinion in *Wallace v. Jaffree.* In *Grand Rapids,* the Court relies heavily on the principles of *Everson* and *McCollum* but declines to discuss the faulty "wall" premise upon which those cases rest. In doing so the Court blinds itself to the first 150 years' history of the Establishment Clause.

The Court today attempts to give content to the "effects" prong of the *Lemon* test by holding that a "symbolic link between government and religion" creates an impermissible effect. But one wonders how the teaching of "Math Topics," "Spanish," and "Gymnastics," which is struck down today, creates a greater "symbolic link" than the municipal creche upheld in *Lynch* or the legislative chaplain upheld in *Marsh.*

A most unfortunate result of *Grand Rapids* is that to support its holding the Court, despite its disclaimers, impugns the integrity of public school teachers. Contrary to the law and the teachers' promises, they are assumed to be eager inculcators of religious dogma requiring, in the Court's words, "ongoing supervision." Not one instance of attempted religious inculcation exists in the records of the school aid cases decided today, even though both the Grand Rapids and New York programs have been in operation for a number of years. I would reverse.

Aguilar v. Felton, 105 S.Ct. 3232 (1985)

Justice Brennan, writing for the majority in this companion case to *Grand Rapids,* struck down a New York program that sent public schoolteachers and other professionals to religious schools to provide remedial instruction and guidance service. He stated: "Despite the well-intentioned efforts . . . the program remains constitutionally flawed owing to the nature of the aid."

In dissent, Justice O'Connor argued that public schoolteachers' "praiseworthy efforts have not eroded and do not threaten the religious liberty assured by the Establishment Clause."

JUSTICE BRENNAN DELIVERED THE OPINION OF THE COURT.

The City of New York uses federal funds to pay the salaries of public employees who teach in parochial schools. In this companion case to *School District of Grand Rapids v. Ball,* we determine whether this practice violates the Establishment Clause of the First Amendment.

I

A

The program at issue in this case authorizes the Secretary of Education to distribute financial assistance to local educational institutions to meet the needs of educationally deprived children from low-income families. The funds are to be appropriated in accordance with programs proposed by local educational agencies and approved by state educational agencies. "To the extent consistent with the number of educationally deprived children in the school district of the local educational agency who are enrolled in private elementary and secondary schools, such agency shall make provisions for including special educational services and arrangements . . . in which such children can participate." The proposed programs must also meet the following statutory requirements: the children involved in the program must be educationally deprived, the children must reside in areas comprising a high concentration of low-income families, and the programs must supplement, not supplant, programs that would exist absent funding under Title I.

Since 1966, the City of New York has provided instructional services funded by Title I to parochial school students on the premises of parochial schools. Of those students eligible to receive funds in 1981–1982, 13.2% were enrolled in private schools. Of that group, 84% were enrolled in schools affiliated with the Roman Catholic Archdiocese of New York and the Diocese of Brooklyn and 8% were enrolled in Hebrew day schools. With respect to the religious atmosphere of these schools, the Court of Appeals concluded that "the picture that emerges is of a system in which religious considerations play a key role in the selection of students and teachers, and which has as its substantial purpose the inculcation of religious values."

The programs conducted at these schools include remedial reading, reading skills, remedial mathematics, English as a second language, and guidance services. These programs are carried out by regular employees of the public schools (teachers, guidance counselors, psychologists, psychiatrists and social workers) who have volunteered to teach in the parochial schools. The amount of time that each professional spends in the parochial school is determined by the number of students in the particular program and the needs of these students.

The City's Bureau of Nonpublic School Reimbursement makes teacher assignments, and the instructors are supervised by field personnel, who attempt to pay at least one unannounced visit per month. The field supervisors, in turn, report to program coordinators, who also pay occasional unannounced supervisory visits to monitor Title I classes in the parochial schools. The professionals involved in the program are directed to avoid involvement with religious activities that are conducted within the private schools and to bar religious materials in their classrooms. All material and equipment used in the programs funded under Title I are supplied by the Government and are used only in those programs. The professional personnel are solely responsible for the selection of the students. Additionally, the professionals are informed that contact with private school personnel should be kept to a minimum. Finally, the administrators of the parochial schools are required to clear the classrooms used by the public school personnel of all religious symbols.

B

In 1978, six taxpayers commenced this action in the District Court for the Eastern District of New York, alleging that the Title I program administered by the City of New York violates the Establishment Clause. These taxpayers, appellees in today's case, sought to enjoin the further distribution of funds to programs involving instruction on the premises of parochial schools. . . . When the District Court in *PEARL* affirmed the constitutionality of the Title I program, and this Court dismissed the appeal for want of jurisdiction, the challenge of the present appellees was renewed. The District Court granted the appellants' motion for summary judgment based upon the evidentiary record developed in *PEARL.**

A unanimous panel of the Court of Appeals for the Second Circuit reversed, holding that

> [t]he Establishment Clause, as it has been interpreted by the Supreme Court in *Public Funds for Public Schools v. Marburger, Meek,* and *Wolman* constitutes an insurmountable barrier to the use of federal funds to send public school teachers and other professionals into religious schools to carry on instruction, remedial or otherwise, or to provide clinical and guidance services of the sort at issue here.

We postponed probable jurisdiction. We conclude that jurisdiction by appeal does not properly lie. Treating the papers as a petition for a writ of certiorari, we grant the petition and now affirm the judgment below.

*National Coalition for Public Education and Religious Liberty.

II

In *School Districts of the City of Grand Rapids v. Ball,* the Court has today held unconstitutional under the Establishment Clause two remedial and enhancement programs operated by the *Grand Rapids Public School District,* in which classes were provided to private school children at public expense in classrooms located in and leased from the local private schools. The New York programs challenged in this case are very similar to the programs we examined in *Ball.* In both cases, publicly funded instructors teach classes composed exclusively of private school students in private school buildings. In both cases, an overwhelming number of the participating private schools are religiously affiliated. In both cases, the publicly funded programs provide not only professional personnel, but also all materials and supplies necessary for the operation of the programs. Finally, the instructors in both cases are told that they are public school employees under the sole control of the public school system.

The appellants attempt to distinguish this case on the ground that the City of New York, unlike the Grand Rapids Public School District, had adopted a system for monitoring the religious content of publicly funded Title I classes in the religious schools. At best, the supervision in this case would assist in preventing the Title I program from being used, intentionally or unwittingly, to inculcate the religious beliefs of the surrounding parochial school. But appellants' argument fails in any event, because the supervisory system established by the City of New York inevitably results in the excessive entanglement of church and state, an Establishment Clause concern distinct from that addressed by the effects doctrine. Even where state aid to parochial institutions does not have the primary effect of advancing religion, the provision of such aid may nonetheless violate the Establishment Clause owing to the nature of the interaction of church and state in the administration of that aid.

The principle that the state should not become too closely entangled with the church in the administration of assistance is rooted in two concerns. When the state becomes enmeshed with a given denomination in matters of religious significance, the freedom of religious belief of those who are not adherents of that denomination suffers, even when the governmental purpose underlying the involvement is largely secular. In addition, the freedom of even the adherents of the denomination is limited by the governmental intrusion into sacred matters. "[T]he First Amendment rests upon the premise that both religion and government can best work to achieve their lofty aims if each is left free from the other within its respective sphere."

In *Lemon v. Kurtzman,* the Court held that the supervision necessary to ensure that teachers in parochial schools were not conveying religious messages to their students would constitute the excessive entanglement of church and state:

> A comprehensive, discriminating, and continuing state surveillance will inevitably be required to ensure that these restrictions are obeyed and the First Amendment otherwise respected. Unlike a book, a teacher cannot be inspected once so as to determine the extent and intent of his or her personal beliefs and subjective acceptance of the limitations imposed by the First Amendment. These prophylactic contacts will involve excessive and enduring entanglement between state and church.

Similarly, in *Meek,* we invalidated a state program that offered guidance, testing, remedial and therapeutic services performed by public employees on the premises of the parochial schools. As in *Lemon,* we observed that though a comprehensive system of supervision might conceivably prevent teachers from having the primary effect of advancing religion, such a system would inevitably lead to an unconstitutional administrative entanglement between church and state.

* * * * *

In *Roemer,* the Court sustained state programs of aid to religiously affiliated institutions of higher learning. The state allowed the grants to be used for any nonsectarian purpose. The Court upheld the grants on the ground that the institutions were not "'pervasively sectarian,'" and therefore a system of supervision was unnecessary to ensure that the grants were not being used to effect a religious end. In so holding, the Court identified "what is crucial to a nonentangling aid program: the ability of the State to identify and subsidize separate secular functions carried out at the school, without on-the-site inspections being necessary to prevent diversion of the funds to sectarian purposes." Similarly, in *Tilton,* the Court upheld one-time grants to sectarian institutions because ongoing supervision was not required.

As the Court of Appeals recognized, the elementary and secondary schools here are far different from the colleges at issue in *Roemer, Hunt,* and *Tilton.* Unlike the colleges, which were found not to be "pervasively sectarian," many of the schools involved in this case are the same sectarian schools which had "'as a substantial purpose the inculcation of religious values'" in *Nyquist.* Moreover, our holding in *Meek* invalidating instructional services much like those at issue in this case rested on the ground that the publicly funded teachers were "performing important educational services in schools in which education is an integral part of the dominant sectarian mission and in which an atmosphere dedicated to the advancement of religious belief is constantly maintained." The court below found that the schools involved in this case were "well within this characterization." Unlike the schools in *Roemer,* many of the schools here receive funds and report back to their affiliated church, require attendance at church religious exercises, begin the school day or class period with prayer, and grant preference in admission to members of the sponsoring denominations. In addition, the Catholic schools at issue here, which constitute the vast majority of the aided schools, are under the general supervision and control of the local parish.

The critical elements of the entanglement proscribed in *Lemon* and *Meek* are thus present in this case. First, as noted above, the aid is provided in a pervasively sectarian environment. Second, because assistance is provided in the form of teachers, ongoing inspection is required to ensure the absence of a religious message. In short, the scope and duration of New York's Title I program would require a permanent and pervasive State presence in the sectarian schools receiving aid.

This pervasive monitoring by public authorities in the sectarian schools infringes precisely those Establishment Clause values at the root of the prohibition of excessive entanglement. Agents of the State must visit and inspect the religious school regularly, alert for the subtle or overt presence of religious matter in Title I classes. In addition, the religious school must obey these same agents when they make determinations as to what is and what is not a "religious symbol" and thus off limits in a Title I classroom. In short, the religious school, which has as a primary purpose the advancement and preservation of a particular religion must endure the ongoing presence of state personnel whose primary purpose is to monitor teachers and students in an attempt to guard against the infiltration of religious thought.

The administrative cooperation that is required to maintain the educational program at issue here entangles Church and State in still another way that infringes interests at the heart of the Establishment Clause. Administrative personnel of the public and parochial school systems must work together in resolving matters related to schedules, classroom assignments, problems that arise in the implementation of the program, requests for additional services, and the dissemination of information regarding the program. Furthermore, the program necessitates "frequent contacts between the regular and the remedial teachers (or other professionals), in which each side reports on individual student needs, problems encountered, and results achieved."

We have long recognized that underlying the Establishment Clause is "the objective . . . to prevent, as far as possible, the intrusion of either [Church or State] into the precincts of the other." Although "[s]eparation in this context cannot mean absence of all contact," the detailed monitoring and close administrative contact required to maintain New York's Title I program can only produce "a kind of continuing day-to-day relationship which the policy of neutrality seeks to minimize." The numerous judgments that must be made by agents of the state concern matters that may be subtle and controversial, yet may be of deep religious significance to the controlling denominations. As government agents must make these judgments, the dangers of political divisiveness along religious lines increase. At the same time, "[t]he picture of state inspectors prowling the halls of parochial schools and auditing classroom instruction surely raises more than an imagined specter of governmental 'secularization of a creed.'"

III

Despite the well-intentioned efforts taken by the City of New York, the program remains constitutionally flawed owing to the nature of the aid, to the institution receiving the aid, and to the constitutional principles that they implicate—that neither the State nor Federal Government shall promote or hinder a particular faith or faith generally through the advancement of benefits or through the excessive entanglement of church and state in the administration of those benefits.

Affirmed.

JUSTICE O'CONNOR, WITH WHOM JUSTICE REHNQUIST JOINS AS TO PARTS II AND III, DISSENTING.

Today the Court affirms the holding of the Court of Appeals that public schoolteachers can offer remedial instruction to disadvantaged students who attend religious schools "only if such instruction . . . [is] afforded at a neutral site off the premises of the religious school." This holding rests on the theory, enunciated in Part V of the Court's opinion in *Meek,* that public school teachers who set foot on parochial school premises are likely to bring religion into their classes, and that the supervision necessary to prevent religious teaching would unduly entangle church and state. Even if this theory were valid in the abstract, it cannot validly be applied to New York City's 19-year-old Title I program. The Court greatly exaggerates the degree of supervision necessary to prevent public school teachers from inculcating religion, and thereby demonstrates the flaws of a test that condemns benign cooperation between church and state. I would uphold Congress' efforts to afford remedial instruction to disadvantaged schoolchildren in both public and parochial schools.

I

As in *Wallace v. Jaffree* and *Thornton v. Caldor,* the Court in this litigation adheres to the three-part Establishment Clause test enunciated in *Lemon v. Kurtzman.* To survive the *Lemon* test, a statute must have both a secular legislative purpose and a principal or primary effect that neither advances nor inhibits religion. Under *Lemon* and its progeny, direct state aid to parochial schools that has the purpose or effect of furthering the religious mission of the schools is unconstitutional. I agree with that principle. According to the Court, however, the New York Title I program is defective not because of any improper purpose or effect, but rather because it fails the third part of the *Lemon* test: the Title I program allegedly fosters excessive government entanglement with religion. I disagree with the Court's analysis of entanglement and I question the utility of entanglement as a separate Establishment Clause standard in most cases. Before discussing entanglement, however, it is worthwhile to explore the purpose and effect of the New York Title I program in greater depth than does the majority opinion.

The purpose of Title I is to provide special educational assistance to disadvantaged children who would not otherwise receive it. Congress recognized that poor academic performance by disadvantaged children is part of the cycle of poverty. Congress sought to break the cycle by providing classes in remedial reading, mathematics, and English to disadvantaged children in parochial as well as public schools, for public schools enjoy no monopoly on education in low income areas. Congress permitted remedial instruction by public school teachers on parochial school premises only if such instruction is "not normally provided by the nonpublic school" and would "contribute particularly to meeting the special educational needs of educationally deprived children. . . ."

* * * * *

After reviewing the text of the statute and its legislative history, the District Court concluded that Title I serves a secular purpose of aiding needy children regardless of where they attend school. The Court of Appeals did not dispute this finding, and no party in this Court contends that the purpose of the statute or of the New York City Title I program is to advance or endorse religion. Indeed, the record demonstrates that New York City public schoolteachers offer Title I classes on the premises of parochial schools solely because alternative means to reach the disadvantaged parochial school students—such as instruction for parochial school students at the nearest public school, either after or during regular school hours—were unsuccessful. As the Court of Appeals acknowledged, New York City "could reasonably have regarded [Title I instruction on parochial school premises] as the most effective way to carry out the purposes of the Act." Whether one looks to the face of the statute or to its implementation, the Title I program is undeniably animated by a legitimate secular purpose.

The Court's discussion of the effect of the New York City Title I program is even more perfunctory than its analysis of the program's purpose. The Court's opinion today in *Grand Rapids,* which strikes down a Grand Rapids scheme that the Court asserts is very similar to the New York program, identifies three ways in which public instruction on parochial school premises may have the impermissible effect of advancing religion. First, "state-paid instructors, influenced by the pervasively sectarian nature of the religious schools in which they work, may subtly or overtly indoctrinate the students in particular religious tenets at public expense." Second, "state-provided instruction in the religious school buildings threatens to convey a message of state support for religion to students and to the general public." Third, "the programs in effect subsidize the religious functions of the parochial schools by taking over a substantial portion of their responsibility for teaching secular subjects." While addressing the effect of the

Grand Rapids program at such length, the Court overlooks the effect of Title I in New York City.

One need not delve too deeply in the record to understand why the Court does not belabor the effect of the Title I program. The abstract theories explaining why on-premises instruction might possibly advance religion dissolve in the face of experience in New York. As the District Court found in 1980:

> New York City has been providing Title I services in nonpublic schools for fourteen years. The evidence presented in this action includes: extensive background information on Title I; an in-depth description of New York City's program; a detailed review of Title I rules and regulations and the ways in which they are enforced; and the testimony and affidavits of federal officials, state officers, school administrators, Title I teachers and supervisors, and parents of children receiving Title I services. The evidence establishes that the result feared in other cases has not materialized in the City's Title I program. The presumption—that the "religious mission" will be advanced by providing educational services on parochial school premises—is not supported by the facts of this case.

Indeed, in 19 years there has never been a single incident in which a Title I instructor "subtly or overtly" attempted to "indoctrinate the students in particular religious tenets at public expense."

Common sense suggests a plausible explanation for this unblemished record. New York City's public Title I instructors are professional educators who can and do follow instructions not to inculcate religion in their classes. They are unlikely to be influenced by the sectarian nature of the parochial schools where they teach, not only because they are carefully supervised by public officials, but also because the vast majority of them visit several different schools each week and are not of the same religion as their parochial students. In light of the ample record, an objective observer of the implementation of the Title I program in New York would hardly view it as endorsing the tenets of the participating parochial schools. To the contrary, the actual and perceived effect of the program is precisely the effect intended by Congress: impoverished school children are being helped to overcome learning deficits, improving their test scores, and receiving a significant boost in their struggle to obtain both a thorough education and the opportunities that flow from it.

The only type of impermissible effect that arguably could carry over from the *Grand Rapids* decision to this litigation, then, is the effect of subsidizing "the religious functions of the parochial schools by taking over a substantial portion of their responsibility for teaching secular subjects." That effect is tenuous, however, in light of the statutory directive that Title I funds may be used only to provide services that otherwise would not be available to the participating students. The Secretary of Education has vigorously enforced the requirement that Title I funds supplement rather than supplant the services of local education agencies.

Even if we were to assume that Title I remedial classes in New York may have duplicated to some extent instruction parochial schools would have offered in the absence of Title I, the Court's delineation of this third type of effect proscribed by the Establishment Clause would be seriously flawed. Our Establishment Clause decisions have not barred remedial assistance to parochial school children, but rather remedial assistance *on the premises of the parochial school.* Under *Wolman,* the New York City classes prohibited by the Court today would have survived Establishment Clause scrutiny if they had been offered in a neutral setting off the property of the private school. Yet is it difficult to understand why a remedial reading class offered on parochial school premises is any more likely to supplant the secular course offerings of the parochial school than the same class offered in a portable classroom next door to the school. Unless *Wolman* was wrongly decided, the defect in the Title I program cannot lie in the risk that it will supplant secular course offerings.

II

Recognizing the weakness of any claim of an improper purpose or effect, the Court today relies entirely on the entanglement prong of *Lemon* to invalidate the New York City Title I program. The Court holds that the occasional presence of peripatetic public schoolteachers on parochial school grounds threatens undue entanglement of church and state because (1) the remedial instruction is afforded in a pervasively sectarian environment; (2) ongoing supervision is required to assure that the public schoolteachers do not attempt to inculcate religion; (3) the administrative personnel of the parochial and public school systems must work together in resolving administrative and scheduling problems; and (4) the instruction is likely to result in political divisiveness over the propriety of direct aid.

This analysis of entanglement, I acknowledge, finds support in some of this Court's precedents. . . .

* * * * *

I would accord these decisions the appropriate deference commanded by the doctrine of *stare decisis* if I could discern logical support for their analysis. But experience has demonstrated that the analysis in Part V of the *Meek* opinion is flawed. At the time *Meek* was decided, thoughtful dissents pointed out the absence of any record support for the notion that public school teachers would attempt to inculcate religion simply because they temporarily occupied a parochial school classroom, or that such instruction would produce political divisiveness. Experience has given greater force to the arguments of the dissenting opinions in *Meek*. It is not intuitively obvious that a dedicated public school teacher will tend to disobey instructions and commence proselytizing students at public expense merely because the classroom is within a parochial school. *Meek* is correct in asserting that a teacher of remedial reading "remains a teacher," but surely it is significant that the teacher involved is a professional, full-time public school employee who is unaccustomed to bringing religion into the classroom. Given that not a single incident of religious indoctrination has been identified as occurring in the thousands of classes offered in Grand Rapids and New York over the past two decades, it is time to acknowledge that the risk identified in *Meek* was greatly exaggerated.

Just as the risk that public school teachers in parochial classrooms will inculcate religion has been exaggerated, so has the degree of supervision required to manage that risk. In this respect the New York Title I program is instructive. What supervision has been necessary in New York to enable public school teachers to help disadvantaged children for 19 years without once proselytizing? Public officials have prepared careful instructions warning public schoolteachers of their exclusively secular mission, and have required Title I teachers to study and observe them. Under the rules, Title I teachers are not accountable to parochial or private school officials; they have sole responsibility for selecting the students who participate in their class, must administer their own tests for determining eligibility, cannot engage in team teaching or cooperative activities with parochial schoolteachers, must make sure that all materials and equipment they use are not otherwise used by the parochial school, and must not participate in religious activities in the schools or introduce any religious matter into their teaching. To ensure compliance with the rules, a field supervisor and a program coordinator, who are full-time public school employees, make unannounced visits to each teacher's classroom at least once a month.

The Court concludes that this degree of supervision of public school employees by other public school employees constitutes excessive entanglement of church and state. I cannot agree. The supervision that occurs in New York's Title I program does not differ significantly from the supervision any public schoolteacher receives, regardless of the location of the classroom. Justice Powell suggests that the required supervision is extensive because the State must be *certain* that public schoolteachers do not inculcate religion. That reasoning would require us to close our public schools, for there is always some chance that a public schoolteacher will bring religion into the classroom, regardless of its location. Even if I remained confident of the usefulness of entanglement as an Establishment Clause test, I would conclude that New York's efforts to prevent religious indoctrination in Title I classes have been adequate and have not caused excessive institutional entanglement of church and state.

The Court's reliance on the potential for political divisiveness as evidence of undue entanglement is also unpersuasive. There is little record support for the proposition that New York's admirable Title I program has ignited any controversy other than this litigation.

* * * * *

I adhere to the doubts about the entanglement test that were expressed in *Lynch.* It is curious indeed to base our interpretation of the Constitution on speculation as to the likelihood of a phenomenon which the parties may create merely by prosecuting a lawsuit. My reservations about the entanglement test, however, have come to encompass its institutional aspects as well. As Justice Rehnquist has pointed out, many of the inconsistencies in our Establishment Clause decisions can be ascribed to our insistence that parochial aid programs with a valid purpose and effect may still be invalid by virtue of undue entanglement. For example, we permit a State to pay for bus transportation to a parochial school, but preclude States from providing buses for parochial school field trips, on the theory such trips involve excessive state supervision of the parochial officials who lead them. To a great extent, the anomalous results in our Establishment Clause cases are "attributable to [the] 'entanglement' prong."

Pervasive institutional involvement of church and state may remain relevant in deciding the *effect* of a statute which is alleged to violate the Establishment Clause, but state efforts to ensure that public resources are used only for nonsectarian ends should not in themselves serve to invalidate an otherwise valid statute. The State requires sectarian organizations to cooperate on a whole range of matters without thereby advancing religion or giving the impression that the government endorses religion. If a statute lacks a purpose or effect of advancing or endorsing religion, I would not invalidate it merely because it requires some ongoing cooperation between church and state or some state supervision to ensure that state funds do not advance religion.

III

Today's ruling does not spell the end of the Title I program of remedial education for disadvantaged children. Children attending public schools may still obtain the benefits of the program. Impoverished children who attend parochial schools may also continue to benefit from Title I programs offered off the premises of their schools—possible in portable classrooms just over the edge of school property. The only disadvantaged children who lose under the Court's holding are those in cities where it is not economically and logistically feasible to provide public facilities for remedial education adjacent to the parochial school. But this subset is significant, for it includes more than 20,000 New York City schoolchildren and uncounted others elsewhere in the country.

For these children, the Court's decision is tragic. The Court deprives them of a program that offers a meaningful chance at success in life, and it does so on the untenable theory that public schoolteachers (most of whom are of different faiths than their students) are likely to start teaching religion merely because they have walked across the threshold of a parochial school. I reject this theory and the analysis in *Meek* on which it is based. I cannot close my eyes to the fact that, over almost two decades, New York's public schoolteachers have helped thousands of impoverished parochial schoolchildren to overcome educational disadvantages without once attempting to inculcate religion. Their praiseworthy efforts have not eroded and do not threaten the religious liberty assured by the Establishment Clause. The contrary judgment of the Court of Appeals should be reversed.

I respectfully dissent.

Public Schools

McCollum v. Board of Education, 333 U.S. 203 (1948)

In this case, with only Justice Reed dissenting, Justice Black, writing for the majority, used *Everson* to demonstrate that the state of Illinois had engaged in religious establishment as opposed to the simple child-benefit guideline accepted in the earlier case. The theory of separation is thus enunciated as a unifying concept reflecting both sides in *Everson.* The decision focused upon Illinois' law that permitted religious groups to use school classrooms during school hours to teach religion. Although students were not compelled to attend such classes, Justice Black concluded, "Here not only are the state's tax-supported public school buildings used for the dissemination of religious doctrines. The State also affords sectarian groups an invaluable aid in that it helps to provide pupils for their religious classes through the use of the state's compulsory public school machinery. This is not separation of Church and State." In Justice Frankfurter's separate opinion, there was a suggestion about "dismissed time" that emerged in the *Zorach* case four years later. Justice Reed, in dissent, noted that Jefferson's wall "did not exclude religious education from" the University of Virginia.

Justice Frankfurter's opinion, joined by the other three justices who dissented in *Everson*, uses that dissent to important effect here. Further, their opinion traces the history of public and parochial schools in the United States as well as the history of "released time." "Separation," they argued, "means separation, not something less."

MR. JUSTICE BLACK DELIVERED THE OPINION OF THE COURT.

This case relates to the power of a state to utilize its tax-supported public school system in aid of religious instruction insofar as that power may be restricted by the First and Fourteenth Amendments to the Federal Constitution.

The appellant, Vashti McCollum, began this action for mandamus against the Champaign Board of Education in the Circuit Court of Champaign County, Illinois. Her asserted interest was that of a resident and taxpayer of Champaign and of a parent whose child was then enrolled in the Champaign public schools. Illinois has a compulsory education law which, with exceptions, requires parents to send their children, aged seven to sixteen, to its tax-supported public schools where the children are to remain in attendance during the hours when the schools are regularly in session. Parents who violate this law commit a misdemeanor punishable by fine unless the children attend private or parochial schools which meet educational standards fixed by the State. District boards of education are given general supervisory powers over the use of the public school buildings within the school districts.

Appellant's petition for mandamus alleged that religious teachers, employed by private religious groups, were permitted to come weekly into the school buildings during the regular hours set apart for secular teaching, and then and there for a period of thirty minutes substitute their religious teaching for the secular education provided under the compulsory education law. The petitioner charged that this joint public-school religious-group program violated the First and Fourteenth Amendments to the United States Constitution. The prayer of her petition was that the Board of Education be ordered to "adopt and enforce rules and regulations prohibiting all instruction in and teaching of all religious education in all public schools in Champaign District Number 71, . . . and in all public school houses and buildings in said district when occupied by public schools."

The board first moved to dismiss the petition on the ground that under Illinois law appellant had no standing to maintain the action. This motion was denied. An answer was then filed, which admitted that regular weekly religious instruction was given during school hours to those pupils whose parents consented and that those pupils were released temporarily from their regular secular classes for the limited purpose of attending the religious classes. The answer denied that this coordinated program of religious instruction violated the State or Federal Constitution. Much evidence was heard, findings of fact were made, after which the petition for mandamus was denied on the ground that the school's religious instruction program violated neither the federal nor state constitutional provisions invoked by the appellant. On appeal the State Supreme Court affirmed.

The appellee presses a motion to dismiss the appeal on several grounds, the first of which is that the judgment of the State Supreme Court does not draw in question the "validity of a statute of any State" as required by 28 U.S.C. 344(a). This contention rests on the admitted fact that the challenged program of religious instruction was not expressly authorized by statute. But the State Supreme Court has sustained the validity of the program on the ground that the Illinois statutes granted the board authority to establish such a program. This holding is sufficient to show that the validity of an Illinois statute was drawn in question within the meaning of 28 U.S.C. 344(a). A second ground for the motion to dismiss is that the appellant lacks standing to maintain the action, a ground which is also without merit. A third ground for the motion is that the appellant failed properly to present in the State Supreme Court her challenge that the state program violated the Federal Constitution. But in view of the express rulings of both state courts on this question, the argument cannot be successfully maintained. The motion to dismiss the appeal is denied.

Although there are disputes between the parties as to various inferences that may or may not properly be drawn from the evidence concerning the religious program, the following facts are shown by the record without dispute. In 1940 interested members of the Jewish, Roman Catholic, and a few of the Protestant faiths formed a voluntary association called the Champaign Council on Religious Education. They obtained permission from the Board of Education to offer classes in religious instruction to public school pupils in grades four to nine inclusive. Classes were made up of pupils whose parents signed printed cards requesting that their children be permitted to attend; they were held weekly, thirty minutes for the lower grades, forty-five minutes for the higher. The council employed the religious teachers at no expense to the school authorities, but the instructors were subject to the approval and supervision of the superintendent of schools. The classes were taught in three separate religious groups by Protestant teachers, Catholic priests, and a Jewish rabbi, although for the past several years there have apparently been no classes instructed in the Jewish religion. Classes were conducted in the regular classrooms of the school building. Students who did not choose to take the religious instruction were not released from public school duties; they were required to leave their classrooms and go to some other place in the school building for pursuit of their secular studies. On the other hand, students who were released from secular study for the religious instructions were required to be present at the religious classes. Reports of their presence or absence were to be made to their secular teachers.

The foregoing facts, without reference to others that appear in the record, show the use of tax-supported property for religious instruction and the close cooperation between the school authorities and the religious council in promoting religious education. The operation of the state's compulsory education system thus assists and is integrated with the program of religious instruction carried on by separate religious sects. Pupils compelled by law to go to school for secular education are released in part from their legal duty upon the condition that they attend the religious classes. This is beyond all question a utilization of the tax-established and tax-supported public school system to aid religious groups to spread their faith. And it falls squarely under the ban of the First Amendment (made applicable to the States by the Fourteenth) as we interpreted it in *Everson v. Board of Education.* There we said: "Neither a state nor the Federal Government can set up a church. Neither can pass laws which aid one religion, aid all religions, or prefer one religion over another. Neither can force or influence a person to go to or to remain away from church against his will or force him to profess a belief or disbelief in any religion. No person can be punished for entertaining or professing religious beliefs or disbeliefs, for church attendance or nonattendance. No tax in any amount, large or small, can be levied to support any religious activities or institutions, whatever they may be called, or whatever form they may adopt to teach or practice religion. Neither a state nor the Federal Government can, openly or secretly, participate in the affairs of any religious organizations or groups, and vice versa. In the words of Jefferson, the clause against establishment of religion by law was intended to erect 'a wall of separation between Church and State.'" The majority in the *Everson* case, and the minority . . . agreed that the First Amendment's language, properly interpreted, had erected a wall of separation between Church and State. They disagreed as to the facts shown by the record and as to the proper application of the First Amendment's language to those facts.

Recognizing that the Illinois program is barred by the First and Fourteenth Amendments if we adhere to the views expressed both by the majority and the minority in the *Everson* case, counsel for the respondents challenge those views as dicta and urge that we reconsider and repudiate them. They argue that historically the First Amendment was intended to forbid only governnment preference of one religion over another, not an impartial governmental assistance of all religions. In addition they ask that we distinguish or overrule our holding in the *Everson* case that the Fourteenth Amendment made the "establishment of religion" clause of the First Amendment applicable as a prohibition against the states. After giving full consideration to the arguments presented we are unable to accept either of these contentions.

To hold that a state cannot consistently with the First and Fourteenth Amendments utilize its public school system to aid any or all religious faiths or sects in the dissemination of their doctrines and ideals does not, as counsel urge, manifest a governmental hostility to religion or religious teachings. A manifestation of such hostility would be at war with our national tradition as embodied in the First Amendment's guaranty of the free exercise of religion. For the First Amendment rests upon the premise that both religion and government can best work to achieve their lofty aims if each is left free from the other within its respective sphere. Or, as we said in the *Everson* case, the First Amendment has erected a wall between Church and State which must be kept high and impregnable.

Here not only are the state's tax-supported public school buildings used for the dissemination of religious doctrines. The State also affords sectarian groups an invaluable aid in that it helps to provide pupils for their religious classes through use of the state's compulsory public school machinery. This is not separation of Church and State.

The cause is reversed and remanded to the State Supreme Court for proceedings not inconsistent with this opinion.

MR. JUSTICE REED, DISSENTING.

The decisions reversing the judgment of the Supreme Court of Illinois interpret the prohibition of the First Amendment against the establishment of religion, made effective as to the states by the Fourteenth Amendment, to forbid pupils of the public schools electing, with the approval of their parents, courses in religious education. The courses are given, under the school laws of Illinois as approved by the

Supreme Court of that State, by lay or clerical teachers supplied and directed by an interdenominational, local council of religious education. The classes are held in the respective school buildings of the pupils at study or released time periods so as to avoid conflict with recitations. The teachers and supplies are paid for by the interdenominational group. As I am convinced that this interpretation of the First Amendment is erroneous, I feel impelled to express the reasons for my disagreement. By directing attention to the many instances of close association of church and state in American society and by recalling that many of these relations are so much a part of our tradition and culture that they are accepted without more, this dissent may help in an appraisal of the meaning of the clause of the First Amendment concerning the establishment of religion and of the reasons which lead to the approval or disapproval of the judgment below.

The reasons for the reversal of the Illinois judgment, as they appear in the respective opinions may be summarized by the following excerpts. The opinion of the Court after stating the facts, says: "the foregoing facts, without reference to others that appear in the record, show the use of tax-supported property for religious instruction and the close cooperation between the school authorities and the religious council in promoting religious education. . . . And it falls squarely under the ban of the First Amendment (made applicable to the States by the Fourteenth) as we interpreted it in *Everson v. Board of Education.*" Another opinion phrases it thus: "We do not now attempt to weigh in the Constitutional scale every separate detail or various combination of factors which may establish a valid 'released time' program. We find that the basic Constitutional principle of absolute separation was violated when the State of Illinois, speaking through its Supreme Court, sustained the school authorities of Champaign in sponsoring and effectively furthering religious beliefs by its educational arrangement." These expressions in the decisions seem to leave open for further litigation variations from the Champaign plan. Actually, however, future cases must run the gantlet not only of the judgment entered but of the accompanying words of the opinions. I find it difficult to extract from the opinions any conclusion as to what it is in the Champaign plan that is unconstitutional. Is it the use of school buildings for religious instruction; the release of pupils by the schools for religious instruction during school hours; the so-called assistance by teachers in handing out the request cards to pupils, in keeping lists of them for release and records of their attendance; or the action of the principals in arranging an opportunity for the classes and the appearance of the Council's instructors? None of the reversing opinions say whether the purpose of the Champaign plan for religious instruction during school hours is unconstitutional or whether it is some ingredient used in or omitted from the formula that makes the plan unconstitutional.

From the tenor of the opinions I conclude that their teachings are that any use of a pupil's school time whether that use is on or off the school grounds, with the necessary school regulations to facilitate attendance, falls under the ban. I reach this conclusion notwithstanding one sentence of indefinite meaning in the second opinion: "We do not consider, as indeed we could not, school programs not before us which, though colloquially characterized as 'released time,' present situations differing in aspects that may well be constitutionally crucial." The use of the words "cooperation," "fusion," "complete hands off," "integrate" and "integrated" to describe the relations between the school and the Council in the plan evidences this. So does the interpretation of the word "aid." The criticized "momentum of the whole school atmosphere," "feeling of separatism" engendered in the non-participating sects, "obvious pressure . . . to attend," and "divisiveness" lead to the stated conclusion. From the holding and the language of the opinions, I can only deduce that religious instruction of public school children during school hours is prohibited. The history of American education is against such an interpretation of the First Amendment.*

The opinions do not say in words that the condemned practice of religious education is a law respecting an establishment of religion contrary to the First Amendment. The practice is accepted as a state law by all. I take it that when the opinion of the Court says that "The operation of the state's compulsory education system thus assists and is integrated with the program of religious instruction carried on by separate religious sects" and concludes "this is beyond all question a utilization of the tax-established and tax-supported public school system to aid religious groups to spread their faith," the intention of its author is to rule that this practice is a law "respecting an establishment

*These citations are from Justice Frankfurter's opinion (not included in this collection).

of religion." That was the basis of *Everson v. Board of Education.* It seems obvious that the action of the School Board in permitting religious education in certain grades of the schools by all faiths did not prohibit the free exercise of religion. Even assuming that certain children who did not elect to take instruction are embarrassed to remain outside of the classes, one can hardly speak of that embarrassment as a prohibition against the free exercise of religion. As no issue of prohibition upon the free exercise of religion is before us, we need only examine the School Board's action to see if it constitutes an establishment of religion.

The facts, as stated in the reversing opinions, are adequately set out if we interpret the abstract words used in the light of the concrete incidents of the record. It is correct to say that the parents "consented" to the religious instruction of the children, if we understand "consent" to mean the signing of a card like the one in the margin. It is correct to say that "instructors were subject to the approval and supervision of the superintendent of schools," if it is understood that there were no definitive written rules and that the practice was as is shown in the excerpts from the findings below. The substance of the religious education course is determined by the members of the various churches on the council, not by the superintendent. The evidence and findings set out in the two preceding notes convince me that the "approval and supervision" referred to above are not of the teachers and the course of studies but of the orderly presentation of the courses to those students who may elect the instruction. The teaching largely covered Biblical incidents. The religious teachers and their teachings in every real sense, were financed, and regulated by the Council of Religious Education, not the School Board.

The phrase "an establishment of religion" may have been intended by Congress to be aimed only at a state church. When the First Amendment was pending in Congress in substantially its present form, "Mr. Madison said, he apprehended the meaning of the words to be, that Congress should not establish a religion, and enforce the legal observation of it by law, nor compel men to worship God in any manner contrary to their conscience." Passing years, however, have brought about acceptance of a broader meaning, although never until today, I believe, has this Court widened its interpretation to any such degree as holding that recognition of the interest of our nation in religion, through the granting, to qualified representatives of the principal faiths, of opportunity to present religion as an optional, extracurricular subject during released school time in public school buildings, was equivalent to an establishment of religion. A reading of the general statements of eminent statesmen of former days, referred to in the opinions in this and *Everson v. Board of Education*, will show that circumstances such as those in this case were far from the minds of the authors. The words and spirit of those statements may be wholeheartedly accepted without in the least impugning the judgment of the State of Illinois.

* * * * *

This Court summarized the amendment's accepted reach into the religious field, as I understand its scope, in *Everson v. Board of Education.* The Court's opinion quotes the gist of the Court's reasoning in *Everson.* I agree as there stated that none of our governmental entities can "set up a church." I agree that they cannot "aid" all or any religions or prefer one "over another." But "aid" must be understood as a purposeful assistance directly to the church itself or to some religious group or organization doing religious work of such a character that it may fairly be said to be performing ecclesiastical functions. "Prefer" must give an advantage to one "over another." I agree that pupils cannot "be released in part from their legal duty" of school attendance upon condition that they attend religious classes. But as Illinois has held that it is within the discretion of the School Board to permit absence from school for religious instruction no legal duty of school attendance is violated. If the sentence in the first opinion, concerning the pupils' release from legal duty, is intended to mean that the Constitution forbids a school to excuse a pupil from secular control during school hours to attend voluntarily a class in religious education, whether in or out of school buildings, I disagree. Of course, no tax can be levied to support organizations intended "to teach or practice religion." I agree too that the state cannot influence one toward religion against his will or punish him for his beliefs. Champaign's religious education course does none of these things.

It seems clear to me that the "aid" referred to by the Court in the *Everson* case could not have been those incidental advantages that religious bodies, with other groups similarly situated, obtain as a by-product of organized society. This explains the well-known fact that all churches receive "aid" from government in the form of freedom from taxation. The *Everson* decision itself justified the transportation of children to church schools by New Jersey for safety reasons. It accords with *Cochran v. Louisiana State Board of Education*, where this Court upheld a free textbook statute of Louisiana against a charge that it aided private schools on the ground that the books were for the education of the children, not to aid religious schools. Likewise the National School Lunch Act aids all school children attending tax exempt schools. In *Bradfield v. Roberts*, this Court held proper the payment of money by the Federal Government to build an addition to a hospital, chartered by individuals who were members of a Roman Catholic sisterhood, and operated under the auspices of the Roman Catholic Church. This was done over the objection that it aided the establishment of religion. While obviously in these instances the respective churches, in a certain sense, were aided, this Court has never held that such "aid" was in violation of the First or Fourteenth Amendments.

* * * * *

With the general statements in the opinions concerning the constitutional requirement that the nation and states, by virtue of the First and Fourteenth Amendments, may "make no law respecting an establishment of religion," I am in agreement. But, in the light of the meaning given to those words by the precedents, customs, and practices which I have detailed above, I cannot agree with the Court's conclusion that when pupils compelled by law to go to school for secular education are released from school so as to attend the religious classes, churches are unconstitutionally aided. Whatever may be the wisdom of the arrangement as to the use of the school buildings made with The Champaign Council of Religious Education, it is clear to me that past practice shows such cooperation between the schools and a nonecclesiastical body is not forbidden by the First Amendment. When actual church services have always been permitted on government property, the mere use of the school buildings by a non-sectarian group for religious education ought not to be condemned as an establishment of religion. For a non-sectarian organization to give the type of instruction here offered cannot be said to violate our rule as to the establishment of religion by the state. The prohibition of enactments respecting the establishment of religion do not bar every friendly gesture between church and state. It is not an absolute prohibition against every conceivable situation where the two may work together any more than the other provisions of the First Amendment—free speech, free press—are absolutes. If abuses occur such as the use of the instruction hour for sectarian purposes, I have no doubt, in view of the Ring case, that Illinois will promptly correct them. If they are of a kind that tend to the establishment of a church or interfere with the free exercise of religion, this Court is open for a review of any erroneous decision. This Court cannot be too cautious in upsetting practices embedded in our society by many years of experience. A state is entitled to have great leeway in its legislation when dealing with the important social problems of its population. A definite violation of legislative limits must be established. The Constitution should not be stretched to forbid national customs in the way courts act to reach arrangements to avoid federal taxation. Devotion to the great principle of religious liberty should not lead us into a rigid interpretation of the constitutional guarantee that conflicts with accepted habits of our people. This is an instance where, for me, the history of past practices is determinative of the meaning of a constitutional clause not a decorous introduction to the study of its text. The judgment should be affirmed.

Zorach v. Clauson, 343 U.S. 306 (1952)

The question addressed by the Court in this decision was whether to extend the *McCollum* ruling. Both majority and minority continued to employ the *Everson* principle of separation. Justice Douglas was firm in asserting, "There cannot be the slightest doubt that the First Amendment reflects the philosophy that Church and State should be separated." Yet he and five fellow justices were satisfied that expanding *McCollum* to apply in *Zorach* would endorse "a philosophy of hostility to religion." Released time off the school property, with no evidence of coercion, they perceived to meet the tests of *Everson* and *McCollum*. Justices Black, Frankfurter, and Jackson saw it differently. Justice Black wrote that "*McCollum* . . . held that Illinois could not constitutionally manipulate the compelled classroom hours . . . so as to channel children into sectarian classes." He was convinced that the Court decision in *Zorach* gave that right to New York. In a more biting mood, Justice Jackson wrote that "the *McCollum* case has passed like a storm in a teacup. . . . Today's judgment will be more interesting to students of psychology and of the judicial process than to students of constitutional law."

MR. JUSTICE DOUGLAS DELIVERED THE OPINION OF THE COURT.

New York City has a program which permits its public schools to release students during the school day so that they may leave the school buildings and school grounds and go to religious centers for religious instruction or devotional exercises. A student is released on written request of his parents. Those not released stay in the classrooms. The churches make weekly reports to the schools, sending a list of children who have been released from public school but who have not reported for religious instruction.

This "released time" program involves neither religious instruction in public school classrooms nor the expenditure of public funds. All costs, including the application blanks, are paid by the religious organizations. The case is therefore unlike *McCollum v. Board of Education* which involved a "released time" program from Illinois. In that case the classrooms were turned over to religious instructors. We accordingly held that the program violated the First Amendment which (by reason of the Fourteenth Amendment) prohibits the states from establishing religion or prohibiting its free exercise.

Appellants, who are taxpayers and residents of New York City and whose children attend its public schools, challenge the present law, contending it is in essence not different from the one involved in the *McCollum* case. Their argument, stated elaborately in various ways, reduces itself to this: the weight and influence of the school is put behind a program for religious instruction; public school teachers police it, keeping tab on students who are released; the classroom activities come to a halt while the students who are released for religious instruction are on leave; the school is a crutch on which the churches are leaning for support in their religious training; without the cooperation of the schools this "released time" program, like the one in the *McCollum* case, would be futile and ineffective. The New York Court of Appeals sustained the law against this claim of unconstitutionality. The case is here on appeal.

The briefs and arguments are replete with data bearing on the merits of this type of "released time" program. Views pro and con are expressed, based on practical experience with these programs and with their implications. We do not stop to summarize these materials nor to burden the opinion with an analysis of them. For they involve considerations not germane to the narrow constitutional issue presented. They largely concern the wisdom of the system, its efficiency from an educational point of view, and the political considerations which have motivated its adoption or rejection in some communities. Those matters are of no concern here, since our problem reduces itself to whether New York by this system has either prohibited the "free exercise" of religion or has made a law "respecting an establishment of religion" within the meaning of the First Amendment.

It takes obtuse reasoning to inject any issue of the "free exercise" of religion into the present case. No one is forced to go to the religious classroom and no religious exercise or instruction is brought to the classrooms of the public schools. A student need not take religious instruction. He is left to his own desires as to the manner or time of his religious devotions, if any.

There is a suggestion that the system involves the use of coercion to get public school students into religious classrooms. There is no evidence in the record before us that supports that conclusion. The present record indeed tells us that the school authorities are neutral in this regard and do no more than release students whose parents so request. If in fact coercion were used, if it were established that any one or more teachers were using their office to persuade or force students to take the religious instruction, a wholly different case would be presented. Hence we put aside that claim of coercion both as respects the "free exercise" of religion and "an establishment of religion" within the meaning of the First Amendment.

Moreover, apart from that claim of coercion, we do not see how New York by this type of "released time" program has made a law respecting an establishment of religion within the meaning of the First Amendment. There is much talk of the separation of Church and State in the history of the Bill of Rights and in the decisions clustering around the First Amendment. See *Everson v. Board of Education; McCollum v. Board of Education.* There cannot be the slightest doubt that the First Amendment reflects the philosophy that Church and State should be separated. And so far as interference with the "free exercise" of religion and an "establishment" of religion are concerned, the separation must be complete and unequivocal. The First Amendment within the scope of its coverage permits no exception; the prohibition is absolute. The First Amendment, however, does not say that in every and all respects there shall be a separation of Church and State. Rather, it studiously defines the manner, the specific ways, in which there shall be no concert or union or dependency one on the other. That is the common sense of the matter. Otherwise the state and religion would be aliens to each other—hostile, suspicious, and even unfriendly. Churches could not be required to pay even property taxes. Municipalities would not be permitted to render police or fire protection to religious groups. Policemen who helped parishioners into their places of worship would violate the Constitution. Prayers in our legislative halls; the appeals to the Almighty in the messages of the Chief Executive; the proclamations making Thanksgiving Day a holiday; "so help me God" in our courtroom oaths—these and all other references to the Almighty that run through our laws, our public rituals, our ceremonies would be flouting the First Amendment. A fastidious atheist or agnostic could even object to the supplication with which the Court opens each session: "God save the United States and this Honorable Court."

We would have to press the concept of separation of Church and State to these extremes to condemn the present law on constitutional grounds. The nullification of this law would have wide and profound effects. A Catholic student applies to his teacher for permission to leave the school during hours on a Holy Day of Obligation to attend a mass. A Jewish student asks his teacher for permission to be excused for Yom Kippur. A Protestant wants the afternoon off for a family baptismal ceremony. In each case the teacher requires parental consent in writing. In each case the teacher, in order to make sure the student is not a truant, goes further and requires a report from the priest, the rabbi, or the minister. The teacher in other words cooperates in a religious program to the extent of making it possible for her students to participate in it. Whether she does it occasionally for a few students, regularly for one, or pursuant to a systematized program designed to further the religious needs of all the students does not alter the character of the act.

We are a religious people whose institutions presuppose a Supreme Being. We guarantee the freedom to worship as one chooses. We make room for as wide a variety of beliefs and creeds as the spiritual needs of man deem necessary. We sponsor an attitude on the part of government that shows no partiality to any one group and that lets each flourish according to the zeal of its adherents and the appeal of its dogma. When the state encourages religious instruction or cooperates with religious authorities by adjusting the schedule of public events to sectarian needs, it follows the best of our traditions. For it then respects the religious nature of our people and accommodates the public service to their spiritual needs. To hold that it may not would be to find in the Constitution a requirement that the government show a callous indifference to religious groups. That would be preferring those who believe in no religion over those who do believe. Government may not finance religious groups nor undertake religious instruction nor blend secular and sectarian education nor use secular institutions to force one or some religion on any person. But we find no constituional requirement which makes it necessary for government to be hostile to religion and to throw its weight against efforts to widen the effective scope of religious influence. The government must be neutral when it comes to competition between sects. It may not thrust any sect on any person. It may not make a religious observance compulsory. It may not coerce anyone to attend church, to observe a religious holiday, or to take religious instruction. But it can close its doors or suspend its operations as to those who want to repair to their religious sanctuary for worship or instruction. No more than that is undertaken here.

This program may be unwise and improvident from an educational or a community viewpoint. That appeal is made to us on a theory, previously advanced, that each case must be decided on the basis of "our own prepossessions." See *McCollum v. Board of Education.* Our individual preferences, however, are not the constitutional standard. The constitutional standard is the separation of Church and State. The problem, like many problems in constitutional law, is one of degree.

In the *McCollum* case the classrooms were used for religious instruction and the force of the public school was used to promote that instruction. Here, as we have said, the public schools do no more than accommodate their schedules to a program of outside religious instruction. We follow the *McCollum* case. But we cannot expand it to cover the present released time program unless separation of Church and State means that public institutions can make no adjustment of their schedules to accommodate the religious needs of the people. We cannot read into the Bill of Rights such a philosophy of hostility to religion.

Affirmed.

MR. JUSTICE BLACK, DISSENTING.

Illinois ex rel. McCollum v. Board of Education held invalid as an "establishment of religion" an Illinois system under which school children, compelled by law to go to public schools, were freed from some hours of required school work on condition that they attend special religious classes held in the school buildings. Although the classes were taught by sectarian teachers neither employed nor paid by the state, the state did use its power to further the program by releasing some of the children from regular class work, insisting that those released attend the religious classes, and requiring that those who remained behind do some kind of academic work while the others received their religious training. We said this about the Illinois system:

> Pupils compelled by law to go to school for secular education are released in part from their legal duty upon the condition that they attend the religious classes. This is beyond all question a utilization of the tax established and tax-supported public school system to aid religious groups to spread their faiths. And it falls squarely under the ban of the First Amendment. . . .

I see no significant difference between the invalid Illinois system and that of New York here sustained. Except for the use of the school buildings in Illinois, there is no difference between the systems which I consider even worthy of mention. In the New York program, as in that of Illinois, the school authorities release some of the children on the condition that they attend the religious classes, get reports on whether they attend, and hold the other children in the school building until the religious hour is over. As we attempted to make categorically clear, the *McCollum* decision would have been the same if the religious classes had not been held in the school buildings. We said:

"Here not only are the State's tax-supported public school buildings used for the dissemination of religious doctrines. The State also affords sectarian groups an invaluable aid in that it helps to provide pupils for their religious classes through the use of the State's compulsory school machinery. This is not separation of Church and State." *McCollum* thus held that Illinois could not constitutionally manipulate the compelled classroom hours of its compulsory school machinery so as to channel children into sectarian classes. Yet that is exactly what the Court holds New York can do.

I am aware that our *McCollum* decision on separation of church and state has been subjected to a most searching examination throughout the country. Probably few opinions from this Court in recent years have attracted more attention or stirred wider debate. Our insistence on "a wall between Church and State which must be kept high and impregnable" has seemed to some a correct exposition of the philosophy and a true interpretation of the language of the First Amendment to which we should strictly adhere. With equal conviction and sincerity, others have thought the *McCollum* decision fundamentally wrong and have pledged continuous warfare against it. The opinions in the court below and the briefs here reflect these diverse viewpoints. In dissenting today, I mean to do more than give routine approval to our *McCollum* decision. I mean also to reaffirm my faith in the fundamental philosophy expressed in *McCollum* and *Everson v. Board of Education.* That reaffirmance can be brief because of the exhaustive opinions in those recent cases.

Difficulty of decision in the hypothetical situations mentioned by the Court, but not now before us, should not confuse the issues in this case. Here the sole question is whether New York can use its compulsory education laws to help religious sects get attendants presumably too unenthusiastic to go unless moved to do so by the pressure of this state machinery. That this is the plan, purpose, design and consequence of the New York program cannot be denied. The state thus makes religious sects beneficiaries of its power to compel children to attend secular schools. Any use of such coercive power by the state to help or hinder some religious sects or to prefer all religious sects over nonbelievers or vice versa is just what I think the First Amendment forbids. In considering whether a state has entered this forbidden field the question is not whether it has entered too far but whether it has entered at all. New York is manipulating its compulsory education laws to help religious sects get pupils. This is not separation but combination of Church and State.

The Court's validation of the New York system rests in part on its statement that Americans are "a religious people whose institutions presuppose a Supreme Being." This was at least as true when the First Amendment was adopted; and it was just as true when eight justices of this Court invalidated the released time system in *McCollum* on the premise that a state can no more "aid all religions" than it can aid one. It was precisely because Eighteenth Century Americans were a religious people divided into many fighting sects that we were given the constitutional mandate to keep church and state completely separate. Colonial history had already shown that, here as elsewhere zealous sectarians entrusted with governmental power to further their causes, would sometimes torture, maim and kill those they branded "heretics," "atheists" or "agnostics." The First Amendment was therefore to insure that no one powerful sect or combination of sects could use political or governmental power to punish dissenters whom they could not convert to their faith. Now as then, it is only by wholly isolating the state from the religious sphere and compelling it to be completely neutral, that the freedom of each and every denomination and of all non-believers can be maintained. It is this neutrality the Court abandons today when it treats New York's coercive system as a program which merely "encourages religious instruction or cooperates with religious authorities." The abandonment is all the more dangerous to liberty because of the Court's legal exaltation of the orthodox and its derogation of unbelievers.

Under our system of religious freedom, people have gone to their religious sanctuaries not because they feared the law but because they loved their God. The choice of all has been as free as the choice of those who answered the call to worship moved only by the music of the old Sunday morning church bells. The spiritual mind of man has thus been free to believe, disbelieve, or doubt, without repression, great or small, by the heavy hand of government. Statutes authorizing such repression have been stricken. Before today, our judicial opinions have refrained from drawing invidious distinctions between those who believe in no religion and those who do believe. The First Amendment has lost much if the religious follower and the atheist are no longer to be judicially regarded as entitled to equal justice under law.

State help to religion injects political and party prejudices into a holy field. It too often substitutes force for prayer, hate for love, and persecution for persuasion. Government should not be allowed, under cover of the soft euphemism of "co-operation," to steal into the sacred area of religious choice.

MR. JUSTICE FRANKFURTER, DISSENTING.

By way of emphasizing my agreement with Mr. Justice Jackson's dissent, I add a few words.

The Court tells us that in the maintenance of its public schools, "(The State government) can close its doors or suspend its operations" so that its citizens may be free for religious devotions or instruction. If that were the issue, it would not rise to the dignity of a constitutional controversy. Of course a State may provide that the classes in its schools shall be dismissed, for any reason, or no reason, on fixed days, or for special occasions. The essence of this case is that the school system did not "close its doors" and did not "suspend its operations." There is all the difference in the world between letting the children out of school and letting some of them out of school into religious classes. If every one is free to make what use he will of time wholly unconnected from schooling required by law—those who wish sectarian instruction devoting it to that purpose, those who have ethical instruction at home, to that, those who study music, to that—then of course there is no conflict with the Fourteenth Amendment.

The pith of the case is that formalized religious instruction is substituted for other school activity which those who do not participate in the released-time program are compelled to attend. The school system is very much in operation during this kind of released time. If its doors are closed, they are closed upon those students who do not attend the religious instruction in order to keep them within the school. That is the very thing which raises the constitutional issue. It is not met by disregarding it. Failure to discuss this issue does not take it out of the case.

Again, the Court relies upon the absence from the record of evidence of coercion in the operation of the system. "If in fact coercion were used," according to the Court, "if it were established that any one or more teachers were using their office to persuade or force students to take the religious instruction, a wholly different case would be presented." Thus, "coercion" in the abstract is acknowledged to be fatal. But the Court disregards the fact that as the case comes to us, there could be no proof of coercion, for the petitioners were not allowed to make proof of it. Petitioners alleged that "The operation of the released time program has resulted and inevitably results in the exercise of pressure and coercion upon parents and children to secure attendance by the children for religious instruction." This allegation—that coercion was in fact present and is inherent in the system, no matter what disavowals might be made in the operating regulations—was denied by respondents. Thus were drawn issues of fact which cannot be determined, on any conceivable view of judicial notice, by judges out of their own knowledge or experience. Petitioners sought an opportunity to adduce evidence in support of these allegations at an appropriate trial. And though the courts below cited the concurring opinion in *McCollum v. Board of Education* to "emphasize the importance of detailed analysis of the facts to which the Constitutional test of Separation is to be applied," they denied that opportunity on the ground that such proof was irrelevant to the issue of constitutionality.

When constitutional issues turn on facts, it is a strange procedure indeed not to permit the facts to be established. When such is the case, there are weighty considerations for us to require the State court to make its determination only after a thorough canvass of all the circumstances and not to bar them from consideration. If we are to decide this case on the present record, however, a strict adherence to the usage of courts in ruling on the sufficiency of pleadings would require us to take as admitted the facts pleaded in the petitioners' complaint, including the fact of coercion, actual and inherent. Even on a more latitudinarian view, I cannot see how a finding that coercion was absent, deemed critical by this Court in sustaining the practice, can be made here, when petitioners were prevented from making a timely showing of coercion because the courts below thought it irrelevant.

The result in the *McCollum* case was based on principles that received unanimous acceptance by this Court, barring only a single vote. I agree with Mr. Justice Black that those principles are disregarded in reaching the result in this case. Happily they are not disavowed by the Court. From this I draw the hope that in future variations of the problem which are bound to come here, these principles may again be honored in the observance.

The deeply divisive controversy aroused by the attempts to secure public school pupils for sectarian instruction would promptly end if the advocates of such instruction were content to have the school "close its doors or suspend operation"—that is, dismiss classes in their entirety, without discrimination—instead of seeking to use the public schools as the instrument for security of attendance at denominational classes. The unwillingness of the promoters of this movement to dispense with such use of the public schools betrays a surprising want of confidence in the inherent power of the various faiths to draw children to outside sectarian classes—an attitude that hardly reflects the faith of the greatest religious spirits.

MR. JUSTICE JACKSON, DISSENTING.

This released time program is founded upon a use of the State's power of coercion, which, for me, determines its unconstitutionality.

Stripped to its essentials, the plan has two stages, first, that the State compel each student to yield a large part of his time for public secular education and, second, that some of it be "released" to him on condition that he devote it to sectarian religious purposes.

No one suggests that the Constitution would permit the State directly to require this "released" time to be spent "under the control of a duly constituted religious body." This program accomplishes that forbidden result by indirection. If public education were taking so much of the pupils' time as to injure the public or the student's welfare by encroaching upon their religious opportunity, simply shortening everyone's school day would facilitate voluntary and optional attendance at Church classes. But that suggestion is rejected upon the ground that if they are made free many students will not go to the Church. Hence, they must be deprived of freedom for this period, with Church attendance put to them as one of the two permissible ways of using it.

The greater effectiveness of this system over voluntary attendance after school hours is due to the truant officer who, if the youngster fails to go to the Church school, dogs him back to the public schoolroom. Here schooling is more or less suspended during the "released time" so the nonreligious attendants will not forge ahead of the Churchgoing absentees. But it serves as a temporary jail for a pupil who will not go to Church. It takes more subtlety of mind than I possess to deny that this is governmental constraint in support of religion. It is as unconstitutional, in my view, when exerted by indirection as when exercised forthrightly.

As one whose children, as a matter of free choice, have been sent to privately supported Church schools, I may challenge the Court's suggestion that opposition to this plan can only be antireligious, atheistic, or agnostic. My evangelistic brethren confuse an objection to compulsion with an objection to religion. It is possible to hold a faith with enough confidence to believe that what should be rendered to God does not need to be decided and collected by Caesar.

The day that this country ceases to be free for irreligion it will cease to be free for religion—except for the sect that can win political power. The same epithetical jurisprudence used by the Court today to beat down those who oppose pressuring children into some religion can devise as good epithets tomorrow against those who object to pressuring them into a favored religion. And, after all, if we concede to the State power and wisdom to single out "duly constituted religious" bodies as exclusive alternatives for compulsory secular instruction, it would be logical to also uphold the power and wisdom to choose the true faith among those "duly constituted." We start down a rough road when we begin to mix compulsory public education with compulsory godliness.

A number of Justices just short of a majority of the majority that promulgates today's passionate dialectics joined in answering them in *Illinois ex rel. McCollum v. Board of Education.* The distinction attempted between that case and this is trivial, almost to the point of cynicism, magnifying its nonessential details and disparaging compulsion which was the underlying reason for invalidity. A reading of the Court's opinion in that case along with its opinion in this case will show such difference of overtones and undertones as to make clear that the *McCollum* case has passed like a storm in a teacup. The wall which the Court was professing to erect between Church and State has become even more warped and twisted than I expected. Today's judgment will be more interesting to students of psychology and of the judicial processes than to students of constitutional law.

Engel v. Vitale, 370 U.S. 421 (1962)

In a decision reached on June 25, 1962, the Court described New York's prescribed program of daily classroom invocation of God's blessings promulgated by the Board of Regents as "a religious activity" inconsistent with the Establishment Clause. This was the first of the prayer cases destined to raise serious objections among many citizens. The storm of protests that resulted has generated a charged public debate that has shown little sign of abatement in twenty-five years. Justice Black, writing for the Court, affirmed that it is "no part of the business of government to compose official prayers." He went on to state that "each separate government in this country should stay out of the business of writing or sanctioning official prayers."

In a concurring opinion Justice Douglas, reflecting upon his previous support for the majority in *Everson,* asserted, "The Everson case seems in retrospect to be out of line with the First Amendment." He went on to quote approvingly part of Justice Rutledge's dissent.

Justice Stewart filed the lone dissent in *Vitale.* Justice Frankfurter took no part in the decision, and Justice White took no part in either the consideration or the decision of this case.

MR. JUSTICE BLACK DELIVERED THE OPINION OF THE COURT.

The respondent Board of Education of Union Free School District No. 9, New Hyde Park, New York, acting in its official capacity under state law, directed the School District's principal to cause the following prayer to be said aloud by each class in the presence of a teacher at the beginning of each school day: "Almighty God, we acknowledge our dependence upon Thee, and we beg Thy blessings upon us, our parents, our teachers and our Country." This daily procedure was adopted on the recommendation of the State Board of Regents, a governmental agency created by the State Constitution to which the New York Legislature has granted broad supervisory, executive, and legislative powers over the State's public school system. These state officials composed the prayer which they recommended and published as a part of their "Statement on Moral and Spiritual Training in the Schools," saying: "We believe that this Statement will be subscribed to by all men and women of good will, and we call upon all of them to aid in giving life to our program."

Shortly after the practice of reciting the Regents' prayer was adopted by the School District, the parents of ten pupils brought this action in a New York State Court insisting that use of this official prayer in the public schools was contrary to the beliefs, religions, or religious practices of both themselves and their children. Among other things, these parents challenged the constitutionality of both the state law authorizing the School District to direct the use of prayer in public schools and the School District's regulation ordering the recitation of this particular prayer on the ground that these actions of official governmental agencies violate that part of the First Amendment of the Federal Constitution which commands that "Congress shall make no law respecting an establishment of religion"—a command which was "made applicable to the State of New York by the Fourteenth Amendment of the said Constitution." The New York Court of Appeals, over the dissents of Judges Dye and Fuld, sustained an order of the lower state courts which had upheld the power of New York to use the Regents' prayer as a part of the daily procedures of its public schools so long as the schools did not compel any pupil to join in the prayer over his or his parents' objection. We granted certiorari to review this important decision involving rights protected by the First and Fourteenth Amendments.

We think that by using its public school system to encourage recitation of the Regents' prayer, the State of New York has adopted a practice wholly inconsistent with the Establishment Clause. There can, of course, be no doubt that New York's program of daily classroom invocation of God's blessings as prescribed in the Regents' prayer is a religious activity. It is a solemn avowal of divine faith and supplication for the blessings of the Almighty. The nature of such a prayer has always been religious, none of the respondents has denied this and the trial court expressly so found:

> The religious nature of prayers was recognized by Jefferson and has been concurred in by theological writers, the United States Supreme Court and state courts and administrative officials, including New York's Commissioner of Education. A committee of the New York Legislature has agreed.
>
> The Board of Regents as *amicus curiae,* the respondents and intervenors all concede the religious nature of prayer, but seek to distinguish this prayer because it is based on our spiritual heritage. . . .

The petitioners contend among other things that the state laws requiring or permitting use of the Regents' prayer must be struck down as a violation of the Establishment Clause because that prayer was composed by governmental officials as a part of a governmental program to further religious beliefs. For this reason, petitioners argue, the State's use of the Regents' prayer in its public school system breaches the constitutional wall of separation between Church and State. We agree with that contention since we think that the constitutional prohibition against laws respecting an establishment of religion must at least mean that in this country it is no part of the business of government to compose official prayers for any group of the American people to recite as a part of a religious program carried on by government.

It is a matter of history that this very practice of establishing governmentally composed prayers for religious services was one of the reasons which caused many of our early colonists to leave England and seek religious freedom in America. The Book of Common Prayer, which was created under governmental direction and which was approved by Acts of Parliament in 1548 and 1549, set out in minute detail the accepted form and content of prayer and other religious ceremonies to be used in the established, tax-supported Church of England. The controversies over the Book and what should be its content repeatedly threatened to disrupt the peace of that country as the accepted forms of prayer in the established church changed with the views of the particular ruler that happened to be in control at the time. Powerful groups representing some of the varying religious views of the people struggled among themselves to impress their particular views upon the Government and obtain amendments of the Book more suitable to their respective notions of how religious services should be conducted in order that the official religious establishment would advance their particular religious beliefs. Other groups, lacking the necessary political power to influence the Government on the matter, decided to leave England and its established church and seek freedom in America from England's governmentally ordained and supported religion.

It is an unfortunate fact of history that when some of the very groups which had most strenuously opposed the established Church of England found themselves sufficiently in control of colonial governments in this country to write their own prayers into law, they passed laws making their own religion the official religion of their respective colonies. Indeed, as late as the time of the Revolutionary War, there were established churches in at least eight of the thirteen former colonies and established religions in at least four of the other five. But the successful Revolution against English political domination was shortly followed by intense opposition to the practice of establishing religion by law. This opposition crystallized rapidly into an effective political force in Virginia where the minority religious groups such as Presbyterians, Lutherans, Quakers and Baptists had gained such strength that the adherents to the established Episcopal Church were actually a minority themselves. In 1785–1786, those opposed to the established Church, led by James Madison and Thomas Jefferson, who, though themselves not members of any of these dissenting religious groups, opposed all religious establishments by law on grounds of principle, obtained the enactment of the famous "Virginia Bill for Religious Liberty" by which all religious groups were placed on an equal footing so far as the State was concerned. Similar though less far-reaching legislation was being considered and passed in other States.

By the time of the adoption of the Constitution, our history shows that there was a widespread awareness among many Americans of the dangers of a union of Church and State. These people knew, some of them from bitter personal experience, that one of the greatest dangers to the freedom of the individual to worship in his own way lay in the Government's placing its official stamp of approval upon one particular kind of prayer or one particular form of religious services. They knew the anguish, hardship and bitter strife that could come when zealous religious groups struggled with one another to obtain the Government's stamp of approval from each King, Queen, or Protector that came to temporary power. The Constitution was intended to avert a part of this danger by leaving the government of this country in the hands of the people rather than in the hands of any monarch. But this safeguard was not enough. Our Founders were no more willing to let the content of their prayers and their privilege of praying whenever they pleased be influenced by the ballot box than they were to let these vital matters of personal conscience depend upon the succession of monarchs. The First Amendment was added to the Constitution to stand as a guarantee that neither the power nor the prestige of the Federal Government would be used to control, support or influence the kinds of prayer the American people can say—that the people's religions must not be subjected to the pressures of government for change each time a new political administration is elected to office. Under that Amendment's prohibition against governmental establishment of religion, as reinforced by the provisions of the Fourteenth Amendment, government in this country, be it state or federal, is without power to prescribe by law any particular form of prayer which is to be used as an official prayer in carrying on any program of governmentally sponsored religious activity.

There can be no doubt that New York's state prayer program officially establishes the religious beliefs embodied in the Regents' prayer. The respondents' argument to the contrary, which is largely based upon the contention that the Regents' prayer is "nondenominational" and the fact that the program, as modified and approved by state courts, does not require all pupils to recite the prayer but permits those who wish to do so to remain silent or be excused from the room, ignores the essential nature of the program's constitutional defects. Neither the fact that prayer may be denominationally neutral nor the fact that its observance on the part of the students is voluntary can serve to free it from the limitations of the Establishment Clause, as it might from the Free Exercise Clause, of the First Amendment, both of which are operative against the States by virtue of the Fourteenth Amendment. Although these two clauses may in certain instances overlap, they forbid two quite different kinds of governmental encroachment upon religious freedom. The Establishment Clause, unlike the Free Exercise Clause, does not depend upon any showing of direct governmental compulsion and is violated by the enactment of laws which establish an official religion whether those laws operate directly to coerce nonobserving individuals or not. This is not to say, of course, that laws officially prescribing a particular form of religious worship do not involve coercion of such individuals. When the power, prestige and financial support of government is placed behind a particular religious belief, the indirect coercive pressure upon religious minorities to conform to the prevailing officially approved religion is plain. But the purposes underlying the Establishment Clause go much further than that. Its first and most immediate purpose rested on the belief that a union of government and religion tends to destroy government and to degrade religion. The history of governmentally established religion, both in England and in this country, showed that whenever government had allied itself with one particular form of religion, the inevitable result had been that it had incurred the hatred, disrespect and even contempt of those who held contrary beliefs. That same history showed that many people had lost their respect for any religion that had relied upon the support of government to spread its faith. The Establishment Clause thus stands as an expression of principle on the part of the Founders of our Constitution that religion is too personal, too sacred, too holy, to permit its "unhallowed perversion" by a civil magistrate. Another purpose of the Establishment Clause rested upon an awareness of the historical fact that governmentally established religions and religious persecutions go hand in hand. The Founders knew that only a few years after the Book of Common Prayer became the only accepted form of religious services in the established Church of England, an Act of Uniformity was passed to compel all Englishmen to attend those services and to make it a criminal offense to conduct or attend religious gatherings of any other kind—a law which was consistently flouted by dissenting religious groups in England and which contributed to widespread persecutions of people like John Bunyan who persisted in holding "unlawful [religious] meetings . . . to the great disturbance and distraction of the good subjects of this kingdom. . . ." And they knew that similar persecutions had received the sanction of law in several of the colonies in this country soon after the establishment of official religions in those colonies. It was in large part to get completely away from this sort of systematic religious persecution that the Founders brought into being our Nation, our Constitution, and our Bill of Rights with its prohibition against any governmental establishment of religion. The New York laws officially prescribing the Regents' prayer are inconsistent both with the purposes of the Establishment Clause and with the Establishment Clause itself.

It has been argued that to apply the Constitution in such a way as to prohibit state laws respecting an establishment of religious services in public schools is to indicate a hostility toward religion or toward prayer. Nothing, of course, could be more wrong. The history of man is inseparable from the history of religion. And perhaps it is not too much to say that since the beginning of that history many people have devoutly believed that "More things are wrought by prayer than this world dreams of." It was doubtless largely due to men who believed this that there grew up a sentiment that caused men to leave the cross-currents of officially established state religions and religious persecution in Europe and come to this country filled with the hope that they could find a place in which they could pray when they pleased to the God of their faith in the language they chose. And there were men of this same faith in the power of prayer who led the fight for adoption of our Constitution and also for our Bill of Rights with the very guarantees of religious freedom that forbid the sort of governmental activity which New York has attempted here. These men knew that the First Amendment, which tried to put an end to governmental control of religion and of prayer, was not written to destroy either. They knew rather that it was written to quiet well-justified fears which nearly all of them felt arising out of an awareness that governments of the past had shackled men's tongues to make them speak only the religious thoughts that government wanted them to speak and to pray only to the God that government wanted them to pray to. It is neither sacrilegious nor antireligious to say that each separate government in this country should stay out of the business of writing or sanctioning official prayers and leave that purely religious function to the people themselves and to those the people choose to look to for religious guidance.*

It is true that New York's establishment of its Regents' prayer as an officially approved religious doctrine of that State does not amount to a total establishment of one particular religious sect to the exclusion of all others—that, indeed, the governmental endorsement of that prayer seems relatively insignificant when compared to the governmental encroachments upon religion which were commonplace 200 years ago. To those who may subscribe to the view that because the Regents' official prayer is so brief and general there can be no danger to religious freedom in its governmental establishment, however, it may be appropriate to say in the words of James Madison, the author of the First Amendment:

> [I]t is proper to take alarm at the first experiment on our liberties. . . . Who does not see that the same authority which can establish Christianity, in exclusion of all other Religions, may establish with the same ease any particular sect of Christians, in exclusion of all other Sects? That the same authority which can force a citizen to contribute three pence only of his property for the support of any one establishment, may force him to conform to any other establishment in all cases whatsoever?

The judgment of the Court of Appeals of New York is reversed and the cause remanded for further proceedings not inconsistent with this opinion.

Reversed and remanded.

MR. JUSTICE STEWART, DISSENTING.

A local school board in New York has provided that those pupils who wish to do so may join in a brief prayer at the beginning of each

*There is of course nothing in the decision reached here that is inconsistent with the fact that school children and others are officially encouraged to express love for our country by reciting historical documents such as the Declaration of Independence which contain references to the Deity or by singing officially espoused anthems which include the composer's professions of faith in a Supreme Being, or with the fact that there are many manifestations in our public life of belief in God. Such patriotic or ceremonial occasions bear no true resemblance to the unquestioned religious exercise that the State of New York has sponsored in this instance.

school day, acknowledging their dependence upon God and asking His blessing upon them and upon their parents, their teachers, and their country. The Court today decides that in permitting this brief non-denominational prayer the school board has violated the Constitution of the United States. I think this decision is wrong.

The Court does not hold, nor could it, that New York has interfered with the free exercise of anybody's religion. For the state courts have made clear that those who object to reciting the prayer must be entirely free of any compulsion to do so, including any "embarrassments and pressures." But the Court says that in permitting school children to say this simple prayer, the New York authorities have established "an official religion."

With all respect, I think the Court has misapplied a great constitutional principle. I cannot see how an "official religion" is established by letting those who want to say a prayer say it. On the contrary, I think that to deny the wish of these school children to join in reciting this prayer is to deny them the opportunity of sharing in the spiritual heritage of our Nation.

The Court's historical review of the quarrels over the Book of Common Prayer in England throws no light for me on the issue before us in this case. England had then and has now an established church. Equally unenlightening, I think, is the history of the early establishment and later rejection of an official church in our own States. For we deal here not with the establishment of a state church, which would, of course, be constitutionally impermissible, but with whether school children who want to begin their day by joining in prayer must be prohibited from doing so. Moreover, I think that the Court's task, in this as in all areas of constitutional adjudication, is not responsibly aided by the uncritical invocation of metaphors like the "wall of separation," a phrase nowhere to be found in the Constitution. What is relevant to the issue here is not the history of an established church in sixteenth century England or in eighteenth century America, but the history of the religious traditions of our people, reflected in countless practices of the institutions and officials of our government.

At the opening of each day's Session of this Court we stand, while one of our officials invokes the protection of God. Since the days of John Marshall our Crier has said, "God save the United States and this Honorable Court." Both the Senate and the House of Representatives open their daily Sessions with prayer. Each of our Presidents, from George Washington to John F. Kennedy, has upon assuming his Office asked the protection and help of God.

The Court today says that the state and federal governments are without constitutional power to prescribe any particular form of words to be recited by any group of the American people on any subject touching religion. One of the stanzas of "The Star-Spangled Banner," made our National Anthem by Act of Congress in 1931, contains these verses:

> Blest with victory and peace, may
> the heav'n rescued land
> Praise the Pow'r that hath made
> and preserved us a nation!
> Then conquer we must, when our
> cause it is just,
> And this be our motto "In God is
> our Trust."

In 1954 Congress added a phrase to the Pledge of Allegiance to the Flag so that it now contains the words "one Nation *under God,* indivisible, with liberty and justice for all." In 1952 Congress enacted legislation calling upon the President each year to proclaim a National Day of Prayer. Since 1865 the words "IN GOD WE TRUST" have been impressed on our coins.

Countless similar examples could be listed, but there is no need to belabor the obvious. It was all summed up by this Court just ten years ago in a single sentence: "We are a religious people whose institutions presuppose a Supreme Being." *Zorach v. Clauson.*

I do not believe that this Court, or the Congress, or the President has by the actions and practices I have mentioned established an "official religion" in violation of the Constitution. And I do not believe the State of New York has done so in this case. What each has done has been to recognize and to follow the deeply entrenched and highly cherished spiritual traditions of our Nation—traditions which come down to us from those who almost two hundred years ago avowed their "firm Reliance on the Protection of divine Providence" when they proclaimed the freedom and independence of this brave new world.

I dissent.

School District of Abington Township v. Schempp, 374 U.S. 203 (1963)

By the decision rendered by Justice Clark, with only a single dissent from Justice Stewart, the Court proscribed public school exercises that are exclusively religious. In extending the *Engel* decision in this instance, the Court established purpose and effect tests regarding the Establishment Clause. Justice Clark stated that two questions had to be asked about a law that is challenged. For a law to be valid, "there must be a secular legislative purpose and a primary effect that neither advances nor inhibits religion." The storm of public protest over this subject continued with serious efforts by members of Congress (Representative Becker, Senator Dirksen) either to amend the First Amendment or to exclude specifically Bible reading and prayer from inclusion under its prohibitions.*

Justice Brennan, in a concurring opinion, laid out a rationale that offered an involved historical analysis in which he detailed the intense public debate, in the nineteenth century, over officially sanctioned sectarian practices in public schools.

Under the title of this case, another—*Murray v. Curlett*—was decided as well. Its singular importance grows from the involvement of Madalyn Murray, who would attain national notoriety as the leader of an atheist movement.

MR. JUSTICE CLARK DELIVERED THE OPINION OF THE COURT.

Once again we are called upon to consider the scope of the provision of the First Amendment to the United States Constitution which declares that "Congress shall make no law respecting an establishment of religion, or prohibiting the free exercise thereof. . . ." These companion cases present the issues in the context of state action requiring that schools begin each day with readings from the Bible. While raising the basic questions under slightly different factual situations, the cases permit of joint treatment. In light of the history of the First Amendment and of our cases interpreting and applying its requirements, we hold that the practices at issue and the laws requiring them are unconstitutional under the Establishment Clause, as applied to the States through the Fourteenth Amendment.

*The deletions noted in this opinion are of lengthy citations of earlier cases.

I

The Facts in Each Case: No. 142. The Commonwealth of Pennsylvania by law requires that "At least ten verses from the Holy Bible shall be read, without comment, at the opening of each public school on each school day. Any child shall be excused from such Bible reading, or attending such Bible reading, upon the written request of his parent or guardian." The Schempp family, husband and wife and two of their three children, brought suit to enjoin enforcement of the statute, contending that their rights under the Fourteenth Amendment to the Constitution of the Untied States are, have been, and will continue to be violated unless this statute be declared unconstitutional as violative of these provisions of the First Amendment. They sought to enjoin the appellant school district, wherein the Schempp children attend school, and its officers and the Superintendent of Public Instruction of the Commonwealth from continuing to conduct such readings and recitation of the Lord's Prayer in the public schools of the district pursuant to the statute. A three-judge statutory District Court for the Eastern District of Pennsylvania held that the statute is violative of the Establishment Clause of the First Amendment as applied to the States by the Due Process Clause of the Fourteenth Amendment and directed that appropriate injunctive relief issue. On appeal by the District, its officials and the Superintendent, we noted probable jurisdiction.

The appellees Edward Lewis Schempp, his wife Sidney, and their children, Roger and Donna, are of the Unitarian faith and are members of the Unitarian Church in Germantown, Philadelphia, Pennsylvania, where they, as well as another son, Ellory, regularly attend religious services. The latter was originally a party but having graduated from the school system *pendente lite* was voluntarily dismissed from the action. The other children attend the Abington Senior High School, which is a public school operated by appellant district.

On each school day at the Abington Senior High School between 8:15 and 8:30 a.m., while the pupils are attending their home rooms or advisory sections, opening exercises are conducted pursuant to the statute. The exercises are broadcast into each room in the school building through an intercommunications system and are conducted under the supervision of a teacher by students attending the school's radio and television workshop. Selected students from this course gather each morning in the school's workshop studio for the exercises, which include readings by one of the students of 10 verses of the Holy Bible, broadcast to each room in the building. This is followed by the recitation of the Lord's Prayer, likewise over the intercommunications system, but also by the students in the various classrooms, who are asked to stand and join in repeating the prayer in unison. The exercises are closed with the flag salute and such pertinent announcements as are of interest to the students. Participation in the opening exercises, as directed by the statute, is voluntary. The student reading the verses from the Bible may select the passages and read from any version he chooses, although the only copies furnished by the school are the King James version, copies of which were circulated to each teacher by the school district. During the period in which the exercises have been conducted the King James, the Douay and the Revised Standard versions of the Bible have been used, as well as the Jewish Holy Scriptures. There are no prefatory statements, no questions asked or solicited, no comments or explanations made and no interpretations given at or during the exercises. The students and parents are advised that the student may absent himself from the classroom or, should he elect to remain, not participate in the exercises.

It appears from the record that in schools not having an intercommunications system the Bible reading and the recitation of the Lord's Prayer were conducted by the home-room teacher, who chose the text of the verses and read them herself or had students read them in rotation or by volunteers. This was followed by a standing recitation of the Lord's Prayer, together with the Pledge of Allegiance to the Flag by the class in unison and a closing announcement of routine school items of interests.

At the first trial Edward Schempp and the children testified as to specific religious doctrines purveyed by a literal reading of the Bible "which were contrary to the religious beliefs which they held and to their familial teaching." The children testified that all of the doctrines to which they referred were read to them at various times as part of the exercises. Edward Schempp testified at the second trial that he had considered having Roger and Donna excused from attendance at the exercises but decided against it for several reasons, including his belief that the children's relationships with their teachers and classmates would be adversely affected.

Expert testimony was introduced by both appellants and appellees at the first trial, which testimony was summarized by the trial court as follows:

> Dr. Solomon Grayzel testified that there were marked differences between the Jewish Holy Scriptures and the Christian Holy Bible, the most obvious of which was the absence of the New Testament in the Jewish Holy Scriptures. Dr. Grayzel testified that portions of the New Testament were offensive to Jewish tradition and that, from the standpoint of Jewish faith, the concept of Jesus Christ as the Son of God was 'practically blasphemous.' He cited instances in the New Testament which, assertedly, were not only sectarian in nature but tended to bring the Jews into ridicule or scorn. Dr. Grayzel gave as his expert opinion that such material from the New Testament could be explained to Jewish children in such a way as to do no harm to them. But if portions of the New Testament were read without explanation, they could be, and in his specific experience with children Dr. Grayzel observed, had been, psychologically harmful to the child and had caused a divisive force within the social media of the school.
>
> Dr. Grayzel also testified that there was significant difference in attitude with regard to the respective Books of the Jewish and Christian Religions in that Judaism attaches no special significance to the reading of the Bible *per se* and that the Jewish Holy Scriptures are source materials to be studied. But Dr. Grayzel did state that many portions of the New, as well as of the Old Testament contained passages of great literary and moral value.
>
> Dr. Luther A. Weigle, an expert witness for the defense, testified in some detail as to the reasons for and the methods employed in developing the King James and the Revised Standard Versions of the Bible. On direct examination, Dr. Weigle stated that the Bible was non-sectarian. He later stated that the phrase 'non-sectarian' meant to him nonsectarian within the Christian faiths. Dr. Weigle stated that his definition of the Holy Bible would include the Jewish Holy Scriptures, but also stated that the 'Holy Bible' would not be complete without the New Testament. He stated that the New Testament 'conveyed the message of Christians.' In his opinion, reading of the Holy Scrip-

> tures to the exclusion of the New Testament would be a sectarian practice. Dr. Weigle stated that the Bible was of great moral, historical and literary value. This is conceded by all the parties and is also the view of the court.

The trial court, in striking down the practices and the statute requiring them, made specific findings of fact that the children's attendance at Abington Senior High School is compulsory and that the practice of reading 10 verses from the Bible is also compelled by law. It also found that:

> The reading of the verses, even without comment, possesses a devotional and religious character and constitutes in effect a religious observance. The devotional and religious nature of the morning exercises is made all the more apparent by the fact that the Bible reading is followed immediately by a recital in unison by the pupils of the Lord's Prayer. The fact that some pupils, or theoretically all pupils, might be excused from attendance at the exercises does not mitigate the obligatory nature of the ceremony for . . . Section 1516 . . . unequivocally requires the exercises to be held every school day in every school in the Commonwealth. The exercises are held in the school buildings and perforce are conducted by and under the authority of the local school authorities and during school sessions. Since the statute requires the reading of the 'Holy Bible,' a Christian document, the practice . . . prefers the Christian religion. The record demonstrates that it was the intention of . . . the Commonwealth . . . to introduce a religious ceremony into the public schools of the Commonwealth.

No. 119. In 1905 the Board of School Commissioners of Baltimore City adopted a rule pursuant to Art. 77, §202 of the Annotated Code of Maryland. The rule provided for the holding of opening exercises in the schools of the city, consisting primarily of the "reading, without comment, of a chapter in the Holy Bible and/or the use of the Lord's Prayer." The petitioners, Mrs. Madalyn Murray and her son, William J. Murray III, are both professed atheists. Following unsuccessful attempts to have the respondent school board rescind the rule, this suit was filed for mandamus to compel its rescission and cancellation. It was alleged that William was a student in a public school of the city and Mrs. Murray, his mother, was a taxpayer therein; that it was the practice under the rule to have a reading on each school morning from the King James version of the Bible; that at petitioners' insistence the rule was amended to permit children to be excused from the exercise on request of the parent and that William had been excused pursuant thereto; that nevertheless the rule as amended was in violation of the petitioners' rights "to freedom of religion under the First and Fourteenth Amendments" and in violation of "the principle of separation between church and state, contained therein. . . ." The petition particularized the petitioners' atheistic beliefs and stated that the rule, as practiced, violated their rights

> in that it threatens their religious liberty by placing a premium on belief as against non-belief and subjects their freedom of conscience to the rule of the majority; it pronounces belief in God as the source of all moral and spiritual values, equating these values with religious values, and thereby renders sinister, alien and suspect the beliefs and ideals of your Petitioners, promoting doubt and question of their morality, good citizenship and good faith.

The respondents demurred and the trial court, recognizing that the demurrer admitted all facts well pleaded, sustained it without leave to amend. The Maryland Court of Appeals affirmed, the majority of four justices holding the exercise not in violation of the First and Fourteenth Amendments, with three justices dissenting. We granted certiorari.

II

It is true that religion has been closely identified with our history and government. As we said in *Engel,* "The history of man is inseparable from the history of religion. And . . . since the beginning of that history many people have devoutly believed that 'More things are wrought by prayer than this world dreams of.'" In *Zorach,* we gave specific recognition to the proposition that "[w]e are a religious people whose institutions presuppose a Supreme Being." The fact that the Founding Fathers believed devotedly that there was a God and that the unalienable rights of man were rooted in Him is clearly evidenced in their writings, from the Mayflower Compact to the Constitution itself. This background is evidenced today in our public life through the continuance in our oaths of office from the Presidency to the Alderman of the final supplication, "So help me God." Likewise each House of the Congress provides through its Chaplain an opening prayer, and the sessions of this Court are declared open by the crier in a short ceremony, the final phrase of which invokes the grace of God. Again, there are such manifestations in our military forces, where those of our citizens who are under the restrictions of military service wish to engage in voluntary worship. Indeed, only last year an official survey of the country indicated that 64% of our people have church membership, Bureau of the Census, U.S. Department of Commerce, Statistical Abstract of the United States 48, while less than 3% profess no religion whatever. It can be truly said, therefore, that today, as in the beginning, our national life reflects a religious people who, in the words of Madison, are "earnestly praying, as . . . in duty bound, that the Supreme Lawgiver of the Universe . . . guide them into every measure which may be worthy of his [blessing. . . .]"

This is not to say, however, that religion has been so identified with our history and government that religious freedom is not likewise as strongly imbedded in our public and private life. Nothing but the most telling of personal experiences in religious persecution suffered by our forebears could have planted our belief in liberty of religious opinion any more deeply in our heritage. It is true that this liberty frequently was not realized by the colonists, but this is readily accountable by their close ties to the Mother Country. However, the views of Madison and Jefferson, preceded by Roger Williams, came to be incorporated not only in the Federal Constitution but likewise in those of most of our States. This freedom to worship was indispensable in a country whose people came from the four quarters of the earth and brought with them a diversity of religious opinion. Today authorities list 83 separate religious bodies, each with membership exceeding 50,000, existing among our people, as well as innumerable smaller groups.

III

Before examining this "neutral" position in which the Establishment and Free Exercise Clauses of the First Amendment place our Government it is well that we discuss the reach of the Amendment under the cases of this Court.

First, this Court has decisively settled that the First Amendment's mandate that "Congress shall make no law respecting an establishment of religion, or prohibiting the free exercise thereof" has been made wholly applicable to the States by the Fourteenth Amendment.

* * * * *

Second, this Court has rejected unequivocally the contention that the Establishment Clause forbids only governmental preference of one religion over another.

* * * * *

IV

The interrelationship of the Establishment and the Free Exercise Clauses was first touched upon by Mr. Justice Roberts for the Court in *Cantwell,* where it was said that their "inhibition of legislation" had

> a double aspect. On the one hand, it forestalls compulsion by law of the acceptance of any creed or the practice of any form of worship. Freedom of conscience and freedom to adhere to such religious organization or form of worship as the individual may choose cannot be restricted by law. On the other hand, it safeguards the free exercise of the chosen form of religion. Thus the Amendment embraces two concepts,—freedom to believe and freedom to act. The first is absolute but, in the nature of things, the second cannot be.

A half dozen years later in *Everson,* this Court, through Mr. Justice Black, stated that the "scope of the First Amendment . . . was designed forever to suppress" the establishment of religion or the prohibition of the free exercise thereof. In short, the Court held that the Amendment

> requires the state to be a neutral in its relations with groups of religious believers and non-believers; it does not require the state to be their adversary. State power is no more to be used so as to handicap religions then it is to favor them.

. . . Only one year later the Court was asked to reconsider and repudiate the doctrine of these cases in *McCollum.* It was argued that "historically the First Amendment was intended to forbid only government preference of one religion over another. . . . In addition they ask that we distinguish or overrule our holding in the *Everson* case that the Fourteenth Amendment made the 'establishment of religion' clause of the First Amendment applicable as a prohibition against the States." The Court, with Mr. Justice Reed alone dissenting, was unable to "accept either of these contentions." Mr. Justice Frankfurter, joined by Justices Jackson, Rutledge and Burton, wrote a very comprehensive and scholarly concurrence in which he said that "[s]eparation is a requirement to abstain from fusing functions of Government and of religious sects, not merely to treat them all equally." Continuing, he stated that:

> the Constitution . . . prohibited the Government common to all from becoming embroiled, however innocently, in the destructive religious conflicts of which the history of even this country records some dark pages.

In 1952 in *Zorach,* Mr. Justice Douglas for the Court reiterated:

> There cannot be the slightest doubt that the First Amendment reflects the philosophy that Church and State should be separated. And so far as interference with the "free exercise" of religion and an "establishment" of religion are concerned, the separation must be complete and unequivocal. The First Amendment within the scope of its coverage permits no exception; the prohibition is absolute. The First Amendment, however, does not say that in every and all respects there shall be a separation of Church and State. Rather, it studiously defines the manner, the specific ways, in which there shall be no concert or union or dependency one on the other. That is the common sense of the matter.

And then in 1961 in *McGowan* and in *Torcaso* each of these cases was discussed and approved. Chief Justice Warren in *McGowan,* for a unanimous Court on this point, said:

> But, the First Amendment, in its final form, did not simply bar a congressional enactment *establishing a church;* it forbade all laws *respecting an establishment of religion.* Thus, this Court has given the Amendment a "broad interpretation . . . in the light of its history and the evils it was designed forever to suppress. . . ."

And Mr. Justice Black for the Court in *Torcaso,* without dissent but with Justices Frankfurter and Harlan concurring in the result, used this language:

> We repeat and again reaffirm that neither a State nor the Federal Government can constitutionally force a person "to profess a belief or disbelief in any religion." Neither can constitutionally pass laws or impose requirements which aid all religions as against non-believers, and neither can aid those religions based on a belief in the existence of God as against those religions founded on different beliefs.

Finally, in *Engel* only last year, these principles were so universally recognized that the Court, without the citation of a single case and over the sole dissent of Mr. Justice Stewart, reaffirmed them. The Court found the 22-word prayer used in "New York's program of daily classroom invocation of God's blessings as prescribed in the Regents' prayer . . . [to be] a religious activity." It held that "it is no part of the business of government to compose official prayers for any group of the American people to recite as a part of a religious program carried on by government." . . .

V

The wholesome "neutrality" of which this Court's cases speak thus stems from a recognition of the teachings of history that powerful sects or groups might bring about a fusion of governmental and religious functions or a concert or dependency of one upon the other to the end that official support of the State or Federal Government would be placed behind the tenets of one or of all orthodoxies. This the Establishment Clause prohibits. And a further reason for neutrality is found in the Free Exercise Clause, which recognizes the value of religious training, teaching and observance and, more particularly, the right of every person to freely choose his own course with reference thereto, free of any compulsion from the state. This the Free Exercise Clause guarantees. Thus, as we have seen, the two clauses may overlap. As we have indicated, the Establishment Clause has been directly considered by this Court eight times in the past score of years and, with only one Justice dissenting on the point, it has consistently held that the clause withdrew all legislative power respecting religious belief or the expression thereof. The test may be stated as follows: what are the purpose and the primary effect of the enactment? If either is the advancement or inhibition of religion then the enactment exceeds the scope of legislative power as circumscribed by the Constitution. That is to say that to withstand the strictures of the Establishment Clause there must be a secular legislative purpose and a primary effect that neither advances nor inhibits religion. The Free Exercise Clause, likewise considered many times here, withdraws from legislative power, state and federal, the exertion of any restraint on the free exercise of religion. Its purpose is to secure religious liberty in the individual by prohibiting any invasions thereof by civil authority. Hence it is necessary in a free exercise case for one to show the coercive effect of the enactment as it operates against him in the practice of his religion. The distinction between the two clauses is apparent—a violation of the Free Exercise Clause is predicated on coercion while the Establishment Clause violation need not be so attended.

Applying the Establishment Clause principles to the cases at bar we find that the States are requiring the selection and reading at the opening of the school day of verses from the Holy Bible and the recitation of the Lord's Prayer by the students in unison. These exercises are prescribed as part of the curricular activities of students who are required by law to attend school. They are held in the school buildings under the supervision and with the participation of teachers employed in those schools. None of these factors, other than compulsory school attendance, was present in the program upheld in *Zorach.* The trial court in No. 142 has found that such an opening exercise is a religious ceremony and was intended by the State to be so. We agree with the trial court's finding as to the religious character of the exercises. Given that finding, the exercises and the law requiring them are in violation of the Establishment Clause.

There is no such specific finding as to the religious character of the exercises in No. 119, and the State contends that the program is an effort to extend its benefits to all public school children without regard to their religious belief. Included within its secular purposes, it says, are the promotion of moral values, the contradiction to the materialistic trends of our times, the perpetuation of our institutions and the teaching of literature. The case came up on demurrer, of course, to a petition which alleged that the uniform practice under the rule had been to read from the King James version of the Bible and that the exercise was sectarian. The short answer, therefore, is that the religious character of the exercise was admitted by the State. But even if its purpose is not strictly religious, it is sought to be accomplished through readings, without comment, from the Bible. Surely the place of the Bible as an instrument of religion cannot be gainsaid, and the State's recognition of the pervading religious character of the ceremony is evident from the rule's specific permission of the alternative use of the Catholic Douay version as well as the recent amendment permitting nonattendance at the exercises. None of these factors is consistent with the contention that the Bible is here used either as an instrument for nonreligious moral inspiration or as a reference for the teaching of secular subjects.

The conclusion follows that in both cases the laws require religious exercises and such exercises are being conducted in direct violation of the rights of the appellees and petitioners. Nor are these required exercises mitigated by the fact that individual students may absent themselves upon parental request, for that fact furnishes no defense to a claim of unconstitutionality under the Establishment Clause. Further, it is no defense to urge that the religious practices here may be relatively minor encroachments on the First Amendment. The breach of neutrality that is today a trickling stream may all too soon become a raging torrent and, in the words of Madison, "it is proper to take alarm at the first experiment on our liberties."

It is insisted that unless these religious exercises are permitted a "religion of secularism" is established in the schools. We agree of course that the State may not establish a "religion of secularism" in the sense of affirmatively opposing or showing hostility to religion, thus "preferring those who believe in no religion over those who do believe." We do not agree, however, that this decision in any sense has that effect. In addition, it might well be said that one's education is not complete without a study of comparative religion or the history of religion and its relationship to the advancement of civilization. It certainly may be said that the Bible is worthy of study for its literary and historic qualities. Nothing we have said here indicates that such study of the Bible or of religion, when presented objectively as part of a secular program of education, may not be effected consistently with the First Amendment. But the exercises here do not fall into those categories. They are religious exercises, required by the States in violation of the command of the First Amendment that the Government maintain strict neutrality, neither aiding nor opposing religion.

Finally, we cannot accept that the concept of neutrality, which does not permit a State to require a religious exercise even with the consent of the majority of those affected, collides with the majority's right to free exercise of religion. While the Free Exercise Clause clearly prohibits the use of state action to deny the rights of free exercise to *anyone,* it has never meant that a majority could use the machinery of the State to practice its beliefs. Such a contention was effectively answered by Mr. Justice Jackson for the Court in *West Virginia Board of Education v. Barnette.*

> The very purpose of a Bill of Rights was to withdraw certain subjects from the vicissitudes of political controversy, to place them beyond the reach of majorities and officials and to establish them as legal principles to be applied by the courts. One's right to . . . freedom of worship . . . and other fundamental rights may not be submitted to vote; they depend on the outcome of no elections.

The place of religion in our society is an exalted one, achieved through a long tradition of reliance on the home, the church and the inviolable citadel of the individual heart and mind. We have come to recognize through bitter experience that it is not within the power of government to invade that citadel, whether its purpose or effect be to aid or oppose, to advance or retard. In the relationship between man and religion, the State is firmly committed to a position of neutrality. Though the application of that rule requires interpretation of a delicate sort, the rule itself is clearly and concisely stated in the words of the First Amendment. Applying that rule to the facts of these cases, we affirm the judgment in No. 142. In No. 119, the judgment is reversed and the cause remanded to the Maryland Court of Appeals for further proceedings consistent with this opinion.

It is so ordered.

MR. JUSTICE STEWART, DISSENTING.

I think the records in the two cases before us are so fundamentally deficient as to make impossible an informed or responsible determination of the constitutional issues presented. Specifically, I cannot agree that on these records we can say that the Establishment Clause has necessarily been violated. But I think there exist serious questions under both that provision and the Free Exercise Clause—insofar as each is imbedded in the Fourteenth Amendment—which require the remand of these cases for the taking of additional evidence.

I

The First Amendment declares that "Congress shall make no law respecting an establishment of religion, or prohibiting the free exercise thereof. . . ." It is, I think, a fallacious oversimplification to regard these two provisions as establishing a single constitutional standard of "separation of church and state," which can be mechanically applied in every case to delineate the required boundaries between government and religion. We err in the first place if we do not recognize, as a matter of history and as a matter of the imperatives of our free society, that religion and government must necessarily interact in countless ways. Secondly, the fact is that while in many contexts the Establishment Clause and the Free Exercise Clause fully complement each other, there are areas in which a doctrinaire reading of the Establishment Clause leads to irreconcilable conflict with the Free Exercise Clause.

A single obvious example should suffice to make the point. Spending federal funds to employ chaplains for the armed forces might be said to violate the Establishment Clause. Yet a lonely soldier stationed at some faraway outpost could surely complain that a government which did *not* provide him the opportunity for pastoral guidance was affirmatively prohibiting the free exercise of his religion. And such examples could readily be multiplied. The short of the matter is simply that the two relevant clauses of the First Amendment cannot accurately be reflected in a sterile metaphor which by its very nature may distort rather than illumine the problems involved in a particular case.

II

As a matter of history, the First Amendment was adopted solely as a limitation upon the newly created National Government. The events leading to its adoption strongly suggest that the Establishment Clause was primarily an attempt to insure that Congress not only would be powerless to establish a national church, but would also be unable to interfere with existing state establishments. Each State was left free to go its own way and pursue its own policy with respect to religion. Thus Virginia from the beginning pursued a policy of disestablishmentarianism. Massachusetts, by contrast, had an established church until well into the nineteenth century.

So matters stood until the adoption of the Fourteenth Amendment, or more accurately, until this Court's decision in *Cantwell.* In that case the Court said: "The First Amendment declares that Congress shall make no law respecting an establishment of religion or prohibiting the free exercise thereof. The Fourteenth Amendment has rendered the legislatures of the states as incompetent as Congress to enact such laws."

I accept without question that the liberty guaranteed by the Fourteenth Amendment against impairment by the States embraces in full the right of free exercise of religion protected by the First Amendment, and I yield to no one in my conception of the breadth of that freedom. I accept too the proposition that the Fourteenth Amendment has somehow absorbed the Establishment Clause, although it is not without irony that a constitutional provision evidently designed to leave the States free to go their own way should now have become a restriction upon their autonomy. But I cannot agree with what seems to me the insensitive definition of the Establishment Clause contained in the Court's opinion, nor with the different but, I think, equally mechanistic definitions contained in the separate opinions which have been filed.

III

Since the *Cantwell* pronouncement in 1940, this Court has only twice held invalid state laws on the ground that they were laws "respecting an establishment of religion" in violation of the Fourteenth Amendment. On the other hand, the Court has upheld against such a challenge laws establishing Sunday as a compulsory day of rest and a law authorizing reimbursement from public funds for the transportation of parochial school pupils.

Unlike other First Amendment guarantees, there is an inherent limitation upon the applicability of the Establishment Clause's ban on state support to religion. That limitation was succintly put in *Everson:* "State power is no more to be used so as to handicap religions than it is to favor them." And in a later case, this Court recognized that the limitation was one which was itself compelled by the free exercise guarantee. "To hold that a state cannot consistently with the First and Fourteenth Amendments utilize its public school system to aid any or all religious faiths or sects in the dissemination of their doctrines and ideals does not . . . manifest a governmental hostility to religion or religious teachings. A manifestation of such hostility would be at war with our national tradition as embodied in the First Amendment's guaranty of the free exercise of religion."

That the central value embodied in the First Amendment—and, more particularly, in the guarantee of "liberty" contained in the Fourteenth—is the safeguarding of an individual's right to free exercise of his religion has been consistently recognized. Thus, in the case of *Hamilton* v. *Regents,* Mr. Justice Cardozo, concurring, assumed that it was " . . . *the religious liberty* protected by the First Amendment against invasion by the nation [which] is protected by the Fourteenth Amendment against invasion by the states." (Emphasis added.) And in *Cantwell,* the purpose of those guarantees was described in the following terms: "On the one hand, it forestalls compulsion by law of the acceptance of any creed or the practice of any form of worship. Freedom of conscience and freedom to adhere to such religious organization or form of worship as the individual may choose cannot be restricted by law. On the other hand, it safeguards the free exercise of the chosen form of religion."

It is this concept of constitutional protection embodied in our decisions which makes the cases before us such difficult ones for me. For there is involved in these cases a substantial free exercise claim on the part of those who affirmatively desire to have their children's school day open with the reading of passages from the Bible.

It has become accepted that the decision in *Pierce,* upholding the right of parents to send their children to nonpublic schools, was ultimately based upon the recognition of the validity of the free exercise claim involved in that situation. It might be argued here that parents who wanted their children to be exposed to religious influences in school could, under *Pierce,* send their children to private or parochial schools. But the consideration which renders this contention too facile to be determinative has already been recognized by the Court: "Freedom of speech, freedom of the press, freedom of religion are available to all, not merely to those who can pay their own way."

It might also be argued that parents who want their children exposed to religious influences can adequately fulfill that wish off school property and outside school time. With all its surface persuasiveness, however, this argument seriously misconceives the basic constitutional justification for permitting the exercises at issue in these cases. For a compulsory state educational system so structures a child's life that if religious exercises are held to be an impermissible activity in schools, religion is placed at an artificial and state-created disadvantage. Viewed in this light, permission of such exercises for those who want them is necessary if the schools are truly to be neutral in the matter of religion. And a refusal to permit religious exercises thus is seen, not as the realization of state neutrality, but rather as the establishment of a religion of secularism, or at the least, as government support of the beliefs of those who think that religious exercises should be conducted only in private.

What seems to me to be of paramount importance, then, is recognition of the fact that the claim advanced here in favor of Bible reading is sufficiently substantial to make simple reference to the constitutional phrase "establishment of religion" as inadequate an analysis of the cases before us as the ritualistic invocation of the nonconstitutional phrase "separation of church and state." What these cases compel, rather, is an analysis of just what the "neutrality" is which is required by the interplay of the Establishment and Free Exercise Clauses of the First Amendment, as imbedded in the Fourteenth.

IV

Our decisions make clear that there is no constitutional bar to the use of government property for religious purposes. On the contrary, this Court has consistently held that the discriminatory barring of religious groups from public property is itself a violation of First and Fourteenth Amendment guarantees. A different standard has been applied to public school property, because of the coercive effect which the use by religious sects of a compulsory school system would necessarily have upon the children involved. But insofar as the *McCollum* decision rests on the Establishment rather than the Free Exercise Clause, it is clear that its effect is limited to religious instruction—to government support of proselytizing activities of religious sects by throwing the weight of secular authority behind the dissemination of religious tenets.

The dangers both to government and to religion inherent in official support of instruction in the tenets of various religious sects are absent in the present cases, which involve only a reading from the Bible unaccompanied by comments which might otherwise constitute instruction. Indeed, since, from all that appears in either record, any teacher who does not wish to do so is free not to participate, it cannot even be contended that some infinitesimal part of the salaries paid by the State are made contingent upon the performance of a religious function.

In the absence of evidence that the legislature or school board intended to prohibit local schools from substituting a different set of readings where parents requested such a change, we should not assume that the provisions before us—as actually administered—may not be construed simply as authorizing religious exercises, nor that the designations may not be treated simply as indications of the promulgating body's view as to the community's preference. We are under a duty to interpret these provisions so as to render them constitutional if reasonably possible. In the *Schempp* case there is evidence which indicates that variations were in fact permitted by the very school there involved, and that further variations were not introduced only because of the absence of requests from parents. And in the *Murray* case the Baltimore rule itself contains a provision permitting another version of the Bible to be substituted for the King James version.

If the provisions are not so construed, I think that their validity under the Establishment Clause would be extremely doubtful, because of the designation of a particular religious book and a denominational prayer. But since, even if the provisions are construed as I believe they must be, I think that the cases before us must be remanded for further evidence on other issues—thus affording the plaintiffs an opportunity to prove that local variations are not in fact permitted—I shall for the balance of this dissenting opinion treat the provisions before us as making the variety and content of the exercises, as well as a choice as to their implementation, matters which ultimately reflect the consensus of each local school community. In the absence of coercion upon those who do not wish to participate—because they hold less strong beliefs, other beliefs, or no beliefs at all—such provisions cannot, in my view, be held to represent the type of support of religion barred by the Establishment Clause. For the only support which such rules provide for religion is the withholding of state hostility—a simple acknowledgment on the part of secular authorities that the Constitution does not require extirpation of all expression of religious belief.

V

I have said that these provisions authorizing religious exercises are properly to be regarded as measures making possible the free exercise of religion. But it is important to stress that, strictly speaking, what is at issue here is a privilege rather than a right. In other words, the question presented is not whether exercises such as those at issue here are constitutionally compelled, but rather whether they are constitutionally invalid. And that issue, in my view, turns on the question of coercion.

It is clear that the dangers of coercion involved in the holding of religious exercises in a schoolroom differ qualitatively from those presented by the use of similar exercises or affirmations in ceremonies attended by adults. Even as to children, however, the duty laid upon government in connection with religious exercises in the public schools is that of refraining from so structuring the school environment as to put any kind of pressure on a child to participate in those exercises; it is not that of providing an atmosphere in which children are kept scrupulously insulated from any awareness that some of their fellows may want to open the school day with prayer, or of the fact that there exist in our pluralistic society differences of religious belief.

These are not, it must be stressed, cases like *Brown* v. *Board of Education,* in which this Court held that, in the sphere of public education, the Fourteenth Amendment's guarantee of equal protection of the laws required that race not be treated as a relevant factor. A segregated school system is not invalid because its operation is coercive; it is invalid simply because our Constitution presupposes that men are created equal, and that therefore racial differences cannot provide a valid basis for governmental action. Accommodation of religious differences on the part of the State, however, is not only permitted but required by that same Constitution.

The governmental neutrality which the First and Fourteenth Amendments require in the cases before us, in other words, is the extension of evenhanded treatment to all who believe, doubt, or disbelieve—a refusal on the part of the State to weight the scales of private choice. In these cases, therefore, what is involved is not state action based on impermissible categories, but rather an attempt by the State to accommodate those differences which the existence in our society of a variety of religious beliefs makes inevitable. The Constitution requires that such efforts be struck down only if they are proven to entail the use of the secular authority of government to coerce a preference among such beliefs.

It may well be, as has been argued to us, that even the supposed benefits to be derived from noncoercive religious exercises in public schools are incommensurate with the administrative problems which they would create. The choice involved, however, is one for each local community and its school board, and not for this Court. For, as I have said, religious exercises are not constitutionally invalid if they simply reflect differences which exist in the society from which the school draws its pupils. They become constitutionally invalid only if their administration places the sanction of secular authority behind one or more particular religious or irreligious beliefs.

To be specific, it seems to me clear that certain types of exercises would present situations in which no possibility of coercion on the part of secular officials could be claimed to exist. Thus, if such exercises were held either before or after the official school day, or if the school schedule were such that participation were merely one among a number of desirable alternatives, it could hardly be contended that the exercises did anything more than to provide an opportunity for the voluntary expression of religious belief. On the other hand, a law which provided for religious exercises during the school day and which contained no excusal provision would obviously be unconstitutionally coercive upon those who did not wish to participate. And even under a law containing an excusal provision, if the exercises were held during the school day, and no equally desirable alternative were provided by the school authorities, the likelihood that children might be under at least some psychological compulsion to participate would be great. In a case such as the latter, however, I think we would err if we *assumed* such coercion in the absence of any evidence.

VI

Viewed in this light, it seems to me clear that the records in both of the cases before us are wholly inadequate to support an informed or responsible decision. Both cases involve provisions which explicitly permit any student who wishes, to be excused from participation in the exercises. There is no evidence in either case as to whether there would exist any coercion of any kind upon a student who did not want to participate. No evidence at all was adduced in the *Murray* case, because it was decided upon a demurrer. All that we have in that case, therefore, is the conclusory language of a pleading. While such conclusory allegations are acceptable for procedural purposes, I think that the nature of the constitutional problem involved here clearly demands that no decision be made except upon evidence. In the *Schempp* case the record shows no more than a subjective prophecy by a parent of what he thought would happen if a request were made to be excused from participation in the exercises under the amended statute. No such request was ever made, and there is no evidence whatever as to what might or would actually happen, nor of what administrative arrangements the school actually might or could make to free from pressure of any kind those who do not want to participate in the exercises. There were no District Court findings on this issue, since the case under the amended statute was decided exclusively on Establishment Clause grounds.

What our Constitution indispensably protects is the freedom of each of us, be he Jew or Agnostic, Christian or Atheist, Buddhist or Freethinker, to believe or disbelieve, to worship or not worship, to pray or keep silent, according to his own conscience, uncoerced and unrestrained by government. It is conceivable that these school boards, or even all school boards, might eventually find it impossible to administer a system of religious exercises during school hours in such a way as to meet this constitutional standard—in such a way as completely to free from any kind of official coercion those who do not affirmatively want to participate. But I think we must not assume that school boards so lack the qualities of inventiveness and good will as to make impossible the achievement of that goal.

I would remand both cases for further hearings.

Epperson v. Arkansas, 393 U.S. 97 (1968)

Justice Fortas wrote the unanimous decision of the Court on this case concerning the teaching of evolution in the public schools of Arkansas. The legislation made it unlawful "to teach the theory or doctrine that mankind ascended or descended from a lower order of animals" or "to adopt or use in any such institution a textbook that teaches" such a theory. The law was found unconstitutional since it failed the "secular purpose" test. The thrust of the decision was to affirm that the curriculum of public schools must be secular. "The law's effort was confined to an attempt to blot out a particular theory because of its supposed conflict with the Biblical account, literally read." Plainly, the Court noted, the law is contrary to the mandate of the First, and in violation of the Fourteenth Amendment to the Constitution.

Following this decision, events in Arkansas focused upon a law that required teaching of "creationism" under a "balanced treatment" theory. An Arkansas federal district court found the statute unconstitutional since it deemed "creationism" to be a religious doctrine based on the biblical account in Genesis *(McLean v. Arkansas)*. The Supreme Court, in *Edwards v. Aguillard* (1987), used similar arguments to strike down a Louisiana Act with the same intent as the Arkansas law.

MR. JUSTICE FORTAS DELIVERED THE OPINION OF THE COURT.

I

This appeal challenges the constitutionality of the "anti-evolution" statute which the State of Arkansas adopted in 1928 to prohibit the teaching in its public schools and universities of the theory that man evolved from other species of life. The statute was a product of the upsurge of "fundamentalist" religious fervor of the twenties. The Arkansas statute was an adaptation of the famous Tennessee "monkey law" which that State adopted in 1925. The constitutionality of the Tennessee law was upheld by the Tennessee Supreme Court in the celebrated *Scopes* case in 1927.

The Arkansas law makes it unlawful for a teacher in any state-supported school or university "to teach the theory or doctrine that mankind ascended or descended from a lower order of animals," or "to adopt or use in any such institution a textbook that teaches" this theory. Violation is a misdemeanor and subjects the violator to dismissal from his position.

The present case concerns the teaching of biology in a high school in Little Rock. According to the testimony, until the events here in litigation, the official textbook furnished for the high school biology course did not have a section on the Darwinian Theory. Then, for the academic year 1965–1966, the school administration, on recommendation of the teachers of biology in the school system, adopted and prescribed a textbook which contained a chapter setting forth "the theory about the origin . . . of man from a lower form of animal."

Susan Epperson, a young woman who graduated from Arkansas' school system and then obtained her master's degree in zoology at the University of Illinois, was employed by the Little Rock school system in the fall of 1964 to teach 10th grade biology at Central High School. At the start of the next academic year, 1965, she was confronted by the new textbook (which one surmises from the record was not unwelcome to her). She faced at least a literal dilemma because she was supposed to use the new textbook for classroom instruction and presumably to teach the statutorily condemned chapter; but to do so would be a criminal offense and subject her to dismissal.

She instituted the present action in the Chancery Court of the State, seeking a declaration that the Arkansas statute is void and enjoining the State and the defendant officials of the Little Rock school system from dismissing her for violation of the statute's provisions. H. H. Blanchard, a parent of children attending the public schools, intervened in support of the action.

The Chancery Court, in an opinion by Chancellor Murray O. Reed, held that the statute violated the Fourteenth Amendment to the United States Constitution. The court noted that this Amendment encompasses the prohibitions upon state interference with freedom of speech and thought which are contained in the First Amendment. Accordingly, it held that the challenged statute is unconstitutional because, in violation of the First Amendment, it "tends to hinder the quest for knowledge, restrict the freedom to learn, and restrain the freedom to teach." In this perspective, the Act, it held, was an unconstitutional and void restraint upon the freedom of speech guaranteed by the Constitution.

On appeal, the Supreme Court of Arkansas reversed. Its two-sentence opinion is set forth in the margin. It sustained the statute as an exercise of the State's power to specify the curriculum in public schools. It did not address itself to the competing constitutional considerations.

Appeal was duly prosecuted to this Court. Only Arkansas and Mississippi have such "anti-evolution" or "monkey" laws on their books. There is no record of any prosecutions in Arkansas under its statute. It is possible that the statute is presently more of a curiosity than a vital fact of life in these States. Nevertheless, the present case was brought, the appeal as of right is properly here, and it is our duty to decide the issues presented.

II

At the outset, it is urged upon us that the challenged statute is vague and uncertain and therefore within the condemnation of the Due Process Clause of the Fourteenth Amendment. The contention that the

Act is vague and uncertain is supported by language in the brief opinion of Arkansas' Supreme Court. That court, perhaps reflecting the discomfort which the statute's quixotic prohibition necessarily engenders in the modern mind, stated that it "expresses no opinion" as to whether the Act prohibits "explanation" of the theory of evolution or merely forbids "teaching that the theory is true." Regardless of this uncertainty, the court held that the statute is constitutional.

On the other hand, counsel for the State, in oral argument in this Court, candidly stated that, despite the State Supreme Court's equivocation, Arkansas would interpret the statute "to mean that to make a student aware of the theory . . . just to teach that there was such a theory" would be grounds for dismissal and for prosecution under the statute; and he said "that the Supreme Court of Arkansas' opinion should be interpreted in that manner." He said: "If Mrs. Epperson would tell her students that 'Here is Darwin's theory, that man ascended or descended from a lower form of being,' then I think she would be under this statute liable for prosecution."

In any event, we do not rest our decision upon the asserted vagueness of the statute. On either interpretation of its language, Arkansas' statute cannot stand. It is of no moment whether the law is deemed to prohibit mention of Darwin's theory, or to forbid any or all of the infinite varieties of communication embraced within the term "teaching." Under either interpretation, the law must be stricken because of its conflict with the constitutional prohibition of state laws respecting an establishment of religion or prohibiting the free exercise thereof. The overriding fact is that Arkansas' law selects from the body of knowledge a particular segment which it proscribes for the sole reason that it is deemed to conflict with a particular religious doctrine; that is, with a particular interpretation of the Book of Genesis by a particular religious group.

III

The antecedents of today's decision are many and unmistakable. They are rooted in the foundation soil of our Nation. They are fundamental to freedom.

Government in our democracy, state and national, must be neutral in matters of religious theory, doctrine, and practice. It may not be hostile to any religion or to the advocacy of no-religion; and it may not aid, foster, or promote one religion or religious theory against another or even against the militant opposite. The First Amendment mandates governmental neutrality between religion and religion, and between religion and nonreligion.

As early as 1872, this Court said: "The law knows no heresy, and is committed to the support of no dogma, the establishment of no sect." This has been the interpretation of the great First Amendment which this Court has applied in the many and subtle problems which the ferment of our national life has presented for decision within the Amendment's broad command.

Judicial interposition in the operation of the public school system of the Nation raises problems requiring care and restraint. Our courts, however, have not failed to apply the First Amendment's mandate in our educational system where essential to safeguard the fundamental values of freedom of speech and inquiry and of belief. By and large, public education in our Nation is committed to the control of state and local authorities. Courts do not and cannot intervene in the resolution of conflicts which arise in the daily operation of school systems and which do not directly and sharply implicate basic constitutional values. On the other hand, "[t]he vigilant protection of constitutional freedoms is nowhere more vital than in the community of American schools." As this Court said in *Keyishian* v. *Board of Regents,* the First Amendment "does not tolerate laws that cast a pall of orthodoxy over the classroom."

The earliest cases in this Court on the subject of the impact of constitutional guarantees upon the classroom were decided before the Court expressly applied the specific prohibitions of the First Amendment to the States. But as early as 1923, the Court did not hesitate to condemn under the Due Process Clause "arbitrary" restrictions upon the freedom of teachers to teach and of students to learn. In that year, the Court, in an opinion by Justice McReynolds, held unconstitutional an Act of the State of Nebraska making it a crime to teach any subject in any language other than English to pupils who had not passed the eighth grade. The State's purpose in enacting the law was to promote civic cohesiveness by encouraging the learning of English and to combat the "baneful effect" of permitting foreigners to rear and educate their children in the language of the parents' native land. The Court recognized these purposes, and it acknowledged the State's power to prescribe the school curriculum, but it held that these were not adequate to support the restriction upon the liberty of teacher and pupil. The challenged statute, it held, unconstitutionally interfered with the right of the individual, guaranteed by the Due Process Clause, to engage in any of the common occupations of life and to acquire useful knowledge.

For purposes of the present case, we need not re-enter the difficult terrain which the Court, in 1923, traversed without apparent misgivings. We need not take advantage of the broad premise which the Court's decision in *Meyer* furnishes, nor need we explore the implications of that decision in terms of the justiciability of the multitude of controversies that beset our campuses today. Today's problem is capable of resolution in the narrower terms of the First Amendment's prohibition of laws respecting an establishment of religion or prohibiting the free exercise thereof.

There is and can be no doubt that the First Amendment does not permit the State to require that teaching and learning must be tailored to the principles or prohibitions of any religious sect or dogma. In *Everson* this Court, in upholding a state law to provide free bus service to school children, including those attending parochial schools, said: "Neither [a State nor the Federal Government] can pass laws which aid one religion, aid all religions, or prefer one religion over another."

At the following Term of Court, in *McCollum,* the Court held that Illinois could not release pupils from class to attend classes of instruction in the school buildings in the religion of their choice. This, it said, would involve the State in using tax-supported property for religious purposes, thereby breaching the "wall of separation" which, according to Jefferson, the First Amendment was intended to erect between church and state. While study of religions and of the Bible from a literary and historic viewpoint, presented objectively as part of a secular program of education, need not collide with the First Amendment's prohibition, the State may not adopt programs or practices in its public schools or colleges which "aid or oppose" any religion. This prohibition is absolute. It forbids alike the preference of a religious doctrine or the prohibition of theory which is deemed antagonistic to a particular dogma. As Mr. Justice Clark stated in *Joseph Burstyn, Inc.* v. *Wilson,* "the state has no legitimate interest in protecting any or all religions from views distasteful to them. . . ." The test was stated as follows in *Schempp:* "[W]hat are the purpose and the primary effect of the enactment? If either is the advancement or inhibition of religion then the enactment exceeds the scope of legislative power as circumscribed by the Constitution."

These precedents inevitably determine the result in the present case.

The State's undoubted right to prescribe the curriculum for its public schools does not carry with it the right to prohibit, on pain of criminal penalty, the teaching of a scientific theory or doctrine where that prohibition is based upon reasons that violate the First Amendment. It is much too late to argue that the State may impose upon the teachers in its schools any conditions that it chooses, however restrictive they may be of constitutional guarantees.

In the present case, there can be no doubt that Arkansas has sought to prevent its teachers from discussing the theory of evolution because it is contrary to the belief of some that the Book of Genesis must be the exclusive source of doctrine as to the origin of man. No suggestion has been made that Arkansas' law may be justified by considerations of state policy other than the religious views of some of its citizens. It is clear that fundamentalist sectarian conviction was and is the law's reason for existence. Its antecedent, Tennessee's "monkey law," candidly stated its purpose: to make it unlawful "to teach any theory that denies the story of the Divine Creation of man as taught in the Bible, and to teach instead that man has descended from a lower order of animals." Perhaps the sensational publicity attendant upon the *Scopes* trial induced Arkansas to adopt less explicit language. It eliminated Tennessee's reference to "the story of the Divine Creation of man" as taught in the Bible, but there is no doubt that the motivation for the law was the same: to suppress the teaching of a theory which, it was thought, "denied" the divine creation of man.

Arkansas' law cannot be defended as an act of religious neutrality. Arkansas did not seek to excise from the curricula of its schools and universities all discussion of the origin of man. The law's effort was confined to an attempt to blot out a particular theory because of its supposed conflict with the Biblical account, literally read. Plainly, the law is contrary to the mandate of the First, and in violation of the Fourteenth, Amendment to the Constitution.

The judgment of the Supreme Court of Arkansas is reversed.

Wallace v. Jaffree, 105 S.Ct. 2479 (1985)

Alabama had sought to establish a moment of silence in its schools that was, in the mind of the majority, patently sectarian. Justice Stevens, for the majority, pointed to the "purpose" test as fundamental. He saw a legislative intent "to return prayer to the public schools." Justice O'Connor, concurring, identified "the peculiar features of the Alabama law that render it invalid." In so arguing, Justice O'Connor left open the possibility that a more carefully worded moment-of-silence law might pass muster.

Justice Rehnquist issued a strong dissent in which he set forth a historical analysis of the origins of the First Amendment. Justice Rehnquist dismissed the Jefferson "separation of church and state" phrase as irrelevant to the First Amendment and saw no violation of the Establishment Clause in a generalized state endorsement of prayer.

Five years earlier, in 1980, the Court had used the "purpose test" in *Stone v. Graham* to declare unconstitutional a Kentucky law requiring the posting of the Ten Commandments in public schoolrooms. Rehnquist, in dissent, argued that the intent of the law was to demonstrate "the secular impact of the Ten Commandments."

JUSTICE STEVENS DELIVERED THE OPINION OF THE COURT.

At an early stage of this litigation, the constitutionality of three Alabama statutes was questioned: (1) § 16–1–20, enacted in 1978, which authorized a one-minute period of silence in all public schools "for meditation"; (2) § 16–1–20.1, enacted in 1981, which authorized a period of silence "for meditation or voluntary prayer"; and (3) § 16–1–20.2 enacted in 1982, which authorized teachers to lead "willing students" in a prescribed prayer to "Almighty God . . . the Creator and Supreme Judge of the world."

At the preliminary-injunction stage of this case, the District Court distinguished § 16–1–20 from the other two statutes. It then held that there was "nothing wrong" with § 16–1–20, but that § 16–1–20.1 and 16–1–20.2 were both invalid because the sole purpose of both was "an effort on the part of the State of Alabama to encourage a religious activity." After the trial on the merits, the District Court did not change its interpretation of these two statutes, but held that they were constitutional because, in its opinion, Alabama has the power to establish a state religion if it chooses to do so.

The Court of Appeals agreed with the District Court's initial interpretation of the purpose of both §§ 16–1–20.1 and 16–1–20.2, and held them both unconstitutional. We have already affirmed the Court of Appeals' holding with respect to § 16–1–20.2. Moreover, appellees have not questioned the holding that § 16–1–20 is valid. Thus, the narrow question for decision is whether § 16–1–20.1, which authorizes a period of silence for "meditation or voluntary prayer," is a law respecting the establishment of religion within the meaning of the First Amendment.

I

Appellee Ishmael Jaffree is a resident of Mobile County, Alabama. On May 28, 1982, he filed a complaint on behalf of three of his minor children; two of them were second-grade students and the third was then in kindergarten. The complaint named members of the Mobile County School Board, various school officials, and the minor plaintiffs' three teachers as defendants. The complaint alleged that the appellees brought the action "seeking principally a declaratory judgment and an injunction restraining the Defendants and each of them from maintaining or allowing the maintenance of regular religious prayer services or other forms of religious observances in the Mobile County Public Schools in violation of the First Amendment as made applicable to states by the Fourteenth Amendment to the United States Constitution." The complaint further alleged that two of the children had been subjected to various acts of religious indoctrination "from the beginning of the school year in September, 1981"; that the defendant teachers had "on a daily basis" led their classes in saying certain prayers in unison; that the minor children were exposed to ostracism from their peer group class members if they did not participate; and that Ishmael Jaffree had repeatedly but unsuccessfully requested that the devotional services be stopped. The original complaint made no reference to any Alabama statute.

On June 4, 1982, appellees filed an amended complaint seeking class certification, and on June 30, 1982, they filed a second amended complaint naming the Governor of Alabama and various State officials as additional defendants. In that amendment the appellees challenged the constitutionality of three Alabama statutes: §§ 16–1–20, 16–1–20.1, and 16–1–20.2.

On August 2, 1982, the District Court held an evidentiary hearing on appellees' motion for a preliminary injunction. At that hearing, State Senator Donald G. Holmes testified that he was the "prime sponsor" of the bill that was enacted in 1981 as § 16–1–20.1. He explained that the bill was an "effort to return voluntary prayer to our public schools . . . it is a beginning and a step in the right direction." Apart from the purpose to return voluntary prayer to public school, Senator Holmes unequivocally testified that he had "no other purpose in mind." A week after the hearing, the District Court entered a preliminary injunction. The court held that appellees were likely to prevail on the merits because the enactment of §§ 16–1–20.1 and 16–1–20.2 did not reflect a clearly secular purpose.

In November 1982, the District Court held a four-day trial on the merits. The evidence related primarily to the 1981–1982 academic year—the year after the enactment of § 16–1–20.1 and prior to the enactment of § 16–1–20.2. The District Court found that during that academic year each of the minor plaintiffs' teachers had led classes in prayer activities, even after being informed of appellees' objections to these activities.

In its lengthy conclusions of law, the District Court reviewed a number of opinions of this Court interpreting the Establishment Clause of the First Amendment, and then embarked on a fresh examination of the question whether the First Amendment imposes any barrier to the establishment of an official religion by the State of Alabama. After reviewing at length what is perceived to be newly discovered historical evidence, the District Court concluded that "the establishment clause of the first amendment to the United States Constitution does not prohibit the state from establishing a religion." In a separate opinion, the District Court dismissed appellees' challenge to the three Alabama statutes because of a failure to state any claim for which relief could be granted. The Court's dismissal of this challenge was also based on its conclusion that the Establishment Clause did not bar the States from establishing a religion.

The Court of Appeals consolidated the two cases; not surprisingly, it reversed. The Court of Appeals noted that this Court had considered and had rejected the historical arguments that the District Court found persuasive, and that the District Court had misapplied the doctrine of *stare decisis.* The Court of Appeals then held that the teachers' religious activities violated the Establishment Clause of the First Amendment. With respect to § 16–1–20.1 and § 16–1–20.2, the Court of Appeals stated that "both statutes advance and encourage religious activities." The Court of Appeals then quoted with approval the District Court's finding that § 16–1–20.1, and § 16–1–20.2, were efforts "'to encourage a religious activity. Even though these statutes are permissive in form, it is nevertheless state involvement respecting an establishment of religion.'" Thus, the Court of Appeals concluded that both statutes were "specifically the type which the Supreme Court addressed in *Engel.*"

A suggestion for rehearing en banc was denied over the dissent of four judges who expressed the opinion that the full court should reconsider the panel decision insofar as it held § 16–1–20.1 unconstitutional. When this Court noted probable jurisdiction, it limited argument to the question that those four judges thought worthy of reconsideration. The judgment of the Court of Appeals with respect to the other issues presented by the appeals was affirmed.

II

Our unanimous affirmance of the Court of Appeals' judgment concerning § 16–1–20.2 makes it unnecessary to comment at length on the District Court's remarkable conclusion that the Federal Constitution imposes no obstacle to Alabama's establishment of a state religion. Before analyzing the precise issue that is presented to us, it is nevertheless appropriate to recall how firmly embedded in our constitutional jurisprudence is the proposition that the several States have no greater power to restrain the individual freedoms protected by the First Amendment than does the Congress of the United States.

As is plain from its text, the First Amendment was adopted to curtail the power of Congress to interfere with the individual's freedom to believe, to worship, and to express himself in accordance with the dictates of his own conscience. Until the Fourteenth Amendment was added to the Constitution, the First Amendment's restraints on the exercise of federal power simply did not apply to the States. But when the Constitution was amended to prohibit any State from depriving any person of liberty without due process of law, that Amendment imposed the same substantive limitations on the States' power to legislate that the First Amendment had always imposed on the Congress' power. This Court has confirmed and endorsed this elementary proposition of law time and time again.

* * * * *

> The Court in *Barnette,* was faced with a state statute which required public school students to participate in daily public ceremonies by honoring the flag both with words and traditional

> salute gestures. In overruling its prior decision in *Gobitis,* the Court held that "a ceremony so touching matters of opinion and political attitude may [not] be imposed upon the individual by official authority under powers committed to any political organization under our Constitution." Compelling the affirmative act of a flag salute involved a more serious infringement upon personal liberties than the passive act of carrying the state motto on a license plate, but the difference is essentially one of degree. Here, as in *Barnette,* we are faced with a state measure which forces an individual, as part of his daily life—indeed constantly while his automobile is in public view—to be an instrument for fostering public adherence to an ideological point of view he finds unacceptable. In doing so, the State "invades the sphere of intellect and spirit which it is the purpose of the First Amendment to our Constitution to reserve from all official control." (*Wooley v. Maynard*)

Just as the right to speak and the right to refrain from speaking are complementary components of a broader concept of individual freedom of mind, so also the individual's freedom to choose his own creed is the counterpart of his right to refrain from accepting the creed established by the majority. At one time it was thought that this right merely proscribed the preference of one Christian sect over another, but would not require equal respect for the conscience of the infidel, the atheist, or the adherent of a non-Christian faith such as Mohammedism or Judaism. But when the underlying principle has been examined in the crucible of litigation, the Court has unambiguously concluded that the individual freedom of conscience protected by the First Amendment embraces the right to select any religious faith or none at all. This conclusion derives support not only from the interest in respecting the individual's freedom of conscience, but also from the conviction that religious beliefs worthy of respect are the product of free and voluntary choice by the faithful, and from recognition of the fact that the political interest in forestalling intolerance extends beyond intolerance among Christian sects—or even intolerance among "religions"—to encompass intolerance of the disbeliever and the uncertain. As Justice Jackson eloquently stated in *Barnette:*

> If there is any fixed star in our constitutional constellation, it is that no official, high or petty, can prescribe what shall be ortho-

> dox in politics, nationalism, religion, or other matters of opinion or force citizens to confess by word or act their faith therein.

The State of Alabama, no less than the Congress of the United States, must respect that basic truth.

When the Court has been called upon to construe the breadth of the Establishment Clause, it has examined the criteria developed over a period of many years. Thus, in *Lemon v. Kurtzman:*

> Every analysis in this area must begin with consideration of the cumulative criteria developed by the Court over many years. Three such tests may be gleaned from our cases. First, the statute must have a secular legislative purpose; second, its principal or primary effect must be one that neither advances nor inhibits religion; finally, the statute must not foster "an excessive government entanglement with religion."

It is the first of these three criteria that is most plainly implicated by this case. As the District Court correctly recognized, no consideration of the second or third criteria is necessary if a statute does not have a clearly secular purpose. For even though a statute that is motivated in part by a religious purpose may satisfy the first criterion, the First Amendment requires that a statute must be invalidated if it is entirely motivated by a purpose to advance religion.

In applying the purpose test, it is appropriate to ask "whether government's actual purpose is to endorse or disapprove of religion." In this case, the answer to that question is dispositive. For the record not only provides us with an unambiguous affirmative answer, but it also reveals that the enactment of § 16–1–20.1 was not motivated by any clearly secular purpose—indeed, the statute had *no* secular purpose.

IV

The sponsor of the bill that became § 16–1–20.1, Senator Donald Holmes, inserted into the legislative record—apparently without dissent—a statement indicating that the legislation was an "effort to return voluntary prayer" to the public schools. Later Senator Holmes confirmed this purpose before the District Court. In response to the question whether he had any purpose for the legislation other than returning voluntary prayer to public schools, he stated, "No, I did not have no other purpose in mind." The State did not present evidence of *any* secular purpose.

The unrebutted evidence of legislative intent contained in the legislative record and in the testimony of the sponsor of § 16–1–20.1 is confirmed by a consideration of the relationship between this statute and the two other measures that were considered in this case. The District Court found that the 1981 statute and its 1982 sequel had a common, nonsecular purpose. The wholly religious character of the later enactment is plainly evident from its text. When the differences between § 16–1–20.1 and its 1978 predecessor, § 16–1–20, are examined, it is equally clear that the 1981 statute has the same wholly religious character. . . .The only significant textual difference is the addition of the words "or voluntary prayer."

The legislative intent to return prayer to the public schools is, of course, quite different from merely protecting every student's right to engage in voluntary prayer during an appropriate moment of silence during the school day. The 1978 statute already protected that right, containing nothing that prevented any student from engaging in voluntary prayer during a silent minute of meditation. Appellants have not identified any secular purpose that was not fully served by § 16–1–20 before the enactment of § 16–1–20.1. Thus, only two conclusions are consistent with the text of § 16–1–20.1: (1) the statute was enacted to convey a message of State endorsement and promotion of prayer; or (2) the statute was enacted for no purpose. No one suggests that the statute was nothing but a meaningless or irrational act.

We must, therefore, conclude that the Alabama Legislature intended to change existing law and that it was motivated by the same purpose that the Governor's Answer to the Second Amended Complaint expresssly admitted; that the statement inserted in the legislative history revealed; and that Senator Holmes' testimony frankly described. The Legislature enacted § 16–1–20.1 despite the existence of § 16–1–20 for the sole purpose of expressing the State's endorsement of prayer activities for one minute at the beginning of each school day. The addition of "or voluntary prayer" indicates that the State intended to characterize prayer as a favored practice. Such an endorsement is not consistent with the established principle that the Government must pursue a course of complete neutrality toward religion.

The importance of that principle does not permit us to treat this as an inconsequential case involving nothing more than a few words of symbolic speech on behalf of the political majority. For whenever the

State itself speaks on a religious subject, one of the questions that we must ask is "whether the Government intends to convey a message of endorsement or disapproval of religion." The well-supported concurrent findings of the District Court and the Court of Appeals—that § 16–1–20.1 was intended to convey a message of State-approval of prayer activities in the public schools—make it unnecessary, and indeed inappropriate, to evaluate the practical significance of the addition of the words "or voluntary prayer" to the statute. Keeping in mind, as we must, "both the fundamental place held by the Establishment Clause in our constitutional scheme and the myriad, subtle ways in which Establishment Clause values can be eroded," we conclude that § 16–1–20.1 violates the First Amendment.

The judgment of the Court of Appeals is affirmed.

It is so ordered.

JUSTICE O'CONNOR, CONCURRING IN THE JUDGMENT.

Nothing in the United States Constitution as interpreted by this Court or in the laws of the State of Alabama prohibits public school students from voluntarily praying at any time before, during, or after the school day. Alabama has facilitated voluntary silent prayers of students who are so inclined by enacting Ala. Code § 16–1–20, which provides a moment of silence in appellees' schools each day. The parties to these proceedings concede the validity of this enactment. At issue in these appeals is the constitutional validity of an additional and subsequent Alabama statute, which both the District Court and the Court of Appeals concluded was enacted solely to officially encourage prayer during the moment of silence. I agree with the judgment of the Court that, in light of the findings of the Courts below and the history of its enactment, the Alabama Code violates the Establishment Clause of the First Amendment. In my view, there can be little doubt that the purpose and likely effect of this subsequent enactment is to endorse and sponsor voluntary prayer in the public schools. I write separately to identify the peculiar features of the Alabama law that render it invalid, and to explain why moment of silence laws in other States do not necessarily manifest the same infirmity. I also write to explain why neither history nor the Free Exercise Clause of the First Amendment validate the Alabama law struck down by the Court today.

I

* * * * *

The endorsement test does not preclude government from acknowledging religion or from taking religion into account in making law and policy. It does preclude government from conveying or attempting to convey a message that religion or a particular religious belief is favored or preferred. Such an endorsement infringes the religious liberty of the nonadherent, for "[w]hen the power, prestige and financial support of government is placed behind a particular religious belief, the indirect coercive pressure upon religious minorities to conform to the prevailing officially approved religion is plain." At issue today is whether state moment of silence statutes in general, and Alabama's moment of silence statute in particular, embody an impermissible endorsement of prayer in public schools.

A

Twenty-five states permit or require public school teachers to have students observe a moment of silence in their classrooms. A few statutes provide that the moment of silence is for the purpose of meditation alone. The typical statute, however, calls for a moment of silence at the beginning of the school day during which students may meditate, pray, or reflect on the activities of the day. Federal trial courts have divided on the constitutionality of these moment of silence laws. Relying on this Court's decisions disapproving vocal prayer and Bible reading in the public schools, the courts that have struck down the moment of silence statutes generally conclude that their purpose and effect is to encourage prayer in public schools.

The *Engel* and *Abington* decisions are not dispositive on the constitutionality of moment of silence laws. In those cases, public school teachers and students led their classes in devotional exercises. In *Engel,* a New York statute required teachers to lead their classes in a vocal prayer. The Court concluded that "it is no part of the business of government to compose official prayers for any group of the American people to recite as part of a religious program carried on by the government." In *Abington,* the Court addressed Pennsylvania and Maryland statutes that authorized morning Bible readings in public schools. The Court reviewed the purpose and effect of the statutes, concluded that they required religious exercises, and therefore found them to violate the Establishment Clause. Under all of these statutes, a student who did not share the religious beliefs expressed in the course of the exercise was left with the choice of participating, thereby compromising the nonadherent's beliefs, or withdrawing, thereby calling attention to his or her non-conformity. The decisions acknowledged the coercion implicit under the statutory schemes, but they expressly turned only on the fact that the government was sponsoring a manifestly religious exercise.

A state sponsored moment of silence in the public schools is different from state sponsored vocal prayer or Bible reading. First, a moment of silence is not inherently religious. Silence, unlike prayer or Bible reading, need not be associated with a religious exercise. Second, a pupil who participates in a moment of silence need not compromise his or her beliefs. During a moment of silence, a student who objects to prayer is left to his or her own thoughts, and is not compelled to listen to the prayers or thoughts of others. For these simple reasons, a moment of silence statute does not stand or fall under the Establishment Clause according to how the Court regards vocal prayer or Bible reading. Scholars and at least one member of this Court have recognized the distinction and suggested that a moment of silence in public schools would be constitutional. As a general matter, I agree. It is difficult to discern a serious threat to religious liberty from a room of silent, thoughtful schoolchildren.

By mandating a moment of silence, a State does not necessarily endorse any activity that might occur during the period. Even if a statute specifies that a student may choose to pray silently during a quiet moment, the State has not thereby encouraged prayer over other specified alternatives. Nonetheless, it is also possible that a moment of silence statute, either as drafted or as actually implemented, could effectively favor the child who prays over the child who does not. For example, the message of endorsement would seem inescapable if the teacher exhorts children to use the designated time to pray. Similarly, the face of the statute or its legislative history may clearly establish that it seeks to encourage or promote voluntary prayer over other alternatives, rather than merely provide a quiet moment that may be dedicated to prayer by those so inclined. The crucial question is whether the State has conveyed or attempted to convey the message that children should use the moment of silence for prayer. This question cannot be answered in the abstract, but instead requires courts to examine the history, language, and administration of a particular statute to determine whether it operates as an endorsement of religion.

* * * * *

B

The analysis above suggests that moment of silence laws in many States should pass Establishment Clause scrutiny because they do not favor the child who chooses to pray during a moment of silence over the child who chooses to meditate or reflect. Alabama Code § 16-1-20.1 does not stand on the same footing. However deferentially one examines its text and legislative history, however objectively one views the message attempted to be conveyed to the public, the conclusion is unavoidable that the purpose of the statute is to endorse prayer in public schools. I accordingly agree with the Court of Appeals that the Alabama statute has a purpose which is in violation of the Establishment Clause, and cannot be upheld.

* * * * *

II

The solution to the conflict between the religion clauses lies not in "neutrality," but rather in identifying workable limits to the Government's license to promote the free exercise of religion. The text of the Free Exercise Clause speaks of laws that prohibit the free exercise of religion. On its face, the Clause is directed at government interference with free exercise. Given that concern, one can plausibly assert that government pursues free exercise clause values when it lifts a government-imposed burden on the free exercise of religion. If a statute falls within this category, then the standard Establishment Clause test should be modified accordingly. It is disingenuous to look for a purely secular purpose when the manifest objective of a statute is to facilitate the free exercise of religion by lifting a government-imposed burden. Instead, the Court should simply acknowledge that the religious purpose of such a statute is legitimated by the Free Exercise Clause. I would also go further. In assessing the effect of such a statute—that is, in determining whether the statute conveys the message of endorsement of religion or a particular religious belief—courts should assume that the "objective observer," is acquainted with the Free Exercise Clause and the values it promotes. Thus individual perceptions, or resentment that a religious observer is exempted from a particular government requirement, would be entitled to little weight if the Free Exercise Clause strongly supported the exemption.

* * * * *

III

The Court does not hold that the Establishment Clause is so hostile to religion that it precludes the States from affording schoolchildren an opportunity for voluntary silent prayer. To the contrary, the moment of silence statutes of many States should satisfy the Establishment Clause standard we have here applied. The Court holds only that Alabama has intentionally crossed the line between creating a quiet moment during which those so inclined may pray, and affirmatively endorsing the particular religious practice of prayer. This line may not be a fine one, but our precedents and the principles of religious liberty require that we draw it. In my view, the judgment of the Court of Appeals must be affirmed.

JUSTICE REHNQUIST, DISSENTING.

Thirty-eight years ago this Court, in *Everson* summarized its exegesis of Establishment Clause doctrine thus:

> In the words of Jefferson, the clause against establishment of religion by law was intended to erect "a wall of separation between church and State."

This language from *Reynolds,* a case involving the Free Exercise Clause of the First Amendment rather than the Establishment Clause, quoted from Thomas Jefferson's letter to the Danbury Baptist Association the phrase "I contemplate with sovereign reverence that act of the whole American people which declared that their legislature should 'make no law respecting an establishment of religion, or prohibiting the free exercise thereof,' thus building a wall of separation between church and State."

It is impossible to build sound constitutional doctrine upon a mistaken understanding of constitutional history, but unfortunately the Establishment Clause has been expressly freighted with Jefferson's misleading metaphor for nearly forty years. Thomas Jefferson was of course in France at the time the constitutional amendments known as the Bill of Rights were passed by Congress and ratified by the states. His letter to the Danbury Baptist Association was a short note of courtesy, written fourteen years after the amendments were passed by Congress. He would seem to any detached observer as a less than ideal source of contemporary history as to the meaning of the Religion Clauses of the First Amendment.

Jefferson's fellow Virginian James Madison, with whom he was joined in the battle for the enactment of the Virginia Statute of Religious Liberty of 1786, did play as large a part as anyone in the drafting of the Bill of Rights. He had two advantages over Jefferson in this regard: he was present in the United States, and he was a leading member of the First Congress. But when we turn to the record of the proceedings in the First Congress leading up to the adoption of the Establishment Clause of the Constitution, including Madison's significant contributions thereto, we see a far different picture of its purpose than the highly simplified "wall of separation between church and State."

During the debates in the thirteen colonies over ratification of the Constitution, one of the arguments frequently used by opponents of ratification was that without a Bill of Rights guaranteeing individual liberty the new general government carried with it a potential for tyranny. The typical response to this argument on the part of those who favored ratification was that the general government established by the Constitution had only delegated powers, and that these delegated powers were so limited that the government would have no occasion to violate individual liberties. This response satisfied some, but not others, and of the eleven colonies which ratified the Constitution by early 1789, five proposed one or another amendments guaranteeing individual liberty. Three—New Hampshire, New York, and Virginia—included in one form or another a declaration of religious freedom. Rhode Island and North Carolina flatly refused to ratify the Constitution in the absence of amendments in the nature of a Bill of Rights. Virginia and North Carolina proposed identical guarantees of religious freedom:

> [A]ll men have an equal, natural and unalienable right to the free exercise of religion, according to the dictates of conscience, and that no particular religious sect or society ought to be favored or established, by law, in preference to others.

On June 8, 1789, James Madison rose in the House of Representatives and "reminded the House that this was the day that he had heretofore named for bringing forward amendments to the Constitution."

Madison's subsequent remarks in urging the House to adopt his drafts of the proposed amendments were less those of a dedicated advocate of the wisdom of such measures than those of a prudent statesman seeking the enactment of measures sought by a number of his fellow citizens which could surely do no harm and might do a great deal of good. He said, *inter alia:*

> It appears to me that this House is bound by every motive of prudence, not to let the first session pass over without proposing to the State Legislatures, some things to be incorporated into the Constitution, that will render it as acceptable to the whole people of the United States, as it has been found acceptable to a majority of them. I wish, among other reasons why something should be done, that those who had been friendly to the adoption of this Constitution may have the opportunity of proving to those who were opposed to it that they were as sincerely devoted to liberty and a Republican Government, as those who charged them with wishing the adoption of this Constitution in order to lay the foundation of an aristocracy or despotism. It will be a desirable thing to extinguish from the bosom of every member of the community, any apprehensions that there are those among his countrymen who wish to deprive them of the liberty for which they valiantly fought and honorably bled. And if there are amendments desired of such a nature as will not injure the Constitution, and they can be ingrafted so as to give satisfaction to the doubting part of our fellow-citizens, the friends of the Federal Government will evince that spirit of deference and concession for which they have hitherto been distinguished.

The language Madison proposed for what ultimately became the Religion Clauses of the First Amendment was this:

> The civil rights of none shall be abridged on account of religious belief or worship, nor shall any national religion be established, nor shall the full and equal rights of conscience be in any manner, or on any pretext, infringed.

On the same day that Madison proposed them, the amendments which formed the basis for the Bill of Rights were referred by the House to a committee of the whole, and after several weeks' delay were then referred to a Select Committee consisting of Madison and ten others. The Committee revised Madison's proposal regarding the establishment of religion to read: "[N]o religion shall be established by law, nor shall the equal rights of conscience be infringed."

The Committee's proposed revisions were debated in the House on August 15, 1789. The entire debate on the Religion Clauses is contained in two full columns of the "Annals," and does not seem particularly illuminating. Representative Peter Sylvester of New York expressed his dislike for the revised version, because it might have a tendency "to abolish religion altogether." Representative John Vining suggested that the two parts of the sentence be transposed; Representative Elbridge Gerry thought the language should be changed to read "that no religious doctrine shall be established by law." Roger Sherman of Connecticut had the traditional reason for opposing provisions of a Bill of Rights—that Congress had no delegated authority to "make religious establishments"—and therefore he opposed the adoption of the amendment. Representative Daniel Carroll of Maryland thought it desirable to adopt the words proposed, saying "[h]e would not contend with gentlemen about the phraseology, his object was to secure the substance in such a manner as to satisfy the wishes of the honest part of the community."

Madison then spoke, and said that "he apprehended the meaning of the words to be, that Congress should not establish a religion, and enforce the legal observation of it by law, nor compel men to worship God in any manner contrary to their conscience." He said that some of the state conventions had thought that Congress might rely on the "necessary and proper" clause to infringe the rights of conscience or to establish a national religion, and "to prevent these effects he presumed the amendment was intended, and he thought it as well expressed as the nature of the language would admit."

Representative Benjamin Huntington then expressed the view that the Committee's language might "be taken in such latitude as to be extremely hurtful to the cause of religion. He understood the amendment to mean what had been expressed by the gentleman from Virginia; but others might find it convenient to put another construction upon it." Huntington, from Connecticut, was concerned that in the New England states, where state established religions were the rule rather than the exception, the federal courts might not be able to entertain claims based upon an obligation under the bylaws of a religious organization to contribute to the support of a minister or the building of a place of worship. He hoped that "the amendment would be made in such a way as to secure the rights of conscience, and a free exercise of the rights of religion, but not to patronise those who professed no religion at all."

Madison responded that the insertion of the word "national" before the word "religion" in the Committee version should satisfy the minds of those who had criticized the language. "He believed that the people feared one sect might obtain a pre-eminence, or two combine together, and establish a religion to which they would compel others to conform. He thought that if the word 'national' was introduced, it would point the amendment directly to the object it was intended to prevent." Representative Samuel Livermore expressed himself as dissatisfied with Madison's proposed amendment, and thought it would be better if the Committee language were altered to read that "Congress shall make no laws touching religion, or infringing the rights of conscience."

Representative Gerry spoke in opposition to the use of the word "national" because of strong feelings expressed during the ratification debates that a federal government, not a national government, was created by the Constitution. Madison thereby withdrew his proposal but insisted that his reference to a "national religion" only referred to a national establishment and did not mean that the government was a national one. The question was taken on Representative Livermore's motion, which passed by a vote of 31 for and 20 against.

The following week, without any apparent debate, the House voted to alter the language of the Religion Clause to read "Congress shall make no law establishing religion, or to prevent the free exercise thereof, or to infringe the rights of conscience." The floor debates in the Senate were secret, and therefore not reported in the Annals. The Senate on September 3, 1789 considered several different forms of the Religion Amendment, and reported this language back to the House: "Congress shall make no law establishing articles of faith or a mode of worship, or prohibiting the free exercise of religion."

The House refused to accept the Senate's changes in the Bill of Rights and asked for a conference; the version which emerged from the conference was that which ultimately found its way into the Constitution as a part of the First Amendment. "Congress shall make no law respecting an establishment of religion, or prohibiting the free exercise thereof." The House and the Senate both accepted this language on successive days, and the amendment was proposed in this form.

On the basis of the record of these proceedings in the House of Representatives, James Madison was undoubtedly the most important architect among the members of the House of the amendments which became the Bill of Rights, but it was James Madison speaking as an advocate of sensible legislative compromise, not as an advocate of incorporating the Virginia Statute of Religious Liberty into the United States Constitution. During the ratification debate in the Virginia Convention, Madison had actually opposed the idea of any Bill of Rights. His sponsorship of the amendments in the House was obviously not that of a zealous believer in the necessity of the Religion Clauses, but of one who felt it might do some good, could do no harm, and would satisfy those who had ratified the Constitution on the condition that Congress propose a Bill of Rights. His original language "nor shall any national religion be established" obviously does not conform to the "wall of separation" between church and State idea which latter day commentators have ascribed to him. His explanation on the floor of the meaning of his language—"that Congress should not establish a religion, and enforce the legal observation of it by law" is of the same ilk. When he replied to Huntington in the debate over the proposal which came from the Select Committee of the House, he urged that the language "no religion shall be established by law" should be amended by inserting the word "national" in front of the word "religion."

It seems indisputable from these glimpses of Madison's thinking, as reflected by actions on the floor of the House in 1789, that he saw the amendment as designed to prohibit the establishment of a national religion, and perhaps to prevent discrimination among sects. He did not see it as requiring neutrality on the part of government between religion and irreligion. Thus the Court's opinion in *Everson*—while correct in bracketing Madison and Jefferson together in their exertions in their home state leading to the enactment of the Virginia Statute of Religious Liberty—is totally incorrect in suggesting that Madison carried these views onto the floor of the United States House of Representatives when he proposed the language which would ultimately become the Bill of Rights.

The repetition of this error in the Court's opinion in *McCollum* does not make it any sounder historically. Finally, in *Schempp* the

Court made the truly remarkable statement that "the views of Madison and Jefferson, preceded by Roger Williams came to be incorporated not only in the Federal Constitution but likewise in those of most of our States." On the basis of what evidence we have, this statement is demonstrably incorrect as a matter of history. And its repetition in varying forms in succeeding opinions of the Court can give it no more authority than it possesses as a matter of fact; *stare decisis* may bind courts as to matters of law, but it cannot bind them as to matters of history.

None of the other Members of Congress who spoke during the August 15th debate expressed the slightest indication that they thought the language before them from the Select Committee, or the evil to be aimed at, would require that the Government be absolutely neutral as between religion and irreligion. The evil to be aimed at, so far as those who spoke were concerned, appears to have been the establishment of a national church, and perhaps the preference of one religious sect over another; but it was definitely not concern about whether the Government might aid all religions evenhandedly. If one were to follow the advice of Justice Brennan, concurring in *Schempp,* and construe the Amendment in the light of what particular "practices . . . challenged threaten those consequences which the Framers deeply feared; whether, in short, they tend to promote that type of interdependence between religion and state which the First Amendment was designed to prevent," one would have to say that the First Amendment Establishment Clause should be read no more broadly than to prevent the establishment of a national religion or the governmental preference of one religious sect over another.

The actions of the First Congress, which re-enacted the Northwest Ordinance for the governance of the Northwest Territory in 1789, confirm the view that Congress did not mean that the Government should be neutral between religion and irreligion. The House of Representatives took up the Northwest Ordinance on the same day as Madison introduced his proposed amendments which became the Bill of Rights; while at that time the Federal Government was of course not bound by draft amendments to the Constitution which had not yet been proposed by Congress, say nothing of ratified by the States, it seems highly unlikely that the House of Representatives would simultaneously consider proposed amendments to the Constitution and enact an important piece of territorial legislation which conflicted with the intent of those proposals. The Northwest Ordinance, 1 Stat. 50, reenacted the Northwest Ordinance of 1787 and provided that "[r]eligion, morality, and knowledge, being necessary to good government and the happiness of mankind, schools and the means of education shall forever be encouraged." Land grants for schools in the Northwest Territory were not limited to public schools. It was not until 1845 that Congress limited land grants in the new States and Territories to nonsectarian schools.

On the day after the House of Representatives voted to adopt the form of the First Amendment Religion Clause which was ultimately proposed and ratified, Representative Elias Boudinot proposed a resolution asking President George Washington to issue a Thanksgiving Day proclamation. Boudinot said he "could not think of letting the session pass over without offering an opportunity to all the citizens of the United States of joining with one voice, in returning to Almighty God their sincere thanks for the many blessings he had poured down upon them." Representative Aedanas Burke objected to the resolution because he did not like "this mimicking of European customs"; Representative Thomas Tucker objected that whether or not the people had reason to be satisfied with the Constitution was something that the states knew better than the Congress, and in any event "it is a religious matter, and, as such, is proscribed to us." Representative Sherman supported the resolution "not only as a laudable one in itself, but as warranted by a number of precedents in Holy Writ: for instance, the solemn thanksgivings and rejoicings which took place in the time of Solomon, after the building of the temple, was a case in point. This example, he thought, worthy of Christian imitation on the present occasion. . . ."

Boudinot's resolution was carried in the affirmative on September 25, 1789. Boudinot and Sherman, who favored the Thanksgiving proclamation, voted in favor of the adoption of the proposed amendments to the Constitution, including the Religion Clause; Tucker, who opposed the Thanksgiving proclamation, voted against the adoption of the amendments which became the Bill of Rights.

Within two weeks of this action by the House, George Washington responded to the Joint Resolution which by now had been changed to include the language that the President "recommend to the people of the United States a day of public thanksgiving and prayer, to be observed by acknowledging with grateful hearts the many and signal favors of Almighty God, especially by affording them an opportunity peaceably to establish a form of government for their safety and happiness."

* * * * *

George Washington, John Adams, and James Madison all issued Thanksgiving proclamations; Thomas Jefferson did not, saying:

> Fasting and prayer are religious exercises; the enjoining them an act of discipline. Every religious society has a right to determine for itself the times for these exercises, and the objects proper for them, according to their own particular tenets; and this right can never be safer than in their own hands, where the Constitution has deposited it.

As the United States moved from the 18th into the 19th century, Congress appropriated time and again public moneys in support of sectarian Indian education carried on by religious organizations. Typical of these was Jefferson's treaty with the Kaskaskia Indians, which provided annual cash support for the Tribe's Roman Catholic priest and church. It was not until 1897, when aid to sectarian education for Indians had reached $500,000 annually, that Congress decided thereafter to cease appropriating money for education in sectarian schools. This history shows the fallacy of the notion found in *Everson* that "no tax in any amount" may be levied for religious activities in any form.

* * * * *

It would seem from this evidence that the Establishment Clause of the First Amendment had acquired a well-accepted meaning: it forbade establishment of a national religion, and forbade preference among religious sects or denominations. Indeed, the first American dictionary defined the word "establishment" as "the act of establishing, founding, ratifying or ordainin(g,") such as in "[t]he episcopal form of religion, so called, in England." The Establishment Clause did not require government neutrality between religion and irreligion nor did it prohibit the federal government from providing non-discriminatory aid to religion. There is simply no historical foundation for the proposition that the Framers intended to build the "wall of separation" that was constitutionalized in *Everson.*

Notwithstanding the absence of an historical basis for this theory of rigid separation, the wall idea might well have served as a useful albeit misguided analytical concept, had it led this Court to unified and principled results in Establishment Clause cases. The opposite, unfortunately, has been true; in the 38 years since *Everson* our Establishment Clause cases have been neither principled nor unified. Our recent opinions, many of them hopelessly divided pluralities, have with embarrassing candor conceded that the "wall of separation" is merely a "blurred, indistinct, and variable barrier," which "is not wholly accurate" and can only be "dimly perceived."

Whether due to its lack of historical support or its practical unworkability, the *Everson* "wall" has proven all but useless as a guide to sound constitutional adjudication. It illustrates only too well the wisdom of Benjamin Cardozo's observation that "[m]etaphors in law are to be narrowly watched, for starting as devices to liberate thought, they end often by enslaving it."

But the greatest injury of the "wall" notion is its mischievous diversion of judges from the actual intentions of the drafters of the Bill of Rights. The "crucible of litigation," is well adapted to adjudicating factual disputes on the basis of testimony presented in court, but no amount of repetition of historical errors in judicial opinions can make the errors true. The "wall of separation between church and State" is a metaphor based on bad history, a metaphor which has proved useless as a guide to judging. It should be frankly and explicitly abandoned.

The Court has more recently attempted to add some mortar to *Everson's* wall through the three-part test of *Lemon v. Kurtzman,* which served at first to offer a more useful test for purposes of the Establishment Clause than did the "wall" metaphor. Generally stated, the *Lemon* test proscribes state action that has a sectarian purpose or effect, or causes an impermissible governmental entanglement with religion.

Lemon cited *Board of Education v. Allen,* as the source of the "purpose" and "effect" prongs of the three-part test. The *Allen* opinion explains, however, how it inherited the purpose and effect elements from *Schempp* and *Everson,* both of which contain the historical errors described above. Thus the purpose and effect prongs have the same historical deficiencies as the wall concept itself: they are in no way based on either the language or intent of the drafters.

The secular purpose prong has proven mercurial in application because it has never been fully defined, and we have never fully stated how the test is to operate. If the purpose prong is intended to void those aids to sectarian institutions accompanied by a stated legislative purpose to aid religion, the prong will condemn nothing so long as the legislature utters a secular purpose and says nothing about aiding religion. Thus the constitutionality of a statute may depend upon what the legislators put into the legislative history and, more importantly, what they leave out. The purpose prong means little if it only requires the legislature to express any secular purpose and omit all sectarian references, because legislators might do just that. Faced with a valid legislative secular purpose, we could not properly ignore that purpose without a factual basis for doing so.

However, if the purpose prong is aimed to void all statutes enacted with the intent to aid sectarian institutions, whether stated or not, then most statutes providing any aid, such as textbooks or bus rides for sectarian school children, will fail because one of the purposes behind every statute, whether stated or not, is to aid the target of its largesse. In other words, if the purpose prong requires an absence of *any* intent to aid sectarian institutions, whether or not expressed, few state laws in this area could pass the test, and we would be required to void some state aids to religion which we have already upheld.

The entanglement prong of the *Lemon* test came from *Walz. Walz* involved a constitutional challenge to New York's time-honored practice of providing state property tax exemptions to church property used in worship. The *Walz* opinion refused to "undermine the ultimate constitutional objective [of the Establishment Clause] as illuminated by history," and upheld the tax exemption. The Court examined the historical relationship between the state and church when church property was in issue, and determined that the challenged tax exemption did not so entangle New York with the Church as to cause an intrusion or interference with religion. Interferences with religion should arguably be dealt with under the Free Exercise Clause, but the entanglement inquiry in *Walz* was consistent with that case's broad survey of the relationship between state taxation and religious property.

We have not always followed *Walz's* reflective inquiry into entanglement, however. One of the difficulties with the entanglement prong is that, when divorced from the logic of *Walz,* it creates an "insoluble paradox" in school aid cases: we have required aid to parochial schools to be closely watched lest it be put to sectarian use, yet this close supervision itself will create an entanglement. For example, in

Wolman, the Court in part struck the State's nondiscriminatory provision of buses for parochial school field trips, because the state supervision of sectarian officials in charge of field trips would be too onerous. This type of self-defeating result is certainly not required to ensure that States do not establish religions.

The entanglement test as applied in cases like *Wolman* also ignores the myriad state administrative regulations properly placed upon sectarian institutions such as curriculum, attendance, and certification requirements for sectarian schools, or fire and safety regulations for churches. Avoiding entanglement between church and State may be an important consideration in a case like *Walz,* but if the entanglement prong were applied to all state and church relations in the automatic manner in which it has been applied to school aid cases, the State could hardly require anything of church-related institutions as a condition for receipt of financial assistance.

These difficulties arise because the *Lemon* test has no more grounding in the history of the First Amendment than does the wall theory upon which it rests. The three-part test represents a determined effort to craft a workable rule from an historically faulty doctrine; but the rule can only be as sound as the doctrine it attempts to service. The three-part test has simply not provided adequate standards for deciding Establishment Clause cases, as this Court has slowly come to realize. Even worse, the *Lemon* test has caused this Court to fracture into unworkable plurality opinions, depending upon how each of the three factors applies to a certain state action. The results from our school services cases show the difficulty we have encountered in making the *Lemon* test yield principled results.

For example, a State may lend to parochial school children geography textbooks that contain maps of the United States, but the State may not lend maps of the United States for use in geography class. A State may lend textbooks on American colonial history, but it may not lend a film on George Washington, or a film projector to show it in history class. A State may lend classroom workbooks, but may not lend workbooks in which the parochial school children write, thus rendering them nonreusable. A State may pay for bus transportation to religious schools but may not pay for bus transportation from the parochial school to the public zoo or natural history museum for a field trip. A State may pay for diagnostic services conducted in the parochial school but therapeutic services must be given in a different building; speech and hearing "services" conducted by the State inside the sectarian school are forbidden, but the State may conduct speech and hearing diagnostic testing inside the sectarian school. Exceptional parochial school students may receive counseling, but it must take place outside of the parochial school, such as in a trailer parked down the street. A State may give cash to a parochial school to pay for the administration of State-written tests and state-ordered reporting services, but it may not provide funds for teacher-prepared tests on secular subjects. Religious instruction may not be given in public school, but the public school may release students during the day for religion classes elsewhere, and may enforce attendance at those classes with its truancy laws.

These results violate the historically sound principle "that the Establishment Clause does not forbid governments . . . to [provide] general welfare under which benefits are distributed to private individuals, even though many of those individuals may elect to use those benefits in ways that 'aid' religious instruction or worship." It is not surprising in the light of this record that our most recent opinions have expressed doubt on the usefulness of the *Lemon* test.

Although the test initially provided helpful assistance, we soon began describing the test as only a "guideline," and lately we have described it as "no more than [a] useful signpos[t]." We have noted that the *Lemon* test is "not easily applied," *(Meek),* and as Justice White noted in *Committee for Public Education v. Regan,* under the *Lemon* test we have "sacrifice[d] clarity and predictability for flexibility." In *Lynch* we reiterated that the *Lemon* test has never been binding on the Court, and we cited two cases where we had declined to apply it.

If a constitutional theory has no basis in the history of the amendment it seeks to interpret, is difficult to apply and yields unprincipled results, I see little use in it. The "crucible of litigation" has produced only consistent unpredictability, and today's effort is just a continuation of "the sisyphean task of trying to patch together the 'blurred, indistinct and variable barrier' described in *Lemon v. Kurtzman.*" We have done much straining since 1947, but still we admit that we can only "dimly perceive" the *Everson* wall. Our perception has been clouded not by the Constitution but by the mists of an unnecessary metaphor.

The true meaning of the Establishment Clause can only be seen in its history. As drafters of our Bill of Rights, the Framers inscribed the principles that control today. Any deviation from their intentions frustrates the permanence of that Charter and will only lead to the type of unprincipled decision making that has plagued our Establishment Clause cases since *Everson.*

The Framers intended the Establishment Clause to prohibit the designation of any church as a "national" one. The Clause was also designed to stop the Federal Government from asserting a preference for one religious denomination or sect over others. Given the "incorporation" of the Establishment Clause as against the States via the Fourteenth Amendment in *Everson,* States are prohibited as well from establishing a religion or discriminating between sects. As its history abundantly shows, however, nothing in the Establishment Clause requires government to be strictly neutral between religion and irreligion, nor does that Clause prohibit Congress or the States from pursuing legitimate secular ends through nondiscriminatory sectarian means.

The Court strikes down the Alabama statute in *Wallace v. Jaffree,* because the State wished to "endorse prayer as a favored practice." It would come as much of a shock to those who drafted the Bill of Rights as it will to a large number of thoughtful Americans today to learn that the Constitution, as construed by the majority, prohibits the Alabama Legislature from "endorsing" prayer. George Washington himself, at the request of the very Congress which passed the Bill of Rights, proclaimed a day of "public thanksgiving and prayer, to be observed by acknowledging with grateful hearts the many and signal favors of Almighty God." History must judge whether it was the father of his country in 1789, or a majority of the Court today, which has strayed from the meaning of the Establishment Clause.

The State surely has a secular interest in regulating the manner in which public schools are conducted. Nothing in the Establishment Clause of the First Amendment, properly understood, prohibits any such generalized "endorsement" of prayer. I would therefore reverse the judgment of the Court of Appeals in *Wallace v. Jaffree.*

Edwards v. Aguillard, 107 S.Ct. 2573 (1987)

On June 19, 1987 the Court handed down a decision respecting the Louisiana Balanced Treatment for Creation-Science and Evolution-Science in Public Instruction Act. In a 7 to 2 decision the Court found the act unconstitutional. Justice Brennan wrote the opinion, and Justice Scalia offered a vigorous dissent in which Justice Rehnquist concurred.

In strong language Brennan described as a "sham" the claim that the Louisiana Act was designed for the purpose of assuring academic freedom and that it was for a secular purpose. In concurring with the majority, Justices Powell and O'Connor concluded that the purpose of the Act "is to advance a particular religious belief." In dissent, Scalia and Rehnquist, while objecting to the *Lemon* three-prong test, insisted that the Act met the first prong since it "had a secular purpose." This position was advanced on the premise that "'creation science' is a body of scientific knowledge rather than revealed belief.'"

Apart from the substance, this decision has two significant aspects. First, it is the last important decision on church/state matters in which Justice Powell will participate. He announced his retirement from the Bench on June 26, 1987, ending two decades of thoughtful commentary by a scholarly Justice committed to a strong separationist position. It opened the way for a confrontation between President Reagan and the Democratic Senate over a new appointment, since the President chose to nominate Judge Robert Bork, who has a long record of writings based on "original intent." Bork's rejection by the Senate was, in large measure, a result of his inability to find a "right of privacy" in the Constitution. Bork's argument from silence recalls a major reason why Madison originally opposed a Bill of Rights. He wrote Jefferson in 1788, "there is great reason to fear that a positive declaration of some of the most essential rights could not be obtained in the requisite latitude." Madison feared restriction of rights not listed or clearly defined. Second, *Edwards v. Aguillard* offers an initial insight into the direction of Justice Scalia's thoughts on church and state matters as they are manifest in his lengthy dissent.

Editorial restraints resulting from the timing of this decision rendered by Justice Brennan require that only portions of the Court's opinion be reproduced here. Every effort has been made to assure fairness both to the majority and minority in this abbreviated presentation.

JUSTICE BRENNAN DELIVERED THE OPINION OF THE COURT.

The question for decision is whether Louisiana's Balanced Treatment for Creation-Science and Evolution-Science in Public School Instruction Act (Creationism Act), is facially invalid as violative of the Establishment Clause of the First Amendment.

I

The Creationism Act forbids the teaching of the theory of evolution in public schools unless accompanied by instruction in "creation science." No school is required to teach evolution or creation science. If either is taught, however, the other must also be taught. The theories of evolution and creation science are statutorily defined as "the scientific evidences for [creation or evolution] and inferences from those scientific evidences."

Appellees, who include parents of children attending Louisiana public schools, Louisiana teachers, and religious leaders, challenged the constitutionality of the Act in District Court, seeking an injunction and declaratory relief. Appellants, Louisiana officials charged with implementing the Act, defended on the ground that the purpose of the Act is to protect a legitimate secular interest, namely, academic freedom. Appellees attacked the Act as facially invalid because it violated the Establishment Clause and made a motion for summary judgment. The District Court granted the motion. . . . The Court of Appeals affirmed. . . . We noted probable jurisdiction, and now affirm.

The Establishment Clause forbids the enactment of any law "respecting an establishment of religion." The Court has applied a three-pronged test to determine whether legislation comports with the Establishment Clause. First, the legislature must have adopted the law with a secular purpose. Second, the statute's principal or primary effect must be one that neither advances nor inhibits religion. Third, the statute must not result in an excessive entanglement of government with religion. (*Lemon v. Kurtzman*) State action violates the Establishment Clause if it fails to satisfy any of these prongs.

Lemon's first prong focuses on the purpose that animated adoption of the Act. "The purpose prong of the *Lemon* test asks whether government's actual purpose is to endorse or disapprove of religion." A governmental intention to promote religion is clear when the State enacts a law to serve a religious purpose. This intention may be evidenced by promotion of religion in general, or by advancement of a particular religious belief. If the law was enacted for the purpose of endorsing religion, "no consideration of the second or third criteria [of *Lemon*] is necessary." In this case, the petitioners have identified no clear secular purpose for the Louisiana Act.

True, the Act's stated purpose is to protect academic freedom. This phrase might, in common parlance, be understood as referring to enhancing the freedom of teachers to teach what they will. The Court of Appeals, however, correctly concluded that the Act was not designed to further that goal. We find no merit in the State's argument that the "legislature may not [have] use[d] the terms 'academic freedom' in the correct legal sense. They might have [had] in mind, instead, a basic concept of fairness; teaching all of the evidence." Even if "academic freedom" is read to mean "teaching all of the evidence" with respect to the origin of human beings, the Act does not further this purpose. The goal of providing a more comprehensive science curriculum is not furthered either by outlawing the teaching of evolution or by requiring the teaching of creation science.

While the Court is normally deferential to a State's articulation of a secular purpose, it is required that the statement of such purpose be sincere and not a sham. As Justice O'Connor stated in *Wallace:* "It is not a trivial matter, however, to require that the legislature manifest a secular purpose and omit all sectarian endorsements from its laws. That requirement is precisely tailored to the Establishment Clause's purpose of assuring that Government not intentionally endorse religion or a religious practice."

It is clear from the legislative history that the purpose of the legislative sponsor, Senator Bill Keith, was to narrow the science curriculum. During the legislative hearings, Senator Keith stated: "My preference would be that neither [creationism nor evolution] be taught." Such a ban on teaching does not promote—indeed, it undermines—the provision of a comprehensive scientific education.

It is equally clear that requiring schools to teach creation science with evolution does not advance academic freedom. . . . The Act provides Louisiana schoolteachers with no new authority. Thus the stated purpose is not furthered by it. . . .

Furthermore, the goal of basic "fairness" is hardly furthered by the Act's discriminatory preference for the teaching of creation science and against the teaching of evolution. While requiring that curriculum guides be developed for creation science, the Act says nothing of comparable guides for evolution. Similarly, research services are supplied for creation science but not for evolution. Only "creation scientists" can serve on the panel that supplies the resource services. The Act forbids school boards to discriminate against anyone who "chooses to be a creation-scientist" or to teach "creationism," but fails to protect those who choose to teach evolution or any other non-creation science theory, or who refuse to teach creation science. . . . Thus we agree with the Court of Appeals' conclusion that the Act does not serve to protect academic freedom, but has the distinctly different purpose of discrediting "evolution by counterbalancing its teaching at every turn with the teaching of creation science. . . . "

Stone v. *Graham,* invalidated the State's requirement that the Ten Commandments be posted in public classrooms. "The Ten Commandments are undeniably sacred text in the Jewish and Christian faiths, and no legislative recitation of a supposed secular purpose can blind us to that fact." As a result, the contention that the law was designed to provide instruction on a "fundamental legal code" was "not sufficient to avoid conflict with the First Amendment." Similarly *Schempp* held unconstitutional a statute "requiring the selection and reading at the opening of the school day of verses from the Holy Bible and the recitation of the Lord's Prayer by the students in unison," despite the proffer of such secular purposes as the "promotion of moral values, the contradiction to the materialistic trends of our times, the perpetuation of our institutions and the teaching of literature."

. . . There is a historic and contemporaneous link between the teachings of certain religious denominations and the teaching of evolution. It was this link that concerned the Court in *Epperson* which also involved a facial challenge to a statute regulating the teaching of evolution.

* * * * *

These same historic and contemporaneous antagonisms between the teachings of certain religious denominations and the teaching of evolution are present in this case. The preeminent purpose of the Louisiana legislature was clearly to advance the religious viewpoint that a supernatural being created humankind. The term "creation science" was defined as embracing this particular religious doctrine by those responsible for the passage of the Creationism Act.

* * * * *

Furthermore, it is not happenstance that the legislature required the teaching of a theory that coincided with this religious view. The legislative history documents that the Act's primary purpose was to change the science curriculum of public schools in order to provide persuasive advantage to a particular religious doctrine that rejects the factual basis of evolution in its entirety. The sponsor of the Creationism Act, Senator Keith, explained during the legislative hearings that his disdain for the theory of evolution resulted from the support that evolution supplied to views contrary to his own religious beliefs. According to Senator Keith, the theory of evolution was consonant with the "cardinal principle[s] of religious humanism, secular humanism, theological liberalism, aetheistism [*sic*]." The state senator repeatedly stated that scientific evidence supporting his religious views should be included in the public school curriculum to redress the fact that the theory of evolution incidentally coincided with what he characterized as religious beliefs antithetical to his own. The legislation therefore sought to alter the science curriculum to reflect endorsement of a religious view that is antagonistic to the theory of evolution.

In this case, the purpose of the Creationism Act was to restructure the science curriculum to conform with a particular religious viewpoint. Out of many possible science subjects taught in the public schools, the legislature chose to affect the teaching of the one scientific theory that historically has been opposed by certain religious sects. As in *Epperson,* the legislature passed the Act to give preference to those religious groups which have as one of their tenets the creation of humankind by a divine creator. The "overriding fact" that confronted the Court in *Epperson* was "that Arkansas' law selects from the body of knowledge a particular segment which it proscribes for the sole reason that it is deemed to conflict with . . . a particular interpretation of the Book of Genesis by a particular religious group." Similarly, the Creationism Act is designed *either* to promote the theory of creation science which embodies a particular religious tenet by requiring that creation science be taught whenever evolution is taught *or* to prohibit the teaching of a scientific theory disfavored by certain religious sects by forbidding the teaching of evolution when creation science is not also taught. The Establishment Clause, however, "forbids *alike* the preference of a religious doctrine *or* the prohibition of theory which is deemed antagonistic to a particular dogma." Because the primary purpose of the Creationism Act is to advance a particular religious belief, the Act endorses religion in violation of the First Amendment.

We do not imply that a legislature could never require that scientific critiques of prevailing scientific theories be taught. Indeed, the Court acknowledged in *Stone* that its decision forbidding the posting of the Ten Commandments did not mean that no use could ever be made of the Ten Commandments, or that the Ten Commandments played an exclusively religious role in the history of Western Civilization. In a similar way, teaching a variety of scientific theories about the origins of humankind to schoolchildren might be validly done with the clear secular intent of enhancing the effectiveness of science instruction. But because the primary purpose of the Creationism Act is to endorse a particular religious doctrine, the Act furthers religion in violation of the Establishment Clause.

* * * * *

The Louisiana Creationism Act advances a religious doctrine by requiring either the banishment of the theory of evolution from public school classrooms or the presentation of a religious viewpoint that rejects evolution in its entirety. The Act violates the Establishment Clause of the First Amendment because it seeks to employ the symbolic and financial support of government to achieve a religious purpose. The judgment of the Court of Appeals therefore is

Affirmed.

JUSTICE POWELL, WITH WHOM JUSTICE O'CONNOR JOINS, CONCURRING.

I write separately to note certain aspects of the legislative history, and to emphasize that nothing in the Court's opinion diminishes the traditionally broad discretion accorded state and local school officials in the selection of the public school curriculum.

* * * * *

A religious purpose alone is not enough to invalidate an act of a state legislature. The religious purpose must predominate. The Act contains a statement of purpose: to "protec[t] academic freedom." This statement is puzzling. Of course, the "academic freedom" of teachers to present information in public schools, and students to receive it is broad. But it necessarily is circumscribed by the Establishment Clause. "Academic freedom" does not encompass the right of a legislature to structure the public school curriculum in order to advance a particular religious belief.

* * * * *

When, as here, "both courts below are unable to discern an arguably valid secular purpose, this Court normally should hesitate to find one." My examination of the language and the legislative history of the Balanced Treatment Act confirms that the intent of the Louisiana legislature was to promote a particular religious belief. The legislative history of the Arkansas statute prohibiting the teaching of evolution examined in *Epperson* was strikingly similar to the legislative history of the Balanced Treatment Act.

* * * * *

Here, it is clear that religious belief is the Balanced Treatment Act's "reason for existence." The tenets of creation-science parallel the Genesis story of creation, and this is a religious belief. "[N]o legislative recitation of a supposed secular purpose can blind us to the fact." Although the Act as finally enacted does not contain explicit reference to its religious purpose, there is no indication in the legislative history that the deletion of "creation *ex nihilo*" and the four primary tenets of the theory were intended to alter the purpose of teaching creation-science. Instead, the statements of purpose of the sources of creation-science in the United States make clear that their purpose is to promote a religious belief. I find no persuasive evidence in the legislative history that the legislature's purpose was any different. The fact that the Louisiana legislature purported to add information to the school curriculum rather than detract from it as in *Epperson* does not affect my analysis. Both legislatures acted with the unconstitutional purpose of structuring the public school curriculum to make it compatible with a particular religious belief: the "divine creation of man."

That the statute is limited to the scientific evidences supporting the theory does not render its purpose secular. In reaching its conclusion that the Act is unconstitutional, the Court of Appeals "[did] not deny that the underpinnings of creationism may be supported by scientific evidence." And there is no need to do so. Whatever the academic merit of particular subjects or theories, the Establishment Clause limits the discretion of state officials to pick and choose among them for the purpose of promoting a particular religious belief. The language of the statute and its legislative history convince me that the Louisiana legislature exercised its discretion for this purpose in this case.

Even though I find Louisiana's Balanced Treatment Act unconstitutional, I adhere to the view "that the States and locally elected school boards should have the responsibility for determining the educational policy of the public schools." . . . In the context of a challenge under the Establishment Clause, interference with the decisions of these authorities is warranted only when the purpose for their decisions is clearly religious.

* * * * *

As a matter of history, school children can and should properly be informed of all aspects of this Nation's religious heritage. I would see no constitutional problem if school children were taught the nature of the Founding Father's religious beliefs and how these beliefs affected the attitudes of the times and the structure of our government. Courses in comparative religion of course are customary and constitutionally appropriate. In fact, since religion permeates our history, a familiarity with the nature of religious beliefs is necessary to understand many historical as well as contemporary events. In addition, it is worth noting that the Establishment Clause does not prohibit *per se* the educational use of religious documents in public school education. Although this Court has recognized that the Bible is "an instrument of religion," it also has made clear that the Bible "may constitutionally be used in an appropriate study of history, civilization, ethics, comparative religion, or the like." The book is, in fact, "the world's all-time best seller" with undoubted literary and historic value apart from its religious content. The Establishment Clause is properly understood to prohibit the use of the Bible and other religious documents in public school education only when the purpose of the use is to advance a particular religious belief.

In sum, I find that the language and the legislative history of the Balanced Treatment Act unquestionably demonstrate that its purpose is to advance a particular religious belief. Although the discretion of state and local authorities over public school curricula is broad, "the First Amendment does not permit the State to require that teaching and learning must be tailored to the principles or prohibitions of any religious sect or dogma." Accordingly, I concur in the opinion of the Court and its judgment that the Balanced Treatment Act violates the Establishment Clause of the Constitution.

JUSTICE SCALIA, WITH WHOM THE CHIEF JUSTICE JOINS, DISSENTING.

Even if I agreed with the questionable premise that legislation can be invalidated under the Establishment Clause on the basis of its motivation alone, without regard to its effects, I would still find no justification for today's decision. The Louisiana legislators who passed the "Balanced Treatment for Creation-Science and Evolution-Science Act" each of whom had sworn to support the Constitution, were well aware of the potential Establishment Clause problems and considered that aspect of the legislation with great care. After seven hearings and several months of study, resulting in substantial revision of the original proposal, they approved the Act overwhelmingly and specifically articulated the secular purpose they meant it to serve. Although the record contains abundant evidence of the sincerity of that purpose (the only issue pertinent to this case), the Court today holds, essentially on the basis of "its visceral knowledge regarding what *must* have motivated the legislators," that the members of the Louisiana Legislature knowingly violated their oaths and then lied about it. I dissent. Had requirements of the Balanced Treatment Act that are not apparent on its face been clarified by an interpretation of the Louisiana Supreme Court, or by the manner of its implementation, the Act might well be found unconstitutional; but the question of its constitutionality cannot rightly be disposed of on the gallop, by impugning the motives of its supporters.

* * * * *

Like the Court of Appeals, the Court finds it necessary to consider only the motives of the legislators who supported the Balanced Treatment Act. After examining the statute, its legislative history, and its historical and social context, the Court holds that the Louisiana Legislature acted without "a secular legislative purpose" and that the Act therefore fails the "purpose" prong of the three-part test set forth in *Lemon.* I doubt whether that "purpose" requirement of *Lemon* is a proper interpretation of the Constitution; but even if it were, I could not agree with the Court's assessment that the requirement was not satisfied here.

* * * * *

At the outset, it is important to note that the Balanced Treatment Act did not fly through the Louisiana Legislature on wings of fundamentalist religious fervor—which would be unlikely, in any event, since only a small minority of the State's citizens belong to fundamentalist religious denominations. The Act had its genesis (so to speak) in legislation introduced by Senator Bill Keith in June 1980. After two hearings before the Senate Committee on Education, Senator Keith asked that his bill be referred to a study commission composed of members of both houses of the Louisiana Legislature. He expressed hope that the joint committee would give the bill careful consideration and determine whether his arguments were "legitimate." The committee met twice during the interim, heard testimony (both for and against the bill) from several witnesses, and received staff reports. Senator Keith introduced his bill again when the legislature reconvened. The Senate Committee on Education held two more hearings and approved the bill after substantially amending it (in part over Senator Keith's objection). After approval by the full Senate, the bill was referred to the House Committee on Education. That committee conducted a lengthy hearing, adopted further amendments, and sent the bill on to the full House, where it received favorable consideration. The Senate concurred in the House amendments and on July 20, 1981, the Governor signed the bill into law.

Senator Keith's statements before the various committees that considered the bill hardly reflect the confidence of a man preaching to the converted. He asked his colleagues to "keep an open mind" and not to be "biased" by misleading characterizations of creation science. He also urged them to "look at this subject on its merits and not on some preconceived idea." Senator Keith's reception was not especially warm. Over his strenuous objection, the Senate Committee on Education voted 5–1 to amend his bill to deprive it of any force; as amended, the bill merely gave teachers *permission* to balance the teaching of creation science or evolution with the other. The House Committee restored the "mandatory" language to the bill by a vote of only 6–5, and both the full House and full Senate had to repel further efforts to gut the bill. . . .

Before summarizing the testimony of Senator Keith and his supporters, I wish to make clear that I by no means intend to endorse its accuracy. But my views (and the views of this Court) about creation science and evolution are (or should be) beside the point. Our task is not to judge the debate about teaching the origins of life, but to ascertain what the members of the Louisiana Legislature believed. The vast majority of them voted to approve a bill which explicitly stated a secular purpose; what is crucial is not their *wisdom* in believing that purpose would be achieved by the bill, but their *sincerity* in believing it would be.

* * * * *

Senator Keith repeatedly and vehemently denied that his purpose was to advance a particular religious doctrine. At the outset of the first hearing on the legislation, he testified, "We are not going to say today that you should have some kind of religious instruction in our schools. . . . We are not talking about religion today. . . . I am not proposing that we take the Bible in each science class and read the first chapter of Genesis." At a later hearing, Senator Keith stressed that "to . . . teach religion and disguise it as creationism . . . is not my intent. My intent is to see to it that our textbooks are not censored." He made many similar statements throughout the hearings.

We have no way of knowing, of course, how many legislators believed the testimony of Senator Keith and his witnesses. But in the absence of evidence to the contrary, we have to assume that many of them did. Given that assumption, the Court today plainly errs in holding that the Louisiana Legislature passed the Balanced Treatment Act for exclusively religious purposes.

Even with nothing more than this legislative history to go on, I think it would be extraordinary to invalidate the Balanced Treatment Act for lack of a valid secular purpose. Striking down a law approved by the democratically elected representatives of the people is no minor matter. "The cardinal principle of statutory construction is to save and not to destroy. We have repeatedly held that as between two possible interpretations of a statute, by one of which it would be unconstitutional and by the other valid, our plain duty is to adopt that which will save the act." So, too, it seems to me, with discerning statutory purpose. Even if the legislative history were silent or ambiguous about the existence of a secular purpose—and here it is not—the statute should survive *Lemon's* purpose test. But even more validation than mere legislative history is present here. The Louisiana Legislature explicitly set forth its secular purpose ("protecting academic freedom") in the very text of the Act. . . .

The Court seeks to evade the force of this expression of purpose by stubbornly misinterpreting it, and then finding that the provisions of the Act do not advance that misinterpreted purpose, thereby showing it to be a sham. The Court first surmises that "academic freedom" means "enhancing the freedom of teachers to teach what they will," even though "academic freedom" in that sense has little scope in the structured elementary and secondary curriculums with which the Act is concerned. Alternatively, the Court suggests that it might mean "maximiz[ing] the comprehensiveness and effectiveness of science instruction," though that is an exceeding strange interpretation of the words, and one that is refuted on the very face of the statute. Had the Court devoted to this central question of the meaning of the legislatively expressed purpose a small fraction of the research into legislative history that produced its quotations of religiously motivated statements by individual legislators, it would have discerned quite readily what "academic freedom" meant: *students'* freedom from *indoctrination.* The legislature wanted to ensure that students would be free to decide for themselves how life began, based upon a fair and balanced presentation of the scientific evidence—that is, to protect "the right of each [student] voluntarily to determine what to believe (and what not to believe) free of any coercive pressures from the State." The legislature did not care *whether* the topic of origins was taught; it simply wished to ensure that *when* the topic was taught, students would receive "'all of the evidence.'"

As originally introduced, the "purpose" section of the Balanced Treatment Act read: "This Chapter is enacted for the purposes of protecting academic freedom . . . *of students* . . . and assisting *students* in their search for truth." Among the proposed findings of fact contained in the original version of the bill was the following: "Public school instruction in only evolution-science . . . *violates the principle of academic freedom because it denies students a choice between scientific models and instead indoctrinates them in evolution science alone.*" Senator Keith unquestionably understood "academic freedom" to mean "freedom from indoctrination."

If one adopts the obviously intended meaning of the statutory terms "academic freedom," there is no basis whatever for concluding that the purpose they express is a "sham." To the contrary, the Act pursues that purpose plainly and consistently. It requires that, whenever the subject of origins is covered, evolution be "taught as a theory, rather than as proven scientific fact" and that scientific evidence inconsistent with the theory of evolution (*viz.*, "creation science") be taught as well.

* * * * *

The Act's reference to "creation" is not convincing evidence of religious purpose. The Act defines creation science as *"scientific evidenc[e],"* and Senator Keith and his witnesses repeatedly stressed that the subject can and should be presented without religious content.

We have no basis on the record to conclude that creation science need be anything other than a collection of scientific data supporting the theory that life abruptly appeared on earth. Creation science, its proponents insist, no more must explain *whence* life came than evolution must explain whence came the inanimate materials from which it says life evolved. But even if that were not so, to posit a past creator is not to posit the eternal and personal God who is the object of religious veneration. Indeed, it is not even to posit the "*unmoved* mover" hypothesized by Aristotle and other notably nonfundamentalist philosophers. Senator Keith suggested this when he referred to "a creator *however you define a creator.*"

The Court cites three provisions of the Act which, it argues, demonstrate a "discriminatory preference for the teaching of creation science" and no interest in "academic freedom." First, the Act prohibits discrimination only against creation scientists and those who teach creation science. Second, the Act requires local school boards to develop and provide to science teachers "a curriculum guide on presentation of creation-science." Finally, the Act requires the governor to designate seven creation scientists who shall, upon request, assist local school boards in developing the curriculum guides. But none of these provisions casts doubt upon the sincerity of the legislators' articulated purpose of "academic freedom"—unless, of course, one gives that term the obviously erroneous meanings preferred by the Court.

* * * * *

It is undoubtedly true that what prompted the Legislature to direct its attention to the misrepresentation of evolution in the schools (rather than the inaccurate presentation of other topics) was its awareness of the tension between evolution and the religious beliefs of many children. But even appellees concede that a valid secular purpose is not rendered impermissible simply because its pursuit is prompted by concern for religious sensitivities. If a history teacher falsely told her students that the bones of Jesus Christ had been discovered, or a physics teacher that the Shroud of Turin had been conclusively established to be inexplicable on the basis of natural causes, I cannot believe (despite the majority's implication to the contrary, see *ante,* at 13) that legislators or school board members would be constitutionally prohibited from taking corrective action, simply because that action was prompted by concern for the religious beliefs of the misinstructed students.

In sum, even if one concedes, for the sake of argument, that a majority of the Louisiana Legislature voted for the Balanced Treatment Act partly in order to foster (rather than merely eliminate discrimination against) Christian fundamentalist beliefs, our cases establish that that alone would not suffice to invalidate the Act, so long as there was a genuine secular purpose as well. We have, moreover, no adequate basis for disbelieving the secular purpose set forth in the Act itself, or for concluding that it is a sham enacted to conceal the legislators' violation of their oaths of office. I am astonished by the Court's unprecedented readiness to reach such a conclusion, which I can only attribute to an intellectual predisposition created by the facts and the legend of *Scopes v. State*—an instinctive reaction that any governmentally imposed requirements bearing upon the teaching of evolution must be a manifestation of Christian fundamentalist repression. In this case, however, it seems to me the Court's position is the repressive one. The people of Louisiana, including those who are Christian fundamentalists, are quite entitled, as a secular matter, to have whatever scientific evidence there may be against evolution presented in their schools, just as Mr. Scopes was entitled to present whatever scientific evidence there was for it. Perhaps what the Louisiana Legislature has done is unconstitutional because there *is* no such evidence, and the scheme they have established will amount to no more than a presentation of the Book of Genesis. But we cannot say that on the evidence before us in this summary judgment context, which includes ample uncontradicted testimony that "creation science" is a body of scientific knowledge rather than revealed belief. *Infinitely less* can we say (or should we say) that the scientific evidence for evolution is so conclusive that no one could be gullible enough to believe that there is any real scientific evidence to the contrary, so that the legislation's stated purpose must be a lie. Yet that illiberal judgment, that *Scopes*-in-reverse, is ultimately the basis on which the Court's facile rejection of the Louisiana Legislature's purpose must rest.

Since the existence of secular purpose is so entirely clear, and thus dispositive, I will not go on to discuss the fact that, even if the Louisiana Legislature's purpose were exclusively to advance religion, some of the well established exceptions to the impermissibility of that purpose might be applicable—the validating intent to eliminate a perceived discrimination against a particular religion, to facilitate its free exercise, or to accommodate it. I am not in any case enamored of those amorphous exceptions, since I think them no more than unpredictable correctives to what is (as the next Part of this opinion will discuss) a fundamentally unsound rule. It is surprising, however, that the Court does not address these exceptions, since the context of the legislature's action gives some reason to believe they may be applicable.

Because I believe that the Balanced Treatment Act had a secular purpose, which is all the first component of the *Lemon* test requires, I would reverse the judgment of the Court of Appeals and remand for further consideration.

* * * * *

Given the many hazards involved in assessing the subjective intent of governmental decisionmakers, the first prong of *Lemon* is defensible, I think, only if the text of the Establishment Clause demands it. That is surely not the case. The Clause states that "Congress shall make no law respecting an establishment of religion." One could argue, I suppose, that any time Congress acts with the *intent* of advancing religion, it has enacted a "law respecting an establishment of religion"; but far from being an unavoidable reading, it is quite an unnatural one. I doubt, for example, that the Clayton Act, as amended, could reasonably be described as a "law respecting an establishment of religion" if bizarre new historical evidence revealed that it lacked a secular purpose, even though it has no discernible nonsecular effect. It is, in short, far from an inevitable reading of the Establishment Clause that it forbids all governmental action intended to advance religion; and if not inevitable, any reading with such untoward consequences must be wrong.

In the past we have attempted to justify our embarrassing Establishment Clause jurisprudence on the ground that it "sacrifices clarity and predictability for flexibility." One commentator has aptly characterized this as "a euphemism . . . for . . . the absence of any principled rationale." I think it time that we sacrifice some "flexibility" for "clarity and predictability." Abandoning *Lemon's* purpose test—a test which exacerbates the tension between the Free Exercise and Establishment Clauses, has no basis in the language or history of the amendment, and, as today's decision shows, has wonderfully flexible consequences—would be a good place to start.

Post-Secondary Education

A Summary of the Significant Cases Related to Colleges

In writing about the Court's attitude toward church-related colleges, Professor A. E. Dick Howard comments that the majority has maintained "a sharp distinction between aid to sectarian primary and secondary schools and aid at the level of higher education."[1] The three major cases were *Tilton v. Richardson*, 403 U.S. 672 (1971); *Hunt v. McNair*, 413 U.S. 734 (1973); and *Roemer v. Board of Public Works*, 426 U.S. 736 (1976). These cases are represented here through a brief summary and selected citations.

On the same day that the Court ruled unconstitutional certain "parochaid" in *Lemon v. Kurtzman,* Justice Burger in *Tilton* spoke for the five-member majority upholding the 1963 Higher Education Facilities Act that provides construction grants and facilities used exclusively for secular purposes in church-related colleges. In justifying the decision, he wrote: "There are generally significant differences between the religious aspects of church-related institutions of higher learning and parochial elementary and secondary schools. . . . The entanglement between church and state is also lessened here by the nonideological character of the aid that the Government provides." Justice Douglas, writing for Justices Black and Marshall, entered a vigorous dissent. He wrote: "It is almost unbelievable that we have made the radical departure from Madison's Remonstrance memorialized in

[1]A. E. Dick Howard, "Up Against the Wall: The Uneasy Separation of Church and State," in *Church, State, and Politics,* J. B. Hensel, ed. (Washington, D.C.: The Roscoe Pound–American Trial Lawyers Foundation, 1981).

today's decision. . . . It should be remembered that in this case we deal with federal grants and with the command that 'Congress shall make no law respecting an establishment of religion, or prohibiting the free exercise thereof.' The million-dollar grants sustained today put Madison's miserable 'three pence' to shame. But he even thought, as I do, that even a small amount coming out of the pocket of taxpayers and going into the coffers of a church was not in keeping with our constitutional ideal."

In 1973 the Court, in *Hunt,* rejected First Amendment challenges to South Carolina issuing revenue bonds to help a Baptist college borrow money. Justice Powell, for the majority, argued that even though the college was owned and operated by the South Carolina Baptist Convention, it was not "pervasively sectarian." Relying upon *Tilton* and convinced that the "scope of the assistance" was to the "secular aspects" of the college, Justice Powell did not believe there was a foreshadowing of "excessive entanglement."

In writing for Justices Douglas and Marshall, Justice Brennan in dissent stated: "Thus, it is crystal clear, I think, that this scheme involves the State in a degree of policing of the affairs of the College far exceeding that called for by the statutes struck down in *Lemon I.*" The problem for the dissenters was how the programs of surveillance and inspection called for in both the current case and *Tilton* "differ from the Pennsylvania and Rhode Island programs invalidated in *Lemon I.*"

Again in *Roemer* the Court addressed for a third time the subject of church-related colleges, this time Catholic institutions in Maryland. Justice Blackmun concluded for the majority that "neutrality is what is required" in the noncategorical grants authorized under state law. He relied upon *Tilton* and *Hunt* to argue that the Maryland law passed the three-part *Lemon I* test. There is, nonetheless, some uncertainty in the language of the decision:

> So the slate we write on is anything but clean. Instead, there is little room for further refinement of the principles governing public aid to church-affiliated private schools. Our purpose is not to unsettle those principles, so recently reaffirmed, or to expand upon them substantially, but merely to insure that they are faithfully applied in this case.

And Justice Blackmun concluded:

> There is no exact science in gauging the entanglement of church and state. The wording of the test, which speaks of '*excessive* entanglement,' itself makes that clear. The relevant factors we have identified are to be considered 'cumulatively' in judging the degree of entanglement. They may cut different ways, as certainly they do here.

Justice Brennan wrote a dissent joined by Justices Marshall, Stewart, and Stevens in which he stated: "The discrete interests of government and religion are mutually best served when each avoids too close a proximity to the other. . . . The Maryland Act requires 'too close a proximity' of government to the subsidized sectarian institutions and in my view creates real dangers of the secularization of a creed."

Quoting once again from Professor Howard: "The Court in brief, takes a pragmatic approach to programs aiding church-related colleges." The Court is content to accept that while church control at the secondary level almost certainly means the schools are "pervasively sectarian," it is not the same at the college level. The Court, by a narrow majority, has accepted the proposition that church-related colleges have a secular mission rather than a sectarian one.

In a continuation of this line of thought, the Court in *Witters v. Washington Department of Services for the Blind* (1986) held that the Establishment Clause does not preclude a state from providing assistance under a vocational rehabilitation program to a blind person at a Christian college studying to become a pastor or youth director. In part the justification for the decision hinged on the fact that the money was paid to the student, not the college.

Sunday Laws

McGowan et al. v. Maryland, 366 U.S. 420 (1961)

McGowan addressed the sensitive issue of Sunday closing laws from the point of view of establishment. The case was brought by employees of a department store who had been convicted under a Maryland law prohibiting the sale of certain items on Sunday. In writing for the majority Justice Warren noted that "what we must decide is whether the present Sunday legislation, having undergone extensive changes from the earliest forms, still retains its religious character." From Justice Frankfurter's extended separate opinion tracing the history of the Sunday laws, we have included his opening premise and his basic conclusions. Justice Douglas reached opposite results in his dissent. In addition to *McGowan,* the Court handed down three other decisions the same day, one dealing primarily with establishment and two addressing the free exercise clause. One of the latter, *Braunfeld v. Brown,* is to be found elsewhere in this volume. It should be noted that both Frankfurter's and Douglas' opinions apply to all four cases. While Douglas provided the only dissent in the two establishment cases *(McGowan, Two Guys From Harrison-Allentown, Inc. v. McGinley),* his dissent was joined in the free exercise cases *(Braunfeld, Gallagher v. Crown Kosher Super Market)* by Justices Brennan and Stewart. In all four the Court majority found Sunday laws to be constitutional. The Frankfurter opinion and Douglas dissent printed here make reference to the entire group of cases.

MR. CHIEF JUSTICE WARREN DELIVERED THE OPINION OF THE COURT.

The issues in this case concern the constitutional validity of Maryland criminal statutes, commonly known as Sunday Closing Laws or Sunday Blue Laws. These statutes, with exceptions to be noted hereafter, generally proscribe all labor, business and other commercial activities on Sunday. The questions presented are whether the classifications within the statutes bring about a denial of equal protection of the law, whether the laws are so vague as to fail to give reasonable notice of the forbidden conduct and therefore violate due process, and whether the statutes are laws respecting an establishment of religion or prohibiting the free exercise thereof.

Appellants are seven employees of a large discount department store located on a highway in Anne Arundel County, Maryland. They were indicted for the Sunday sale of a three-ring loose-leaf binder, a can of floor wax, a stapler and staples, and a toy submarine in violation of Md. Ann. Code, Art. 27, § 521. Generally, this section prohibited, throughout the State, the Sunday sale of all merchandise except the retail sale of tobacco products, confectioneries, milk, bread, fruits, gasoline, oils, greases, drugs and medicines, and newspapers and periodicals. Recently amended, this section also now excepts from the general prohibition the retail sale in Anne Arundel County of all foodstuffs, automobile and boating accessories, flowers, toilet goods, hospital supplies and souvenirs. It now further provides that any retail establishment in Anne Arundel County which does not employ more than one person other than the owner may operate on Sunday.

Although appellants were indicted only under § 521, in order properly to consider several of the broad constitutional contentions, we must examine the whole body of Maryland Sunday laws. Several sections of the Maryland statutes are particularly relevant to evaluation of the issues presented. Section 492, Art. 27, forbids all persons from doing any work or bodily labor on Sunday and forbids permitting children or servants to work on that day or to engage in fishing, hunting and unlawful pastimes or recreations. The section excepts all works of necessity and charity. Section 522 disallows the opening or use of any dancing saloon, opera house, bowling alley or barber shop on Sunday. However, in addition to the exceptions noted above, Art. 27, § 509, exempts, for Anne Arundel County, the Sunday operation of any bathing beach, bathhouse, dancing saloon and amusement park, and activities incident thereto and retail sales of merchandise customarily sold at, or incidental to, the operation of the aforesaid occupations and businesses. Section 90 makes generally unlawful the sale of alcoholic beverages on Sunday. However, this section and immediately succeeding ones, provide various immunities for the Sunday sale of different kinds of alcoholic beverages, at different hours during the day, by vendors holding different types of licenses, in different political divisions of the State—particularly in Anne Arundel County.

The remaining statutory sections concern a myriad of exceptions for various counties, districts of counties, cities and towns throughout the State. Among the activities allowed in certain areas on Sunday are such sports as football, baseball, golf, tennis, bowling, croquet, basketball, lacrosse, soccer, hockey, swimming, softball, boating, fishing, skating, horseback riding, stock car racing and pool or billiards. Other immunized activities permitted in some regions of the State include group singing or playing of musical instruments; the exhibition of motion pictures; dancing; the operation of recreation centers, picnic grounds, swimming pools, skating rinks and miniature golf courses. The taking of oysters and the hunting or killing of game is generally forbidden, but shooting conducted by organized rod and gun clubs is permitted in one county. In some of the subdivisions within the State, the exempted Sunday activities are sanctioned throughout the day; in others, they may not commence until early afternoon or evening; in many, the activities may only be conducted during the afternoon and late in the evening. Certain localities do not permit the allowed Sunday activity to be carried on within one hundred yards of any church where religious services are being held. Local ordinances and regulations concerning certain limited activities supplement the State's statutory scheme. In Anne Arundel County, for example, slot machines, pinball machines and bingo may be played on Sunday.

Among other things, appellants contended at the trial that the Maryland statutes under which they were charged were contrary to the Fourteenth Amendent for the reasons stated at the outset of this opinion. Appellants were convicted and each was fined five dollars and costs. The Maryland Court of Appeals affirmed; on appeal we noted probable jurisdiction.

I

Appellants argue that the Maryland statutes violate the "Equal Protection" Clause of the Fourteenth Amendment on several counts. First, they contend that the classifications contained in the statutes concerning which commodities may or may not be sold on Sunday are without rational and substantial relation to the object of the legislation. Specifically, appellants allege that the statutory exemptions for the Sunday sale of the merchandise mentioned above render arbitrary the statute under which they were convicted. Appellants further allege that § 521 is capricious because of the exemptions for the operation of the various amusements that have been listed and because slot machines, pin-ball machines, and bingo are legalized and are freely played on Sunday.

The standards under which this proposition is to be evaluated have been set forth many times by this Court. Although no precise formula has been developed, the Court has held that the Fourteenth Amendment permits the States a wide scope of discretion in enacting laws which affect some groups of citizens differently than others. The constitutional safeguard is offended only if the classification rests on grounds wholly irrelevant to the achievement of the State's objective. State legislatures are presumed to have acted within their constitutional power despite the fact, that in practice, their laws result in some inequality. A statutory discrimination will not be set aside if any state of facts reasonably may be conceived to justify it.

It would seem that a legislature could reasonably find that the Sunday sale of the exempted commodities was necessary either for the health of the populace or for the enhancement of the recreational atmosphere of the day—that a family which takes a Sunday ride into the country will need gasoline for the automobile and may find pleasant a soft drink or fresh fruit; that those who go to the beach may wish ice cream or some other item normally sold there; that some people will prefer alcoholic beverages or games of chance to add to their relaxation; that newspapers and drug products should always be available to the public.

The record is barren of any indication that this apparently reasonable basis does not exist, that the statutory distinctions are invidious, that local tradition and custom might not rationally call for this legislative treatment. Likewise, the fact that these exemptions exist and deny some vendors and operators the day of rest and recreation contemplated by the legislature does not render the statutes violative of equal protection since there would appear to be many valid reasons for these exemptions, as stated above, and no evidence to dispel them.

Secondly, appellants contend that the statutory arrangement which permits only certain Anne Arundel County retailers to sell merchandise essential to, or customarily sold at, or incidental to, the operation of bathing beaches, amusement parks et cetera is contrary to the

"Equal Protection" Clause because it discriminates unreasonably against retailers in other Maryland counties. But we have held that the Equal Protection Clause relates to equality between persons as such, rather than between areas and that territorial uniformity is not a constitutional prerequisite. With particular reference to the State of Maryland, we have noted that the prescription of different substantive offenses in different counties is generally a matter for legislative discretion. We find no invidious discrimination here.

Thirdly, appellants contend that this same statutory provision violates the "Equal Protection" Clause because it permits only certain merchants within Anne Arundel County (operators of bathing beaches and amusement parks et cetera) to sell merchandise customarily sold at these places while forbidding its sale by other vendors of this merchandise, such as appellants' employer. Here again, it would seem that a legislature could reasonably find that these commodities, necessary for the health and recreation of its citizens, should only be sold on Sunday by those vendors at the locations where the commodities are most likely to be immediately put to use. Such a determination would seem to serve the consuming public and at the same time secure Sunday rest for those employees, like appellants, of all other retail establishments. In addition, the enforcement problems which would accrue if large retail establishments, like appellants' employer, were permitted to remain open on Sunday but were restricted to the sale of the merchandise in question would be far greater than the problems accruing if only beach and amusement park vendors were exempted. Here again, there has been no indication of the unreasonableness of this differentiation. On the record before us, we cannot say that these statutes do not provide equal protection of the laws.

II

Another question presented by appellants is whether Art. 27, § 509, which exempts the Sunday retail sale of "merchandise essential to, or customarily sold at, or incidental to, the operation of" bathing beaches, amusement parks et cetera in Anne Arundel County, is unconstitutionally vague. We believe that business people of ordinary intelligence in the position of appellants' employer would be able to know what exceptions are encompassed by the statute either as a matter of ordinary commercial knowledge or by simply making a reasonable investigation at a nearby bathing beach or amusement park within the county. Under these circumstances, there is no necessity to guess at the statute's meaning in order to determine what conduct it makes criminal. Questions concerning proof that the items appellants sold were customarily sold at, or incidental to the operation of, a bathing beach or amusement park were not raised in the Maryland Court of Appeals, nor are they raised here. Thus, we cannot consider the matter.

III

The final questions for decisions are whether the Maryland Sunday Closing Laws conflict with the Federal Constitution's provisions for religious liberty. First, appellants contend here that the statutes applicable to Anne Arundel County violate the constitutional guarantee of freedom of religion in that the statutes' effect is to prohibit the free exercise of religion in contravention of the First Amendment, made applicable to the States by the Fourteenth Amendment. But appellants allege only economic injury to themselves; they do not allege any infringement of their own religious freedoms due to Sunday closing. In fact, the record is silent as to what appellants' religious beliefs are. Since the general rule is that "a litigant may only assert his own constitutional rights or immunities," we hold that appellants have no standing to raise this contention. Furthermore, since appellants do not specifically allege that the statutes infringe upon the religious beliefs of the department store's present or prospective patrons, we have no occasion here to consider the standing question of *Pierce.* Those persons whose religious rights are allegedly impaired by the statutes are not without effective ways to assert these rights. Appellants present no weighty countervailing policies here to cause an exception to our general principles.

Secondly, appellants contend that the statutes violate the guarantee of separation of church and state in that the statutes are laws respecting an establishment of religion contrary to the First Amendment, made applicable to the States by the Fourteenth Amendment. If the purpose of the "establishment" clause was only to insure protection for the "free exercise" of religion, then what we have said above concerning appellants' standing to raise the "free exercise" contention would appear to be true here. However, the writings of Madison, who was the First Amendment's architect, demonstrate that the establishment of a religion was equally feared because of its tendencies to political tyranny and subversion of civil authority. Thus, in *Everson* the Court permitted a district taxpayer to challenge, on "establishment" grounds, a state statute which authorized district boards of education to reimburse parents for fares paid for the transportation of their children to both public and Catholic schools. Appellants here concededly have suffered direct economic injury, allegedly due to the imposition on them of the tenets of the Christian religion. We find that, in these circumstances, these appellants have standing to complain that the statutes are laws respecting an establishment of religion.

The essence of appellants' "establishment" argument is that Sunday is the Sabbath day of the predominant Christian sects; that the purpose of the enforced stoppage of labor on that day is to facilitate and encourage church attendance; that the purpose of setting Sunday as a day of universal rest is to induce people with no religion or people with marginal religious beliefs to join the predominant Christian sects; that the purpose of the atmosphere of tranquility created by Sunday closing is to aid the conduct of church services and religious observance of the sacred day. In substantiating their "establishment" argument, appellants rely on the wording of the present Maryland statutes, on earlier versions of the current Sunday laws and on prior judicial characterizations of these laws by the Maryland Court of Appeals. Although only the constitutionality of § 521, the section under which appellants have been convicted, is immediately before us in this litigation, inquiry into the history of Sunday Closing Laws in our country, in addition to an examination of the Maryland Sunday closing statutes in their entirety and of their history, is relevant to the decision of whether the Maryland Sunday law in question is one respecting an establishment of religion. There is no dispute that the original laws which dealt with Sunday labor were motivated by religious forces. But what we must decide is whether present Sunday legislation, having undergone extensive changes from the earliest forms, still retains its religious character.

Sunday Closing Laws go far back into American history, having been brought to the colonies with a background of English legislation dating to the thirteenth century. In 1237, Henry III forbade the frequenting of markets on Sunday; the Sunday showing of wools at the staple was banned by Edward III in 1354; in 1409, Henry IV prohibited the playing of unlawful games on Sunday; Henry VI proscribed Sunday fairs in churchyards in 1444 and, four years later, made unlawful all fairs and markets and all showings of any goods or merchandise; Edward VI disallowed Sunday bodily labor by several injunctions in the mid-sixteenth century; various Sunday sports and amusements were restricted in 1625 by Charles I. The law of the colonies to the time of the Revolution and the basis of the Sunday laws in the States was 29 Charles II, c. 7 (1677). It provided, in part:

> For the better observation and keeping holy the Lord's day, commonly called Sunday: be it enacted . . . that all the laws enacted and in force concerning the observation of the day, *and repairing to the church thereon,* be carefully put in execution; and that all and every person and persons whatsoever shall upon every Lord's day apply themselves to the observation of the same, by exercising themselves thereon in the duties of piety and true religion, publicly and privately; and that no tradesman, artificer, workman, laborer, or other person whatsoever, *shall do or exercise any worldly labor or business or work* of their ordinary callings upon the Lord's day, or any part thereof (works of necessity and charity only excepted); . . . and that no person or persons whatsoever shall publicly cry, show forth, or expose for sale any wares, merchandise, fruit, herbs, goods, or chattels, whatsoever, upon the Lord's day, or any part thereof. . . . (Emphasis added.)

Observation of the above language, and of that of the prior mandates, reveals clearly that the English Sunday legislation was in aid of the established church.

The American colonial Sunday restrictions arose soon after settlement. Starting in 1650, the Plymouth Colony proscribed servile work, unnecessary travelling, sports, and the sale of alcoholic beverages on the Lord's day and enacted laws concerning church attendance. The Massachusetts Bay Colony and the Connecticut and New Haven Colonies enacted similar prohibitions, some even earlier in the seventeenth century. The religious orientation of the colonial statutes was equally apparent. For example, a 1629 Massachusetts Bay instruction began, "And to the end the Sabbath may be celebrated in a religious manner. . . . " A 1653 enactment spoke of Sunday activities "which things tend much to the dishonor of God, the reproach of religion, and the profanation of his holy Sabbath, the sanctification whereof is sometimes put for all duties immediately respecting the service of

God. . . . "These laws persevered after the Revolution and, at about the time of the First Amendment's adoption, each of the colonies had laws of some sort restricting Sunday labor.

But, despite the strongly religious origin of these laws, beginning before the eighteenth century, nonreligious arguments for Sunday closing began to be heard more distinctly and the statutes began to lose some of their totally religious flavor. In the middle 1700's, Blackstone wrote, "[T]he keeping one day in the seven holy, as a time of relaxation and refreshment as well as for public worship, is of admirable service to a state considered merely as a civil institution. It humanizes, by the help of conversation and society, the manners of the lower classes; which would otherwise degenerate into a sordid ferocity and savage selfishness of spirit; it enables the industrious workman to pursue his occupation in the ensuing week with health and cheerfulness." A 1788 English statute dealing with chimney sweeps, in addition to providing for their Sunday religious affairs, also regulated their hours of work. The preamble to a 1679 Rhode Island enactment stated that the reason for the ban on Sunday employment was that "persons being evill minded, have presumed to employ in servile labor, more than necessity requireth, their servants. . . . " The New York law of 1788 omitted the term "Lord's day" and substituted "the first day of the week commonly called Sunday." Similar changes marked the Maryland statutes, discussed below. With the advent of the First Amendment, the colonial provisions requiring church attendance were soon repealed.

More recently, further secular justifications have been advanced for making Sunday a day of rest, a day when people may recover from the labors of the week just passed and may physically and mentally prepare for the week's work to come. In England, during the First World War, a committee investigating the health conditions of munitions workers reported that "if the maximum output is to be secured and maintained for any length of time, a weekly period of rest must be allowed. . . . On economic and social grounds alike this weekly period of rest is best provided on Sunday."

The proponents of Sunday closing legislation are no longer exclusively representatives of religious interests. Recent New Jersey Sunday legislation was supported by labor groups and trade associations; modern English Sunday legislation was promoted by the National Federation of Grocers and supported by the National Chamber of Trade, the Drapers' Chamber of Trade, and the National Union of Shop Assistants.

Throughout the years, state legislatures have modified, deleted from and added to their Sunday statutes. As evidenced by the New Jersey laws mentioned above, current changes are commonplace. Almost every State in our country presently has some type of Sunday regulation and over forty possess a relatively comprehensive system. Some of our States now enforce their Sunday legislation through Departments of Labor. Thus have Sunday laws evolved from the wholly religious sanctions that originally were enacted.

Moreover, litigation over Sunday closing laws is not novel. Scores of cases may be found in the state appellate courts relating to sundry phases of Sunday enactments. Religious objections have been raised there on numerous occasions but sustained only once, in *Ex parte Newman,* and that decision was overruled three years later, in *Ex parte Andrews.* A substantial number of cases in varying postures bearing on state Sunday legislation have reached this Court. Although none raising the issues now presented have gained plenary hearing, language used in some of these cases further evidences the evolution of Sunday laws as temporal statutes.

* * * * *

Before turning to the Maryland legislation now here under attack, an investigation of what historical position Sunday Closing Laws have occupied with reference to the First Amendment should be undertaken.

This Court has considered the happenings surrounding the Virginia General Assembly's enactment of "An act for establishing religious freedom," written by Thomas Jefferson and sponsored by James Madison, as best reflecting the long and intensive struggle for religious freedom in America, as particularly relevant in the search for the First Amendment's meaning. In 1776, nine years before the bill's passage, Madison co-authored Virginia's Declaration of Rights which provided that "all men are equally entitled to the free exercise of religion, according to the dictates of conscience. . . . " Virginia had had Sunday legislation since early in the seventeenth century; in 1776, the laws penalizing "maintaining any opinions in matters of religion, *forbearing to repair to church,* or the exercising any mode of worship whatsoever" were repealed, and all dissenters were freed from the taxes levied for the support of the established church. (Emphasis added.)

The Sunday labor prohibitions remained; apparently, they were not believed to be inconsistent with the newly enacted Declaration of Rights. Madison had sought also to have the Declaration expressly condemn the existing Virginia establishment. This hope was finally realized when "A Bill for Establishing Religious Freedom" was passed in 1785. In this same year, Madison presented to Virginia legislators "A Bill for Punishing . . . Sabbath Breakers" which provided in part:

> If any person on Sunday shall himself be found labouring at his own or any other trade or calling, or shall employ his apprentices, servants or slaves in labour, or other business, except it be in the ordinary houshold offices of daily necessity, or other work of necessity or charity, he shall forfeit the sum of ten shillings for every such offence, deeming every apprentice, servant, or slave so employed, and every day he shall be so employed as constituting a distinct offence.

This became law the following year and remained during the time that Madison fought for the First Amendment in the Congress. It was the law of Virginia, and similar laws were in force in other States, when Madison stated at the Virginia ratification convention:

> Happily for the states, they enjoy the utmost freedom of religion. . . . Fortunately for this commonwealth, a majority of the people are decidedly against any exclusive establishment. I believe it to be so in the other states. . . . I can appeal to my uniform conduct on this subject, that I have warmly supported religious freedom.

In 1799, Virginia pronounced "An act for establishing religious freedom" as "a true exposition of the principles of the bill of rights and constitution," and repealed all subsequently enacted legislation deemed inconsistent with it. Virginia's statute banning Sunday labor stood.

In *Reynolds* the Court relied heavily on the history of the Virginia bill. That case concerned a Mormon's attack on a statute making bigamy a crime. . . . In the case at bar, we find the place of Sunday Closing Laws in the First Amendment's history both enlightening and persuasive.

* * * * *

An early commentator opined that the "real object of the amendment was . . . to prevent any national ecclesiastical establishment, which should give to an hierarchy the exclusive patronage of the national government." But, the First Amendment, in its final form, did not simply bar a congressional enactment *establishing a church;* it forbade all laws *respecting an establishment of religion.* Thus, this Court has given the Amendment a "broad interpretation . . . in the light of its history and the evils it was designed forever to suppress. . . . " It has found that the First and Fourteenth Amendments afford protection against religious establishment far more extensive than merely to forbid a national or state church. Thus, in *McCollum* the Court held that the action of a board of education, permitting religious instruction during school hours in public school buildings and requiring those children who chose not to attend to remain in their classrooms, to be contrary to the "Establishment" Clause.

However, it is equally true that the "Establishment" Clause does not ban federal or state regulation of conduct whose reason or effect merely happens to coincide or harmonize with the tenets of some or all religions. In many instances, the Congress or state legislatures conclude that the general welfare of society, wholly apart from any religious considerations, demands such regulation. Thus, for temporal purposes, murder is illegal. And the fact that this agrees with the dictates of the Judaeo-Christian religions while it may disagree with others does not invalidate the regulation. So too with the questions of adultery and polygamy. The same could be said of theft, fraud, etc., because those offenses were also proscribed in the Decalogue.

Thus, these broad principles have been set forth by this Court. Those cases dealing with the specific problems arising under the "Establishment" Clause which have reached this Court are few in number. The most extensive discussion of the "Establishment" Clause's latitude is to be found in *Everson.*

Under challenge was a statute authorizing repayment to parents of their children's transportation expenses to public and Catholic schools. The Court, speaking through Mr. Justice Black, recognized that "it is undoubtedly true that children are helped to get to church schools," and "[t]here is even a possibility that some of the children might not be sent to the church schools if the parents were compelled to pay their children's bus fares out of their own pockets when transportation to a public school would have been paid for by the State."

But the Court found that the purpose and effect of the statute in question was general "public welfare legislation," that it was to protect all school children from the "very real hazards of traffic," that the expenditure of public funds for school transportation, to religious schools or to any others; was like the expenditure of public funds to provide policemen to safeguard these same children or to provide "such general government services as ordinary police and fire protection, connections for sewage disposal, public highways and sidewalks."

In light of the evolution of our Sunday Closing Laws through the centuries, and of their more or less recent emphasis upon secular considerations, it is not difficult to discern that as presently written and administered, most of them, at least, are of a secular rather than of a religious character, and that presently they bear no relationship to establishment of religion as those words are used in the Constitution of the United States.

Throughout this century and longer, both the federal and state governments have oriented their activities very largely toward improvement of the health, safety, recreation and general well-being of our citizens. Numerous laws affecting public health, safety factors in industry, laws affecting hours and conditions of labor of women and children, week-end diversion at parks and beaches, and cultural activities of various kinds, now point the way toward the good life for all. Sunday Closing Laws, like those before us, have become part and parcel of this great governmental concern wholly apart from their original purposes or connotations. The present purpose and effect of most of them is to provide a uniform day of rest for all citizens; the fact that this day is Sunday, a day of particular significance for the dominant Christian sects, does not bar the State from achieving its secular goals. To say that the States cannot prescribe Sunday as a day of rest for these purposes solely because centuries ago such laws had their genesis in religion would give a constitutional interpretation of hostility to the public welfare rather than one of mere separation of church and State.

We now reach the Maryland statutes under review. The title of the major series of sections of the Maryland Code dealing with Sunday closing is "Sabbath Breaking"; § 492 proscribes work or bodily labor on the "Lord's day," and forbids persons to "profane the Lord's day" by gaming, fishing et cetera; § 522 refers to Sunday as the "Sabbath day." As has been mentioned above, many of the exempted Sunday activities in the various localities of the State may only be conducted during the afternoon and late evening; most Christian church services, of course, are held on Sunday morning and early Sunday evening.

Finally, as previously noted, certain localities do not permit the allowed Sunday activities to be carried on within one hundred yards of any church where religious services are being held. This is the totality of the evidence of religious purpose which may be gleaned from the face of the present statute and from its operative effect.

The predecessors of the existing Maryland Sunday laws are undeniably religious in origin. The first Maryland statute dealing with Sunday activities, enacted in 1649, was entitled "An Act concerning Religion." It made it criminal to "profane the Sabbath or Lords day called Sunday by frequent swearing, drunkennes or by any uncivill or disorderly recreation, or by working on that day when absolute necessity doth not require it." A 1692 statute entitled "An Act for the Service of Almighty God and the Establishment of the Protestant Religion within this Province," after first stating the importance of keeping the Lord's Day holy and sanctified and expressing concern with the breach of its observance throughout the State, then enacted a Sunday labor prohibition which was the obvious precursor of the present § 492. There was a re-enactment in 1696 entitled "An Act for Sanctifying & keeping holy the Lord's Day Commonly called Sunday." By 1723, the Sabbath-breaking section of the statute assumed the present form of § 492, omitting the specific prohibition against Sunday swearing and the patently religiously motivated title.

There are judicial statements in early Maryland decisions which tend to support appellants' position. In an 1834 case involving a contract calling for delivery on Sunday, the Maryland Court of Appeals remarked that "Ours is a christian community, and a day set apart as the day of rest, is the day consecrated by the resurrection of our Saviour, and embraces the twenty-four hours next ensuing the midnight of Saturday."This language was cited with approval in *Judefind* v. *State.*

* * * * *

But it should be noted that, throughout the *Judefind* decision, the Maryland court specifically rejected the contention that the laws interfered with religious liberty and stated that the laws' purpose was to provide the "advantages of having a weekly day of rest, 'from a mere physical and political standpoint.'"

Considering the language and operative effect of the current statutes, we no longer find the blanket prohibition against Sunday work or bodily labor. To the contrary, we find that § 521 of Art. 27, the section which appellants violated, permits the Sunday sale of tobaccos and sweets and a long list of sundry articles which we have enumerated above; we find that § 509 of Art. 27 permits the Sunday operation of bathing beaches, amusement parks and similar facilities; we find that Art. 2B, § 28, permits the Sunday sale of alcoholic beverages, products strictly forbidden by predecessor statutes; we are told that Anne Arundel County allows Sunday bingo and the Sunday playing of pinball machines and slot machines, activities generally condemned by prior Maryland Sunday legislation. Certainly, these are not works of charity or necessity. Section 521's current stipulation that shops with only one employee may remain open on Sunday does not coincide with a religious purpose. These provisions, along with those which permit various sports and entertainments on Sunday, seem clearly to be fashioned for the purpose of providing a Sunday atmosphere of recreation, cheerfulness, repose and enjoyment. Coupled with the general proscription against other types of work, we believe that the air of the day is one of relaxation rather than one of religion.

The existing Maryland Sunday laws are not simply verbatim re-enactments of their religiously oriented antecedents. Only § 492 retains the appellation of "Lord's day" and even that section no longer makes recitation of religious purpose. It does talk in terms of "profan[ing] the Lord's day," but other sections permit the activities previously thought to be profane. Prior denunciation of Sunday drunkenness is now gone. Contemporary concern with these statutes is evidenced by the dozen changes made in 1959 and by the recent enactment of a majority of the exceptions.

Finally, the relevant pronouncements of the Maryland Court of Appeals dispel any argument that the statutes' announced purpose is religious. In *Hiller* v. *Maryland* (1914), the court had before it a Baltimore ordinance prohibiting Sunday baseball. The court said:

> What the eminent chief judge said with respect to police enactments which deal with the protection of the public health, morals and safety apply with equal force to those which are concerned with the peace, order and quiet of the community on Sunday, for these social conditions are well recognized heads of the police power. Can the Court say that this ordinance has no real and substantial relation to the peace and order and quiet of Sunday, as a day of rest, in the City of Baltimore?

And the Maryland court declared in its decision in the instant case: "The legislative plan is plain. It is to compel a day of rest from work, permitting only activities which are necessary or recreational." After engaging in the close scrutiny demanded of us when First Amendment liberties are at issue, we accept the State Supreme Court's determination that the statutes' present purpose and effect is not to aid religion but to set aside a day of rest and recreation.

But this does not answer all of the appellants' contentions. We are told that the State has other means at its disposal to accomplish its secular purpose, other courses that would not even remotely or incidentally give state aid to religion. On this basis, we are asked to hold these statutes invalid on the ground that the State's power to regulate conduct in the public interest may only be executed in a way that does not unduly or unnecessarily infringe upon the religious provisions of the First Amendment. However relevant this argument may be, we believe that the factual basis on which it rests is not supportable. It is true that if the State's interest were simply to provide for its citizens a periodic respite from work, a regulation demanding that everyone rest one day in seven, leaving the choice of the day to the individual, would suffice.

However, the State's purpose is not merely to provide a one-day-in-seven work stoppage. In addition to this, the State seeks to set one day apart from all others as a day of rest, repose, recreation and tranquility—a day which all members of the family and community have the opportunity to spend and enjoy together, a day on which there exists relative quiet and disassociation from the everyday intensity of commercial activities, a day on which people may visit friends and relatives who are not available during working days.

Obviously, a State is empowered to determine that a rest-one-day-in-seven statute would not accomplish this purpose; that it would not provide for a general cessation of activity, a special atmosphere of tranquility, a day which all members of the family or friends and relatives might spend together. Furthermore, it seems plain that the problems involved in enforcing such a provision would be exceedingly more difficult than those in enforcing a common-day-of-rest provision.

Moreover, it is common knowledge that the first day of the week has come to have special significance as a rest day in this country. People of all religions and people with no religion regard Sunday as a time for family activity, for visiting friends and relatives, for late sleeping, for passive and active entertainments, for dining out, and the like. . . . Sunday is a day apart from all others. The cause is irrelevant; the fact exists. It would seem unrealistic for enforcement purposes and perhaps detrimental to the general welfare to require a State to choose a common day of rest other than that which most persons would select of their own accord. For these reasons, we hold that the Maryland statutes are not laws respecting an establishment of religion.

The distinctions between the statutes in the case before us and the state action in *McCollum,* the only case in this Court finding a violation of the "Establishment" Clause, lend further substantiation to our conclusion. In *McCollum,* state action permitted religious instruction in public school buildings during school hours and required students not attending the religious instruction to remain in their classrooms during that time. The Court found that this system had the effect of coercing the children to attend religious classes; no such coercion to attend church services is present in the situation at bar. In *McCollum,* the only alternative available to the nonattending students was to remain in their classrooms; the alternatives open to nonlaboring persons in the instant case are far more diverse. In *McCollum,* there was direct cooperation between state officials and religious ministers; no such direct participation exists under the Maryland laws. In *McCollum,* tax-supported buildings were used to aid religion; in the instant case, no tax monies are being used in aid of religion.

Finally, we should make clear that this case deals only with the constitutionality of § 521 of the Maryland statute before us. We do not hold that Sunday legislation may not be a violation of the "Establishment" Clause if it can be demonstrated that its purpose—evidenced either on the face of the legislation, in conjunction with its legislative history, or in its operative effect—is to use the State's coercive power to aid religion.

Accordingly, the decision is affirmed.

SEPARATE OPINION OF MR. JUSTICE FRANKFURTER, WHOM MR. JUSTICE HARLAN JOINS.

So deeply do the issues raised by these cases cut that it is not surprising that no one opinion can wholly express the views even of all the members of the Court who join in its result. Individual opinions in constitutional controversies have been the practice throughout the

Court's history. Such expression of differences in view or even in emphasis converging toward the same result makes for the clarity of candor and thereby enhances the authority of the judicial process.

For me considerations are determinative here which call for separate statement. The long history of Sunday legislation, so decisive if we are to view the statutes now attacked in a perspective wider than that which is furnished by our own necessarily limited outlook, cannot be conveyed by a partial recital of isolated instances or events. The importance of that history derives from its continuity and fullness—from the massive testimony which it bears to the evolution of statutes controlling Sunday labor and to the forces which have, during three hundred years of Anglo-American history at the least, changed those laws, transmuted them, made them the vehicle of mixed and complicated aspirations. Since I find in the history of these statutes insights controllingly relevant to the constitutional issues before us, I am constrained to set that history forth in detail. And I also deem it incumbent to state how I arrive at concurrence with The Chief Justice's principal conclusions without drawing on *Everson.*

* * * * *

It cannot, therefore, be said that Massachusetts and Pennsylvania have imposed gratuitous restrictions upon the Sunday activities of persons observing the Orthodox Jewish Sabbath in achieving the legitimate secular ends at which their Sunday statutes may aim. The remaining question is whether the importance to the public of those ends is sufficient to outweigh the restraint upon the religious exercise of Orthodox Jewish practicants which the restriction entails. The nature of the legislative purpose is the preservation of a traditional institution which assures to the community a time during which the mind and body are released from the demands and distractions of an increasingly mechanized and competition-driven society. The right to this release has been claimed by workers and by small enterprisers, especially by retail merchandisers, over centuries, and finds contemporary expression in legislation in three-quarters of the States. The nature of the injury which must be balanced against it is the economic disadvantage to the enterpriser, and the inconvenience to the consumer, which Sunday regulations impose upon those who choose to adhere to the Sabbatarian tenets of their faith.

These statutes do not make criminal, do not place under the onus of civil or criminal disability, any act which is itself prescribed by the duties of the Jewish or other religions. They do create an undeniable financial burden upon the observers of one of the fundamental tenets of certain religious creeds, a burden which does not fall equally upon other forms of observance. This was true of the tax which this Court held an unconstitutional infringement of the free exercise of religion in *Follett* v. *Town of McCormick.* But unlike the tax in *Follett,* the burden which the Sunday statutes impose is an incident of the only feasible means to achievement of their particular goal. And again unlike *Follett,* the measure of the burden is not determined by fixed legislative decree, beyond the power of the individual to alter. Upon persons who earn their livelihood by activities not prohibited on Sunday, and upon those whose jobs require only a five-day week, the burden is not considerable. Like the customers of Crown Kosher Super Market in the *Gallagher* case, they are inconvenienced in their shopping. This is hardly to be assessed as an injury of preponderant constitutional weight. The burden on retail sellers competing with Sunday-observing and non-observing retailers is considerably greater. But, without minimizing the fact of this disadvantage, the legislature may have concluded that its severity might be offset by the industry and commercial initiative of the individual merchant. More is demanded of him, admittedly, whether in the form of additional labor or of material sacrifices, than is demanded of those who do not choose to keep his Sabbath. More would be demanded of him, of course, in a State in which there were no Sunday laws and in which his competitors chose—like "Two Guys from Harrison-Allentown"—to do business seven days a week. In view of the importance of the community interests which must be weighed in the balance, is the disadvantage wrought by the non-exempting Sunday statutes an impermissible imposition upon the Sabbatarian's religious freedom? Every court which has considered the question during a century and a half has concluded that it is not. This Court so concluded in *Friedman v. New York.* On the basis of the criteria for determining constitutionality, as opposed to what one might desire as a matter of legislative policy, a contrary conclusion cannot be reached.

* * * * *

MR. JUSTICE DOUGLAS, DISSENTING.

The question is not whether one day out of seven can be imposed by a State as a day of rest. The question is not whether Sunday can by force of custom and habit be retained as day of rest. The question is whether a State can impose criminal sanctions on those who, unlike the Christian majority that makes up our society, worship on a different day or do not share the religious scruples of the majority.

If the "free exercise" of religion were subject to reasonable regulations, as it is under some constitutions, or if all laws "respecting the establishment of religion" were not proscribed, I could understand how rational men, representing a predominantly Christian civilization, might think these Sunday laws did not unreasonably interfere with anyone's free exercise of religion and took no step toward a burdensome establishment of any religion.

But that is not the premise from which we start, as there is agreement that the fact that a State, and not the Federal Government, has promulgated these Sunday laws does not change the scope of the power asserted. For the classic view is that the First Amendment should be applied to the States with the same firmness as it is enforced against the Federal Government. The most explicit statement perhaps was in *Barnette*. . . .

With that as my starting point I do not see how a State can make protesting citizens refrain from doing innocent acts on Sunday because the doing of those acts offends sentiments of their Christian neighbors.

The institutions of our society are founded on the belief that there is an authority higher than the authority of the State; that there is a moral law which the State is powerless to alter; that the individual possesses rights, conferred by the Creator, which government must respect.

But those who fashioned the First Amendment decided that if and when God is to be served, His service will not be motivated by coercive measures of government. "Congress shall make no law respecting an establishment of religion, or prohibiting the free exercise thereof"—such is the command of the First Amendment made applicable to the State by reason of the Due Process Clause of the Fourteenth. This means, as I understand it, that if a religious leaven is to be worked into the affairs of our people, it is to be done by individuals and groups, not by the Government. This necessarily means, *first,* that the dogma, creed, scruples, or practices of no religious group or sect are to be preferred over those of any others; *second,* that no one shall be interfered with by government for practicing the religion of his choice; *third,* that the State may not require anyone to practice a religion or even any religion; and *fourth,* that the State cannot compel one so to conduct himself as not to offend the religious scruples of another. The idea, as I understand it, was to limit the power of government to act in religious matters not to limit the freedom of religious men to act religiously nor to restrict the freedom of atheists or agnostics.

The First Amendment commands government to have no interest in theology or ritual; it admonishes government to be interested in allowing religious freedom to flourish—whether the result is to produce Catholics, Jews, or Protestants, or to turn the people toward the path of Buddha, or to end in a predominantly Moslem nation, or to produce in the long run atheists or agnostics. On matters of this kind government must be neutral. This freedom plainly includes freedom *from* religion with the right to believe, speak, write, publish and advocate antireligious programs. Certainly the "free exercise" clause does not require that everyone embrace the theology of some church or of some faith, or observe the religious practices of any majority or minority sect. The First Amendment by its "establishment" clause prevents, of course, the selection by government of an "official" church. Yet the ban plainly extends farther than that. We said in *Everson* that it would be an "establishment" of a religion if the Government financed one church or several churches. For what better way to "establish" an institution than to find the fund that will support it? The "establishment" clause protects citizens also against any law which selects any religious custom, practice, or ritual, puts the force of government behind it, and fines, imprisons, or otherwise penalizes a person for not observing it. The Government plainly could not join forces with one religious group and decree a universal and symbolic circumcision. Nor could it require all children to be baptized or give tax exemptions only to those whose children were baptized.

Could it require a fast from sunrise to sunset throughout the Moslem month of Ramadan? I should think not. Yet why then can it make criminal the doing of other acts, as innocent as eating, during the day that Christians revere?

Sunday is a word heavily overlaid with connotations and traditions deriving from the Christian roots of our civilization that color all judgments concerning it. This is what the philosophers call "word magic."

> For most judges, for most lawyers, for most human beings, we are as unconscious of our value patterns as we are of the oxygen that we breathe.

* * * * *

. . . The Court picks and chooses language from various decisions to bolster its conclusion that these Sunday laws in the modern setting are "civil regulations." No matter how much is written, no matter what is said, the parentage of these laws is the Fourth Commandment; and they serve and satisfy the religious predispositions of our Christian communities. After all, the labels a State places on its laws are not binding on us when we are confronted with a constitutional decision. We reach our own conclusion as to the character, effect, and practical operation of the regulation in determining its constitutionality.

It seems to me plain that by these laws the States compel one, under sanction of law, to refrain from work or recreation on Sunday because of the majority's religious views about that day. The State by law makes Sunday a symbol of respect or adherence. Refraining from work or recreation in deference to the majority's religious feelings about Sunday is within every person's choice. By what authority can government compel it?

Cases are put where acts that are immoral by our standards but not by the standards of other religious groups are made criminal. That category of cases, until today, has been a very restricted one confined to polygamy and other extreme situations. The latest example is *Prince* v. *Massachusetts,* which upheld a statute making it criminal for a child under twelve to sell papers, periodicals, or merchandise on a street or in any public place. It was sustained in spite of the finding that the child thought it was her religious duty to perform the act. But that was a narrow holding which turned on the effect which street solicitation might have on the child-solicitor.

* * * * *

None of the acts involved here implicates minors. None of the actions made constitutionally criminal today involves the doing of any act that any society has deemed to be immoral.

The conduct held constitutionally criminal today embraces the selling of a pure, not impure, food; wholesome, not noxious, articles. Adults, not minors, are involved. The innocent acts, now constitutionally classified as criminal, emphasize the drastic break we make with tradition.

These laws are sustained because, it is said, the First Amendment is concerned with religious convictions or opinion, not with conduct. But it is a strange Bill of Rights that makes it possible for the dominant religious group to bring the minority to heel because the minority, in the doing of acts which intrinsically are wholesome and not antisocial, does not defer to the majority's religious beliefs. Some have religious scruples against eating pork. Those scruples, no matter how bizarre they might seem to some, are within the ambit of the First Amendment. Is it possible that a majority of a state legislature having those religious scruples could make it criminal for the nonbeliever to sell pork? Some have religious scruples against slaughtering cattle. Could a state legislature, dominated by that group, make it criminal to run an abattoir?

The Court balances the need of the people for rest, recreation, late sleeping, family visiting and the like against the command of the First Amendment that no one need bow to the religious beliefs of another. There is in this realm no room for balancing. I see no place for it in the constitutional scheme. A legislature of Christians can no more make minorities conform to their weekly regime than a legislature of Moslems, or a legislature of Hindus. The religious regime of every group must be respected—unless it crosses the line of criminal conduct. But no one can be forced to come to a halt before it, or refrain from doing things that would offend it. That is my reading of the Establishment Clause and the Free Exercise Clause. Any other reading imports, I fear, an element common in other societies but foreign to us.

* * * * *

The State can, of course, require one day of rest a week: one day when every shop or factory is closed. Quite a few States make that requirement. Then the "day of rest" becomes purely and simply a health measure. But the Sunday laws operate differently. They force minorities to obey the majority's religious feelings of what is due and proper for a Christian community; they provide a coercive spur to the "weaker brethren," to those who are indifferent to the claims of a Sabbath through apathy or scruple. Can there be any doubt that Christians, now aligned vigorously in favor of these laws, would be as strongly opposed if they were prosecuted under a Moslem law that forbade them from engaging in secular activities on days that violated Moslem scruples?

There is an "establishment" of religion in the constitutional sense if any practice of any religious group has the sanction of law behind it. There is an interference with the "free exercise" of religion if what in conscience one can do or omit doing is required because of the religious scruples of the community. Hence I would declare each of those laws unconstitutional as applied to the complaining parties, whether or not they are members of a sect which observes as its Sabbath a day other than Sunday.

When these laws are applied to Orthodox Jews, as they are in No. 11 and in No. 67, or to Sabbatarians their vice is accentuated. If the Sunday laws are constitutional, kosher markets are on a five-day week. Thus those laws put an economic penalty on those who observe Saturday rather than Sunday as the Sabbath. For the economic pressures on these minorities, created by the fact that our communities are predominantly Sunday-minded, there is no recourse. When, however, the State uses its coercive powers—here the criminal law—to compel minorities to observe a second Sabbath, not their own, the State undertakes to aid and "prefer one religion over another"—contrary to the command of the Constitution.

In large measure the history of the religious clause of the First Amendment was a struggle to be free of economic sanctions for adherence to one's religion. A small tax was imposed in Virginia for religious education. Jefferson and Madison led the fight against the tax, Madison writing his famous Memorial and Remonstrance against that law. As a result, the tax measure was defeated and instead Virginia's famous "Bill for Religious Liberty," written by Jefferson, was enacted.

* * * * *

The reverse side of an "establishment" is a burden on the "free exercise" of religion. Receipt of funds from the State benefits the established church directly; laying an extra tax on nonmembers benefits the established church indirectly. Certainly the present Sunday laws place Orthodox Jews and Sabbatarians under extra burdens because of their religious opinions or beliefs. Requiring them to abstain from their trade or business on Sunday reduces their work-week to five days, unless they violate their religious scruples. This places them at a competitive disadvantage and penalizes them for adhering to their religious beliefs.

"The sanction imposed by the state for observing a day other than Sunday as holy time is certainly more serious economically than the imposition of a license tax for preaching," which we struck down in *Murdock* v. *Pennsylvania* and in *Follett* v. *McCormick.* The special protection which Sunday laws give the dominant religious groups and the penalty they place on minorities whose holy day is Saturday constitute, in my view, state interference with the "free exercise" of religion.

I dissent from applying criminal sanctions against any of these complainants since to do so implicates the States in religious matters contrary to the constitutional mandate.

* * * * *

Other Establishment Cases

Marsh v. Chambers, 463 U.S. 783 (1983)

This case concerns the services of a chaplain to the Nebraska legislature. Chief Justice Burger, writing for the Court, held that the chaplaincy practice did not violate the Establishment Clause. He stated: "We do not doubt the sincerity of those, who like respondents, believe that to have prayer in this context risks the beginning of the establishment the Founding Fathers feared. . . . The unbroken practice for two centuries in the National Congress, for more than a century in Nebraska and in many other states, gives abundant assurance that there is no real threat 'while this Court sits.'"

Justice Brennan, one of three dissenters, remarked: "Legislative prayer clearly violates the principles of neutrality and separation that are embedded within the Establishment Clause." He found fault with the Court's dependence upon history to justify current practice.

CHIEF JUSTICE BURGER DELIVERED THE OPINION OF THE COURT.

The question presented is whether the Nebraska Legislature's practice of opening each legislative day with a prayer by a chaplain paid by the State violates the Establishment Clause of the First Amendment.

I

The Nebraska Legislature begins each of its sessions with a prayer offered by a chaplain who is chosen biennially by the Executive Board of the Legislative Council and paid out of public funds. Robert E. Palmer, a Presbyterian minister, has served as chaplain since 1965 at a salary of $319.75 per month for each month the legislature is in session.

Ernest Chambers is a member of the Nebraska Legislature and a taxpayer of Nebraska. Claiming that the Nebraska Legislature's chaplaincy practice violates the Establishment Clause of the First Amendment, he brought this action seeking to enjoin enforcement of the practice. After denying a motion to dismiss on the ground of legislative immunity, the District Court held that the Establishment Clause was not breached by the prayers, but was violated by paying the chaplain from public funds. It therefore enjoined the legislature from using public funds to pay the chaplain; it declined to enjoin the policy of beginning sessions with prayers. Cross-appeals were taken.

The Court of Appeals for the Eighth Circuit rejected arguments that the case should be dismissed on Tenth Amendment, legislative immunity, standing, or federalism grounds. On the merits of the chaplaincy issue, the court refused to treat respondent's challenges as separable issues as the District Court had done. Instead, the Court of Appeals assessed the practice as a whole because "[p]arsing out [the] elements" would lead to "an incongruous result."

Applying the three-part test of *Kurtzman,* as set out in *Nyquist,* the court held that the chaplaincy practice violated all three elements of the test: the purpose and primary effect of selecting the same minister for 16 years and publishing his prayers was to promote a particular religious expression; use of state money for compensation and publication led to entanglement. Accordingly, the Court of Appeals modified the District Court's injunction and prohibited the State from engaging in any aspect of its established chaplaincy practice.

We granted certiorari limited to the challenge to the practice of opening sessions with prayers by a state-employed clergyman, and we reverse.

II

The opening of sessions of legislative and other deliberative public bodies with prayer is deeply embedded in the history and tradition of this country. From colonial times through the founding of the Republic and ever since, the practice of legislative prayer has coexisted with the principles of disestablishment and religious freedom. In the very courtrooms in which the United States District Judge and later three Circuit Judges heard and decided this case, the proceedings opened with an announcement that concluded "God save the United States and this Honorable Court." The same invocation occurs at all sessions of this Court.

The tradition in many of the Colonies was, of course, linked to an established church, but the Continental Congress, beginning in 1774, adopted the traditional procedure of opening its sessions with a prayer offered by a paid chaplain. Although prayers were not offered during the Constitutional Convention, the First Congress, as one of its early items of business, adopted the policy of selecting a chaplain to open each session with prayer. Thus, on April 7, 1789, the Senate appointed a committee "to take under consideration the manner of electing Chaplains." On April 9, 1789, a similar committee was appointed by the House of Representatives. On April 25, 1789, the Senate elected its first chaplain, the House followed suit on May 1, 1789. A statute providing for the payment of these chaplains was enacted into law on September 22, 1789.

On September 25, 1789, three days after Congress authorized the appointment of paid chaplains, final agreement was reached on the language of the Bill of Rights. Clearly the men who wrote the First Amendment Religion Clause did not view paid legislative chaplains and opening prayers as a violation of that Amendment, for the practice of opening sessions with prayer has continued without interruption ever since that early session of Congress. It has also been followed consistently in most of the states, including Nebraska, where the institution of opening legislative sessions with prayer was adopted even before the State attained statehood.

Standing alone, historical patterns cannot justify contemporary violations of constitutional guarantees, but there is far more here than simply historical patterns. In this context, historical evidence sheds light not only on what the draftsmen intended the Establishment Clause to mean, but also on how they thought that Clause applied to the practice authorized by the First Congress—their actions reveal their intent. An Act

> passed by the first Congress assembled under the Constitution, many of whose members had taken part in framing that instrument, . . . is contemporaneous and weighty evidence of its true meaning.

In *Walz* we considered the weight to be accorded to history.

* * * * *

No more is Nebraska's practice of over a century, consistent with two centuries of national practice, to be cast aside. It can hardly be thought that in the same week Members of the First Congress voted to appoint and to pay a chaplain for each House and also voted to approve the draft of the First Amendment for submission to the states, they intended the Establishment Clause of the Amendment to forbid what they had just declared acceptable. In applying the First Amendment to the states through the Fourteenth Amendment, it would be incongruous to interpret that Clause as imposing more stringent First Amendment limits on the states than the draftsmen imposed on the Federal Government.

This unique history leads us to accept the interpretation of the First Amendment draftsmen who saw no real threat to the Establishment Clause arising from a practice of prayer similar to that now challenged. We conclude that legislative prayer presents no more potential for establishment than the provision of school transportation, beneficial grants for higher education, or tax exemptions for religious organizations.

Respondent cites Justice Brennan's concurring opinion in *Schempp,* and argues that we should not rely too heavily on "the advice of the Founding Fathers" because the messages of history often tend to be ambiguous and not relevant to a society far more heterogeneous than that of the Framers. Respondent also points out that John Jay and John Rutledge opposed the motion to begin the first session of the Continental Congress with prayer.

We do not agree that evidence of opposition to a measure weakens the force of the historical argument; indeed it infuses it with power by demonstrating that the subject was considered carefully and the action not taken thoughtlessly, by force of long tradition and without regard to the problems posed by a pluralistic society. Jay and Rutledge specifically grounded their objection on the fact that the delegates to the Congress "were so divided in religious sentiments . . . that [they] could not join in the same act of worship." Their objection was met by Samuel Adams, who stated that "he was no bigot, and could hear a prayer from a gentleman of piety and virtue, who was at the same time a friend to his country."

This interchange emphasizes that the delegates did not consider opening prayers as a proselytizing activity or as symbolically placing the government's "official seal of approval on one religious view." Rather, the Founding Fathers looked at invocations as "conduct whose . . . effect . . . harmonize[d] with the tenets of some or all religions."The Establishment Clause does not always bar a state from regulating conduct simply because it "harmonizes with religious canons." Here, the individual claiming injury by the practice is an adult, presumably not readily susceptible to "religious indoctrination," or peer pressure.

In light of the unambiguous and unbroken history of more than 200 years, there can be no doubt that the practice of opening legislative sessions with prayer has become part of the fabric of our society. To invoke Divine guidance on a public body entrusted with making the laws is not, in these circumstances, an "establishment" of religion or a step toward establishment; it is simply a tolerable acknowledgment of beliefs widely held among the people of this country. . . .

III

We turn then to the question of whether any features of the Nebraska practice violate the Establishment Clause. Beyond the bare fact that a prayer is offered, three points have been made: first, that a clergyman of only one denomination—Presbyterian—has been selected for 16 years; second, that the chaplain is paid at public expense; and third, that the prayers are in the Judeo-Christian tradition. Weighed against the historical background, these factors do not serve to invalidate Nebraska's practice.

The Court of Appeals was concerned that Palmer's long tenure has the effect of giving preference to his religious views. We cannot, any more than Members of the Congresses of this century, perceive any suggestion that choosing a clergyman of one denomination advances the beliefs of a particular church. To the contrary, the evidence indicates that Palmer was reappointed because his performance and personal qualities were acceptable to the body appointing him. Palmer was not the only clergyman heard by the legislature; guest chaplains have officiated at the request of various legislators and as substitutes during Palmer's absences. Absent proof that the chaplain's reappointment stemmed from an impermissible motive, we conclude that his long tenure does not in itself conflict with the Establishment Clause.

Nor is the compensation of the chaplain from public funds a reason to invalidate the Nebraska Legislature's chaplaincy; remuneration is grounded in historic practice initiated, as we noted earlier, by the same Congress that drafted the Establishment Clause of the First Amendment. The Continental Congress paid its chaplain, as did some of the states. Currently, many state legislatures and the United States Congress provide compensation for their chaplains. Nebraska has paid its chaplain for well over a century. The content of the prayer is not of concern to judges where, as here, there is no indication that the prayer opportunity has been exploited to proselytize or advance any one, or to disparage any other, faith or belief. That being so, it is not for us to embark on a sensitive evaluation or to parse the content of a particular prayer.

We do not doubt the sincerity of those, who like respondent, believe that to have prayer in this context risks the beginning of the establishment the Founding Fathers feared. But this concern is not well founded, for as Justice Goldberg aptly observed in his concurring opinion in *Abington:*

> It is of course true that great consequences can grow from small beginnings, but the measure of constitutional adjudication is the ability and willingness to distinguish between real threat and mere shadow.

The unbroken practice for two centuries in the National Congress, for more than a century in Nebraska and in many other states, gives abundant assurance that there is no real threat "while this Court sits."

The judgment of the Court of Appeals is reversed.

JUSTICE BRENNAN, WITH WHOM JUSTICE MARSHALL JOINS, DISSENTING.

The Court today has written a narrow and, on the whole, careful opinion. In effect, the Court holds that officially sponsored legislative prayer, primarily on account of its "unique history," is generally exempted from the First Amendment's prohibition against "an establishment of religion." The Court's opinion is consistent with dictum in at least one of our prior decisions, and its limited rationale should pose little threat to the overall fate of the Establishment Clause. Moreover, disagreement with the Court requires that I confront the fact that some 20 years ago, in a concurring opinion in one of the cases striking down official prayer and ceremonial Bible reading in the public schools, I came very close to endorsing essentially the result reached by the Court today. Nevertheless, after much reflection, I have come to the conclusion that I was wrong then and that the Court is wrong today. I now believe that the practice of official invocational prayer, as it exists in Nebraska and most other state legislatures, is unconstitutional. It is contrary to the doctrine as well the underlying purposes of the Establishment Clause, and it is not saved either by its history or by any of the other considerations suggested in the Court's opinion.

I respectfully dissent.

I

The Court makes no pretense of subjecting Nebraska's practice of legislative prayer to any of the formal "tests" that have traditionally structured our inquiry under the Establishment Clause. That it fails to do so is, in a sense, a good thing, for it simply confirms that the Court is carving out an exception to the Establishment Clause rather than reshaping Establishment Clause doctrine to accommodate legislative prayer. For my purposes, however, I must begin by demonstrating what should be obvious: that, if the Court were to judge legislative prayer through the unsentimental eye of our settled doctrine, it would have to strike it down as a clear violation of the Establishment Clause.

The most commonly cited formulation of prevailing Establishment Clause doctrine is found in *Lemon:*

> Every analysis in this area must begin with consideration of the cumulative criteria developed by the Court over many years. Three such tests may be gleaned from our cases. First, the statute [at issue] must have a secular legislative purpose; second, its principal or primary effect must be one that neither advances nor inhibits religion; finally, the statute must not foster "an excessive government entanglement with religion."

That the "purpose" of legislative prayer is pre-eminently religious rather than secular seems to me to be self-evident. "To invoke Divine guidance on a public body entrusted with making the laws" is nothing but a religious act. Moreover, whatever secular functions legislative prayer might play—formally opening the legislative session, getting the members of the body to quiet down, and imbuing them with a sense of seriousness and high purpose—could so plainly be performed in a purely nonreligious fashion that to claim a secular purpose for the prayer is an insult to the perfectly honorable individuals who instituted and continue the practice.

The "primary effect" of legislative prayer is also clearly religious. As we said in the context of officially sponsored prayers in the public schools, "prescribing a particular form of religious worship," even if the individuals involved have the choice not to participate, places "indirect coercive pressure upon religious minorities to conform to the prevailing officially approved religion. . . . " More importantly, invocations in Nebraska's legislative halls explicitly link religious belief and observance to the power and prestige of the State. "[T]he mere appearance of a joint exercise of legislative authority by Church and State provides a significant symbolic benefit to religion in the minds of some by reason of the power conferred."

Finally, there can be no doubt that the practice of legislative prayer leads to excessive "entanglement" between the State and religion. *Lemon* pointed out that "entanglement" can take two forms: First, a state statute or program might involve the state impermissibly in monitoring and overseeing religious affairs. In the case of legislative prayer, the process of choosing a "suitable" chaplain, whether on a permanent or rotating basis, and insuring that the chaplain limits himself or herself to "suitable" prayers, involves precisely the sort of supervision that agencies of government should if at all possible avoid.

Second, excessive "entanglement" might arise out of "the divisive political potential" of a state statute or program.

> Ordinarily political debate and division, however vigorous or even partisan, are normal and healthy manifestations of our democratic system of government, but political division along religious lines was one of the principal evils against which the First Amendment was intended to protect. The potential divisiveness of such conflict is a threat to the normal political process.

In this case, this second aspect of entanglement is also clear. The controversy between Senator Chambers and his colleagues, which had reached the stage of difficulty and rancor long before this lawsuit was brought, has split the Nebraska Legislature precisely on issues of religion and religious conformity. The record in this case also reports a series of instances, involving legislators other than Senator Chambers, in which invocations by Reverend Palmer and others led to controversy along religious lines. And in general, the history of legislative prayer has been far more eventful—and divisive—than a hasty reading of the Court's opinion might indicate.

In sum, I have no doubt that, if any group of law students were asked to apply the principles of *Lemon* to the question of legislative prayer, they would nearly unanimously find the practice to be unconstitutional.

II

The path of formal doctrine, however, can only imperfectly capture the nature and importance of the issues at stake in this case. A more adequate analysis must therefore take into account the underlying function of the Establishment Clause, and the forces that have shaped its doctrine.

A

Most of the provisions of the Bill of Rights, even if they are not generally enforceable in the absence of state action, nevertheless arise out of moral intuitions applicable to individuals as well as governments. The Establishment Clause, however, is quite different. It is, to its core, nothing less and nothing more than a statement about the proper role of *government* in the society that we have shaped for ourselves in this land.

The Establishment Clause embodies a judgment, born of a long and turbulent history, that, in our society, religion "must be a private matter for the individual, the family, and the institutions of private choice. . . . "

* * * * *

The principles of "separation" and "neutrality" implicit in the Establishment Clause serve many purposes. Four of these are particularly relevant here.

The first, which is most closely related to the more general conceptions of liberty found in the remainder of the First Amendment, is to guarantee the individual right to conscience. The right to conscience, in the religious sphere, is not only implicated when the government engages in direct or indirect coercion. It is also implicated when the government requires individuals to support the practices of a faith with which they do not agree.

The second purpose of separation and neutrality is to keep the state from interfering in the essential autonomy of religious life, either by taking upon itself the decision of religious issues, or by unduly involving itself in the supervision of religious institutions or officials.

The third purpose of separation and neutrality is to prevent the trivialization and degradation of religion by too close an attachment to the organs of government. The Establishment Clause "stands as an expression of principle on the part of the Founders of our Constitution that religion is too personal, too sacred, too holy, to permit its 'unhallowed perversion' by a civil magistrate."

Finally, the principles of separation and neutrality help assure that essentially religious issues, precisely because of their importance and sensitivity, not become the occasion for battle in the political arena. With regard to most issues, the government may be influenced by partisan argument and may act as a partisan itself. In each case, there will be winners and losers in the political battle, and the losers' most common recourse is the right to dissent and the right to fight the battle again another day. With regard to matters that are essentially religious, however, the Establishment Clause seeks that there should be no political battles, and that no American should at any point feel alienated from his government because that government has declared or acted upon some "official" or "authorized" point of view on a matter of religion.

B

The imperatives of separation and neutrality are not limited to the relationship of government to religious institutions or denominations, but extend as well to the relationship of government to religious beliefs and practices. In *Torcaso,* for example, we struck down a state provision requiring a religious oath as a qualification to hold office, not only because it violated principles of free exercise of religion, but also because it violated the principles of nonestablishment of religion. And, of course, in the pair of cases that hang over this one like a reproachful set of parents, we held that official prayer and prescribed Bible reading in the public schools represent a serious encroachment on the Establishment Clause. As we said in *Engel,* "[i]t is neither sacrilegious nor antireligious to say that each separate government in this country should stay out of the business of writing or sanctioning official prayers and leave that purely religious function to the people themselves and to those the people choose to look to for religious guidance."

Nor should it be thought that this view of the Establishment Clause is a recent concoction of an overreaching judiciary. Even before the

First Amendment was written, the Framers of the Constitution broke with the practice of the Articles of Confederation and many state constitutions, and did not invoke the name of God in the document. This "omission of a reference to the Deity was not inadvertent; nor did it remain unnoticed." Moreover, Thomas Jefferson and Andrew Jackson, during their respective terms as President, both refused on Establishment Clause grounds to declare national days of thanksgiving or fasting. And James Madison, writing subsequent to his own Presidency on essentially the very issue we face today, stated:

> Is the appointment of Chaplains to the two Houses of Congress consistent with the Constitution, and with the pure principle of religious freedom?
>
> In strictness, the answer on both points must be in the negative. The Constitution of the U.S. forbids everything like an establishment of a national religion. The law appointing Chaplains establishes a religious worship for the national representatives, to be performed by Ministers of religion, elected by a majority of them; and these are to be paid out of the national taxes. Does not this involve the principle of a national establishment, applicable to a provision for a religious worship for the Constituent as well as of the representative Body, approved by the majority, and conducted by Ministers of religion paid by the entire nation.

C

Legislative prayer clearly violates the principles of neutrality and separation that are embedded within the Establishment Clause. It is contrary to the fundamental message of *Engel* and *Schempp.* It intrudes on the right to conscience by forcing some legislators either to participate in a "prayer opportunity" with which they are in basic disagreement, or to make their disagreement a matter of public comment by declining to participate. It forces all residents of the State to support a religious exercise that may be contrary to their own beliefs. It requires the State to commit itself on fundamental theological issues. It has the potential for degrading religion by allowing a religious call to worship to be intermeshed with a secular call to order. And it injects religion into the political sphere by creating the potential that each and every selection of a chaplain, or consideration of a particular prayer, or even reconsideration of the practice itself, will provoke a political battle along religious lines and ultimately alienate some religiously identified group of citizens.

D

One response to the foregoing account, of course, is that "neutrality" and "separation" do not exhaust the full meaning of the Establishment Clause as it has developed in our cases. It is indeed true that there are certain tensions inherent in the First Amendment itself, or inherent in the role of religion and religious belief in any free society, that have shaped the doctrine of the Establishment Clause, and required us to deviate from an absolute adherence to separation and neutrality. Nevertheless, these considerations, although very important, are also quite specific, and where none of them is present, the Establishment Clause gives us no warrant simply to look the other way and treat an unconstitutional practice as if it were constitutional. Because the Court occasionally suggests that some of these considerations might apply here, it becomes important that I briefly identify the most prominent of them and explain why they do not in fact have any relevance to legislative prayer.

(1)

A number of our cases have recognized that religious institutions and religious practices may, in certain contexts, receive the benefit of government programs and policies generally available, on the basis of some secular criterion, to a wide class of similarly situated nonreligious beneficiaries, and the precise cataloging of those contexts is not necessarily an easy task. I need not tarry long here, however, because the provision for a daily official invocation by a nonmember officer of a legislative body could by no stretch of the imagination appear anywhere in that catalog.

(2)

Conversely, our cases have recognized that religion can encompass a broad, if not total, spectrum of concerns, overlapping considerably with the range of secular concerns, and that not every governmental act which coincides with or conflicts with a particular religious belief is for that reason an establishment of religion. The Court seems to suggest at one point that the practice of legislative prayer may be excused on this ground, but I cannot really believe that it takes this position seriously. The practice of legislative prayer is nothing like the statutes we considered in *McGowan* and *Harris* v. *McRae;* prayer is not merely "conduct whose . . . effect . . . harmonize[s] with the tenets of some or all religions," prayer is fundamentally and necessarily religious. "It is prayer which distinguishes religious phenomena from all those which resemble them or lie near to them, from the moral sense, for instance, or aesthetic feeling."

(3)

We have also recognized that government cannot, without adopting a decidedly *anti*-religious point of view, be forbidden to recognize the religious beliefs and practices of the American people as an aspect of our history and culture. Certainly, bona fide classes in comparative religion can be offered in the public schools. And certainly, the text of Abraham Lincoln's Second Inaugural Address which is inscribed on a wall of the Lincoln Memorial need not be purged of its profound theological content. The practice of offering invocations at legislative sessions cannot, however, simply be dismissed as "a tolerable *acknowledgment of beliefs* widely held among the people of this country." "Prayer is religion *in act.*" "Praying means to take hold of a word, the end, so to speak, of a line that leads to God." Reverend Palmer and other members of the clergy who offer invocations at legislative sessions are not museum pieces, put on display once a day for the edification of the legislature. Rather, they are engaged by the legislature to lead it—as a body—in an act of religious worship. If upholding the practice requires denial of this fact, I suspect that many supporters of legislative prayer would feel that they had been handed a pyrrhic victory.

(4)

Our cases have recognized that the purposes of the Establishment Clause can sometimes conflict. For example, in *Walz* we upheld tax exemptions for religious institutions in part because subjecting those institutions to taxation might foster serious administrative entanglement. Here, however, no such tension exists; the State can vindicate *all* the purposes of the Establishment Clause by abolishing legislative prayer.

(5)

Finally, our cases recognize that, in one important respect, the Constitution is *not* neutral on the subject of religion: Under the Free Exercise Clause, religiously motivated claims of conscience may give rise to constitutional rights that other strongly held beliefs do not. Moreover, even when the government is not compelled to do so by the Free Exercise Clause, it may to some extent act to facilitate the opportunities of individuals to practice their religion . . . ("hostility, not neutrality, would characterize the refusal to provide chaplains and places of worship for prisoners and soldiers cut off by the State from all civilian opportunities for public communion"). This is not, however, a case in which a State is accommodating individual religious interests. We are not faced here with the right of the legislature to allow its members to offer prayers during the course of general legislative debate. We are certainly not faced with the right of legislators to form voluntary groups for prayer or worship. We are not even faced with the right of the State to employ members of the clergy to minister to the private religious needs of individual legislators. Rather, we are faced here with the regularized practice of conducting official prayers, on behalf of the entire legislature, as part of the order of business constituting the formal opening of every single session of the legislative term. If this is Free Exercise, the Establishment Clause has no meaning whatsoever.

III

With the exception of the few lapses I have already noted, each of which is commendably qualified so as to be limited to the facts of this case, the Court says almost nothing contrary to the above analysis. Instead, it holds that "the practice of opening legislative sessions with prayer has become part of the fabric of our society," and chooses not to interfere. I sympathize with the Court's reluctance to strike down a practice so prevalent and so ingrained as legislative prayer. I am, however, unconvinced by the Court's arguments, and cannot shake my conviction that legislative prayer violates both the letter and the spirit of the Establishment Clause.

A

The Court's main argument for carving out an exception sustaining legislative prayer is historical. The Court cannot—and does not—purport to find a pattern of "undeviating acceptance" of legislative prayer. It also disclaims exclusive reliance on the mere longevity of legislative prayer. The Court does, however, point out that, only three days before the First Congress reached agreement on the final wording of the Bill of Rights, it authorized the appointment of paid chaplains for its own proceedings, and the Court argues that in light of this "unique history," the actions of Congress reveal its intent as to the meaning of the Establishment Clause. I agree that historical practice is "of considerable import in the interpretation of abstract constitutional language." This is a case, however, in which—absent the Court's invocation of history—there would be no question that the practice at issue was unconstitutional. And despite the surface appeal of the Court's argument, there are at least three reasons why specific historical practice should not in this case override that clear constitutional imperative.

First, it is significant that the Court's historical argument does not rely on the legislative history of the Establishment Clause itself. Indeed, that formal history is profoundly unilluminating on this and most other subjects. Rather, the Court assumes that the Framers of the Establishment Clause would not have themselves authorized a practice that they thought violated the guarantees contained in the Clause. This assumption, however, is questionable. Legislators, influenced by the passions and exigencies of the moment, the pressure of constituents and colleagues, and the press of business, do not always pass sober constitutional judgment on every piece of legislation they enact, and this must be assumed to be as true of the Members of the First Congress as any other. Indeed, the fact that James Madison, who voted for the bill authorizing the payment of the first congressional chaplains, later expressed the view that the practice was unconstitutional is instructive on precisely this point. Madison's later views may not have represented so much a change of *mind* as a change of *role,* from a Member of Congress engaged in the hurley-burley of legislative activity to a detached observer engaged in unpressured reflection. Since the latter role is precisely the one with which this Court is charged, I am not at all sure that Madison's later writings should be any less influential in our deliberations than his earlier vote.

Second, the Court's analysis treats the First Amendment simply as an Act of Congress, as to whose meaning the intent of Congress is the single touchstone. Both the Constitution and its Amendments, however, became supreme law only by virtue of their ratification by the States, and the understanding of the States should be as relevant to our analysis as the understanding of Congress. This observation is especially compelling in considering the meaning of the Bill of Rights. The first 10 Amendments were not enacted because the Members of the First Congress came up with a bright idea one morning; rather, their enactment was forced upon Congress by a number of the States as a condition for their ratification of the original Constitution. To treat any practice authorized by the First Congress as presumptively consistent with the Bill of Rights is therefore somewhat akin to treating any action of a party to a contract as presumptively consistent with the terms of the contract. The latter proposition, if it were accepted, would of course resolve many of the heretofore perplexing issues in contract law.

Finally, and most importantly, the argument tendered by the Court is misguided because the Constitution is not a static document whose meaning on every detail is fixed for all time by the life experience of the Framers. We have recognized in a wide variety of constitutional contexts that the practices that were in place at the time any particular guarantee was enacted into the Constitution do not necessarily fix forever the meaning of that guarantee. To be truly faithful to the Framers, "our use of the history of their time must limit itself to broad purposes, not specific practices." Our primary task must be to translate "the majestic generalities of the Bill of Rights, conceived as part of the pattern of liberal government in the eighteenth century, into concrete restraints on officials dealing with the problems of the twentieth century. . . . "

The inherent adaptability of the Constitution and its amendments is particularly important with respect to the Establishment Clause. "[O]ur religious composition makes us a vastly more diverse people than were our forefathers. . . . In the face of such profound changes, practices which may have been objectionable to no one in the time of Jefferson and Madison may today be highly offensive to many persons, the deeply devout and the nonbelievers alike." President John Adams issued during his Presidency a number of official proclamations calling on all Americans to engage in Christian prayer. Justice Story, in his treatise on the Constitution, contended that the "real object" of the First Amendment "was, not to countenance, much less to advance Mahometanism, or Judaism, or infidelity, by prostrating

Christianity; but to exclude all rivalry among Christian sects. . . . " Whatever deference Adams' actions and Story's views might once have deserved in this Court, the Establishment Clause must now be read in a very different light. Similarly, the Members of the First Congress should be treated, not as sacred figures whose every action must be emulated, but as the authors of a document meant to last for the ages. Indeed, a proper respect for the Framers themselves forbids us to give so static and lifeless a meaning to their work. To my mind, the Court's focus here on a narrow piece of history is, in a fundamental sense, a betrayal of the lessons of history.

B

Of course, the Court does not rely entirely on the practice of the First Congress in order to validate legislative prayer. There is another theme which, although implicit, also pervades the Court's opinion. It is exemplified by the Court's comparison of legislative prayer with the formulaic recitation of "God save the United States and this Honorable Court." It is also exemplified by the Court's apparent conclusion that legislative prayer is, at worst, a "'mere shadow'" on the Establishment Clause rather than a "'real threat'" to it. Simply put, the Court seems to regard legislative prayer as at most a *de minimis* violation, somehow unworthy of our attention. I frankly do not know what should be the proper disposition of features of our public life such as "God save the United States and this Honorable Court." "In God We Trust," "One Nation Under God," and the like. I might well adhere to the view expressed in *Schempp* that such mottos are consistent with the Establishment Clause, not because their import is *de minimis,* but because they have lost any true religious significance. Legislative invocations, however, are very different.

First of all, as Justice Stevens' dissent so effectively highlights, legislative prayer, unlike mottos with fixed wordings, can easily turn narrowly and obviously sectarian. I agree with the Court that the federal judiciary should not sit as a board of censors on individual prayers, but to my mind the better way of avoiding that task is by striking down all official legislative invocations.

More fundamentally, however, *any* practice of legislative prayer, even if it might look "nonsectarian" to nine Justices of the Supreme Court, will inevitably and continuously involve the State in one or another religious debate. Prayer is serious business—serious theological business—and it is not a mere "acknowledgment of beliefs widely held among the people of this country" for the State to immerse itself in that business. Some religious individuals or groups find it theologically problematic to engage in joint religious exercises predominantly influenced by faiths not their own. Some might object even to the attempt to fashion a "nonsectarian" prayer. Some would find it impossible to participate in any "prayer opportunity" marked by Trinitarian references. Some would find a prayer *not* invoking the name of Christ to represent a flawed view of the relationship between human beings and God. Some might find any petitionary prayer to be improper. Some might find any prayer that lacked a petitionary element to be deficient. Some might be troubled by what they consider shallow public prayer, or nonspontaneous prayer, or prayer without adequate spiritual preparation or concentration. Some might, of course, have *theological* objections to any prayer sponsored by an organ of government. Some might object on theological grounds to the level of political neutrality generally expected of government-sponsored invocational prayer. And some might object on theological grounds to the Court's requirement that prayer, even though religious, not be proselytizing. If these problems arose in the context of a religious objection to some otherwise decidedly secular activity, then whatever remedy there is would have to be found in the Free Exercise Clause. But, in this case, we are faced with potential religious objections to an activity at the very center of religious life, and it is simply beyond the competence of government, and inconsistent with our conceptions of liberty, for the State to take upon itself the role of ecclesiastical arbiter.

IV

The argument is made occasionally that a strict separation of religion and state robs the Nation of its spiritual identity. I believe quite the contrary. It may be true that individuals cannot be "neutral" on the question of religion. But the judgment of the Establishment Clause is that neutrality by the organs of *government* on questions of religion is both possible and imperative. Alexis de Tocqueville wrote the following concerning his travels through this land in the early 1830's:

> The religious atmosphere of the country was the first thing that struck me on arrival in the United States. . . .

> In France I had seen the spirits of religion and of freedom almost always marching in opposite directions. In America I found them intimately linked together in joint reign over the same land.
>
> My longing to understand the reason for this phenomenon increased daily.
>
> To find this out, I questioned the faithful of all communions; I particularly sought the society of clergymen, who are the depositaries of the various creeds and have a personal interest in their survival.... I expressed my astonishment and revealed my doubts to each of them; I found that they all agreed with each other except about details; all thought that the main reason for the quiet sway of religion over their country was the complete separation of church and state. I have no hesitation in stating that throughout my stay in America I met nobody, lay or cleric, who did not agree about that.

More recent history has only confirmed de Tocqueville's observations. If the Court had struck down the legislative prayer today, it would likely have stimulated a furious reaction. But it would also, I am convinced, have invigorated both the "spirit of religion" and the "spirit of freedom."

I respectfully dissent.

Lynch v. Donnelly, 465 U.S. 668 (1984)

Chief Justice Burger wrote for the Court that there is "an unbroken history of official acknowledgement by all three branches of government of the role of religion in American life from at least 1789." Arguing from that history and from a distaste for absolutist readings of the Establishment Clause, he upheld the city of Pawtucket as not having violated that Clause, notwithstanding the religious significance of the crèche displayed on public property.

The four dissenters rejected the proposition that inserting a religious symbol into a secular holiday event avoided the religious import. Justice Brennan held out the hope that the decision in *Marsh* and this case were "aberrant departure[s] from our settled method of analyzing Establishment Clause cases." At Christmas 1987, a number of purely religious displays, appeared on public property. *Lynch* was cited as precedent and, ignored a 1986 Court denial of certiorari on a lower court prohibition against a purely religious Christmas display in Birmingham, Michigan.

CHIEF JUSTICE BURGER DELIVERED THE OPINION OF THE COURT.

We granted certiorari to decide whether the Establishment Clause of the First Amendment prohibits a municipality from including a crèche, or Nativity scene, in its annual Christmas display.

I

Each year, in cooperation with the downtown retail merchants' association, the city of Pawtucket, R.I., erects a Christmas display as part of its observance of the Christmas holiday season. The display is situated in a park owned by a nonprofit organization and located in the heart of the shopping district. The display is essentially like those to be found in hundreds of towns or cities across the Nation—often on public grounds—during the Christmas season. The Pawtucket display comprises many of the figures and decorations traditionally associated with Christmas, including, among other things, a Santa Claus house, reindeer pulling Santa's sleigh, candy-striped poles, a Christmas tree, carolers, cutout figures representing such characters as a clown, an elephant, and a teddy bear, hundreds of colored lights, a large banner that reads "SEASONS GREETINGS," and the crèche at issue here. All components of this display are owned by the city.

The crèche, which has been included in the display for 40 or more years, consists of the traditional figures, including the Infant Jesus, Mary and Joseph, angels, shepherds, kings, and animals, all ranging in height from 5″ to 5′. In 1973, when the present crèche was acquired, it cost the city $1,365; it now is valued at $200. The erection and dismantling of the crèche costs the city about $20 per year; nominal expenses are incurred in lighting the crèche. No money has been expended on its maintenance for the past 10 years.

Respondents, Pawtucket residents and individual members of the Rhode Island affiliate of the American Civil Liberties Union, and the affiliate itself, brought this action in the United States District Court for Rhode Island, challenging the city's inclusion of the crèche in the annual display. The District Court held that the city's inclusion of the crèche in the display violates the Establishment Clause, which is binding on the states through the Fourteenth Amendment. The District Court found that, by including the crèche in the Christmas display, the city has "tried to endorse and promulgate religious beliefs," and that "erection of the crèche has the real and substantial effect of affiliating the City with the Christian beliefs that the crèche represents." This "appearance of official sponsorship," it believed, "confers more than a remote and incidental benefit on Christianity." Last, although the court acknowledged the absence of administrative entanglement, it found that excessive entanglement has been fostered as a result of the political divisiveness of including the crèche in the celebration. The city was permanently enjoined from including the crèche in the display.

A divided panel of the Court of Appeals for the First Circuit affirmed. We granted certiorari, and we reverse.

II

A

This Court has explained that the purpose of the Establishment and Free Exercise Clauses of the First Amendment is

> to prevent, as far as possible, the intrusion of either [the church or the state] into the precincts of the other.

At the same time, however, the Court has recognized that

> total separation is not possible in an absolute sense. Some relationship between government and religious organizations is inevitable.

In every Establishment Clause case, we must reconcile the inescapable tension between the objective of preventing unnecessary intrusion of either the church or the state upon the other, and the reality that, as the Court has so often noted, total separation of the two is not possible.

The Court has sometimes described the Religion Clauses as erecting a "wall" between church and state. The concept of a "wall" of separation is a useful figure of speech probably deriving from views of Thomas Jefferson. The metaphor has served as a reminder that the Establishment Clause forbids an established church or anything approaching it. But the metaphor itself is not a wholly accurate description of the practical aspects of the relationship that in fact exists between church and state.

No significant segment of our society and no institution within it can exist in a vacuum or in total or absolute isolation from all the other parts, much less from government. "It has never been thought either possible or desirable to enforce a regime of total separation. . . ." Nor does the Constitution require complete separation of church and state; it affirmatively mandates accommodation, not merely tolerance, of all religions, and forbids hostility toward any. Anything less would require the "callous indifference" we have said was never intended by the Establishment Clause. Indeed, we have observed, such hostility would bring us into "war with our national tradition as embodied in the First Amendment's guaranty of the free exercise of religion."

B

The Court's interpretation of the Establishment Clause has comported with what history reveals was the contemporaneous understanding of its guarantees. A significant example of the contemporaneous understanding of that Clause is found in the events of the first week of the First Session of the First Congress in 1789. In the very week that Congress approved the Establishment Clause as part of the Bill of Rights for submission to the states, it enacted legislation providing for paid chaplains for the House and Senate. In *Marsh* we noted that 17 Members of the First Congress had been Delegates to the Constitutional Convention where freedom of speech, press, and religion and antagonism toward an established church were subjects of frequent discussion. We saw no conflict with the Establishment Clause when Nebraska employed members of the clergy as official legislative Chaplains to give opening prayers at sessions of the state legislature.

The interpretation of the Establishment Clause by Congress in 1789 takes on special significance in light of the Court's emphasis that the First Congress

> was a Congress whose constitutional decisions have always been regarded, as they should be regarded, as of the greatest weight in the interpretation of that fundamental instrument.

It is clear that neither the 17 draftsmen of the Constitution who were Members of the First Congress, nor the Congress of 1789, saw any establishment problem in the employment of congressional Chaplains to offer daily prayers in the Congress, a practice that has continued for nearly two centuries. It would be difficult to identify a more striking example of the accommodation of religious belief intended by the Framers.

C

There is an unbroken history of official acknowledgment by all three branches of government of the role of religion in American life from at least 1789. Seldom in our opinions was this more affirmatively expressed than in Justice Douglas' opinion for the Court validating a program allowing release of public school students from classes to attend off-campus religious exercises. Rejecting a claim that the program violated the Establishment Clause, the Court asserted pointedly:

> We are a religious people whose institutions presuppose a Supreme Being.

Our history is replete with official references to the value and invocation of Divine guidance in deliberations and pronouncements of the Founding Fathers and contemporary leaders. Beginning in the early colonial period long before Independence, a day of Thanksgiving was celebrated as a religious holiday to give thanks for the bounties of Nature as gifts from God. President Washington and his successors proclaimed Thanksgiving, with all its religious overtones, a day of national celebration and Congress made it a National Holiday more than a century ago. That holiday has not lost its theme of expressing thanks for Divine aid any more than has Christmas lost its religious significance.

Executive Orders and other official announcements of Presidents and of the Congress have proclaimed both Christmas and Thanksgiving National Holidays in religious terms. And, by Acts of Congress, it has long been the practice that federal employees are released from duties on these National Holidays, while being paid from the same public revenues that provide the compensation of the Chaplains of the Senate and the House and the military services. Thus, it is clear that Government has long recognized—indeed it has subsidized—holidays with religious significance.

Other examples of reference to our religious heritage are found in the statutorily prescribed national motto "In God We Trust," which Congress and the President mandated for our currency, and in the language "One nation under God," as part of the Pledge of Allegiance to the American flag. That pledge is recited by many thousands of public school children—and adults—every year.

Art galleries supported by public revenues display religious paintings of the 15th and 16th centuries, predominantly inspired by one religious faith. The National Gallery in Washington, maintained with Government support, for example, has long exhibited masterpieces with religious messages, notably the Last Supper, and paintings depicting the Birth of Christ, the Crucifixion, and the Resurrection, among many others with explicit Christian themes and messages. The very chamber in which oral arguments on this case were heard is decorated with a notable and permanent—not seasonal—symbol of religion: Moses with the Ten Commandments. Congress has long provided chapels in the Capitol for religious worship and meditation.

There are countless other illustrations of the Government's acknowledgment of our religious heritage and governmental sponsorship of graphic manifestations of that heritage. Congress has directed the President to proclaim a National Day of Prayer each year "on which [day] the people of the United States may turn to God in prayer and meditation at churches, in groups, and as individuals." Our Presidents have repeatedly issued such Proclamations. Presidential Proclamations and messages have been issued to commemorate Jewish Heritage Week and the Jewish High Holy Days. One cannot look at even this brief résumé without finding that our history is pervaded by expressions of religious beliefs such as are found in *Zorach.* Equally pervasive is the evidence of accommodation of all faiths and all forms of religious expression, and hostility toward none. Through this accommodation, as Justice Douglas observed, governmental action has "follow[ed] the best of our traditions" and "respect[ed] the religious nature of our people."

III

This history may help explain why the Court consistently has declined to take a rigid, absolutist view of the Establishment Clause. We have refused "to construe the Religion Clauses with a literalness that would undermine the ultimate constitutional objective *as illuminated by history.*" In our modern, complex society, whose traditions and constitutional underpinnings rest on and encourage diversity and pluralism in all areas, an absolutist approach in applying the

Establishment Clause is simplistic and has been uniformly rejected by the Court.

Rather than mechanically invalidating all governmental conduct or statutes that confer benefits or give special recognition to religion in general or to one faith—as an absolutist approach would dictate—the Court has scrutinized challenged legislation or official conduct to determine whether, in reality, it establishes a religion or religious faith, or tends to do so.

In each case, the inquiry calls for the line-drawing; no fixed, *per se* rule can be framed. The Establishment Clause like the Due Process Clauses is not a precise, detailed provision in a legal code capable of ready application. The purpose of the Establishment Clause "was to state an objective, not to write a statute." The line between permissible relationships and those barred by the Clause can no more be straight and unwavering than due process can be defined in a single stroke or phrase or test. The Clause erects a "blurred, indistinct, and variable barrier depending on all the circumstances of a particular relationship."

In the line-drawing process we have often found it useful to inquire whether the challenged law or conduct has a secular purpose, whether its principal or primary effect is to advance or inhibit religion, and whether it creates an excessive entanglement of government with religion. But, we have repeatedly emphasized our unwillingness to be confined to any single test or criterion in this sensitive area. In two cases, the Court did not even apply the *Lemon* "test." We did not, for example, consider that analysis relevant in *Marsh*. Nor did we find *Lemon* useful in *Larson* v. *Valente,* where there was substantial evidence of overt discrimination against a particular church.

In this case, the focus of our inquiry must be on the crèche in the context of the Christmas season. In *Stone,* for example, we invalidated a state statute requiring the posting of a copy of the Ten Commandments on public classroom walls. But the Court carefully pointed out that the Commandments were posted purely as a religious admonition, not "integrated into the school curriculum, where the Bible may constitutionally be used in an appropriate study of history, civilization, ethics, comparative religion, or the like." Similarly, in *Abington,* although the Court struck down the practices in two States requiring daily Bible readings in public schools, it specifically noted that nothing in the Court's holding was intended to "indicat[e] that such study of the Bible or of religion, when presented objectively as part of a secular program of education, may not be effected consistently with the First Amendment." Focus exclusively on the religious component of any activity would inevitably lead to its invalidation under the Establishment Clause.

The Court has invalidated legislation or governmental action on the ground that a secular purpose was lacking, but only when it has concluded there was no question that the statute or activity was motivated wholly by religious considerations. Even where the benefits to religion were substantial, as in *Everson, Allen, Walz,* and *Tilton,* we saw a secular purpose and no conflict with the Establishment Clause.

The District Court inferred from the religious nature of the crèche that the city has no secular purpose for the display. In so doing, it rejected the city's claim that its reasons for including the crèche are essentially the same as its reasons for sponsoring the display as a whole. The District Court plainly erred by focusing almost exclusively on the crèche. When viewed in the proper context of the Christmas Holiday season, it is apparent that, on this record, there is insufficient evidence to establish that the inclusion of the crèche is a purposeful or surreptitious effort to express some kind of subtle governmental advocacy of a particular religious message. In a pluralistic society a variety of motives and purposes are implicated. The city, like the Congresses and Presidents, however, has principally taken note of a significant historical religious event long celebrated in the Western World. The crèche in the display depicts the historical origins of this traditional event long recognized as a National Holiday.

The narrow question is whether there is a secular purpose for Pawtucket's display of the crèche. The display is sponsored by the city to celebrate the Holiday and to depict the origins of that Holiday. These are legitimate secular purposes. The District Court's inference, drawn from the religious nature of the crèche, that the city has no secular purpose was, on this record, clearly erroneous.

The District Court found that the primary effect of including the crèche is to confer a substantial and impermissible benefit on religion in general and on the Christian faith in particular. Comparisons of the relative benefits to religion of different forms of governmental support are elusive and difficult to make. But to conclude that the primary effect of including the crèche is to advance religion in violation of the Establishment Clause would require that we view it as more beneficial to and more an endorsement of religion, for example, than expenditure of large sums of public money for textbooks supplied throughout the country to students attending church-sponsored schools, expenditure of public funds for transportation of students to church-sponsored schools, *Everson,* federal grants for college buildings of church-sponsored institutions of higher education combining secular and religious education, noncategorical grants to church-sponsored colleges and universities, *Roemer,* and the tax exemptions for church properties sanctioned in *Walz.* It would also require that we view it as more of an endorsement of religion than the Sunday Closing Laws upheld in *McGowan,* the release time program for religious training in *Zorach,* and the legislative prayers upheld in *Marsh.*

We are unable to discern a greater aid to religion deriving from inclusion of the crèche than from these benefits and endorsements previously held not violative of the Establishment Clause. What was said about the legislative prayers in *Marsh,* and implied about the Sunday Closing Laws in *McGowan* is true of the city's inclusion of the crèche: its "reason or effect merely happens to coincide or harmonize with the tenets of some . . . religions."

This case differs significantly from *Grendel's Den* and *McCollum,* where religion was substantially aided. In *Grendel's Den,* important governmental power—a licensing veto authority—had been vested in churches. In *McCollum* government had made religious instruction available in public school classrooms; the State had not only used the public school buildings for the teaching of religion, it had "afford[ed] sectarian groups an invaluable aid . . . [by] provid[ing] pupils for their religious classes through use of the State's compulsory public school machinery." No comparable benefit to religion is discernible here.

The dissent asserts some observers may perceive that the city has aligned itself with the Christian faith by including a Christian symbol in its display and that this serves to advance religion. We can assume, *arguendo,* that the display advances religion in a sense; but our precedents plainly contemplate that on occasion some advancement of religion will result from governmental action. The Court has made it abundantly clear, however, that "not every law that confers an 'indirect,' 'remote,' or 'incidental' benefit upon [religion] is, for that reason alone, constitutionally invalid." Here, whatever benefit to one faith or religion or to all religions, is indirect, remote, and incidental; display of the crèche is no more an advancement or endorsement of religion than the Congressional and Executive recognition of the origins of the Holiday itself as "Christ's Mass," or the exhibition of literally hundreds of religious paintings in governmentally supported museums.

The District Court found that there had been no administrative entanglement between religion and state resulting from the city's ownership and use of the crèche. But it went on to hold that some political divisiveness was engendered by this litigation. Coupled with its finding of an impermissible sectarian purpose and effect, this persuaded the court that there was "excessive entanglement." The Court of Appeals expressly declined to accept the District Court's finding that inclusion of the crèche has caused political divisiveness along religious lines, and noted that this Court has never held that political divisiveness alone was sufficient to invalidate government conduct.

Entanglement is a question of kind and degree. In this case, however, there is no reason to disturb the District Court's finding on the absence of administrative entanglement. There is no evidence of contact with church authorities concerning the content of design or the exhibit prior to or since Pawtucket's purchase of the crèche. No expenditures for maintenance of the crèche have been necessary; and since the city owns the crèche, now valued at $200, the tangible material it contributes is *de minimis.* In many respects the display requires far less ongoing, day-to-day interaction between church and state than religious paintings in public galleries. There is nothing here, of course, like the "comprehensive, discriminating, and continuing state surveillance" or the "enduring entanglement" present in *Lemon.*

The Court of Appeals correctly observed that this Court has not held that political divisiveness alone can serve to invalidate otherwise permissible conduct. And we decline to so hold today. This case does not involve a direct subsidy to church-sponsored schools or colleges, or other religious institutions, and hence no inquiry into potential political divisiveness is even called for, *Mueller* v. *Allen.* In any event, apart from this litigation there is no evidence of political friction or divisiveness over the crèche in the 40-year history of Pawtucket's Christmas celebration. The District Court stated that the inclusion of the crèche for the 40 years has been "marked by no apparent dissension" and that the display has had a "calm history. " Curiously, it went on to hold that the political divisiveness engendered by this lawsuit was evidence of excessive entanglement. A litigant cannot, by the very act of commencing a lawsuit, however, create the appearance of divisiveness and then exploit it as evidence of entanglement.

We are satisfied that the city has a secular purpose for including the crèche, that the city has not impermissibly advanced religion, and that including the crèche does not create excessive entanglement between religion and government.

IV

Justice Brennan describes the crèche as a "re-creation of an event that lies at the heart of Christian faith." The crèche, like a painting, is passive; admittedly it is a reminder of the origins of Christmas. Even the traditional, purely secular displays extant at Christmas, with or without a crèche, would inevitably recall the religious nature of the Holiday. The display engenders a friendly community spirit of goodwill in keeping with the season. The crèche may well have special meaning to those whose faith includes the celebration of religious Masses, but none who sense the origins of the Christmas celebration would fail to be aware of its religious implications. That the display brings people into the central city, and serves commercial interests and benefits merchants and their employees, does not, as the dissent points out, determine the character of the display. That a prayer invoking Divine guidance in Congress is preceded and followed by debate and partisan conflict over taxes, budgets, national defense, and myriad mundane subjects, for example, has never been thought to demean or taint the sacredness of the invocation.

Of course the crèche is identified with one religious faith but no more so than the examples we have set out from prior cases in which we found no conflict with the Establishment Clause. It would be ironic, however, if the inclusion of a single symbol of a particular historic religious event, as part of a celebration acknowledged in the Western World for 20 centuries, and in this country by the people, by the Executive Branch, by the Congress, and the courts for 2 centuries, would so "taint" the city's exhibit as to render it violative of the Establishment Clause. To forbid the use of this one passive symbol—the crèche—at the very time people are taking note of the season with Christmas hymns and carols in public schools and other public places, and while the Congress and legislatures open sessions with prayers by paid chaplains would be a stilted overreaction contrary to our history and to our holdings. If the presence of the crèche in this display violates the Establishment Clause, a host of other forms of taking official note of Christmas, and of our religious heritage, are equally offensive to the Constitution.

The Court has acknowledged that the "fears and political problems" that gave rise to the Religion Clauses in the 18th century are of far less concern today. We are unable to perceive the Archbishop of Canterbury, the Bishop of Rome, or other powerful religious leaders behind every public acknowledgment of the religious heritage long officially recognized by the three constitutional branches of government. Any notion that these symbols pose a real danger of establishment of a state church is farfetched indeed.

V

That this Court has been alert to the constitutionally expressed opposition to the establishment of religion is shown in numerous holdings striking down statutes or programs as violative of the Establishment Clause. The most recent example of this careful scrutiny is found in the case invalidating a municipal ordinance granting to a church a virtual veto power over the licensing of liquor establishments near the church. Taken together these cases abundantly demonstrate the Court's concern to protect the genuine objectives of the Establishment Clause. It is far too late in the day to impose a crabbed reading of the Clause on the country.

VI

We hold that, notwithstanding the religious significance of the crèche, the city of Pawtucket has not violated the Establishment Clause of the First Amendment. Accordingly, the judgment of the Court of Appeals is reversed.

It is so ordered.

JUSTICE BRENNAN, WITH WHOM JUSTICE MARSHALL, JUSTICE BLACKMUN, AND JUSTICE STEVENS JOIN, DISSENTING.

The principles announced in the compact phrases of the Religion Clauses have, as the Court today reminds us, proved difficult to apply. Faced with that uncertainty, the Court properly looks for guidance to the settled test announced in *Lemon* v. *Kurtzman,* for assessing whether a challenged governmental practice involves an impermissible step toward the establishment of religion. Applying that test to this case, the Court reaches an essentially narrow result which turns largely upon the particular holiday context in which the city of Pawtucket's nativity scene appeared. The Court's decision implicitly leaves open questions concerning the constitutionality of the public display on public property of a crèche standing alone, or the public display of other distinctively religious symbols such as a cross. Despite the narrow contours of the Court's opinion, our precedents in my view compel the holding that Pawtucket's inclusion of a life-sized display depicting the biblical description of the birth of Christ as part of its annual Christmas celebration is unconstitutional. Nothing in the history of such practices or the setting in which the city's crèche is presented obscures or diminishes the plain fact that Pawtucket's action amounts to an impermissible governmental endorsement of a particular faith.

I

Last Term, I expressed the hope that the Court's decision in *Marsh* would prove to be only a single, aberrant departure from our settled method of analyzing Establishment Clause cases. That the Court today returns to the settled analysis of our prior cases gratifies that hope. At the same time, the Court's less-than-vigorous application of the *Lemon* test suggests that its commitment to those standards may only be superficial. After reviewing the Court's opinion, I am convinced that this case appears hard not because the principles of decision are obscure, but because the Christmas holiday seems so familiar and agreeable. Although the Court's reluctance to disturb a community's chosen method of celebrating such an agreeable holiday is understandable, that cannot justify the Court's departure from controlling precedent. In my view, Pawtucket's maintenance and display at public expense of a symbol as distinctively sectarian as a crèche simply cannot be squared with our prior cases. And it is plainly contrary to the purposes and values of the Establishment Clause to pretend, as the Court does, that the otherwise secular setting of Pawtucket's nativity scene dilutes in some fashion the crèche's singular religiosity, or that the city's annual display reflects nothing more than an "acknowledgment" of our shared national heritage. Neither the character of the Christmas holiday itself, nor our heritage of religious expression supports this result. Indeed, our remarkable and precious religious diversity as a Nation, which the Establishment Clause seeks to protect, runs directly counter to today's decision.

A

As we have sought to meet new problems arising under the Establishment Clause, our decisions, with few exceptions, have demanded that a challenged governmental practice satisfy the following criteria:

> First, the [practice] must have a secular legislative purpose; second, its principal or primary effect must be one that neither advances nor inhibits religion; finally, [it] must not foster "an excessive government entanglement with religion."

This well-defined three-part test expresses the essential concerns animating the Establishment Clause. Thus, the test is designed to ensure that the organs of government remain strictly separate and apart from religious affairs, for "a union of government and religion tends to destroy government and degrade religion." And it seeks to guarantee that government maintains a position of neutrality with respect to religion and neither advances nor inhibits the promulgation and practice of religious beliefs. In this regard, we must be alert in our examination of any challenged practice not only for an official establishment of religion, but also for those other evils at which the Clause was aimed— "'sponsorship, financial support, and active involvement of the sovereign in religious activity.'"

Applying the three-part test to Pawtucket's crèche, I am persuaded that the city's inclusion of the crèche in its Christmas display simply does not reflect a "clearly secular . . . purpose." Unlike the typical case in which the record reveals some contemporaneous expression of a clear purpose to advance religion, or, conversely, a clear secular purpose, here we have no explicit statement of purpose by Pawtucket's municipal government accompanying its decision to purchase, display, and maintain the crèche. Governmental purpose may nevertheless be inferred. For instance, in *Stone* v. *Graham,* this Court found, despite the State's avowed purpose of reminding schoolchildren of the secular application of the commands of the Decalogue, that the "preeminent purpose for posting the Ten Commandments on schoolroom walls is plainly religious in nature." In the present case, the city claims that its purposes were exclusively secular. Pawtucket sought, according to this view, only to participate in the celebration of a national holiday and to attract people to the downtown area in order to promote pre-Christmas retail sales and to help engender the spirit of goodwill and neighborliness commonly associated with the Christmas season.

Despite these assertions, two compelling aspects of this case indicate that our generally prudent "reluctance to attribute unconstitutional motives" to a governmental body, should be overcome. First, as was true in *Grendel's Den,* all of Pawtucket's "valid secular objectives can be readily accomplished by other means." Plainly, the city's interest in celebrating the holiday and in promoting both retail sales and goodwill are fully served by the elaborate display of Santa Claus, reindeer, and wishing wells that are already a part of Pawtucket's annual Christmas display. More importantly, the nativity scene, unlike every other element of the Hodgson Park display, reflects a sectarian exclusivity that the avowed purposes of celebrating the holiday season and promoting retail commerce simply do not encompass. To be found constitutional, Pawtucket's seasonal celebration must at least be nondenominational and not serve to promote religion. The inclusion of a distinctively religious element like the crèche, however, demonstrates that a narrower sectarian purpose lay behind the decision to include a nativity scene. That the crèche retained this religious character for the people and municipal government of Pawtucket is suggested by the Mayor's testimony at trial in which he stated that for him, as well as others in the city, the effort to eliminate the nativity scene from Pawtucket's Christmas celebration "is a step towards establishing another religion, non-religion that it may be." Plainly, the city and its leaders understood that the inclusion of the crèche in its display would serve the wholly religious purpose of "keep[ing] 'Christ in Christmas.'" From this record, therefore, it is impossible to say with the kind of confidence that was possible in *McGowan* that a wholly secular goal predominates.

The "primary effect" of including a nativity scene in the city's display is, as the District Court found, to place the government's imprimatur of approval on the particular religious beliefs exemplified by the crèche. Those who believe in the message of the nativity receive the unique and exclusive benefit of public recognition and approval of their views. For many, the city's decision to include the crèche as part of its extensive and costly efforts to celebrate Christmas can only mean that the prestige of the government has been conferred on the beliefs associated with the crèche, thereby providing "a significant symbolic benefit to religion. . . . " The effect on minority religious groups, as well as on those who may reject all religion, is to convey the message that their views are not similarly worthy of public recognition nor entitled to public support. It was precisely this sort of religious chauvinism that the Establishment Clause was intended forever to prohibit. In this case, as in *Engel,* "[w]hen the power, prestige and financial support of government is placed behind a particular religious belief, the indirect coercive pressure upon religious minorities to conform to the prevailing officially approved religion is plain." Our decision in *Widmar* v. *Vincent* rests upon the same principle. There the Court noted that a state university policy of "equal access" for both secular and religious groups would "not confer any imprimatur of state approval" on the religious groups permitted to use the facilities because "a broad spectrum of groups" would be served and there was no evidence that religious groups would dominate the forum. Here, by contrast, Pawtucket itself owns the crèche and instead of extending similar attention to a "broad spectrum" of religious and secular groups, it has singled out Christianity for special treatment.

Finally, it is evident that Pawtucket's inclusion of a crèche as part of its annual Christmas display does pose a significant threat of fostering "excessive entanglement." As the Court notes, the District Court found no administrative entanglement in this case, primarily because the city had been able to administer the annual display without extensive consultation with religious officials. Of course, there is no reason to disturb that finding, but it is worth noting that after today's decision, administrative entanglements may well develop. Jews and other non-Christian groups, prompted perhaps by the Mayor's remark that he will include a Menorah in future displays, can be expected to press government for inclusion of their symbols, and faced with such requests, government will have to become involved in accommodating the various demands. More importantly, although no political divisiveness was apparent in Pawtucket prior to the filing of respondents' lawsuit, that act, as the District Court found, unleashed powerful emotional reactions which divided the city along religious lines. The fact that calm had prevailed prior to this suit does not immediately suggest the absence of any division on the point for, as the District Court observed, the quiescence of those opposed to the crèche may have reflected nothing more than their sense of futility in opposing the majority. Of course, the Court is correct to note that we have never held that the potential for divisiveness alone is sufficient to invalidate a challenged governmental practice; we have, nevertheless, repeatedly emphasized that "too close a proximity" between religious and civil authorities may represent a "warning signal" that the values embodied in the Establishment Clause are at risk. Furthermore, the Court should not blind itself to the fact that because communities differ in religious composition, the controversy over whether local governments may adopt religious symbols will continue to fester. In many communities, non-Christian groups can be expected to combat practices similar to Pawtucket's; this will be so especially in areas where there are substantial non-Christian minorities.

In sum, considering the District Court's careful findings of fact under the three-part analysis called for by our prior cases, I have no difficulty concluding that Pawtucket's display of the crèche is unconstitutional.

B

The Court advances two principal arguments to support its conclusion that the Pawtucket crèche satisfies the *Lemon* test. Neither is persuasive.

First. The Court, by focusing on the holiday "context" in which the nativity scene appeared, seeks to explain away the clear religious import of the crèche and the findings of the District Court that most observers understood the crèche as both a symbol of Christian beliefs and a symbol of the city's support for those beliefs. Thus, although the Court concedes that the city's inclusion of the nativity scene plainly serves "to depict the origins" of Christmas as a "significant historical religious event," and that the crèche "is identified with one religious faith," we are nevertheless expected to believe that Pawtucket's use of the crèche does not signal the city's support for the sectarian symbolism that the nativity scene evokes. The effect of the crèche, of course, must be gauged not only by its inherent religious significance but also by the overall setting in which it appears. But it blinks reality to claim, as the Court does, that by including such a distinctively religious object as the crèche in its Christmas display, Pawtucket has done no more than make use of a "traditional" symbol of the holiday, and has thereby purged the crèche of its religious content and conferred only an "incidental and indirect" benefit on religion.

The Court's struggle to ignore the clear religious effect of the crèche seems to me misguided for several reasons. In the first place, the city has positioned the crèche in a central and highly visible location within the Hodgson Park display.

* * * * *

Moreover, the city has done nothing to disclaim government approval of the religious significance of the crèche, to suggest that the crèche represents only one religious symbol among many others that might be included in a seasonal display truly aimed at providing a wide catalog of ethnic and religious celebrations, or to disassociate itself from the religious content of the crèche. In *Schempp,* we noted that reading aloud from the Bible would be a permissible schoolroom exercise only if it was "presented objectively as part of a secular program of education" that would remove any message of governmental endorsement of religion. Similarly, when the Court of Appeals for the District of Columbia Circuit approved the inclusion of a crèche as part of a national "Pageant of Peace" on federal parkland adjacent to the White House, it did so on the express condition that the Government would erect "explanatory plaques" disclaiming any sponsorship of religious beliefs associated with the crèche. In this case, by contrast, Pawtucket has made no effort whatever to provide a similar cautionary message.

Third, we have consistently acknowledged that an otherwise secular setting alone does not suffice to justify a governmental practice that has the effect of aiding religion. In *Hunt* v. *McNair,* for instance, we observed that "[a]id normally may be thought to have a primary effect of advancing religion . . . when it [supports] a specifically religious activity in an otherwise substantially secular setting." The demonstrably secular context of public education, therefore, did not save the challenged practice of school prayer in *Engel* or in *Schempp.* Similarly, in *Tilton,* despite the generally secular thrust of the financing legislation under review, the Court unanimously struck down that aspect of the program which permitted church-related institutions eventually to assume total control over the use of buildings constructed with federal aid.

Finally, and most importantly, even in the context of Pawtucket's seasonal celebration, the crèche retains a specifically Christian religious meaning. I refuse to accept the notion implicit in today's decision that non-Christians would find that the religious content of the crèche is eliminated by the fact that it appears as part of the city's otherwise secular celebration of the Christmas holiday. The nativity scene is clearly distinct in its purpose and effect from the rest of the Hodgson Park display for the simple reason that it is the only one rooted in a biblical account of Christ's birth. It is the chief symbol of the characteristically Christian belief that a divine Savior was brought into the world and that the purpose of this miraculous birth was to illuminate a path toward salvation and redemption. For Christians, that path is exclusive, precious, and holy. But for those who do not share these beliefs, the symbolic reenactment of the birth of a divine being who has been miraculously incarnated as a man stands as a dramatic reminder of their differences with Christian faith. When government appears to sponsor such religiously inspired views, we cannot say that the practice is "'so separate and so indisputably marked off from the religious function,' . . . that [it] may fairly be viewed as reflect[ing] a neutral posture toward religious institutions." To be so excluded on religious grounds by one's elected government is an insult and an injury that, until today, could not be countenanced by the Establishment Clause.

Second. The Court also attempts to justify the crèche by entertaining a beguilingly simple, yet faulty syllogism. The Court begins by noting that government may recognize Christmas Day as a public holiday; the Court then asserts that the crèche is nothing more than a traditional element of Christmas celebrations; and it concludes that the inclusion of a crèche as part of a government's annual Christmas celebration is constitutionally permissible. The Court apparently believes that once it finds that the designation of Christmas as a public holiday is constitutionally acceptable, it is then free to conclude that virtually every form of governmental association with the celebration of the holiday is also constitutional. The vice of this dangerously superficial argument is that it overlooks the fact that the Christmas holiday in our national culture contains both secular and sectarian elements. To say that government may recognize the holiday's traditional, secular elements of gift-giving, public festivities, and community spirit, does not mean that government may indiscriminately embrace the distinctively sectarian aspects of the holiday. Indeed, in its eagerness to approve the crèche, the Court has advanced a rationale so simplistic that it would appear to allow the Mayor of Pawtucket to participate in the celebration of a Christmas Mass, since this would be just another unobjectionable way for the city to "celebrate the holiday." As is demonstrated below, the Court's logic is fundamentally flawed both because it obscures the reason why public designation of Christmas Day as a holiday is constitutionally acceptable, and blurs the distinction between the secular aspects of Christmas and its distinctively religious character, as exemplified by the crèche.

When government decides to recognize Christmas Day as a public holiday, it does no more than accommodate the calendar of public activities to the plain fact that many Americans will expect on that day to spend time visiting with their families, attending religious services, and perhaps enjoying some respite from preholiday activities. The Free Exercise Clause, of course, does not necessarily compel the government to provide this accommodation, but neither is the Establishment Clause offended by such a step. Because it is clear that the celebration of Christmas has both secular and sectarian elements, it may well be that by taking note of the holiday, the government is simply seeking to serve the same kinds of wholly secular goals—for instance, promoting goodwill and a common day of rest—that were found to justify Sunday Closing Laws in *McGowan.* If public officials go further and participate in the *secular* celebration of Christmas—by, for example, decorating public places with such secular images as wreaths, garlands, or Santa Claus figures—they move closer to the limits of their constitutional power but nevertheless remain within the boundaries set by the Establishment Clause. But when those officials participate in or appear to endorse the distinctively religious elements of this otherwise secular event, they encroach upon First Amendment freedoms. For it is at that point that the government brings to the forefront the theological content of the holiday, and places the prestige, power, and financial support of a civil authority in the service of a particular faith.

The inclusion of a crèche in Pawtucket's otherwise secular celebration of Christmas clearly violates these principles. Unlike such secular figures as Santa Claus, reindeer, and carolers, a nativity scene represents far more than a mere "traditional" symbol of Christmas. The essence of the crèche's symbolic purpose and effect is to prompt the observer to experience a sense of simple awe and wonder appropriate to the contemplation of one of the central elements of Christian dogma—that God sent His Son into the world to be a Messiah. Contrary to the Court's suggestion, the crèche is far from a mere representation of a "particular historic religious event." It is, instead, best understood as a mystical re-creation of an event that lies at the heart of Christian faith. To suggest, as the Court does, that such a symbol is merely "traditional" and therefore no different from Santa's house or reindeer is not only offensive to those for whom the crèche has profound significance, but insulting to those who insist for religious or personal reasons that the story of Christ is in no sense a part of "history" nor an unavoidable element of our national "heritage."

For these reasons, the crèche in this context simply cannot be viewed as playing the same role that an ordinary museum display does. The Court seems to assume that prohibiting Pawtucket from displaying a crèche would be tantamount to prohibiting a state college from including the Bible or Milton's Paradise Lost in a course on English literature. But in those cases the religiously inspired materials are being considered solely as literature. The purpose is plainly not to single out the particular religious beliefs that may have inspired the authors, but to see in these writings the outlines of a larger imaginative universe shared with other forms of literary expression. The same may be said of a course devoted to the study of art; when the course turns to Gothic architecture, the emphasis is not on the religious beliefs which the cathedrals exalt, but rather upon the "aesthetic consequences of [such religious] thought."

In this case, by contrast, the crèche plays no comparable secular role. Unlike the poetry of Paradise Lost which students in a literature course will seek to appreciate primarily for esthetic or historical reasons, the angels, shepherds, Magi, and infant of Pawtucket's nativity scene can only be viewed as symbols of a particular set of religious beliefs. It would be another matter if the crèche were displayed in a museum setting, in the company of other religiously inspired artifacts, as an example, among many, of the symbolic representation of religious myths. In that setting, we would have objective guarantees that the crèche could not suggest that a particular faith had been singled out for public favor and recognition. The effect of Pawtucket's crèche, however, is not confined by any of these limiting attributes. In the absence of any other religious symbols or of any neutral disclaimer, the inescapable effect of the crèche will be to remind the average observer of the religious roots of the celebration he is witnessing and to call to mind the scriptural message that the nativity symbolizes. The fact that Pawtucket has gone to the trouble of making such an elaborate public celebration and of including a crèche in that otherwise secular setting inevitably serves to reinforce the sense that the city means to express solidarity with the Christian message of the crèche and to dismiss other faiths as unworthy of similar attention and support.

II

Although the Court's relaxed application of the *Lemon* test to Pawtucket's crèche is regrettable, it is at least understandable and properly limited to the particular facts of this case. The Court's opinion, however, also sounds a broader and more troubling theme. Invoking the celebration of Thanksgiving as a public holiday, the legend "In God We Trust" on our coins, and the proclamation "God save the United States and this Honorable Court" at the opening of judicial sessions, the Court asserts, without explanation, that Pawtucket's inclusion of a crèche in its annual Christmas display poses no more of a threat to Establishment Clause values than these other official "acknowledgments" of religion.

Intuition tells us that some official "acknowledgment" is inevitable in a religious society if government is not to adopt a stilted indifference to the religious life of the people. It is equally true, however, that if government is to remain scrupulously neutral in matters of religious conscience, as our Constitution requires, then it must avoid those overly broad acknowledgments of religious practices that may imply governmental favoritism toward one set of religious beliefs. This does not mean, of course, that public officials may not take account, when necessary, of the separate existence and significance of the religious institutions and practices in the society they govern. Should government choose to incorporate some arguably religious element into its public ceremonies, that acknowledgment must be impartial; it must not tend to promote one faith or handicap another; and it should not sponsor religion generally over nonreligion. Thus, in a series of decisions concerned with such acknowledgments, we have repeatedly held that any active form of public acknowledgment of religion indicating sponsorship or endorsement is forbidden.

Despite this body of case law, the Court has never comprehensively addressed the extent to which government may acknowledge religion by, for example, incorporating religious references into public ceremonies and proclamations, and I do not presume to offer a comprehensive approach. Nevertheless, it appears from our prior decisions that at least three principles—tracing the narrow channels which government acknowledgments must follow to satisfy the Establishment Clause—may be identified. First, although the government may not be compelled to do so by the Free Exercise Clause, it may, consistently with the Establishment Clause, act to accommodate to some extent the opportunities of individuals to practice their religion. That is the essential meaning, I submit, of this Court's decision in *Zorach,* finding that government does not violate the Establishment Clause when it simply chooses to "close its doors or suspend its operations as to those who want to repair to their religious sanctuary for worship or instruction." And for me that principle would justify government's decision to declare December 25th a public holiday.

Second, our cases recognize that while a particular governmental practice may have derived from religious motivations and retain certain religious connotations, it is nonetheless permissible for the government to pursue the practice when it is continued today solely for secular reasons. As this Court noted with reference to Sunday Closing Laws in *McGowan,* the mere fact that a governmental practice coincides to some extent with certain religious beliefs does not render it unconstitutional. Thanksgiving Day, in my view, fits easily within this principle, for despite its religious antecedents, the current practice of celebrating Thanksgiving is unquestionably secular and patriotic. We all may gather with our families on that day to give thanks both for personal and national good fortune, but we are free, given the secular character of the holiday, to address that gratitude either to a divine beneficence or to such mundane sources as good luck or the country's abundant natural wealth.

Finally, we have noted that government cannot be completely prohibited from recognizing in its public actions the religious beliefs and practices of the American people as an aspect of our national history and culture. While I remain uncertian about these questions, I would suggest that such practices as the designation of "In God We Trust" as our national motto, or the references to God contained in the Pledge of Allegiance can best be understood, in Dean Rostow's apt phrase, as a form a "ceremonial deism," protected from Establishment Clause scrutiny chiefly because they have lost through rote repetition any significant religious content. Moreover, these references are uniquely suited to serve such wholly secular purposes as solemnizing public occasions, or inspiring commitment to meet some national challenge in a manner that simply could not be fully served in our culture if government were limited to purely nonreligious phrases. The practices by which the government has long acknowledged religion are therefore probably necessary to serve certain secular functions, and that necessity, coupled with their long history, gives those practices an essentially secular meaning.

The crèche fits none of these categories. Inclusion of the crèche is not necessary to accommodate individual religious expression. This is plainly not a case in which individual residents of Pawtucket have claimed the right to place a crèche as part of a wholly private display on public land. Nor is the inclusion of the crèche necessary to serve wholly secular goals; it is clear that the city's secular purposes of celebrating the Christmas holiday and promoting retail commerce can be fully served without the crèche. And the crèche, because of its unique association with Christianity, is clearly more sectarian than those references to God that we accept in ceremonial phrases or in other contexts that assure neutrality. The religious works on display at the National Gallery, Presidential references to God during an Inaugural Address, or the national motto present no risk of establishing religion. To be sure, our understanding of these expressions may begin in contemplation of some religious element, but it does not end there. Their message is dominantly secular. In contrast, the message of the crèche begins and ends with reverence for a particular image of the divine.

By insisting that such a distinctively sectarian message is merely an unobjectionable part of our "religious heritage," the Court takes a long step backwards to the days when Justice Brewer could arrogantly declare for the Court that "this is a Christian nation." Those days, I had thought, were forever put behind us by the Court's decision in *Engel,* in which we rejected a similar argument advanced by the State of New York that its Regent's Prayer was simply an acceptable part of our "spiritual heritage."

III

The American historical experience concerning the public celebration of Christmas, if carefully examined, provides no support for the Court's decision. The opening sections of the Court's opinion, while seeking to rely on historical evidence, do no more than recognize the obvious: because of the strong religious currents that run through our history, an inflexible or absolutistic enforcement of the Establishment

Clause would be both imprudent and impossible. This observation is at once uncontroversial and unilluminating. Simply enumerating the various ways in which the Federal Government has recognized the vital role religion plays in our society does nothing to help decide the question presented in *this* case.

Indeed, the Court's approach suggests a fundamental misapprehension of the proper uses of history in constitutional interpretation. Certainly, our decisions reflect the fact that an awareness of historical practice often can provide a useful guide in interpreting the abstract language of the Establishment Clause. But historical acceptance of a particular practice alone is never sufficient to justify a challenged governmental action, since, as the Court has rightly observed, "no one acquires a vested or protected right in violation of the Constitution by long use, even when that span of time covers our entire national existence and indeed predates it." Attention to the details of history should not blind us to the cardinal purposes of the Establishment Clause, nor limit our central inquiry in these cases—whether the challenged practices "threaten those consequences which the Framers deeply feared." In recognition of this, the Court has, until today, consistently limited its historical inquiry to the particular practice under review.

In *McGowan,* for instance, the Court carefully canvassed the entire history of Sunday Closing Laws from the colonial period up to modern times. On the basis of this analysis, we concluded that while such laws were rooted in religious motivations, the current purpose was to serve the wholly secular goal of providing a uniform day of rest for all citizens. Our inquiry in *Walz* was similarly confined to the special history of the practice under review. There the Court found a pattern of "undeviating acceptance" over the entire course of the Nation's history of according property-tax exemptions to religious organizations, a pattern which supported our finding that the practice did not violate the Religion Clauses. Finally, where direct inquiry into the Framer's intent reveals that the First Amendment was not understood to prohibit a particular practice, we have found such an understanding compelling. Thus, in *Marsh,* after marshaling the historical evidence which indicated that the First Congress had authorized the appointment of paid chaplains for its own proceedings only three days before it reached agreement on the final wording of the Bill of Rights, the

Court concluded on the basis of this "unique history" that the modern-day practice of opening legislative sessions with prayer was constitutional.

Although invoking these decisions in support of its result, the Court wholly fails to discuss the history of the public celebration of Christmas or the use of publicly displayed nativity scenes. The Court, instead, simply asserts, without any historical analysis or support whatsoever, that the now familiar celebration of Christmas springs from an unbroken history of acknowledgment "by the people, by the Executive Branch, by the Congress, and the courts for 2 centuries. . . . " The Court's complete failure to offer any explanation of its assertion is perhaps understandable, however, because the historical record points in precisely the opposite direction. Two features of this history are worth noting. First, at the time of the adoption of the Constitution and the Bill of Rights, there was no settled pattern of celebrating Christmas, either as a purely religious holiday or as a public event. Second, the historical evidence, such as it is, offers no uniform pattern of widespread acceptance of the holiday and indeed suggests that the development of Christmas as a public holiday is a comparatively recent phenomenon.

The intent of the Framers with respect to the public display of nativity scenes is virtually impossible to discern primarily because the widespread celebration of Christmas did not emerge in its present form until well into the nineteenth century. Carrying a well-defined Puritan hostility to the celebration of Christ's birth with them to the New World, the founders of the Massachusetts Bay Colony pursued a vigilant policy of opposition to any public celebration of the holiday. To the Puritans, the celebration of Christmas represented a "Popish" practice lacking any foundation in Scripture. This opposition took legal form in 1659 when the Massachusetts Bay Colony made the observance of Christmas Day, "by abstinence from labor, feasting, or any other way," an offense punishable by fine. Although the Colony eventually repealed this ban in 1681, the Puritan objection remained firm.

During the 18th century, sectarian division over the celebration of the holiday continued. As increasing numbers of members of the Anglican and the Dutch and German Reformed Churches arrived, the practice of celebrating Christmas as a purely religious holiday grew. But denominational differences continued to dictate differences in attitude toward the holiday. American Anglicans, who carried with them the Church of England's acceptance of the holiday, Roman Catholics, and various German groups all made the celebration of Christmas a vital part of their religious life. By contrast, many nonconforming Protestant groups, including the Presbyterians, Congregationalists, Baptists, and Methodists, continued to regard the holiday with suspicion and antagonism well into the 19th century. This pattern of sectarian division concerning the holiday suggests that for the Framers of the Establishment Clause, who were acutely sensitive to such sectarian controversies, no single view of how government should approach the celebration of Christmas would be possible.

Many of the same religious sects that were devotedly opposed to the celebration of Christmas on purely religious grounds, were also some of the most vocal and dedicated foes of established religions in the period just prior to the Revolutionary War. The Puritans, and later the Presbyterians, Baptists, and Methodists, generally associated the celebration of Christmas with the elaborate and, in their view, sacrilegious celebration of the holiday by the Church of England, and also with, for them, the more sinister theology of "Popery." In the eyes of these dissenting religious sects, therefore, the groups most closely associated with established religion—the Churches of England and of Rome—were also most closely linked to the profane practice of publicly celebrating Christmas. For those who authored the Bill of Rights, it seems reasonable to suppose that the public celebration of Christmas would have been regarded as at least a sensitive matter, if not deeply controversial. As we have repeatedly observed, the Religion Clauses were intended to ensure a benign regime of competitive disorder among all denominations, so that each sect was free to vie against the others for the allegiance of its followers without state interference. The historical record, contrary to the Court's uninformed assumption, suggests that at the very least conflicting views toward the celebration of Christmas were an important element of that competition at the time of the adoption of the Constitution.

Furthermore, unlike the religious tax exemptions upheld in *Walz,* the public display of nativity scenes as part of governmental celebrations of Christmas does not come to us supported by an unbroken history of widespread acceptance. It was not until 1836 that a State first granted legal recognition to Christmas as a public holiday. This was followed in the period between 1845 and 1865, by 28 jurisdictions which included Christmas Day as a legal holiday. Congress did not follow the States' lead until 1870 when it established December 25th, along with the Fourth of July, New Year's Day, and Thanksgiving, as a legal holiday in the District of Columbia. This pattern of legal recognition tells us only that public acceptance of the holiday was gradual and that the practice—in stark contrast to the record presented in either *Walz* or *Marsh*—did not take on the character of a widely recognized holiday until the middle of the 19th century.

The historical evidence with respect to public financing and support for governmental displays of nativity scenes is even more difficult to gauge. What is known suggests that German immigrants who settled in Pennsylvania early in the 18th century, presumably drawing upon European traditions, were probably the first to introduce nativity scenes to the American celebration of Christmas. It also appears likely that this practice expanded as more Roman Catholic immigrants settled during the 19th century. From these modest beginnings, the familiar crèche scene developed and gained wider recognition by the late 19th century. It is simply impossible to tell, however, whether the practice ever gained widespread acceptance, much less official endorsement, until the 20th century.

In sum, there is no evidence whatsoever that the Framers would have expressly approved a federal celebration of the Christmas holiday including public displays of a nativity scene; accordingly, the Court's repeated invocation of the decision in *Marsh* is not only baffling, it is utterly irrelevant. Nor is there any suggestion that publicly financed and supported displays of Christmas crèches are supported by a record of widespread, undeviating acceptances that extends throughout our history. Therefore, our prior decisions which relied upon concrete, specific historical evidence to support a particular practice simply have no bearing on the question presented in this case. Contrary to today's careless decision, those prior cases have all recognized that the "illumination" provided by history must always be focused on the particular practice at issue in a given case. Without that guiding principle and the intellectual discipline it imposes, the Court is at sea, free to select random elements of America's varied history solely to suit the views of five Members of this Court.

IV

Under our constitutional scheme, the role of safeguarding our "religious heritage" and of promoting religious beliefs is reserved as the exclusive prerogative of our Nation's churches, religious institutions, and spiritual leaders. Because the Framers of the Establishment Clause understood that "religion is too personal, too sacred, too holy to permit its 'unhallowed perversion' by civil [authorities]," the Clause demands that government play no role in this effort. The Court today brushes aside these concerns by insisting that Pawtucket has done nothing more than include a "traditional" symbol of Christmas in its celebration of this national holiday, thereby muting the religious content of the crèche. But the city's action should be recognized for what it is: a coercive, though perhaps small, step toward establishing the sectarian preferences of the majority at the expense of the minority, accomplished by placing public facilities and funds in support of the religious symbolism and theological tidings that the crèche conveys. As Justice Frankfurter, writing in *McGowan,* observed, the Establishment Clause "withdr[aws] from the sphere of legitimate legislative concern and competence a specific, but comprehensive, area of human conduct: man's belief or disbelief in the verity of some transcendental idea and man's expression in action of that belief or disbelief." That the Constitution sets this realm of thought and feeling apart from the pressures and antagonisms of government is one of its supreme achievements. Regrettably, the Court today tarnishes that achievement.

I dissent.

THE FREE EXERCISE CLAUSE

Reynolds v. United States, 98 U.S. 145 (1879)

The first of the free exercise cases concerned the Church of Jesus Christ of Latter-Day Saints. The Court found that the state's compelling interest in protecting morals outweighed the freedom of the individual to practice an act. A similar decision later led the Court to uphold a state ban on "snakehandling" cults in order to protect its citizens' health and safety.

It is in this decision that the Court first employed Jefferson's "wall" phrase.

MR. CHIEF JUSTICE WAITE DELIVERED THE OPINION OF THE COURT.

This is an indictment for bigamy under Section 5352, Revised Statutes, which, omitting its exceptions, is as follows:

> Every person having a husband or wife living, who marries another, whether married or single, in a Territory, or other place over which the United States have exclusive jurisdiction, is guilty of bigamy, and shall be punished by a fine of not more than $500, and by imprisonment for a term of not more than five years.

The assignments of error, when grouped, present the following questions:

1. Was the indictment bad because found by a grand jury of less than sixteen persons?
2. Were the challenges of certain petit jurors by the accused improperly overruled?
3. Were the challenges of certain other jurors by the Government improperly sustained?
4. Was the testimony of Amelia Jane Schofield, given at a former trial for the same offense, but under another indictment, improperly admitted in evidence?

5. Should the accused have been acquitted if he married the second time, because he believed it to be his religious duty?

6. Did the court err in that part of the charge which directed the attention of the jury to the consequences of polygamy?

These questions will be considered in their order . . . [*Editor's Note:* We omit discussion of first four points.]

5. As to the defense of religious belief or duty.

On the trial, the plaintiff in error, the accused, proved that at the time of his alleged second marriage he was, and for many years before had been, a member of the Church of Jesus Christ of Latter-Day Saints, commonly called the Mormon Church, and a believer in its doctrines: that it was an accepted doctrine of that Church

> That it was the duty of male members of said Church, circumstances permitting, to practice polygamy: . . . that this duty was enjoined by different books which the members of said Church believed to be of divine origin, and among others the Holy Bible, and also that the members of the Church believed that the practice of polygamy was directly enjoined upon the male members thereof by the Almighty God, in a revelation to Joseph Smith, the founder and prophet of said Church; that the failing or refusing to practice polygamy by such male members of said Church, when circumstances would admit, would be punished, and that the penalty for such failure and refusal would be damnation in the life to come.

He also proved

> That he had received permission from the recognized authorities in said Church to enter into polygamous marriage; . . . that Daniel H. Wells, one having authority in said Church to perform the marriage ceremony, married the said defendant on or about the time the crime is alleged to have been committed, to some woman by the name of Schofield, and that such marriage ceremony was performed under and pursuant to the doctrines of said Church.

Upon this proof he asked the court to instruct the jury that if they found from the evidence that he "was married as charged (if he was married) in pursuance of and in conformity with what he believed at the time to be a religious duty, that the verdict must be 'not guilty.'"

This request was refused, and the court did charge "That there must have been a criminal intent, but that if the defendant, under the influence of a religious belief that it was right—under an inspiration, if you please, that it was right—deliberately married a second time, having a first wife living, the want of consciousness of evil intent, the want of understanding on his part that he was committing a crime, did not excuse him; but the law inexorably in such case implies the criminal intent."

Upon this charge and refusal to charge the question is raised, whether religious belief can be accepted as a justification of an overt act made criminal by the law of the land. The inquiry is not as to the power of Congress to prescribe criminal laws for the Territories, but as to the guilt of one who knowingly violates a law which has been properly enacted, if he entertains a belief that the law is wrong.

Congress cannot pass a law for the government of the Territories which shall prohibit the free exercise of religion. The first amendment to the Constitution expressly forbids such legislation. Religious freedom is guaranteed everywhere throughout the United States, so far as congressional interference is concerned. The question to be determined is, whether the law now under consideration comes within the prohibition.

The word "religion" is not defined in the Constitution. We must go elsewhere, therefore, to ascertain its meaning, and nowhere more appropriately, we think, than to the history of the times in the midst of which the provision was adopted. The precise point of the inquiry is, what is the religious freedom which has been guaranteed?

Before the adoption of the Constitution, attempts were made in some of the Colonies and States to legislate not only in respect to the establishment of religion, but in respect to its doctrines and precepts as well. The people were taxed, against their will, for the support of religion, and sometimes for the support of particular sects to whose tenets they could not and did not subscribe. Punishments were prescribed for a failure to attend upon public worship, and sometimes for entertaining heretical opinions. The controversy upon this general subject was animated in many of the States, but seemed at last to culminate in Virginia. In 1784, the House of Delegates of that State having under consideration "A bill establishing provision for teachers of the Christian religion," postponed it until the next session, and directed that the bill should be published and distributed, and that the

People be requested "to signify their opinion respecting the adoption of such a bill at the next session of Assembly."

This brought out a determined opposition. Amongst others, Mr. Madison prepared a "Memorial and Remonstrance," which was widely circulated and signed, and in which he demonstrated "that religion, or the duty we owe the Creator," was not within the cognizance of civil government. At the next session the proposed bill was not only defeated, but another, "for establishing religious freedom," drafted by Mr. Jefferson was passed. In the preamble of this Act, religious freedom is defined; and after a recital "That to suffer the civil magistrate to intrude his powers into the field of opinion, and to restrain the profession or propagation of principles on supposition of their ill tendency, is a dangerous fallacy which at once destroys all religious liberty," it is declared "that it is time enough for the rightful purposes of civil government for its officers to interfere when principles break out into overt acts against peace and good order." In these two sentences is found the true distinction between what properly belongs to the Church and what to the State.

In a little more than a year after the passage of this statute the convention met which prepared the Constitution of the United States. Of this convention Mr. Jefferson was not a member, he being then absent as minister to France. As soon as he saw the draft of the Constitution proposed for adoption, he, in a letter to a friend, expressed his disappointment at the absence of an express declaration insuring the freedom of religion, but was willing to accept it as it was, trusting that the good sense and honest intentions of the people would bring about the necessary alterations. Five of the States, while adopting the Constitution, proposed amendments. Three, New Hampshire, New York and Virginia, included in one form or another a declaration of religious freedom in the changes they desired to have made, as did also North Carolina, where the convention at first declined to ratify the Constitution until the proposed amendments were acted upon. Accordingly, at the first session of the first Congress the amendment now under consideration was proposed with others by Mr. Madison. It met the views of the advocates of religious freedom, and was adopted. Mr. Jefferson afterwards, in reply to an address to him by a committee of the Danbury Baptist Association, took occasion to say: "Believing with you that religion is a matter which lies solely between man and his God; that he owes account to none other for his faith or his worship;

that the legislative powers of the Government reach actions only, and not opinions, I contemplate with sovereign reverence that act of the whole American people which declared that their Legislature should 'make no law respecting an establishment of religion or prohibiting the free exercise thereof,' thus building a wall of separation between Church and State. Adhering to this expression of the Supreme will of the Nation in behalf of the rights of conscience, I shall see, with sincere satisfaction, the progress of those sentiments which tend to restore man to all his natural rights, convinced he has no natural right in opposition to his social duties." Coming as this does from an acknowledged leader of the advocates of the measure, it may be accepted almost as an authoritative declaration of the scope and effect of the amendment thus secured. Congress was deprived of all legislative power over mere opinion, but was left free to reach actions which were in violation of social duties or subversive of good order.

Polygamy has always been odious among the Northern and Western Nations of Europe and, until the establishment of the Mormon Church, was almost exclusively a feature of the life of Asiatic and African people. At common law, the second marriage was always void, and from the earliest history of England polygamy has been treated as an offense against society. After the establishment of the ecclesiastical courts, and until the time of James I., it was punished through the instrumentality of those tribunals, not merely because ecclesiastical rights had been violated, but because upon the separation of the ecclesiastical courts from the civil, the ecclesiastical were supposed to be the most appropriate for the trial of matrimonial causes and offenses against the rights of marriage; just as they were for testamentary causes and the settlement of the estates of deceased persons.

By the Statute of 1 James I, ch. 11, the offense, if committed in England or Wales, was made punishable in the civil courts, and the penalty was death. As this statute was limited in its operation to England and Wales, it was at a very early period re-enacted, generally with some modifications, in all the Colonies. In connection with the case we are now considering, it is a significant fact that on the 8th of December, 1788, after the passage of the Act establishing religious freedom, and after the convention of Virginia had recommended as an amendment to the Constitution of the United States the declaration in a Bill of Rights that "All men have an equal, natural and unalienable right to the free exercise of religion, according to the dictates of conscience," the Legislature of that State substantially enacted the Statute of James I., death penalty included, because as recited in the preamble, "It hath been doubted whether bigamy or polygamy be punishable by the laws of this Commonwealth." From that day to this we think it may safely be said there never has been a time in any State of the Union when polygamy has not been an offense against society, cognizable by the civil courts and punishable with more or less severity. In the face of all this evidence, it is impossible to believe that the constitutional guaranty of religious freedom was intended to prohibit legislation in respect to this most important feature of social life. Marriage, while from its very nature a sacred obligation, is, nevertheless, in most civilized nations, a civil contract, and usually regulated by law. Upon it society may be said to be built, and out of its fruits spring social relations and social obligations and duties, with which government is necessarily required to deal. In fact, according as monogamous or polygamous marriages are allowed, do we find the principles on which the Government of the People, to a greater or less extent, rests. Professor Lieber says: polygamy leads to the patriarchal principle, and which, when applied to large communities, fetters the people in stationary despotism, while that principle cannot long exist in connection with monogamy. Chancellor Kent observes that this remark is equally striking and profound. An exceptional colony of polygamists under an exceptional leadership may sometimes exist for a time without appearing to disturb the social condition of the people who surround it; but there cannot be a doubt that, unless restricted by some form of constitution, it is within the legitimate scope of the power of every civil government to determine whether polygamy or monogamy shall be the law of social life under its dominion.

In our opinion the statute immediately under consideration is within the legislative power of Congress. It is constitutional and valid as prescribing a rule of action for all those residing in the Territories, and in places over which the United States have exclusive control. This being so, the only question which remains is, whether those who make polygamy a part of their religion are excepted from the operation of the statute. If they are, then those who do not make polygamy a part of their religious belief may be found guilty and punished, while those who do must be acquitted and go free. This would be introducing a new element into criminal law. Laws are made for the government of actions, and while they cannot interfere with mere religious belief and opinions, they may with practices. Suppose one believed that human sacrifices were a necessary part of religious worship, would it be seriously contended that the civil government under which he lived could not interfere to prevent a sacrifice? Or if a wife religiously believed it was her duty to burn herself upon the funeral pile of her dead husband, would it be beyond the power of the civil government to prevent her carrying her belief into practice?

So here, as a law of the organization of society under the exclusive dominion of the United States, it is provided that plural marriages shall not be allowed. Can a man excuse his practices to the contrary because of his religious beliefs? To permit this would be to make the professed doctrines of religious belief superior to the law of the land, and in effect to permit every citizen to become a law unto himself. Government could exist only in name under such circumstances.

A criminal intent is generally an element of crime, but every man is presumed to intend the necessary and legitimate consequences of what he knowingly does. Here the accused knew he had been once married, and that his first wife was living. He also knew that his second marriage was forbidden by law. When, therefore, he married the second time, he is presumed to have intended to break the law. And the breaking of the law is the crime. Every act necessary to constitute the crime was knowingly done, and the crime was, therefore, knowingly committed. Ignorance of a fact may sometimes be taken as evidence of a want of criminal intent, but not ignorance of the law. The only defense of the accused in this case is his belief that the law ought not to have been enacted. It matters not that his belief was a part of his professed religion; it was still belief, and belief only.

In *Regina v. Wagstaffe*, the parents of a sick child, who omitted to call in medical attendance because of their religious belief that what they did for its cure would be effective, were held not to be guilty of manslaughter, while it was said the contrary would have been the result if the child had actually been starved to death by the parents, under the notion that it was their religious duty to abstain from giving it food. But when the offense consists of a positive act which is knowingly done, it would be dangerous to hold that the offender might escape punishment because he religiously believed the law which he had broken ought never to have been made. No case, we believe, can be found that has gone so far.

6. As to that part of the charge which directed the attention of the jury to the consequences of polygamy.

The passage complained of is as follows: "I think it not improper, in the discharge of your duties in this case, that you should consider what are to be the consequences to the innocent victims of this delusion. As this contest goes on, they multiply, and there are pure-minded women and there are innocent children; innocent in a sense even beyond the degree of the innocence of childhood itself. These are to be the sufferers; and as jurors fail to do their duty, and as these cases come up in the Territory of Utah, just so do these victims multiply and spread themselves over the land."

While every appeal by the court to the passions or the prejudices of a jury should be promptly rebuked, and while it is the imperative duty of a reviewing court to take care that wrong is not done in this way, we see no just cause for complaint in this case. Congress, in 1862, saw fit to make bigamy a crime in the Territories. This was done because of the evil consequences that were supposed to flow from plural marriages. All the court did was to call the attention of the jury to the peculiar character of the crime for which the accused was on trial, and to remind them of the duty they had to perform. There was no appeal to the passions, no instigation of prejudice. Upon the showing made by the accused himself, he was guilty of a violation of the law under which he had been indicted: and the effort of the court seems to have been not to withdraw the minds of the jury from the issue to be tried, but to bring them to it; not to make them partial, but to keep them impartial.

Upon a careful consideration of the whole case, we are satisfied that no error was committed by the court below, and the judgment is consequently affirmed.

Cantwell v. Connecticut, 310 U.S. 296 (1940)

The first in the Jehovah's Witness cases, *Cantwell* is a milestone, for it laid down the application of the Religion Clauses to the states through the Fourteenth Amendment and it is here that Justice Roberts notes that the Free Exercise Clause "embraces two concepts,—freedom to believe and freedom to act. The first is absolute but, in the nature of things, the second cannot be."

MR. JUSTICE ROBERTS DELIVERED THE OPINION OF THE COURT.

Newton Cantwell and his two sons, Jesse and Russell, members of a group known as Jehovah's Witnesses, and claiming to be ordained ministers were arrested in New Haven, Connecticut, and each was charged by information in five counts, with statutory and common law offenses. After trial in the Court of Common Pleas of New Haven County each of them was convicted on the third count, which charged a violation of 6294 of the General Statutes of Connecticut, and on the fifth count, which charged commission of the common law offenses of inciting a breach of the peace. On appeal to the Supreme Court the conviction of all three on the third count was affirmed. The conviction of Jesse Cantwell, on the fifth count, was also affirmed, but the conviction of Newton and Russell on that count was reversed and a new trial ordered as to them.

By demurrers to the information, by requests for rulings of law at the trial, and by their assignments of error in the State Supreme Court, the appellants pressed the contention that the statute under which the third count was drawn was offensive to the due process clause of the Fourteenth Amendment because, on its face and as construed and applied, it denied them freedom of speech and prohibited their free exercise of religion. In like manner they made the point that they could not be found guilty on the fifth count, without violation of the Amendment.

We have jurisdiction on appeal from the judgments on the third count, as there was drawn in question the validity of a state statute under the Federal Constitution, and the decision was in favor of validity. Since the conviction on the fifth count was not based upon a statute, but presents a substantial question under the Federal Constitution, we granted the writ of certiorari in respect of it.

The facts adduced to sustain the convictions on the third count follow. On the day of their arrest the appellants were engaged in going singly from house to house on Cassius Street in New Haven. They were individually equipped with a bag containing books and pamphlets on religious subjects, a portable phonograph and a set of records, each of which, when played, introduced, and was a description of, one of the books. Each appellant asked the person who responded to his call for permission to play one of the records. If permission was granted he asked the person to buy the book described and, upon refusal, he solicited such contribution towards the publications of the pamphlets as the listener was willing to make. If a contribution was received a pamphlet was delivered upon condition that it would be read.

Cassius Street is in a thickly populated neighborhood, where about ninety per cent of the residents are Roman Catholics. A phonograph record, describing a book entitled "Enemies," included an attack on the Catholic religion. None of the persons interviewed were members of Jehovah's Witnesses.

The statute under which the appellants were charged provides:

"No person shall solicit money, services, subscriptions or any valuable thing for any alleged religious, charitable or philanthropic cause, from other than a member of the organization for whose benefit such person is soliciting or within the county in which such person or organization is located unless such cause shall have been approved by the secretary of the public welfare council. Upon application of any person in behalf of such cause, the secretary shall determine whether such cause is a religious one or is a bona fide object of charity or philanthropy and conforms to reasonable standards of efficiency and integrity, and, if he shall so find, shall approve the same and issue to the authority in charge a certificate to that effect. Such certificate may be revoked at any time. Any person violating any provision of this section shall be fined not more than one hundred dollars or imprisoned not more than thirty days or both."

The appellants claimed that their activities were not within the statute but consisted only of distribution of books, pamphlets, and periodicals. The State Supreme Court construed the finding of the trial court to be that "in addition to the sale of the books and the distribution of the pamphlets the defendants were also soliciting contributions or donations of money for an alleged religious cause, and thereby came within the purview of the statute." It overruled the contention that the Act, as applied to the appellants, offends the due process clause of the Fourteenth Amendment, because it abridges or denies religious freedom and liberty of speech and press. The court stated that it was the solicitation that brought the appellants within the sweep of the Act and not their other activities in the dissemination of literature. It declared the legislation constitutional as an effort by the State to protect the public against fraud and imposition in the solicitation of funds for what purported to be religious, charitable, or philanthropic causes.

The facts which were held to support the conviction of Jesse Cantwell on the fifth count were that he stopped two men in the street, asked, and received, permission to play a phonograph record, and played the record "Enemies," which attacked the religion and church of the two men, who were Catholics. Both were incensed by the contents of the record and were tempted to strike Cantwell unless he went away. On being told to be on his way he left their presence. There was no evidence that he was personally offensive or entered into any argument with those he interviewed.

The court held that the charge was not assault or breach of the peace or threats on Cantwell's part, but invoking or inciting others to breach of the peace, and that the facts supported the conviction of that offense.

First. We hold that the statute, as construed and applied to the appellants, deprives them of their liberty without due process of law in contravention of the Fourteenth Amendment. The fundamental concept of liberty embodied in that Amendment embraces the liberties guaranteed by the First Amendment. The First Amendment declares that Congress shall make no law respecting an establishment of religion or prohibiting the free exercise thereof. The Fourteenth Amendment has rendered the legislatures of the states as incompetent as Congress to enact such laws. The constitutional inhibition of legislation on the subject of religion has a double aspect. On the one hand, it forestalls compulsion by law of the acceptance of any creed or the practice of any form of worship. Freedom of conscience and freedom to adhere to such religious organization or form of worship as the individual may choose cannot be restricted by law. On the other hand, it safeguards the free exercise of the chosen form of religion. Thus the Amendment embraces two concepts–freedom to believe and freedom to act. The first is absolute but, in the nature of things, the second cannot be. Conduct remains subject to regulation for the protection of society. The freedom to act must have appropriate definition to preserve the enforcement of that protection. In every case the power to regulate must be so exercised as not, in attaining a permissible end, unduly to infringe the protected freedom. No one would contest the proposition that a State may not, by statute, wholly deny the right to preach or to disseminate religious views. Plainly such a previous and absolute restraint would violate the terms of the guarantee. It is equally clear that a State may by general and non-discriminatory legislation regulate the times, the places, and the manner of soliciting upon its streets, and of holding meetings thereon; and may in other respects safeguard the peace, good order and comfort of the community without unconstitutionally invading the liberties protected by the Fourteenth Amendment. The appellants are right in their insistence that the Act in question is not such a regulation. If a certificate is procured, solicitation is permitted without restraint but, in the absence of a certificate, solicitation is altogether prohibited.

The appellants urge that to require them to obtain a certificate as a condition of soliciting support for their views amounts to a prior restraint on the exercise of their religion within the meaning of the Constitution. The State insists that the Act, as construed by the Supreme Court of Connecticut, imposes no previous restraint upon the dissemination of religious views or teaching but merely safeguards against the perpetration of frauds under the cloak of religion. Conceding that this is so, the question remains whether the method adopted by Connecticut to that end transgresses the liberty safeguarded by the Constitution.

The general regulation, in the public interest, of solicitation, which does not involve any religious test and does not unreasonably obstruct or delay the collection of funds, is not open to any constitutional objection, even though the collection be for a religious purpose. Such regulation would not constitute a prohibited previous restraint on the free exercise of religion or interpose an inadmissible obstacle to its exercise.

It will be noted, however, that the Act requires an application to the secretary of the public welfare council of the State; that he is empowered to determine whether the cause is a religious one, and that the issue of a certificate depends upon his affirmative action. If he finds that the cause is not that of religion, to solicit for it becomes a crime. He is not to issue a certificate as a matter of course. His decision to issue or refuse it involves appraisal of facts, the exercise of judgment, and the formation of an opinion. He is authorized to withhold his approval if he determines that the cause is not a religious one. Such a censorship of religion as the means of determining its right to survive is a denial of liberty protected by the First Amendment and included in the liberty which is within the protection of the Fourteenth.

The State asserts that if the licensing office acts arbitrarily, capriciously, or corruptly, his action is subject to judicial correction. Counsel refer to the rule prevailing in Connecticut that the decision of a commission or an administrative official will be reviewed upon a claim that "it works material damage to individual or corporate rights, or invades or threatens such rights, or is so unreasonable as to justify judicial intervention, or is not consonant with justice, or that a legal duty has not been performed." It is suggested that the statute is to be read as requiring the officer to issue a certificate unless the cause in question is clearly not a religious one; and that if he violates his duty his action will be corrected by a court.

To this suggestion there are several sufficient answers. The line between a discretionary and a ministerial act is not always easy to mark and the statute has not been construed by the state court to impose a mere ministerial duty on the secretary of the welfare council. Upon his decision as to the nature of the cause, the right to solicit depends. Moreover, the availability of a judicial remedy for abuses in the system of licensing still leaves that system one of previous restraint which, in the field of free speech and press, we have held inadmissible. A statute authorizing previous restraint upon the exercise of the guaranteed freedom by judicial decision after trial is as obnoxious to the Constitution as one providing for like restraint by administrative action.

Nothing we have said is intended even remotely to imply that, under the cloak of religion, persons may, with impunity, commit frauds upon the public. Certainly penal laws are available to punish such conduct. Even the exercise of religion may be at some slight inconvenience in order that the state may protect its citizens from injury. Without doubt a state may protect its citizens from injury. Without doubt a State may protect its citizens from fraudulent solicitation by requiring a stranger in the community, before permitting him publicly to solicit funds for any purpose, to establish his identity and his authority to act for the cause which he purports to represent. The State is likewise free to regulate the time and manner of solicitation generally, in the interest of public safety, peace, comfort or convenience. But to condition the solicitation of aid for the perpetuation of religious views or systems upon a license, the grant of which rests in the exercise of a determination by state authority as to what is a religious cause, is to lay a forbidden burden upon the exercise of liberty protected by the Constitution.

Second. We hold that, in the circumstances disclosed, the conviction of Jesse Cantwell on the fifth count must be set aside. Decision as to the lawfulness of the conviction demands the weighing of two conflicting interests. The fundamental law declares the interest of the

United States that the free exercise of religion be not prohibited and that freedom to communicate information and opinion be not abridged. The State of Connecticut has an obvious interest in the preservation and protection of peace and good order within her borders. We must determine whether the alleged protection of the State's interest, means to which end would, in the absence of limitation by the Federal Constitution, lie wholly within the State's discretion, has been pressed, in this instance, to a point where it has come into fatal collision with the overriding interest protected by the federal compact.

Conviction on the fifth count was not pursuant to a statute evincing a legislative judgment that street discussion of religious affairs, because of its tendency to provoke disorder, should be regulated, or a judgment that the playing of a phonograph on the streets should in the interest of comfort or privacy be limited or prevented. Violation of an Act exhibiting such a legislative judgment and narrowly drawn to prevent the supposed evil, would pose a question differing from that we must here answer. Such a declaration of the State's policy would weigh heavily in any challenge of the law as infringing constitutional limitations. Here, however, the judgment is based on a common law concept of the most general and undefined nature. The court below has held that the petitioner's conduct constituted the commission of an offense under the state law, and we accept its decision as binding upon us to that extent.

The offense known as breach of the peace embraces a great variety of conduct destroying or menacing public order and tranquility. It includes not only violent acts but acts and words likely to produce violence in others. No one would have the hardihood to suggest that the principle of freedom of speech sanctions incitement to riot or that religious liberty connotes the privilege to exhort others to physical attack upon those belonging to another sect. When clear and present danger of riot, disorder, interference with traffic upon the public streets, or other immediate threat to public safety, peace, or order, appears, the power of the State to prevent or punish is obvious. Equally obvious is it that a State may not unduly suppress free communication of views, religious or other, under the guise of conserving desirable conditions. Here we have a situation analogous to a conviction under a statute sweeping in a great variety of conduct under a general and indefinite characterization, and leaving to the executive and judicial branches too wide a discretion in its application.

Having these considerations in mind, we note that Jesse Cantwell, on April 25, 1938, was upon a public street, where he had a right to be, and where he had a right peacefully to impart his views to others. There is no showing that his deportment was noisy, truculent, overbearing or offensive. He requested of two pedestrians permission to play to them a phonograph record. The permission was granted. It is not claimed that he intended to insult or affront the hearers by playing the record. It is plain that he wished only to interest them in his propaganda. The sound of the phonograph is not shown to have disturbed residents of the street, to have drawn a crowd, or to have impeded traffic. Thus far he had invaded no right or interest of the public or of the men accosted.

The record played by Cantwell embodies a general attack on all organized religious systems as instruments of Satan and injurious to man; it then singles out the Roman Catholic Church for strictures couched in terms which naturally would offend not only persons of that persuasion, but all others who respect the honestly held religious faith of their fellows. The hearers were in fact highly offended. One of them said he felt like hitting Cantwell and the other that he was tempted to throw Cantwell off the street. The one who testified he felt like hitting Cantwell said, in answer to the question "Did you do anything else or have any other reaction?" "No, sir, because he said he would take the victrola and he went." The other witness testified that he told Cantwell he had better get off the street before something happened to him and that was the end of the matter as Cantwell picked up his books and walked up the street.

Cantwell's conduct, in the view of the court below, considered apart from the effect of his communication upon his hearers, did not amount to a breach of the peace. One may, however, be guilty of the offense if he commit acts or make statements likely to provoke violence and disturbance of good order, even though no such eventuality be intended. Decisions to this effect are many, but examination discloses that, in practically all, the provocative language which was held to amount to a breach of the peace consisted of profane, indecent, or abusive remarks directed to the person of the hearer. Resort to epithets or personal abuse is not in any proper sense communication of information or opinion safeguarded by the Constitution, and its punishment as a criminal act would raise no question under the instrument.

We find in the instant case no assault or threatening of bodily harm, no truculent bearing, no intentional discourtesy, no personal abuse. On the contrary, we find only an effort to persuade a willing listener to buy a book or to contribute money in the interest of what Cantwell, however misguided others may think him, conceived to be true religion.

In the realm of religious faith, and in that of political belief, sharp differences arise. In both fields the tenets of one man may seem the rankest error to his neighbor. To persuade others to his own point of view, the pleader, as we know, at times, resorts to exaggeration, to vilification of men who have been, or are, prominent in church or state, and even to false statement. But the people of this nation have ordained in the light of history, that, in spite of the probability of excesses and abuses, these liberties are, in the long view, essential to enlightened opinion and right conduct on the part of the citizens of a democracy.

The essential characteristic of these liberties is, that under their shield many types of life, character, opinion and belief can develop unmolested and unobstructed. Nowhere is this shield more necessary than in our own country for a people composed of many races and of many creeds. There are limits to the exercise of these liberties. The danger in these times from the coercive activities of those who in the delusion of racial or religious conceit would incite violence and breaches of the peace in order to deprive others of their equal right to the exercise of their liberties, is emphasized by events familiar to all. These and other transgressions of those limits the States appropriately may punish.

Although the contents of the record not unnaturally aroused animosity, we think that, in the absence of a statute narrowly drawn to define and punish specific conduct as constituting a clear and present danger to a substantial interest of the State, the petitioner's communication, considered in the light of the constitutional guarantees, raised no such clear and present menace to public peace and order as to render him liable to conviction of the common law offense in question.

The judgment affirming the convictions on the third and fifth counts is reversed and the cause is remanded for further proceedings not inconsistent with this opinion. Reversed.

Minersville School District v. Gobitis, 310 U.S. 586 (1940)

The opinion here delivered by Justice Frankfurter concerned children of parents who were Jehovah's Witnesses. The children were excluded by Pennsylvania public schools because they refused, on purely religious grounds, to recite the pledge of allegiance to the flag. Referring to the state's right to provide for gestures of "respect for the symbol of our national life," the Court saw its role as encouraging "the formative period in the development of citizenship."

Justice Stone dissented, insisting that "by this law the state seeks to coerce these children to express a sentiment which violates their deepest religious convictions."

MR. JUSTICE FRANKFURTER DELIVERED THE OPINION OF THE COURT.

A grave responsibility confronts this Court whenever in course of litigation it must reconcile the conflicting claims of liberty and authority. But when the liberty invoked is liberty of conscience, and the authority is authority to safeguard the nation's fellowship, judicial conscience is put to its severest test. Of such nature is the present controversy.

Lillian Gobitis, aged twelve, and her brother William, aged ten, were expelled from the public schools of Minersville, Pennsylvania, for refusing to salute the national flag as part of a daily school exercise. The local Board of Education required both teachers and pupils to participate in this ceremony. The ceremony is a familiar one. The right hand is placed on the breast and the following pledge recited in unison: "I pledge allegiance to my flag, and to the Republic for which it stands; one nation indivisible, with liberty and justice for all." While the words are spoken; teachers and pupils extend their right hands in salute to the flag. The Gobitis family are affiliated with "Jehovah's Witnesses," for whom the Bible as the Word of God is the supreme authority. The children had been brought up conscientiously to believe that such a gesture of respect for the flag was forbidden by command of Scripture.

The Gobitis children were of an age for which Pennsylvania makes school attendance compulsory. Thus they were denied a free education, and their parents had to put them into private schools. To be relieved of the financial burden thereby entailed, their father, on behalf of the children and in his own behalf, brought this suit. He sought to enjoin the authorities from continuing to exact participation in the flag-salute ceremony as a condition of his children's attendance at the Minersville school. After trial of the issues, Judge Maris gave relief in the District Court, on the basis of a thoughtful opinion at a preliminary stage of the litigation, his decree was affirmed by the Circuit Court of Appeals. Since this decision ran counter to several per curiam dispositions of this Court, we granted certiorari to give the matter full reconsideration. By their able submissions, the Committee on the Bill of Rights of the American Bar Association and the American Civil Liberties Union, as friends of the Court, have helped us to our conclusion.

We must decide whether the requirement of participation in such a ceremony, exacted from a child who refuses upon sincere religious grounds, infringes without due process of law the liberty guaranteed by the Fourteenth Amendment.

Centuries of strife over the erection of particular dogmas as exclusive or all-comprehending faiths led to the inclusion of a guarantee for religious freedom in the Bill of Rights. The First Amendment, and the Fourteenth through its absorption of the First, sought to guard against repetition of those bitter religious struggles by prohibiting the establishment of a state religion and by securing to every sect the free exercise of its faith. So pervasive is the acceptance of this precious right that its scope is brought into question, as here, only when the conscience of individuals collides with the felt necessities of society.

Certainly the affirmative pursuit of one's convictions about the ultimate mystery of the universe and man's relation to it is placed beyond the reach of law. Government may not interfere with organized or individual expression of belief or disbelief. Propagation of belief—or even of disbelief—in the supernatural is protected, whether in church or chapel, mosque or synagogue, tabernacle or meeting-house. Likewise the Constitution assures generous immunity to the individual from imposition of penalties for offending, in the course of his own religious activities, the religious views of others, be they a minority or those who are dominant in government.

But the manifold character of man's relations may bring his conception of religious duty into conflict with the secular interests of his fellow-men. When does the constitutional guarantee control exemption from doing what society thinks necessary for the promotion of some great common end, or from a penalty for conduct which appears dangerous to the general good? To state the problem is to recall the truth that no single principle can answer all of life's complexities. The right to freedom of religious belief, however dissident and however obnoxious to the cherished beliefs of others—even of a majority—is itself the denial of an absolute. But to affirm that the freedom to follow conscience has itself no limits in the life of a society would deny that very plurality of principles which, as a matter of history, underlies protection of religious toleration. Our present task, then, as so often the case with courts, is to reconcile two rights in order to prevent either from destroying the other. But, because in safe-guarding conscience we are dealing with interests so subtle and so dear, every possible leeway should be given to the claims of religious faith.

In the judicial enforcement of religious freedom we are concerned with a historic concept. The religious liberty which the Constitution protects has never excluded legislation of general scope not directed against doctrinal loyalties of particular sects. Judicial nullification of legislation cannot be justified by attributing to the framers of the Bill of Rights views for which there is no historic warrant. Conscientious scruples have not, in the course of the long struggle for religious toleration, relieved the individual from obedience to a general law not aimed at the promotion or restriction of religious beliefs. The mere possession of religious convictions which contradict the relevant concerns of a political society does not relieve the citizen from the discharge of political responsibilities. The necessity for this adjustment has again and again been recognized. In a number of situations the exertion of political authority has been sustained, while basic considerations of religious freedom have been left inviolate. *Reynolds v. United States; Davis v. Beason; Selective Draft Law Cases; Hamilton v. Regents.* In all these cases the general laws in question, upheld in their application to those who refused obedience from religious conviction, were manifestations of specific powers of government deemed by the legislature essential to secure and maintain the orderly, tranquil, and free society without which religious toleration itself is unattainable. Nor does the freedom of speech assured by Due Process move in a more absolute circle of immunity than that enjoyed by religious freedom. Even if it were assumed that freedom of speech goes beyond the historic concept of full opportunity to utter and to disseminate views, however heretical or offensive to dominant opinion, and includes freedom from conveying what may be deemed an implied but rejected affirmation, the question remains whether school children, like the Gobitis children, must be excused from conduct required of all the other children in the promotion of national cohesion. We are dealing with an interest inferior to none in the hierarchy of legal values. National unity is the basis of national security. To deny the legislature the right to select appropriate means for its attainment presents a totally different order of problem from that of the propriety of subordinating the possible ugliness of littered streets to the free expression of opinion through distribution of handbills.

Situations like the present are phases of the profoundest problem confronting a democracy—the problem which Lincoln cast in memorable dilemma. "Must a government of necessity be too strong for the liberties of its people, or too weak to maintain its own existence?" No mere textual reading or logical talisman can solve the dilemma. And when the issue demands judicial determination, it is not the personal notion of judges of what wise adjustment requires which must prevail.

Unlike the instances we have cited, the case before us is not concerned with an exertion of legislative power for the promotion of some specific need or interest of secular society—the protection of the family, the promotion of health, the common defense, the raising of public revenues to defray the cost of government. But all these specific activities of government presuppose the existence of an organized political society. The ultimate foundation of a free society is the binding tie of cohesive sentiment. Such sentiment is fostered by all those agencies of the mind and spirit which may serve to gather up the traditions of a people, transmit them from generation to generation, and thereby create that continuity of a treasured common life which constitutes a civilization. "We live by symbols." The flag is the symbol of our national unity, transcending all internal differences, however large, within the framework of the Constitution. This Court has had occasion to say that " . . . the flag is the symbol of the Nation's power, the emblem of freedom in its truest, best sense . . . it signifies government resting on the consent of the governed; liberty regulated by law; the protection of the weak against the strong; security against the exercise of arbitrary power; and absolute safety for free institutions against foreign aggression." *Halter v. Nebraska.*

The case before us must be viewed as though the legislature of Pennsylvania had itself formally directed the flag-salute for the children of Minersville; had made no exemption for children whose parents were possessed of conscientious scruples like those of the Gobitis family; and had indicated its belief in the desirable ends to be secured by having its public school children share a common experience at those periods of development when their minds are supposedly receptive to its assimilation, by an exercise appropriate in time and place and setting and one designed to evoke in them appreciation of the nation's hopes and dreams, its sufferings and sacrifices. The precise issue, then, for us to decide is whether the legislatures of the various states and the authorities in a thousand counties and school districts of this country are barred from determining the appropriateness of various means to evoke that unifying sentiment without which there can ultimately be no liberties, civil or religious.

To stigmatize legislative judgment in providing for this universal gesture of respect for the symbol of our national life in the setting of the common school as a lawless inroad on that freedom of conscience which the Constitution protects, would amount to no less than the pronouncement of pedagogical and psychological dogma in a field where courts possess no marked and certainly no controlling competence. The influences which help toward a common feeling for the common country are manifold. Some may seem harsh and others no doubt are foolish. Surely, however, the end is legitimate. And the effective means for its attainment are still so uncertain and so unauthenticated by science as to preclude us from putting the widely prevalent belief in flag-saluting beyond the pale of legislative power. It mocks reason and denies our whole history to find in the allowance of a requirement to salute our flag on fitting occasions the seeds of sanction for obeisance to a leader.

The wisdom of training children in patriotic impulses by those compulsions which necessarily pervade so much of the educational process is not for our independent judgment. Even were we convinced of the folly of such a measure, such belief would be no proof of its unconstitutionality. For ourselves, we might be tempted to say that the deepest patriotism is best engendered by giving unfettered scope to the most crochety beliefs. Perhaps it is best, even from the standpoint of those interests which ordinances like the one under review seek to promote, to give to the least popular sect leave from conformities like those here in issue. But the courtroom is not the arena for debating issues of educational policy. It is not our province to choose among competing considerations in the subtle process of securing effective loyalty to the traditional ideals of democracy, while respecting at the same time individual idiosyncracies among a people so diversified in racial origins and religious allegiances. So to hold would in effect make us the school board for the country. That authority has not been given to this Court, nor should we assume it.

We are dealing here with the formative period in the development of citizenship. Great diversity of psychological and ethical opinion exists among us concerning the best way to train children for their place in society. Because of these differences and because of reluctance to permit a single, iron-cast system of education to be imposed upon a nation compounded of so many strains, we have held that, even though public education is one of our most cherished democratic institutions, the Bill of Rights bars a state from compelling all children to attend the public schools. *Pierce v. Society of Sisters.* But it is a very different thing for this Court to exercise censorship over the conviction of legislatures that a particular program or exercise will best promote in the minds of children who attend the common schools an attachment to the institutions of their country.

What the school authorities are really asserting is the right to awaken in the child's mind considerations as to the significance of the flag contrary to those implanted by the parent. In such an attempt the state is normally at a disadvantage in competing with the parent's authority, so long—and this is the vital aspect of religious toleration—as parents are unmolested in their right to counteract by their own persuasiveness the wisdom and rightness of those loyalties which the state's educational system is seeking to promote. Except where the transgression of constitutional liberty is too plain for argument, personal freedom is best maintained—so long as the remedial channels of the democratic process remain open and unobstructed—when it is ingrained in a people's habits and not enforced against popular policy by the coercion of adjudicated law. That the flag-salute is an allowable portion of a school program for those who do not invoke conscientious scruples is surely not debatable. But for us to insist that, though the ceremony may be required, exceptional immunity must be given to dissidents, is to maintain that there is no basis for a legislative judgment that such an exemption might introduce elements of difficulty into the school discipline, might cast doubts in the minds of the other children which would themselves weaken the effect of the exercise.

The preciousness of the family relation, the authority and independence which give dignity to parenthood, indeed the enjoyment of all freedom, presuppose the kind of ordered society which is summarized by our flag. A society which is dedicated to the preservation of these ultimate values of civilization may in self-protection utilize the educational process for inculcating those almost unconscious feelings which bind men together in a comprehending loyalty, whatever may be their lesser differences and difficulties. That is to say, the process may be utilized so long as men's right to believe as they please, to win others to their way of belief, and their right to assemble in their chosen places of worship for the devotional ceremonies of their faith, are fully respected.

Judicial review, itself a limitation on popular government, is a fundamental part of our constitutional scheme. But to the legislature no less than to courts is committed the guardianship of deeply-cherished liberties. Where all the effective means of inducing political changes are left free from interference, education in the abandonment of foolish legislation is itself a training in liberty. To fight out the wise use of legislative authority in the forum of public opinion and before legislative assemblies rather than to transfer such a contest to the judicial arena, serves to vindicate the self-confidence of a free people.

MR. JUSTICE STONE, DISSENTING.

I think the judgment below should be affirmed.

Two youths, now fifteen and sixteen years of age, are by the judgment of this Court held liable to expulsion from the public schools and to denial of all publicly supported educational privileges because of their refusal to yield to the compulsion of a law which commands their participation in a school ceremony contrary to their religious convictions. They and their father are citizens and have not exhibited by any action or statement of opinion, any disloyalty to the Government of the United States. They are ready and willing to obey all its laws which do not conflict with what they sincerely believe to be the higher commandments of God. It is not doubted that these convictions are religious, that they are genuine, or that the refusal to yield to the compulsion of the law is in good faith and with all sincerity. It would be a denial of their faith as well as the teachings of most religions to say that children of their age could not have religious convictions.

The law which is thus sustained is unique in the history of Anglo-American legislation. It does more than suppress freedom of speech and more than prohibit the free exercise of religion, which concededly are forbidden by the First Amendment and are violations of the liberty guaranteed by the Fourteenth. For by this law the state seeks to coerce these children to express a sentiment which violates their deepest religious convictions. It is not denied that such compulsion is a prohibited infringement of personal liberty, freedom of speech and religion, guaranteed by the Bill of Rights, except in so far as it may be justified and supported as a proper exercise of the state's power over public education. Since the state, in competition with parents, may through teaching in the public schools indoctrinate to inspire loyalty and devotion to constituted authority and the flag which symbolizes it, it may coerce the pupil to make affirmation contrary to his belief and in violation of his religious faith. And, finally, it is said that since the Minersville School Board and others are of the opinion that the country will be better served by conformity than by the observance of religious liberty which the Constitution prescribes, the courts are not free to pass judgment on the Board's choice.

Concededly the constitutional guaranties of personal liberty are not always absolutes. Government has a right to survive and powers conferred upon it are not necessarily set at naught by the express prohibitions of the Bill of Rights. It may make war and raise armies. To that end it may compel citizens to give military service, and subject them to military training despite their religious objections.

It may suppress religious practices dangerous to morals, and presumably those also which are inimical to public safety, health and good order. But it is a long step, and one which I am unable to take, to the position that government may, as a supposed educational measure and as a means of disciplining the young, compel public affirmations which violate their religious conscience.

The very fact that we have constitutional guaranties of civil liberties and the specificity of their command where freedom of speech and of religion are concerned require some accommodation of the powers which government normally exercises, when no question of civil liberty is involved, to the constitutional demand that those liberties be protected against the action of government itself. The state concededly has power to require and control the education of its citizens, but it cannot by a general law compelling attendance to public schools preclude attendance at a private school adequate in its instruction, where the parent seeks to secure for the child the benefits of religious instruction not provided by the public school. And only recently we have held that the state's authority to control its public streets by generally applicable regulations is not an absolute to which free speech must yield, and cannot be made the medium of its suppression, any more than can its authority to penalize littering of the streets by a general law be used to suppress the distribution of handbills as a means of communicating ideas to their recipients.

In these cases it was pointed out that where there are competing demands of the interests of government and of liberty under the Constitution, and where the performance of governmental functions is brought into conflict with specific constitutional restrictions, there must, when that is possible, be reasonable accommodation between them so as to preserve the essentials of both and that it is the function of courts to determine whether such accommodation is reasonably possible. In the cases just mentioned the Court was of opinion that there were ways enough to secure the legitimate state end without infringing the asserted immunity, or that the inconvenience caused by the inability to secure that end satisfactorily through other means, did not outweigh freedom of speech or religion. So here, even if we believe that such compulsions will contribute to national unity, there are other ways to teach loyalty and patriotism which are the sources of national unity, than by compelling the pupil to affirm that which he does not believe and by commanding a form of affirmance which violates his religious convictions. Without recourse to such compulsion the state is free to compel attendance at school and require teaching by instruction and study of all in our history and in the structure and organization of our government, including the guaranties of civil liberty which tend to inspire patriotism and love of country. I cannot say that government here is deprived of any interest or function which it is entitled to maintain at the expense of the protection of civil liberties by requiring it to resort to the alternatives which do not coerce an affirmation of belief.

The guaranties of civil liberty are but guaranties of freedom of the human mind and spirit and of reasonable freedom and opportunity to express them. They presuppose the right of the individual to hold such opinions as he will and to give them reasonably free expression, and his freedom, and that of the state as well, to teach and persuade others by the communication of ideas. The very essence of the liberty which they guarantee is the freedom of the individual from compulsion as to what he shall think and what he shall say, at least where the compulsion is to bear false witness to his religion. If these guaranties are to have any meaning they must, I think, be deemed to withhold from the state any authority to compel belief or the expression of it where that expression violates religious convictions, whatever may be the legislative view of the desirability of such compulsion.

History teaches us that there have been but few infringements of personal liberty by the state which have not been justified, as they are here, in the name of righteousness and the public good, and few which have not been directed, as they are now, at politically helpless minorities. The framers were not unaware that under the system which they created most governmental curtailments of personal liberty would have the support of a legislative judgment that the public interest would be better served by its curtailment than by its constitutional protection. I cannot conceive that in prescribing, as limitations upon the powers of government, the freedom of the mind and spirit secured by the explicit guaranties of freedom of speech and religion, they intended or rightly could have left any latitude for a legislative judgment that the compulsory expression of belief which violates religious convictions would better serve the public interest than their protection. The Constitution may well elicit expressions of loyalty to it and to the government which it created, but it does not command such expressions or otherwise give any indication that compulsory expressions of loyalty play any such part in our scheme of government as to override the constitutional protection of freedom of speech and religion. And while such expressions of loyalty, when voluntarily given, may promote national unity, it is quite another matter to say that their own and their parents' religious convictions can be regarded as playing so important a part in our national unity as to leave school boards free to exact it despite the constitutional guarantee of freedom of religion. The very terms of the Bill of Rights preclude, it seems to me, any reconciliation of such compulsions with the constitutional guaranties by a legislative declaration that they are more important to the public welfare than the Bill of Rights.

But even if this view be rejected and it is considered that there is some scope for the determination by legislatures whether the citizen shall be compelled to give public expression of such sentiments contrary to his religion, I am not persuaded that we should refrain from passing upon the legislative judgment "as long as the remedial channels of the democratic process remain open and unobstructed." This seems to me no less than the surrender of the constitutional protection of the liberty of small minorities to the popular will. We have previously pointed to the importance of a searching judicial inquiry into the legislative judgment in situations where prejudice against discrete and insular minorities may tend to curtail the operation of those political processes ordinarily to be relied on to protect minorities. And until now we have not hesitated similarly to scrutinize legislation restricting the civil liberty of racial and religious minorities although no political process was affected. Here we have such a small minority entertaining in good faith a religious belief, which is such a departure from the usual course of human conduct, that most persons are disposed to regard it with little toleration or concern. In such circumstances careful scrutiny of legislative efforts to secure conformity of belief and opinion by a compulsory affirmation of the desired belief, is especially needful if civil rights are to receive any protection. Tested by this standard, I am not prepared to say that the right of this small and helpless minority, including children having a strong religious conviction, whether they understand its nature or not, to refrain from an expression obnoxious to their religion, is to be overborne by the interest of the state in maintaining discipline in the schools.

The Constitution expresses more than the conviction of the people that democratic processes must be preserved at all costs. It is also an expression of faith and a command that freedom of mind and spirit must be preserved, which government must obey, if it is to adhere to that justice and moderation without which no free government can exist. For this reason it would seem that legislation which operates to repress the religious freedom of small minorities, which is admittedly within the scope of the protection of the Bill of Rights, must at least be subject to the same judicial scrutiny as legislation which we have recently held to infringe the constitutional liberty of religious and racial minorities.

With such scrutiny I cannot say that the inconveniences which may attend some sensible adjustment of school discipline in order that the religious convictions of these children may be spared, presents a problem so momentous or pressing as to outweigh the freedom from compulsory violation of religious faith which has been thought worthy of constitutional protection.

West Virginia State Board of Education v. Barnette, 319 U.S. 624 (1943)

Justice Jackson, representing the majority in this reversal of the *Gobitis* decision, wrote his classic description of religious freedom: "If there is any fixed star in our constitutional constellation, it is that no official, high or petty, can prescribe what shall be orthodox in politics, nationalism, religion, or other matters of opinion or force citizens to confess by word or act their faith therein."

Justice Frankfurter, who had written the *Gobitis* decision, dissented in the West Virginia decision, insisting that the Court had no jurisdiction "to restrict the powers of democratic government." He offers an extensive case for "judicial restraint."

Perhaps the most remarkable feature of this decision was its timing. *Gobitis* was decided before the United States entered World War II. In contrast, in the midst of that same war, the Court was prepared to support the religious freedom of a minority at the very moment when the country was in its most nationalistic mood.

MR. JUSTICE JACKSON DELIVERED THE OPINION OF THE COURT.

Following the decision by this Court on June 3, 1940, in *Minersville School District v. Gobitis*, the West Virginia legislature amended its statutes to require all schools therein to conduct courses of instruction in history, civics, and in the Constitution of the United States and of the State "for the purpose of teaching, fostering and perpetuating the ideals, principles and spirit of Americanism, and increasing the knowledge of the organization and machinery of the government."

Appellant Board of Education was directed, with advice of the State Superintendent of Schools, to "prescribe the course of study covering these subjects" for public schools. The Act made it the duty of private, parochial and denominational schools to prescribe courses of study "similar to those required for the public schools."

The Board of Education on January 9, 1942, adopted a resolution containing recitals taken largely from the Court's *Gobitis* opinion and ordering that the salute of the Flag become "a regular part of the program of activities in the public schools," that all teachers and pupils "shall be required to participate in the salute honoring the Nation represented by the Flag; provided, however, that refusal to salute the Flag be regarded as an Act of insubordination, and shall be dealt with accordingly."

The resolution originally required the "commonly accepted salute to the Flag" which it defined. Objections to the salute as "being too much like Hitler's" were raised by the Parent and Teacher's Association, the Boy and Girl Scouts, the Red Cross, and the federation of Women's Clubs. Some modification appears to have been made in deference to these objections, but no concession was made to Jehovah's Witnesses. What is now required is the "stiff-arm" salute, the saluter to keep the right hand raised with palm turned up while the following is repeated: "I pledge allegiance to the Flag of the United States of America and to the Republic for which it stands; one Nation, indivisible, with liberty and justice for all."

Failure to conform is "insubordination" dealt with by expulsion. Readmission is denied by statute until compliance. Meanwhile, the expelled child is "unlawfully absent" and may be proceeded against as a delinquent. His parents or guardians are liable to prosecution, and if convicted are subject to fine not exceeding $50 and jail term not exceeding thirty days.

Appellees, citizens of the United States and of West Virigina, brought suit in the United States District Court for themselves and others similarly situated asking its injunction to restrain enforcement of these laws and regulations against Jehovah's Witnesses. The Witnesses are an unincorporated body teaching that the obligation imposed by law of God is superior to that of laws enacted by temporal government. Their religious beliefs include a literal version of Exodus, Chapter 20, verses 4 and 5, which says: "Thou shalt not make unto thee any graven image, or any likeness of anything that is in heaven above, or that is in the earth beneath, or that is in the water under the earth; thou shalt not bow down thyself to them nor serve them." They consider that the flag is an "image" within this command. For this reason they refuse to salute it.

Children of this faith have been expelled from school and are threatened with exclusion for no other cause. Officials threaten to send them to reformatories maintained for criminally inclined juveniles. Parents of such children have been prosecuted and are threatened with prosecutions for causing delinquency.

The Board of Education moved to dismiss the complaint setting forth these facts and alleging that the law and regulations are an unconstitutional denial of religious freedom, and of freedom of speech, and are invalid under the "due process" and "equal protection" clauses of the Fourteenth Amendment of the Federal Constitution. The cause was submitted on the pleadings to a District Court of three judges. It restrained enforcement as to the plaintiffs and those of that class. The Board of Education brought the case here by direct appeal.

This case calls upon us to reconsider a precedent decision, as the Court throughout its history often has been required to do. Before turning to the *Gobitis* case, however, it is desirable to notice certain characteristics by which this controversy is distinguished.

The freedom asserted by these appelles does not bring them into collision with rights asserted by any other individual. It is such conflicts which most frequently require intervention of the State to determine where the rights of one end and those of another begin. But the refusal of these persons to participate in the ceremony does not interfere with or deny rights of others to do so. Nor is there any question in this case that their behavior is peaceable and orderly. The sole conflict is between authority and rights of the individual. The State asserts power to condition access to public education on making a prescribed sign and profession and at the same time to coerce attendance by punishing both parent and child. The latter stand on a right of self-determination in matters that touch individual opinion and personal attitude.

As the present Chief Justice said in dissent in the *Gobitis* case, the State may "require teaching by instruction and study of all in our history and in the structure and organization of our government, including the guaranties of civil liberty which tend to inspire patriotism and love of country." Here, however, we are dealing with a compulsion of students to declare a belief. They are not merely made acquainted with the flag salute so that they may be informed as to what it is or even what it means. The issue here is whether this slow and easily neglected route to aroused loyalties constitutionally may be short-cut by substituting a compulsory salute and slogan. This issue is not prejudiced by the Court's previous holding that where a State, without compelling attendance, extends college facilities to pupils who voluntarily enroll, it may prescribe military training as part of the course without offense to the Constitution. It was held that those who take advantage of its opportunities may not on ground of conscience refuse compliance with such conditions. In the present case attendance is not optional. That case is also to be distinguished from the present one because, independently of college privileges or requirements, the State has power to raise militia and impose the duties of service therein upon its citizens.

There is no doubt that, in connection with the pledges, the flag salute is a form of utterance. Symbolism is a primitive but effective way of communicating ideas. The use of an emblem or flag to symbolize some system, idea, institution, or personality, is a short cut from mind to mind. Causes and nations, political parties, lodges and ecclesiastical groups seek to knit the loyalty of their followings to a flag or banner, a color or design. The State announces rank, function, and authority through crowns and maces, uniforms and black robes; the church speaks through the Cross, the Crucifix, the altar and shrine, and clerical raiment. Symbols of State often convey political ideas just as religious symbols come to convey theological ones. Associated with many of these symbols are appropriate gestures of acceptance or respect: a salute, a bowed or bared head, a bended knee. A person gets from a symbol the meaning he puts into it, and what is one man's comfort and inspiration is another's jest and scorn.

Over a decade ago Chief Justice Hughes led this Court in holding that the display of a red flag as a symbol of opposition by peaceful and legal means to organized government was protected by the free speech guaranties of the Constitution. Here it is the State that employs a flag as a symbol of adherence to government as presently organized. It requires the individual to communicate by word and sign his acceptance of the political ideas it thus bespeaks. Objection to this form of communication when coerced is an old one, well known to the framers of the Bill of Rights.

It is also to be noted that the compulsory flag salute and pledge requires affirmation of a belief and an attitude of mind. It is not clear whether the regulation contemplates that pupils forego any contrary convictions of their own and become unwilling converts to the prescribed ceremony or whether it will be acceptable if they simulate assent by words without belief and by a gesture barren of meaning. It is now a commonplace that censorship or suppression of expression of opinion is tolerated by our Constitution only when the expression presents a clear and present danger of action of a kind the State is empowered to prevent and punish. It would seem that involuntary affirmation could be commanded only on even more immediate and urgent grounds than silence. But here the power of compulsion is invoked without any allegation that remaining passive during a flag salute ritual creates a clear and present danger that would justify an effort even to muffle expression. To sustain the compulsory flag salute we are required to say that a Bill of Rights which guard the individual's right to speak his own mind, left it open to public authorities to compel him to utter what is not in his mind.

Whether the First Amendment to the Constitution will permit officials to order observance of ritual of this nature does not depend upon whether as a voluntary exercise we would think it to be good, bad or merely innocuous. Any credo of nationalism is likely to include what some disapprove or to omit what others think essential, and to give off different overtones as it takes on different accents or interpretations. If official power exists to coerce acceptance of any patriotic creed, what it shall contain cannot be decided by courts, but must be largely discretionary with the ordaining authority, whose power to prescribe would no doubt include power to amend. Hence validity of the asserted power to force an American citizen publicly to profess any statement of belief or to engage in any ceremony of assent to one presents questions of power that must be considered independently of any idea we may have as to the utility of the ceremony in question.

Nor does the issue as we see it turn on one's possession of particular religious views or the sincerity with which they are held. While religion supplies appellees' motive for enduring the discomforts of making the issue in this case, many citizens who do not share these religious views hold such a compulsory rite to infringe constitutional liberty of the individual. It is not necessary to inquire whether nonconformist beliefs will exempt from the duty to salute unless we first find power to make the salute a legal duty.

The *Gobitis* decision, however, assumed, as did the argument in that case and in this, that power exists in the State to impose the flag salute discipline upon school children in general. The Court only examined and rejected a claim based on religious beliefs of immunity from an unquesitoned general rule. The question which underlies the flag salute controversy is whether such a ceremony so touching matters of opinion and political attitude may be imposed upon the individual by official authority under powers committed to any political organization under our Constitution. We examine rather than assume existence of this power and, against this broader definition of issues in this case, re-examine specific grounds assigned for the *Gobitis* decision.

1. It was said that the flag-salute controversy confronted the Court with "the problem which Lincoln cast in memorable dilemma: 'Must a government of necessity be too strong for the liberties of its people, or too weak to maintain its own existence?'" and that the answer must be in favor of strength.

We think these issues may be examined free of pressure or restraint growing out of such considerations.

It may be doubted whether Mr. Lincoln would have thought that the strength of government to maintain itself would be impressively vindicated by our confirming power of the state to expel a handful of children from school. Such oversimplification, so handy in political debate, often lacks the precision necessary to postulates of judicial reasoning. If validly applied to this problem, the utterance cited would resolve every issue of power in favor of those in authority and would require us to override every liberty thought to weaken or delay execution of their policies.

Government of limited power need not be anemic government. Assurance that rights are secure tends to diminish fear and jealousy of strong government, and by making us feel safe to live under it makes for its better support. Without promise of a limiting Bill of Rights it is doubtful if our Constitution could have mustered enough strength to enable its ratification. To enforce those rights today is not to choose weak government over strong government. It is only to adhere as a means of strength to individual freedom of mind in preference to officially disciplined uniformity for which history indicates a disappointing and disastrous end.

The subject now before us exemplifies this principle. Free public education, if faithful to the ideal of secular instruction and political neutrality, will not be partisan or enemy of any class, creed, party, or faction. If it is to impose any ideological discipline, however, each party or denomination must seek to control, or failing that, to weaken the influence of the educational system. Observance of the limitations of the Constitution will not weaken government in the field appropriate for its exercise.

2. It was also considered in the *Gobitis* case that functions of educational officers in states, counties and school districts were such that to interfere with their authority "would in effect make us the school board for the country."

The Fourteenth Amendment, as now applied to the States, protects the citizen against the State itself and all of its creatures—Boards of Education not excepted. These have, of course, important, delicate, and highly discretionary functions, but none that they may not perform within the limits of the Bill of Rights. That they are educating the young for citizenship is reason for scrupulous protection of Constitutional Freedoms of the individual, if we are not to strangle the free mind at its source and teach youth to discount important principles of our government as mere platitudes.

Such Boards are numerous and their territorial jurisdiction often small. But small and local authority may feel less sense of responsibility to the Constitution, and agencies of publicity may be less vigilant in calling it to account. The action of Congress in making flag observance voluntary and respecting the conscience of the objector in a matter so vital as raising the Army contrasts sharply with these local regulations in matters relatively trivial to the welfare of the nation. There are village tyrants as well as village Hampdens, but none who acts under color of law is beyond reach of the Constitution.

3. The *Gobitis* opinion reasoned that this is a field "where courts possess no marked and certainly no controlling competence," that it is committed to the legislatures as well as the courts to guard cherished liberties and that it is constitutionally appropriate to "fight out the wise use of legislative authority in the form of public opinion and before legislative assemblies rather than to transfer such a contest to the judicial arena," since all the "effective means of inducing political changes are left free."

The very purpose of a Bill of Rights was to withdraw certain subjects from the vicissitudes of political controversy, to place them beyond the reach of majorities and officials and to establish them as legal principles to be applied by the courts. One's right to life, liberty, and property, to free speech, a free press, freedom of worship and assembly, and other fundamental rights may not be submitted to vote; they depend on the outcome of no elections.

In weighing arguments of the parties it is important to distinguish between the due process clause of the Fourteenth Amendment as an instrument for transmitting the principles of the First Amendment and those cases in which it is applied for its own sake. The test of legislation which collides with the Fourteenth Amendment, because it also collides with the principles of the First, is much more definite than the test when only the Fourteenth is involved. Much of the vagueness of the due process clause disappears when the specific prohibitions of the First become its standard. The right of a State to regulate, for example, a public utility may well include, so far as the due process test is concerned, power to impose all of the restrictions which a legislature may have a "rational basis" for adopting. But freedom of speech and of press, of assembly, and of worship may not be infringed on such slender grounds. They are susceptible of restriction only to prevent grave and immediate danger to interests which the state may lawfully protect. It is important to note that while it is the Fourteenth Amendment which bears directly upon the State it is the more specific limiting principles of the First Amendment that finally govern this case.

Nor does our duty to apply the Bill of Rights to assertions of official authority depend upon our possession of marked competence in the field where the invasion of rights occurs. True, the task of translating the majestic generalities of the Bill of Rights, conceived as part of the pattern of liberal government in the eighteenth century, into concrete restraints on officials dealing with the problems of the twentieth century, is one to disturb self-confidence. These principles grew in soil which also produced a philosophy that the individual was the center of society, that his liberty was attainable through mere absence of governmental restraints, and that government should be entrusted with few controls and only the mildest supervision over men's affairs. We must transplant these rights to a soil in which the laissez-faire concept or principle of non-interference has withered at least as to economic affairs, and social advancements are increasingly sought through closer integration of society and through expanded and strengthened governmental controls. These changed conditions often deprive precedents of reliability and cast us more than we would choose upon our own judgment. But we act in these matters not by authority of our competence but by force of our commissions. We cannot, because of modest estimates of our competence in such specialities as public education, withhold the judgment that history authenticates as the function of this Court when liberty is infringed.

4. Lastly, and this is the very heart of the *Gobitis* opinion, it reasons that "National unity is the basis of national security," that the authorities have "the right to select appropriate means for its attainment," and hence reaches the conclusion that such compulsory measures toward "national unity" are constitutional. Upon the verity of this assumption depends our answer in this case.

National unity as an end which officials may foster by persuasion and example is not in question. The problem is whether under our Constitution compulsion as here employed is a permissible means for its achievement.

Struggles to coerce uniformity of sentiment in support of some end thought essential to their time and country have been waged by many good as well as by evil men. Nationalism is a relatively recent phenomenon but at other times and places the ends have been racial or territorial security, support of a dynasty or regime, and particular plans for saving souls. As first and moderate methods to attain unity have failed, those bent on its accomplishment must resort to an ever increasing severity. As governmental pressure toward unity becomes greater, so strife becomes more bitter as to whose unity it shall be. Probably no deeper division of our people could proceed from any provocation than from finding it necessary to choose what doctrine and whose program public educational officials shall compel youth to unite in embracing. Ultimate futility of such attempts to compel coherence is the lesson of every such effort from the Roman drive to stamp out Christianity as a disturber of its pagan unity, the Inquisition, as a means to religious and dynastic unity, the Siberian exiles as a means to Russian unity, down to the fast failing efforts of our present totalitarian enemies. Those who begin coercive elimination of dissent soon find themselves exterminating dissenters. Compulsory unification of opinion achieves only the unanimity of the graveyard.

It seems trite but necessary to say that the First Amendment to our Constitution was designed to avoid these ends by avoiding these beginnings. There is no mysticism in the American concept of the State or of the nature or origin of its authority. We set up government by consent of the governed, and the Bill of Rights denies those in power any legal opportunity to coerce that consent. Authority here is to be controlled by public opinion, not public opinion by authority.

The case is made difficult not because the principles of its decision are obscure but because the flag involved is our own. Nevertheless, we apply the limitations of the Constitution with no fear that freedom to be intellectually and spiritually diverse or even contrary will disintegrate the social organization. To believe that patriotism will not flourish if patriotic ceremonies are voluntary and spontaneous instead of a compulsory routine is to make an unflattering estimate of the appeal of our institutions to free minds. We can have intellectual individualism and the rich cultural diversities that we owe to exceptional minds only at the price of occasional eccentricity and abnormal attitudes. When they are so harmless to others or to the State as those we deal with here, the price is not too great. But freedom to differ is not limited to things that do not matter much. That would be a mere shadow of freedom. The test of its substance is the right to differ as to things that touch the heart of the existing order.

If there is any fixed star in our constitutional constellation, it is that no official, high or petty, can prescribe what shall be orthodox in politics, nationalism, religion, or other matters of opinion or force citizens to confess by word or act their faith therein. If there are any circumstances which permit an exception, they do not now occur to us.

We think the action of the local authorities in compelling the flag salute and pledge transcends constitutional limitations on their power and invades the sphere of intellect and spirit which it is the purpose of the First Amendment to our Constitution to reserve from all official control.

The decision of this Court in *Minersville School District v. Gobitis* and the holdings of those few per curiam decisions which preceded and foreshadowed it are over-ruled, and the judgment enjoining enforcement of the West Virginia Regulation is affirmed.

Mr. Justice Roberts and Mr. Justice Reed adhere to the views expressed by the Court in *Minersville School District v. Gobitis* and are of the opinion that the judgment below should be reversed.

MR. JUSTICE FRANKFURTER, DISSENTING.

One who belongs to the most vilified and persecuted minority in history is not likely to be insensible to the freedoms guaranteed by our Constitution. Were my purely personal attitude relevant I should whole-heartedly associate myself with the general libertarian views in the Court's opinion, representing as they do the thought and action of a lifetime. But as judges we are neither Jew nor Gentile, neither Catholic nor agnostic. We owe equal attachment to the Constitution and are equally bound by our judicial obligations whether we derive our citizenship from the earliest or the latest immigrants to these shores. As a member of this Court I am not justified in writing my private notions of policy into the Constitution, no matter how deeply I may cherish them or how mischievous I may deem their disregard. The duty of a judge who must decide which of two claims before the Court shall prevail, that of a State to enact and enforce laws within its general competence or that of an individual to refuse obedience because of the demands of his conscience, is not that of the ordinary person. It can never be emphasized too much that one's own opinion about the wisdom or evil of a law should be excluded altogether when one is doing one's duty on the bench. The only opinion of our own even looking in that direction that is material is our opinion whether legislators could in reason have enacted such a law. In the light of all the circumstances, including the history of this question in this Court, it would require more daring than I possess to deny that reasonable legislators could have taken the action which is before us for review. Most unwillingly, therefore, I must differ from my brethren with regard to legislation like this. I cannot bring my mind to believe that the "liberty" secured by the Due Process Clause gives this Court authority to deny to the State of West Virginia the attainment of that which we all recognize as a legitimate legislative end, namely, the promotion of good citizenship, by employment of the means here chosen.

Not long ago we were admonished that "the only check upon our own exercise of power is our own sense of self-restraint. For the removal of unwise laws from the statute books appeal lies, not to the courts, but to the ballot and to the processes of democratic government." We have been told that generalities do not decide concrete cases. But the intensity with which a general principle is held may determine a particular issue, and whether we put first things first may decide a specific controversy.

The admonition that judicial self-restraint alone limits arbitrary exercise of our authority is relevant every time we are asked to nullify legislation. The Constitution does not give us greater veto power when dealing with one phase of "liberty" than with another, or when dealing with grade school regulations than with college regulations that offend conscience, as was the case in *Hamilton v. Regents.* In neither situation is our function comparable to that of a legislature or are we free to act as though we were a super-legislature. Judicial self-restraint is equally necessary whenever an exercise of political or legislative power is challenged. There is no warrant in the constitutional basis of this Court's authority for attributing different roles to it depending upon the nature of the challenge to the legislation. Our power does not vary according to the particular provision of the Bill of Rights which is invoked. The right not to have property taken without just compensation has, so far as the scope of judicial power is concerned, the same constitutional dignity as the right to be protected against unreasonable searches and seizures, and the latter has no less claim than freedom of the press or freedom of speech or religious freedom. In no instance is this Court the primary protector of the particular liberty that is invoked. This Court has recognized, what hardly could be denied, that all the provisions of the first ten Amendments are "specific" prohibitions. But each specific Amendment, in so far as embraced within the Fourteenth Amendment, must be equally respected, and the function of this Court does not differ in passing on the constitutionality of legislation challenged under different Amendments.

When Mr. Justice Holmes, speaking for this Court, wrote that "it must be remembered that legislatures are ultimate guardians of the liberties and welfare of the people in quite as great a degree as the courts," he went to the very essence of our constitutional system and the democratic conception of our society. He did not mean that for only some phases of civil government this Court was not to supplant legislatures and sit in judgment upon the right or wrong of a challenged measure. He was stating the comprehensive judicial duty and role of this Court in our constitutional scheme whenever legislation is sought to be nullified on any ground, namely, that responsibility for legislation lies with legislatures, answerable as they are directly to the people, and this Court's only and very narrow function is to determine whether within the broad grant of authority vested in legislatures they have exercised a judgment for which reasonable justification can be offered.

The framers of the federal Constitution might have chosen to assign an active share in the process of legislation to this Court. They had before them the well known example of New York's Council of Revision, which had been functioning since 1777. After stating that "laws inconsistent with the spirit of this constitution, or with the public good, may be hastily and unadvisedly passed," the state constitution made the judges of New York part of the legislative process by providing that "all bills which have passed the senate and assembly shall, before they become law," be presented to a Council of which the judges constituted a majority, "for their revisal and consideration." But the framers of the Constitution denied such legislative powers to the federal judiciary. They chose instead to insulate the judiciary from the legislative function. They did not grant to this Court supervision over legislation.

The reason why from the beginning even the narrow judicial authority to nullify legislation has been viewed with a jealous eye is that it serves to prevent the full play of the democratic process. The fact that it may be an undemocratic aspect of our scheme of government does not call for its rejection or its disuse. But it is the best of reasons, as this Court has frequently recognized, for the greatest caution in its use.

The precise scope of the question before us defines the limits of the constitutional power that is in issue. The State of West Virginia requires all pupils to share in the salute to the flag as part of school training in citizenship. The present action is one to enjoin the enforcement of this requirement by those in school attendance. We have not before us any attempt by the State to punish disobedient children or visit penal consequences on their parents. All that is in question is the right of the state to compel participation in this exercise by those who choose to attend the public schools.

We are not reviewing merely the action of a local school board. The flag salute requirement in this case comes before us with the full authority of the State of West Virginia. We are in fact passing judgment on the "the power of the State as a whole." Practically we are passing upon the political power of each of the forty-eight states. Moreover, since the First Amendment has been read into the Fourteenth, our problem is precisely the same as it would be if we had before us an Act of Congress for the District of Columbia. To suggest that we are here concerned with the heedless action of some village tyrants is to distort the augustness of the Constitutional issue and the reach of the consequences of our decision.

Under our constitutional system the legislature is charged solely with civil concerns of society. If the avowed or intrinsic legislative purpose is either to promote or to discourage some religious community or creed, it is clearly within the constitutional restrictions imposed on legislatures and cannot stand. But it by no means follows that legislative power is wanting whenever a general nondiscriminatory civil regulation in fact touches conscientious scruples or religious beliefs of an individual or a group. Regard for such scruples or beliefs undoubtedly presents one of the most reasonable claims for the exertion of legislative accommodation. It is, of course, beyond our power to rewrite the state's requirement, by providing exemptions for those who do not wish to participate in the flag salute or by making some other accommodations to meet their scruples. That wisdom might suggest the making of such accommodations and that the school administration would not find it too difficult to make them and yet maintain the ceremony for those not refusing to conform, is outside our province to suggest. Tact, respect, and generosity toward variant views will always commend themselves to those charged with the duties of legislation so as to achieve a maximum of good will and to require a minimum of unwilling submission to a general law. But the real question is who is to make such accommodations, the courts or the legislature?

This is no dry, technical matter. It cuts deep into one's conception of the democratic process—it concerns no less the practical differences between the means for making these accommodations that are open to courts and to legislatures. A court can only strike down. It can only say "This or that law is void." It cannot modify or qualify, it cannot make exceptions to a general requirement. And it strikes down not merely for a day. At least the finding of unconstitutionality ought not to have ephemeral significance unless the Constitution is to be reduced to the fugitive importance of mere legislation. When we are dealing with the Constitution of the United States, and more particularly with the great safeguards of the Bill of Rights, we are dealing with principles of liberty and justice "so rooted in the traditions and conscience of our people as to be ranked as fundamental"—something without which "a fair and enlightened system of justice would be impossible." If the function of this Court is to be essentially no different from that of a legislature, if the considerations governing constitutional construction are to be substantially those that underlie legislation, then indeed judges should not have life tenure and they should be made directly responsible to the electorate. There have been many but unsuccessful proposals in the last sixty years to amend the Constitution to that end.

Conscientious scruples, all would admit, cannot stand against every legislative compulsion to do positive acts in conflict with such scruples. We have been told that such compulsions override religious scruples only as to major concerns of the state. But the determination of what is major and what is minor itself raises questions of policy. For the way in which men equally guided by reason appraise importance goes to the very heart of policy. Judges should be very diffident in setting their judgment against that of a state in determining what is and what is not a major concern, what means are appropriate to proper ends, and what is the total social cost in striking the balance of imponderables.

What one can say with assurance is that the history out of which grew constitutional provisions for religious equality, and the writings of the great exponents of religious freedom—Jefferson, Madison, John Adams, Benjamin Franklin—are totally wanting in justification for a claim by dissidents of exceptional immunity from civic measures of general applicability, measures not in fact disguised assaults upon such dissident views. The great leaders of the American Revolution were determined to remove political support from every religious establishment. They put on an equality the different religious sects—Episcopalians, Presbyterians, Catholics, Baptists, Methodists, Quakers, Huguenots,—which as dissenters, had been under the heel of the various orthodoxies that prevailed in different colonies. So far as the state was concerned, there was to be neither orthodoxy nor heterodoxy. And so Jefferson and those who followed him wrote guaranties of religious freedom into our constitutions. Religious minorities as well as religious majorities were to be equal in the eyes of the political state. But Jefferson and the others also knew that minorities may disrupt society. It never would have occurred to them to write into the Constitution the subordination of the general civil authority of the state to sectarian scruples.

The constitutional protection of religious freedom terminated disabilities, it did not create new privileges. It gave religious equality, not civil immunity. Its essence is freedom from conformity to religious dogma, not freedom from conformity to law because of religious dogma. Religious loyalties may be exercised without hindrance from the state, not the state may not exercise that which except by leave of religious loyalties is within the domain of temporal power. Otherwise each individual could set up his own censor against obedience to laws conscientiously deemed for the public good by those whose business it is to make laws.

The prohibition against any religious establishment by the government placed denominations on an equal footing—it assured freedom from support by the government to any mode of worship and the freedom of individuals to support any mode of worship. Any person may therefore believe or disbelieve what he pleases. He may practice what he will in his own house of worship or publicly within the limits of public order. But the lawmaking authority is not circumscribed by the variety of religious beliefs, otherwise the constitutional guaranty would be not a protection of the free exercise of religion but a denial of the exercise of legislation.

The essence of the religious freedom guaranteed by our Constitution is therefore this: no religion shall either receive the state's support or incur its hostility. Religion is outside the sphere of political government. This does not mean that all matters on which religious organizations or beliefs may pronounce are outside the sphere of government. Were this so, instead of the separation of church and state, there would be the subordination of the state on any matter deemed within the sovereignty of the religious conscience. Much that is the concern of temporal authority affects the spiritual interests of men. But it is not enough to strike down a non-discriminatory law that it may hurt or offend some dissident view. It would be too easy to cite numerous prohibitions and injunctions to which laws run counter if the variant interpretations of the Bible were made the tests of the obedience to law. The validity of secular laws cannot be measured by their conformity to religious doctrines. It is only in a theocratic state that ecclesiastical doctrines measure legal right or wrong.

An act compelling profession of allegiance to a religion, no matter how subtly or tenuously promoted, is bad. But an act promoting good citizenship and national allegiance is within the domain of governmental authority and is therefore to be judged by the same considerations of power and of constitutionality as those involved in the many claims of immunity from civil obedience because of religious scruples.

That claims are pressed on behalf of sincere religious convictions does not of itself establish their constitutional validity. Nor does waving the banner of religious freedom relieve us from examining the power we are asked to deny the states. Otherwise the doctrine of separation of church and state, so cardinal in the history of this nation and for the liberty of our people, would mean not the disestablishment of a state church but the establishment of all churches and of all religious groups.

The subjection of dissidents to the general requirement of saluting the flag, as a measure conducive to the training of children in good citizenship, is very far from being the first instance of exacting obedience to general laws that have offended deep religious scruples. Compulsory vaccination, compulsory medical treatment, these are but illustrations of conduct that has often been compelled in the enforcement of legislation of general applicability even though the religous consciences of particular individuals rebelled at the exaction.

Law is concerned with external behavior and not with the inner life of man. It rests in large measure upon compulsion. Socrates lives in history partly because he gave his life for the conviction that duty of obedience to secular law does not pre-suppose consent to its enactment or belief in its virtue. The consent upon which free government rests is the consent that comes from sharing in the process of making and unmaking laws. The state is not shut out from a domain because the individual conscience may deny the state's claim. The individual conscience may profess what faith it chooses. It may affirm and promote that faith—in the language of the Constitution, it may "exercise" it freely—but it cannot thereby restrict community action through political organs in matters of community concern, so long as the action is not asserted in a discriminatory way either openly or by stealth. One may have the right to practice one's religion and at the same time owe the duty of formal obedience to laws that run counter to one's beliefs. Compelling belief implies denial of opportunity to combat it and to assert dissident views. Such compulsion is one thing. Quite another matter is submission to conformity of action while denying its wisdom or virtue and with ample opportunity for seeking its change or abrogation.

* * * * *

Parents have the privilege of choosing which schools they wish their children to attend. And the question here is whether the state may make certain requirements that seem to it desirable or important for the proper education of those future citizens who go to schools maintained by the states, or whether the pupils in those schools may be relieved from those requirements if they run counter to the consciences of their parents. Not only have parents the right to send children to schools of their own choosing but the state has no right to bring such schools "under a strict governmental control" or give "affirmative direction concerning the intimate and essential details of such schools, intrust their control to public officers, and deny both owners and patrons reasonable choice and discretion in respect of teachers, curriculum and textbooks." Why should not the state likewise have constitutional power to make reasonable provisions for the proper instruction of children in schools maintained by it?

When dealing with religious scruples we are dealing with an almost numberless variety of doctrines and beliefs, entertained with equal sincerity by the particular groups for which they satisfy man's needs in his relation to the mysteries of the universe. There are in the United States more than 250 distinctive established religious denominations. In the State of Pennsylvania there are 120 of these, and in West Virginia as many as 65. But if religious scruples afford immunity from civic obedience to laws, they may be invoked by the religious beliefs of any individual even though he holds no membership in any sect or organized denomination. Certainly this Court cannot be called upon to determine what claims of conscience should be recognized and what should be rejected as satisfying the "religion" which the Constitution protects. That would indeed resurrect the very discriminatory treatment of religion which the Constitution sought forever to forbid. And so, when confronted with the task of considering the claims of immunity from obedience to a law dealing with civil affairs because of religious scruples, we cannot conceive religion more narrowly than in the terms in which Judge Augustus N. Hand recently characterized it: "It is unnecessary to attempt a definition of religion; the content of the term is found in the history of the human race and is incapable of compression into a few words. Religious belief arises from a sense of the inadequacy of reason as a means of relating the individual to his fellow-men and to his universe . . . [It] may justly be regarded as a response of the individual to an inward mentor, call it conscience or God, that is for many persons at the present time the equivalent of what has always been thought a religious impulse."

Consider the controversial issue of compulsory Bible-reading in public schools. The educational policies of the states are in great conflict over this, and the state courts are divided in their decisions on the issue whether the requirement of Bible-reading offends constitutional provisions dealing with religious freedom. The requirement of Bible-reading has been justified by various state courts as an appropriate means of inculcating ethical precepts and familiarizing pupils with the most lasting expression of great English literature. Is this Court to overthrow such variant state educational policies by denying states the right to entertain such convictions in regard to their school systems because of a belief that the King James version is in fact a sectarian text which parents of the Catholic and Jewish faiths and of some Protestant persuasions may rightly object to having their children exposed? On the other hand the religious consciences of some parents may rebel at the absence of any Bible-reading in the schools. Or is this Court to enter the old controversy between science and religion by unduly defining the limits within which a state may experiment with its school curricula? The religious consciences of some parents may be offended by subjecting their children to the Biblical account of creation, while another state may offend parents by prohibiting a teaching of biology that contradicts such Biblical account. What of conscientious objections to what is devoutly felt by parents to be the poisoning of impressionable minds of children by chauvinistic teaching of history? This is very far from a fanciful suggestion for in the belief of many thoughtful people nationalism is the seed-bed of war.

There are other issues in the offing which admonish us of the difficulties and complexities that confront states in the duty of administering their local school systems. All citizens are taxed for the support of public schools although this Court has denied the right of a state to compel all children to go to such schools and has recognized the right of parents to send children to privately maintained schools. Parents who are dissatisfied with the public schools thus carry a double educational burden. Children who go to public school enjoy in many states derivative advantages such as free textbooks, free lunch, and free transportation in going to and from school. What of the claims for equality of treatment of those parents who, because of religious scruples, cannot send their children to public schools? What of the claim that if the right to send children to privately maintained schools is partly an exercise of religious conviction, to render effective this right it should be accompanied by equality of treatment by the state in supplying free textbooks, free lunch, and free transportation to children who go to private schools? What of the claim that such grants are offensive to the cardinal constitutional doctrine of separation of church and state?

These questions assume increasing importance in view of the steady growth of parochial schools both in number and in population. I am not borrowing trouble by adumbrating these issues nor am I parading horrible examples of the consequences of today's decision. I am aware that we must decide the case before us and not some other case. But that does not mean that a case is dissociated from the past and unrelated to the future. We must decide this case with due regard for what went before and no less regard for what may come after. Is it really a fair construction of such a fundamental concept as the right freely to exercise one's religion that a state cannot choose to require all children who attend public school to make the same gesture of allegiance to the symbol of our national life because it may offend the conscience of some children, but that it may compel all children to attend public school to listen to the King James version although it may offend the consciences of their parents? And what of the larger issue of claiming immunity from obedience to a general civil regulation that has a reasonable relation to a public purpose within the general competence of the state? Another member of the sect now before us insisted that in forbidding her two little girls, aged nine and twelve, to distribute pamphlets Oregon infringed her and their freedom of religion in that the children were engaged in "preaching the gospel of God's Kingdom." A procedural technicality led to the dismissal of the case, but the problem remains.

These questions are not lightly stirred. They touch the most delicate issue and their solution challenges the best wisdom of political and religious statesmen. But it presents awful possibilities to try to encase the solution of these problems within the rigid prohibitions of unconstitutionality.

We are told that a flag salute is a doubtful substitute for adequate understanding of our institutions. The states that require such a school exercise do not have to justify it as the only means for promoting good citizenship in children, but merely as one of diverse means for accomplishing a worthy end. We may deem it a foolish measure, but the point is that this Court is not the organ of government to resolve doubts as to whether it will fulfill its purpose. Only if there be no doubt that any reasonable mind could entertain can we deny to the states the right to resolve doubts their way and not ours.

That which to the majority may seem essential for the welfare of the state may offend the conscience of a minority. But, so long as no inroads are made upon the actual exercise of religion by the minority, to deny the political power of the majority to enact laws concerned with civil matter, simply because they may offend the consciences of a minority, really means that the consciences of a minority are more sacred and more enshrined in the Constitution than the consciences of a majority.

We are told that symbolism is a dramatic but primitive way of communicating ideas. Symbolism is inescapable. Even the most sophisticated live by symbols. But it is not for this Court to make psychological judgments as to the effectiveness of a particular symbol in inculcating concededly indispensable feeling, particularly if the state happens to see fit to utilize the symbol that represents our heritage and our hopes. And surely only flippancy could be responsible for the suggestion that constitutional validity of a requirement to salute our flag implies equal validity of a requirement to salute a dictator. The significance of a symbol lies in what it represents. To reject the swastika does not imply rejection of the Cross. And so it bears repetition to say that it mocks reason and denies our whole history to find in the allowance of a requirement to salute our flag on fitting occasions the seeds of sanction for obeisance to a leader. To deny the power to employ educational symbols is to say that the state's educational system may not stimulate the imagination because this may lead to unwise stimulation.

The right of West Virginia to utilize the flag salute as part of its educational process is denied because, so it is argued, it cannot be justified as a means of meeting a "clear and present danger" to national unity. In passing it deserves to be noted that the four cases which unanimously sustained the power of states to utilize such an educational measure arose and were all decided before the present World War. But to measure the state's power to make such regulations as are here resisted by the imminence of national danger is wholly to misconceive the origin and purpose of the concept of "clear and present danger." To apply such a test is for the Court to assume, however unwittingly, a legislative responsibility that does not belong to it. To talk about "clear and present danger" as the touchstone of allowable educational policy by the states whenever school curricula may impinge upon the boundaries of individual conscience, is to take a felicitous phrase out of the context of the particular situation where it arose and for which it was adapted. Mr. Justice Holmes used the phrase "clear and present danger" in a case involving mere speech as a means by which alone to accomplish sedition in time of war. By that phrase he meant merely to indicate that, in view of the protection given to utterance by the First Amendment, in order that mere utterance may not be prescribed, "the words used are used in such circumstances and are of such a nature as to create a clear and present danger that they will bring about the substantive evils that Congress has a right to prevent." The "substantive evils" about which he was speaking were inducement of insubordination in the military and naval forces of the United States and obstruction of enlistment while the country was at war. He was not enunciating a formal rule that there can be no restriction upon speech and, still less, no compulsion where conscience balks, unless imminent danger would thereby be wrought "to our institutions or our government."

The flag salute exercise has no kinship whatever to the oath tests so odious in history. For the oath test was one of the instruments for suppressing heretical beliefs. Saluting the flag suppresses no belief nor curbs it. Children and their parents may believe what they please, avow their belief and practice it. It is not even remotely suggested that the requirement for saluting the flag involves the slightest restriction against the fullest opportunity on the part both of the children and of their parents to disavow as publicly as they choose to do so the meaning that others attach to the gesture of salute. All channels of affirmative free expression are open to both children and parents. Had we before us any act of the state putting the slightest curbs upon such free expression, I should not lag behind any member of this Court in striking down such an invasion of the right to freedom of thought and freedom of speech protected by the Constitution.

I am fortified in my view of this case by the history of the flag salute controversy in this Court. Five times has the precise question now before us been adjudicated. Four times the Court unanimously found that the requirement of such a school exercise was not beyond the powers of the states. Indeed in the first three cases to come before the Court the constitutional claim now sustained was deemed so clearly unmeritorious that this Court dismissed the appeals for want of a substantial federal question. In the fourth case the judgment of the district court upholding the state law was summarily affirmed on the authority of the earlier cases. The fifth case, *Minersville District v. Gobitis*, was brought here because the decision of the Circuit Court of Appeals for the Third Circuit ran counter to our rulings. They were reaffirmed after full consideration, with one Justice dissenting.

What may be even more significant than this uniform recognition of state authority is the fact that every Justice—thirteen in all—who has hitherto participated in judging this matter has at one or more times found no constitutional infirmity in what is now condemned. Only the two Justices sitting for the first time on this matter have not heretofore found this legislation inoffensive to the "liberty" guaranteed by the Constitution. And among the Justices who sustained this measure were outstanding judicial leaders in the zealous enforcement of constitutional safeguards of civil liberties—men like Chief Justice Hughes, Mr. Justice Brandeis, and Mr. Justice Cardozo, to mention only those no longer on the Court.

One's conception of the Constitution cannot be severed from one's conception of a judge's function in applying it. The Court has no reason for existence if it merely reflects the pressures of the day. Our system is built on the faith that men set apart for this special function, freed from the influences of immediacy and from the deflections of worldly ambition, will become able to take a view of longer range than the period of responsibility entrusted to Congress and legislatures. We are dealing with matters as to which legislators and voters have conflicting views. Are we as judges to impose our strong convictions on where wisdom lies? That which three years ago had seemed to five successive Courts to lie within permissible areas of legislation is now outlawed by the deciding shift of opinion of two Justices. What reason is there to believe that they or their successors may not have another view a few years hence? Is that which was deemed to be of so fundamental a nature as to be written into the Constitution to endure for all times to be the sport of shifting winds of doctrine? Of course, judicial opinions, even as to questions of constitutionality, are not immutable. As has been true in the past, the Court will from time to time reverse its position. But I believe that never before these Jehovah's Witnesses Cases (except for minor deviations subsequently retraced) has this Court overruled decisions so as to restrict the powers of democratic government. Always heretofore, it has withdrawn narrow views of legislative authority so as to authorize what formerly it had denied.

In view of this history it must be plain that what thirteen Justices found to be within the constitutional authority of a state, legislators can not be deemed unreasonable in enacting. Therefore, in denying the states what heretofore has received such impressive judicial sanction, some other tests of unconstitutionality must surely be guiding the Court than the absence of a rational justification for the legislation. But I know of no other test which this Court is authorized to apply in nullifying legislation.

In the past this Court has from time to time set its views of policy against that embodied in legislation by finding laws in conflict with what was called the "spirit of the Constitution." Such undefined destructive power was not conferred on this Court by the Constitution. Before a duly enacted law can be judicially nullified, it must be forbidden by some explicit restriction upon political authority in the Constitution. Equally inadmissible is the claim to strike down legislation because to us as individuals it seems opposed to the "plan and purpose" of the Constitution. That is too tempting a basis for finding in one's personal views the purposes of the Founders.

The uncontrollable power wielded by this Court brings it very close to the most sensitive areas of public affairs. As appeal from legislation to adjudication becomes more frequent, and its consequences more far-reaching, judicial self-restraint becomes more and not less important, lest we unwarrantably enter social and political domain wholly outside our concern. I think I appreciate fully the objections to the law before us. But to deny that it presents a question upon which men might reasonably differ appears to me to be intolerance. And since men may so reasonably differ, I deem it beyond my constitutional power to assert my view of the wisdom of this law against the view of the State of West Virginia.

Jefferson's opposition to judicial review has not been accepted by history, but it still serves as an admonition against confusion between judicial and political functions. As a rule of judicial self-restriant, it is still as valid as Lincoln's admonition. For those who pass laws not only are under duty to pass laws. They are also under duty to observe the Constitution. And even though legislation relates to civil liberties, our duty of deference to those who have the responsibility for making the laws is no less relevant or less exacting. And this is so especially when we consider the accidential contingencies by which one man may determine constitutionality and thereby confine the political power of the Congress of the United States and the legislatures of forty-eight states. The attitude of judicial humility which these considerations enjoin is not an abdication of the judicial function. It is a due observance of its limits. Moreover, it is to be borne in mind that in a question like this we are not passing on the proper distribution of political power as between the states and the central government. We are not discharging the basic function of this Court as the mediator of powers within the federal system. To strike down a law like this is to deny a power to all government.

* * * * *

Of course patriotism cannot be enforced by the flag salute. But neither can the liberal spirit be enforced by judicial invalidation of illiberal legislation. Our constant preoccupation with the constitutionality of legislation rather than with its wisdom tends to preoccupation of the American mind with a false value. The tendency of focusing attention on constitutionality is to make constitutionality synonymous with wisdom, to regard a law as all right if it is constitutional. Such an attitude is a great enemy of liberalism. Particularly in legislation affecting freedom of thought and freedom of speech much which should offend a free-spirited society is constitutional. Reliance for the most precious interests of civilization, therefore, must be found outside of their vindication in courts of law. Only a persistent positive translation of the faith of a free society into the convictions and habits and actions of a community is the ultimate reliance against unabated temptations to fetter the human spirit.

Braunfeld v. Brown, 366 U.S. 599 (1961)

This case is a companion to *McGowan,* dealing as it does with Sunday laws. It addresses the subject from the standpoint of the Free Exercise Clause. It concerned a group of Orthodox Jewish businessmen who challenged the Pennsylvania Sunday closing law as interfering with their free exercise of religion by imposing serious economic disadvantages on them. Chief Justice Warren wrote the Court's opinion upholding the state statute. Justice Stewart in dissent wrote: "I think the impact of this law upon these appellants grossly violates their constitutional right to the free exercise of their religion."

MR. CHIEF JUSTICE WARREN ANNOUNCED THE JUDGMENT OF THE COURT AND AN OPINION IN WHICH MR. JUSTICE BLACK, MR. JUSTICE CLARK, AND MR. JUSTICE WHITTAKER CONCUR.

This case concerns the constitutional validity of the application to appellants of the Pennsylvania criminal statute, enacted in 1959, which proscribes the Sunday retail sale of certain enumerated commodities. Among the questions presented are whether the statute is a law respecting an establishment of religion and whether the statute violates equal protection. Since both of these questions, in reference to this very statute, have already been answered in the negative, *Two Guys from Harrison-Allentown, Inc.,* and since appellants present nothing new regarding them, they need not be considered here. Thus, the only question for consideration is whether the statute interferes with the free exercise of appellants' religion.

Appellants are merchants in Philadelphia who engage in the retail sale of clothing and home furnishings within the proscription of the statute in issue. Each of the appellants is a member of the Orthodox Jewish faith, which requires the closing of their places of business and a total abstention from all manner of work from nightfall each Friday until nightfall each Saturday. They instituted a suit in the court below seeking a permanent injunction against the enforcement of the 1959 statute. Their complaint, as amended, alleged that appellants had previously kept their places of business open on Sunday; that each of appellants had done a substantial amount of business on Sunday, compensating somewhat for their closing on Saturday; that Sunday closing will result in impairing the ability of all appellants to earn a livelihood and will render appellant Braunfeld unable to continue in his business, thereby losing his capital investment; that the statute is unconstitutional for the reasons stated above.

A three-judge court was properly convened and it dismissed the complaint on the authority of the *Two Guys from Harrison* case. On appeal we noted probable jurisdiction.

Appellants contend that the enforcement against them of the Pennsylvania statute will prohibit the free exercise of their religion because, due to the statute's compulsion to close on Sunday, appellants will suffer substantial economic loss, to the benefit of their non-Sabbatarian competitors, if appellants also continue their Sabbath observance by closing their businesses on Saturday; that this result will either compel appellants to give up their Sabbath observance, a basic tenet of the Orthodox Jewish faith, or will put appellants at a serious economic disadvantage if they continue to adhere to their Sabbath. Appellants also assert that the statute will operate so as to hinder the Orthodox Jewish faith in gaining new adherents. And the corollary to these arguments is that if the free exercise of appellants' religion is impeded, that religion is being subjected to discriminatory treatment by the State.

In *McGowan* we noted the significance that this Court has attributed to the development of religious freedom in Virginia in determining the scope of the First Amendment's protection. We observed that when Virginia passed its Declaration of Rights in 1776, providing that "all men are equally entitled to the free exercise of religion," Virginia repealed its laws which in any way penalized "maintaining any opinions in matters of religion, forbearing to repair to church, or the exercising any mode of worship whatsoever." But Virginia retained its laws prohibiting Sunday labor.

We also took cognizance, in *McGowan,* of the evolution of Sunday Closing Laws from wholly religious sanctions to legislation concerned with the establishment of a day of community tranquility, respite and recreation, a day when the atmosphere is one of calm and relaxation rather than one of commercialism, as it is during the other six days of the week. We reviewed the still growing state preoccupation with improving the health, safety, morals and general well-being of our citizens.

Concededly, appellants and all other persons who wish to work on Sunday will be burdened economically by the State's day of rest mandate; and appellants point out that their religion requires them to refrain from work on Saturday as well. Our inquiry then is whether, in these circumstances, the First and Fourteenth Amendments forbid application of the Sunday Closing Law to appellants.

Certain aspects of religious exercise cannot, in any way, be restricted or burdened by either federal or state legislation. Compulsion by law of the acceptance of any creed or the practice of any form of worship is strictly forbidden. The freedom to hold religious beliefs and opinions is absolute. Thus, in *Barnette,* this Court held that state action compelling school children to salute the flag, on pain of expulsion from public school, was contrary to the First and Fourteenth Amendments when applied to those students whose religious beliefs forbade saluting a flag. But this is not the case at bar; the statute before us does not make criminal the holding of any religious belief or opinion, nor does it force anyone to embrace any religious belief or to say or believe anything in conflict with his religious tenets.

However, the freedom to act, even when the action is in accord with one's religious convictions, is not totally free from legislative restrictions. As pointed out in *Reynolds,* legislative power over mere opinion is forbidden but it may reach people's actions when they are found to be in violation of important social duties or subversive of good order, even when the actions are demanded by one's religion.

And, in the *Barnette* case, the Court was careful to point out that "The freedom asserted by these appellees does not bring them into collision with rights asserted by any other individual. It is such conflicts which most frequently require intervention of the State to determine where the rights of one end and those of another begin. . . . It is . . . to be noted that the compulsory flag salute and pledge requires *affirmation of a belief* and an *attitude of mind.*" (Emphasis added.)

Thus, in *Reynolds,* this Court upheld the polygamy conviction of a member of the Mormon faith despite the fact that an accepted doctrine of his church then imposed upon its male members the *duty* to practice polygamy. And, in *Prince* v. *Massachusetts,* this Court upheld a statute making it a crime for a girl under eighteen years of age to sell any newspapers, periodicals or merchandise in public places despite the fact that a child of the Jehovah's Witnesses faith believed that it was her religious *duty* to perform this work.

It is to be noted that, in the two cases just mentioned, the religious practices themselves conflicted with the public interest. In such cases, to make accommodation between the religious action and an exercise of state authority is a particularly delicate task, because resolution in favor of the State results in the choice to the individual of either abandoning his religious principle or facing criminal prosecution.

But, again, this is not the case before us because the statute at bar does not make unlawful any religious practices of appellants; the Sunday law simply regulates a secular activity and, as applied to appellants, operates so as to make the practice of their religious beliefs more expensive. Furthermore, the law's effect does not inconvenience all members of the Orthodox Jewish faith but only those who believe it necessary to work on Sunday. And even these are not faced with as serious a choice as forsaking their religious practices or subjecting themselves to criminal prosecution. Fully recognizing that the alternatives open to appellants and others similarly situated—retaining their present occupations and incurring economic disadvantage or engaging in some other commercial activity which does not call for either Saturday or Sunday labor—may well result in some financial sacrifice in order to observe their religious beliefs, still the option is wholly different than when the legislation attempts to make a religious practice itself unlawful.

To strike down, without the most critical scrutiny, legislation which imposes only an indirect burden on the exercise of religion, *i.e.*, legislation which does not make unlawful the religious practice itself, would radically restrict the operating latitude of the legislature. Statutes which tax income and limit the amount which may be deducted for religious contributions impose an indirect economic burden on the observance of the religion of the citizen whose religion requires him to donate a greater amount to his church; statutes which require the courts to be closed on Saturday and Sunday impose a similar indirect burden on the observance of the religion of the trial lawyer whose religion requires him to rest on a weekday. The list of legislation of this nature is nearly limitless.

Needless to say, when entering the area of religious freedom, we must be fully cognizant of the particular protection that the Constitution has accorded it. Abhorrence of religious persecution and intolerance is a basic part of our heritage. But we are a cosmopolitan nation made up of people of almost every conceivable religious preference. These denominations number almost three hundred. Consequently, it cannot be expected, much less required, that legislators enact no law regulating conduct that may in some way result in an economic disadvantage to some religous sects and not to others because of the special practices of the various religions. We do not believe that such an effect is an absolute test for determining whether the legislation violates the freedom of religion protected by the First Amendment.

Of course, to hold unassailable all legislation regulating conduct which imposes solely an indirect burden on the observance of religion would be a gross oversimplification. If the purpose or effect of a law is to impede the observance of one or all religions or is to discriminate invidiously between religions, that law is constitutionally invalid even though the burden may be characterized as being only indirect. But if the State regulates conduct by enacting a general law within its power, the purpose and effect of which is to advance the State's secular goals, the statute is valid despite its indirect burden on religious observance unless the State may accomplish its purpose by means which do not impose such a burden.

As we pointed out in *McGowan,* we cannot find a State without power to provide a weekly respite from all labor and, at the same time, to set one day of the week apart from the others as a day of rest, repose, recreation and tranquility—a day when the hectic tempo of everyday existence ceases and a more pleasant atmosphere is created, a day which all members of the family and community have the opportunity to spend and enjoy together, a day on which people may visit friends and relatives who are not available during working days, a day when the weekly laborer may best regenerate himself. This is particularly true in this day and age of increasing state concern with public welfare legislation.

Also, in *McGowan,* we examined several suggested alternative means by which it was argued that the State might accomplish its secular goals without even remotely or incidentally affecting religious freedom. We found there that a State might well find that those alternatives would not accomplish bringing about a general day of rest. We need not examine them again here.

However, appellants advance yet another means at the State's disposal which they would find unobjectionable. They contend that the State should cut an exception from the Sunday labor proscription for those people who, because of religious conviction, observe a day of rest other than Sunday. By such regulation, appellants contend, the economic disadvantages imposed by the present system would be removed and the State's interest in having all people rest one day would be satisfied.

A number of States provide such an exemption, and this may well be the wiser solution to the problem. But our concern is not with the wisdom of legislation but with its constitutional limitation. Thus, reason and experience teach that to permit the exemption might well undermine the State's goal of providing a day that, as best possible, eliminates the atmosphere of commercial noise and activity. Although not dispositive of the issue, enforcement problems would be more difficult since there would be two or more days to police rather than one and it would be more difficult to observe whether violations were occurring.

Additional problems might also be presented by a regulation of this sort. To allow only people who rest on a day other than Sunday to keep their businesses open on that day might well provide these people with an economic advantage over their competitors who must remain closed on that day; this might cause the Sunday-observers to complain that their religions are being discriminated against. With this competitive advantage existing, there could well be the temptation for some, in order to keep their businesses open on Sunday, to assert that they have religious convictions which compel them to close their businesses on what had formerly been their least profitable day. This might make necessary a state-conducted inquiry into the sincerity of the individual's religious beliefs, a practice which a State might believe would itself run afoul of the spirit of constitutionally protected religious guarantees. Finally, in order to keep the disruption of the day at a minimum, exempted employers would probably have to hire employees who themselves qualified for the exemption because of their own religious beliefs, a practice which a State might feel to be opposed to its general policy prohibiting religious discrimination in hiring. For all of these reasons, we cannot say that the Pennsylvania statute before us is invalid, either on its face or as applied.

Mr. Justice Harlan concurs in the judgment. Mr. Justice Brennan and Mr. Justice Stewart concur in our disposition of appellants' claims under the Establishment Clause and the Equal Protection Clause. Mr. Justice Frankfurter and Mr. Justice Harlan have rejected appellants' claim under the Free Exercise Clause in a separate opinion.

Accordingly, the decision is affirmed.

MR. JUSTICE BRENNAN, CONCURRING AND DISSENTING.

I agree with the Chief Justice that there is no merit in appellants' establishment and equal-protection claims. I dissent, however, as to the claim that Pennsylvania has prohibited the free exercise of appellants' religion.

The Court has demonstrated the public need for a weekly surcease from worldly labor, and set forth the considerations of convenience which have led the Commonwealth of Pennsylvania to fix Sunday as the time for that respite. I would approach this case differently, from the point of view of the individuals whose liberty is—concededly—curtailed by these enactments. For the values of the First Amendment, as embodied in the Fourteenth, look primarily towards the preservation of personal liberty, rather than towards the fulfillment of collective goals.

The appellants are small retail merchants, faithful practitioners of the Orthodox Jewish faith. They allege—and the allegation must be taken as true, since the case comes to us on a motion to dismiss the complaint—that " . . . one who does not observe the Sabbath [by refraining from labor] . . . cannot be an Orthodox Jew." In appellants' business area Friday night and Saturday are busy times; yet appellants, true to their faith, close during the Jewish Sabbath, and make up some, but not all, of the business thus lost by opening on Sunday. "Each of the plaintiffs," the complaint continues, "does a substantial amount of business on Sundays, and the ability of the plaintiffs to earn a livelihood will be greatly impaired by closing their business establishment on Sundays." Consequences even more drastic are alleged. "Plaintiff, Abraham Braunfeld, will be unable to continue in his business if he may not stay open on Sunday and he will thereby lose his capital investment." In other words, the issue in this case—and we do not understand either appellees or the Court to contend otherwise—is whether a State may put an individual to a choice between his business and his religion. The Court today holds that it may. But I dissent, believing that such a law prohibits the free exercise of religion.

The first question to be resolved, however, is somewhat broader than the facts of this case. That question concerns the appropriate standard of constitutional adjudication in cases in which a statute is assertedly in conflict with the First Amendment, whether that limitation applies of its own force, or as absorbed through the less definite words of the Fourteenth Amendment. The Court in such cases is not confined to the narrow inquiry whether the challenged law is rationally related to some legitimate legislative end. Nor is the case decided by a finding that the State's interest is substantial and important, as well as rationally justifiable. This canon of adjudication was clearly stated by Mr. Justice Jackson, speaking for the Court in *Barnette.*

This exacting standard has been consistently applied by this Court as the test of legislation under all clauses of the First Amendment, not only those specifically dealing with freedom of speech and of the press. For religious freedom—the freedom to believe and to practice strange and, it may be, foreign creeds—has classically been one of the highest values of our society. Even the most concentrated and fully articulated attack on this high standard has seemingly admitted its validity in principle, while deploring some incidental phraseology. The honored place of religious freedom in our constitutional hierarchy, suggested long ago by the argument of counsel in *Permoli* v. *Municipality No. 1 of the City of New Orleans,* and foreshadowed by a prescient footnote in *United States* v. *Carolene Products Co.,* must now be taken to be settled. Or at least so it appeared until today. For in this case the Court seems to say, without so much as a deferential nod towards that high place which we have accorded religious freedom in the past, that any substantial state interest will justify encroachments on religious practice, at least if those encroachments are cloaked in the guise of some nonreligious public purpose.

Admittedly, these laws do not compel overt affirmation of a repugnant belief, as in *Barnette,* nor do they prohibit outright any of appellants' religious practices, as did the federal law upheld in *Reynolds* cited by the Court. That is, the laws do not say that appellants must work on Saturday. But their effect is that appellants may not simultaneously practice their religion and their trade, without being hampered by a substantial competitive disadvantage. Their effect is that no one may at one and the same time be an Orthodox Jew and compete effectively with his Sunday-observing fellow tradesmen. This clog upon the exercise of religion, this state-imposed burden on Orthodox Judaism, has exactly the same economic effect as a tax levied upon the sale of religious literature. And yet, such a tax, when applied in the form of an excise or license fee, was held invalid in *Follett* v. *Town of McCormick.* All this the Court, as I read its opinion, concedes.

What, then, is the compelling state interest which impels the Commonwealth of Pennsylvania to impede appellants' freedom of worship? What overbalancing need is so weighty in the consttutional scale that it justifies this substantial, though indirect, limitation of appellants' freedom? It is not the desire to stamp out a practice deeply abhorred by society, such as polygamy, as in *Reynolds,* for the custom of resting one day a week is universally honored, as the Court has amply shown. Nor is it the State's traditional protection of children, as in *Prince* v. *Massachusetts,* for appellants are reasoning and fully autonomous adults. It is not even the interest in seeing that everyone rests one day a week, for appellants' religion requires that they take such a rest. It is the mere convenience of having everyone rest on the same day. It is to defend this interest that the Court holds that a State need not follow the alternative route of granting an exemption for those who in good faith observe a day of rest other than Sunday.

It is true, I suppose, that the granting of such an exemption would make Sundays a little noisier, and the task of police and prosecutor a little more difficult. It is also true that a majority—21—of the 34 States which have general Sunday regulations have exemptions of this kind. We are not told that those States are significantly noisier, or that their police are significantly more burdened, than Pennsylvania's. Even England, not under the compulsion of a written constitution, but simply influenced by considerations of fairness, has such an exemption for some activities. The Court conjures up several difficulties with such a system which seem to me more fanciful than real. Non-Sunday observers might get an unfair advantage, it is said. A similar contention against the draft exemption for conscientious objectors (another example of the exemption technique) was rejected with the observation that "its unsoundness is too apparent to require" discussion. However widespread the complaint, it is legally baseless, and the State's reliance upon it cannot withstand a First Amendment claim. We are told that an official inquiry into the good faith with which religious beliefs are held might be itself unconstitutional. But this Court indicated otherwise in *United States* v. *Ballard.* Such an inquiry is no more an infringement of religious freedom than the requirement imposed by the Court itself in *McGowan,* decided this day, that a plaintiff show that his good-faith religious beliefs are hampered before he acquires standing to attack a statute under the Free-Exercise Clause of the First Amendment. Finally, I find the Court's mention of a problem under state antidiscrimination statutes almost chimerical. Most such statutes provide that hiring may be made on a religious basis if religion is a *bona fide* occupational qualification. It happens, moreover, that Pennsylvania's statute has such a provision.

In fine, the Court, in my view, has exalted administrative convenience to a constitutional level high enough to justify making one religion economically disadvantageous. The Court would justify this result on the ground that the effect on religion, though substantial, is indirect. The Court forgets, I think, a warning uttered during the congressional discussion of the First Amendment itself: " . . . the rights of conscience are, in their nature, of peculiar delicacy, and will little bear the gentlest touch of governmental hand. . . ."

I would reverse this judgment and remand for a trial of appellants' allegations, limited to the free-exercise-of-religion issue.

MR. JUSTICE STEWART, DISSENTING.

I agree with substantially all that Mr. Justice Brennan has written. Pennsylvania has passed a law which compels an Orthodox Jew to choose between his religious faith and his economic survival. That is a cruel choice. It is a choice which I think no State can constitutionally demand. For me this is not something that can be swept under the rug and forgotten in the interest of enforced Sunday togetherness. I think the impact of this law upon these appellants grossly violates their constitutional right to the free exercise of their religion.

Torcaso v. Watkins, 367 U.S. 488 (1961)

In a simple, long-overdue case, Justice Black wrote the decision of the Court concerning a Maryland citizen denied a notary commission in the state of Maryland because he would not declare his belief in God. Justice Black stated: "This Maryland religious test for public office unconstitutionally invades the appellant's freedom of belief and religion."

MR. JUSTICE BLACK DELIVERED THE OPINION OF THE COURT.

Article 37 of the Declaration of Rights of the Maryland Constitution provides:

> [N]o religious test ought to be required as a qualification for any office of profit or trust in this State, other than a declaration of belief in the existence of God. . . .

The appellant Torcaso was appointed to the office of Notary Public by the Governor of Maryland but was refused a commission to serve because he would not declare his belief in God. He then brought this action in a Maryland Circuit Court to compel issuance of his commission, charging that the State's requirement that he declare this belief violated "the First and Fourteenth Amendments to the Constitution of the United States. . . ." The Circuit Court rejected these federal constitutional contentions, and the highest court of the State, the Court of Appeals, affirmed, holding that the state constitutional provision is self-executing and requires declaration of belief in God as a qualification for office without need for implementing legislation. The case is therefore properly here on appeal.

There is, and can be, no dispute about the purpose or effect of the Maryland Declaration of Rights requirement before us—it sets up a religious test which was designed to and, if valid, does bar every person who refuses to declare a belief in God from holding a public "office of profit or trust" in Maryland. The power and authority of the State of Maryland thus is put on the side of one particular sort of believers—those who are willing to say they believe in "the existence of God." It is true that there is much historical precedent for such laws. Indeed, it was largely to escape religious test oaths and declarations that a great many of the early colonists left Europe and came here hoping to worship in their own way. It soon developed, however, that many of those who had fled to escape religious test oaths turned out to be perfectly willing, when they had the power to do so, to force dissenters from their faith to take test oaths in conformity with that faith. This brought on a host of laws in the new Colonies imposing burdens and disabilities of various kinds upon varied beliefs depending largely upon what group happened to be politically strong enough to legislate in favor of its own beliefs. The effect of all this was the formal or practical "establishment" of particular religious faiths in most of the Colonies, with consequent burdens imposed on the free exercise of the faiths of nonfavored believers.

There were, however, wise and far-seeing men in the Colonies—too many to mention—who spoke out against test oaths and all the philosophy of intolerance behind them. One of these, it so happens, was George Calvert (the first Lord Baltimore), who took a most important part in the original establishment of the Colony of Maryland. He was a Catholic and had, for this reason, felt compelled by his conscience to refuse to take the Oath of Supremacy in England at the cost of resigning from high governmental office. He again refused to take that oath when it was demanded by the Council of the Colony of Virginia, and as a result he was denied settlement in that Colony. A recent historian of the early period of Maryland's life has said that it was Calvert's hope and purpose to establish in Maryland a colonial government free from the religious persecutions he had known—one "securely beyond the reach of oaths. . . . "

When our Constitution was adopted, the desire to put the people "securely beyond the reach" of religious test oaths brought about the inclusion in Article VI of that document of a provision that "no religious Test shall ever be required as a Qualification to any Office or public Trust under the United States." Article VI supports the accuracy of our observation in *Girouard* v. *United States,* that "[t]he test oath is abhorrent to our tradition." Not satisfied, however, with Article VI and other guarantees in the original Constitution, the First Congress proposed and the States very shortly thereafter adopted our Bill of Rights, including the First Amendment. That Amendment broke new constitutional ground in the protection it sought to afford to freedom of religion, speech, press, petition and assembly. Since prior cases in this Court have thoroughly explored and documented the history behind the First Amendment, the reasons for it, and the scope of the religious freedom it protects, we need not cover that ground again. What was said in our prior cases we think controls our decision here.

In *Cantwell* we said:

> The First Amendment declares that Congress shall make no law respecting an establishment of religion or prohibiting the free exercise thereof. The Fourteenth Amendment has rendered the legislatures of the states as incompetent as Congress to enact such laws. . . . Thus the Amendment embraces two concepts,—freedom to believe and freedom to act. The first is absolute but, in the nature of things, the second cannot be.

Later we decided *Everson* and said this:

> The "establishment of religion" clause of the First Amendment means at least this: Neither a state nor the Federal Government can set up a church. Neither can pass laws which aid one religion, aid all religions, or prefer one religion over another. Neither can force nor influence a person to go to or to remain away from church against his will or force him to profess a belief or disbelief in any religion. No person can be punished for entertaining or professing religious beliefs or disbeliefs, for church attendance or non-attendance. No tax in any amount, large or small, can be levied to support any religious activities or institutions, whatever they may be called, or whatever form they may adopt to teach or practice religion. Neither a state nor the Federal Government can, openly or secretly, participate in the affairs of any religious organizations or groups and *vice versa.* In

> the words of Jefferson, the clause against establishment of religion by law was intended to erect "a wall of separation between church and State."

While there were strong dissents in the *Everson* case, they did not challenge the Court's interpretation of the First Amendment's coverage as being too broad, but thought the Court was applying that interpretation too narrowly to the facts of that case. Not long afterward, in *McCollum,* we were urged to repudiate as dicta the above-quoted *Everson* interpretation of the scope of the First Amendment's coverage. We declined to do this, but instead strongly reaffirmed what had been said in *Everson,* calling attention to the fact that both the majority and the minority in *Everson* had agreed on the principles declared in this part of the *Everson* opinion. And a concurring opinion in *McCollum,* written by Mr. Justice Frankfurter and joined by the other *Everson* dissenters, said this:

> We are all agreed that the First and Fourteenth Amendments have a secular reach far more penetrating in the conduct of Government than merely to forbid an "established church." . . . We renew our conviction that "we have staked the very existence of our country on the faith that complete separation between the state and religion is best for the state and best for religion."

The Maryland Court of Appeals thought, and it is argued here, that this Court's later holding and opinion in *Zorach* had in part repudiated the statement in the *Everson* opinion quoted above and previously reaffirmed in *McCollum.* But the Court's opinion in *Zorach* specifically stated: "We follow the *McCollum* case." Nothing decided or written in *Zorach* lends support to the idea that the Court there intended to open up the way for government, state or federal, to restore the historically and constitutionally discredited policy of probing religious beliefs by test oaths or limiting public offices to persons who have, or perhaps more properly profess to have, a belief in some particular kind of religious concept.

We repeat and again reaffirm that neither a State nor Federal Government can constitutionally force a person "to profess a belief or disbelief in any religion." Neither can constitutionally pass laws or impose requirements which aid all religions as against non-believers, and neither can aid those religions based on a belief in the existence of God as against those religions founded on different beliefs.*

In upholding the State's religious test for public office the highest court of Maryland said:

> The petitioner is not compelled to believe or disbelieve, under threat of punishment or other compulsion. True, unless he makes the declaration of belief he cannot hold public office in Maryland, but he is not compelled to hold office.

The fact, however, that a person is not compelled to hold public office cannot possibly be an excuse for barring him from office by state-imposed criteria forbidden by the Constitution. This was settled by our holding in *Wieman* v. *Updegraff.* We there pointed out that whether or not "an abstract right to public employment exists," Congress could not pass a law providing "' . . . that no federal employee shall attend Mass or take any active part in missionary work.'"

This Maryland religious test for public office unconstitutionally invades the appellant's freedom of belief and religion and therefore cannot be enforced against him.

The judgment of the Court of Appeals of Maryland is accordingly reversed and the cause is remanded for further proceedings not inconsistent with this opinion.

Reversed and remanded. Mr. Justice Frankfurter and Mr. Justice Harlan concur in the result.

Sherbert v. Verner, 374 U.S. 398 (1963)

This case concerned a woman in South Carolina denied unemployment benefits because she had failed to accept suitable work when offered. A Seventh-day Adventist, she would not work on Saturday. The Court decision, written by Justice Brennan, invalidated the state law because it abridged appellant's right to free exercise of her religion.

One analyst of the Court suggests that with *Sherbert* "the Court cast substantial doubt on the continued viability of *Braun-*

*Among religions in this country which do not teach what would generally be considered a belief in the existence of God are Buddhism, Taoism, Ethical Culture, Secular Humanism and others.

feld."[1] The Court decision sought to dispel this idea by noting that "the present case is wholly dissimilar to the interests which were found to justify the less direct burden upon religious practices in *Braunfeld.*"

MR. JUSTICE BRENNAN DELIVERED THE OPINION OF THE COURT.

Appellant, a member of the Seventh-day Adventist Church, was discharged by her South Carolina employer because she would not work on Saturday, the Sabbath Day of her faith. When she was unable to obtain other employment because from conscientious scruples she would not take Saturday work, she filed a claim for unemployment compensation benefits under the South Carolina Unemployment Compensation Act. That law provides that, to be eligible for benefits, a claimant must be "able to work and . . . available for work"; and, further, that a claimant is ineligible for benefits "[i]f . . . he has failed, without good cause . . . to accept available suitable work when offered him by the employment office or the employer. . . ." The appellee Employment Security Commission, in administrative proceedings under the statute, found that appellant's restriction upon her availability for Saturday work brought her within the provision disqualifying for benefits insured workers who fail, without good cause, to accept "suitable work when offered . . . by employment office or the employer. . . . " The Commission's finding was sustained by the Court of Common Pleas for Spartanburg County. That court's judgment was in turn affirmed by the South Carolina Supreme Court, which rejected appellant's contention that, as applied to her, the disqualifying provisions of the South Carolina statute abridged her right to the free exercise of her religion secured under the Free Exercise Clause of the First Amendment through the Fourteenth Amendment. The State Supreme Court held specifically that appellant's ineligibility infringed no constitutional liberties because such a construction of the statute "places no restriction upon the appellant's freedom of religion nor does it in any way prevent her in the exercise of her right and freedom to observe her religious beliefs in accordance with the dictates of her conscience." We noted probable jurisdiction of appellant's appeal. We

[1] John W. Baker, "Belief and Action: Limitations on the Free Exercise of Religion," in *Church, State, and Politics*, J. B. Hensel, ed. (Washington, D.C.: The Roscoe Pound–American Trial Lawyers Foundation, 1981).

reverse the judgment of the South Carolina Supreme Court and remand for further proceedings not inconsistent with this opinion.

I

The door of the Free Exercise Clause stands tightly closed against any governmental regulation of religious *beliefs* as such. Government may neither compel affirmation of a repugnant belief, nor penalize or discriminate against individuals or groups because they hold religious views abhorrent to the authorities, nor employ the taxing power to inhibit the dissemination of particular religious views. On the other hand the Court has rejected challenges under the Free Exercise Clause to governmental regulation of certain overt acts prompted by religious beliefs or principles, for "even when the action is in accord with one's religious convictions, [it] is not totally free from legislative restrictions." The conduct or actions so regulated have invariably posed some substantial threat to public safety, peace or order.

Plainly enough, appellant's conscientious objection to Saturday work constitutes no conduct prompted by religious principles of a kind within the reach of state legislation. If, therefore, the decision of the South Carolina Supreme Court is to withstand appellant's constitutional challenge, it must be either because her disqualification as a beneficiary represents no infringement by the State of her constitutional rights of free exercise, or because any incidental burden on the free exercise of appellant's religion may be justified by a "compelling state interest in the regulation of a subject within the State's constitutional power to regulate. . . . "

II

We turn first to the question whether the disqualification for benefits imposes any burden on the free exrecise of appellant's religion. We think it is clear that it does. In a sense the consequences of such a disqualification to religious principles and practices may be only an indirect result of welfare legislation within the State's general competence to enact; it is true that no criminal sanctions directly compel appellant to work a six-day week. But this is only the beginning, not the end, of our inquiry. For "[i]f the purpose or effect of a law is to impede the observance of one or all religions or is to discriminate invidiously between religions, that law is constitutionally invalid even though the burden may be characterized as being only indirect." Here not only is it apparent that appellant's declared ineligibility for benefits derives solely from the practice of her religion, but the pressure upon her to forego that practice is unmistakable. The ruling forces her to choose between following the precepts of her religion and forfeiting benefits, on the one hand, and abandoning one of the precepts of her religion in order to accept work, on the other hand. Governmental imposition of such a choice puts the same kind of burden upon the free exercise of religion as would a fine imposed against appellant for her Saturday worship.

Nor may the South Carolina court's construction of the statute be saved from constitutional infirmity on the ground that unemployment compensation benefits are not appellant's "right" but merely a "privilege." . . . For example, in *Flemming* v. *Nestor,* the Court recognized with respect to Federal Social Security benefits that "[t]he interest of a covered employee under the Act is of sufficient substance to fall within the protection from arbitrary governmental action afforded by the Due Process Clause." In *Speiser* v. *Randall,* we emphasized that conditions upon public benefits cannot be sustained if they so operate, whatever their purpose, as to inhibit or deter the exercise of First Amendment freedoms. We there struck down a condition which limited the availability of a tax exemption to those members of the exempted class who affirmed their loyalty to the state government granting the exemption. While the State was surely under no obligation to afford such an exemption, we held that the imposition of such a condition upon even a gratuitous benefit inevitably deterred or discouraged the exercise of First Amendment rights of expression and thereby threatened to "produce a result which the State could not command directly."

"To deny an exemption to claimants who engage in certain forms of speech is in effect to penalize them for such speech." Likewise, to condition the availability of benefits upon this appellant's willingness to violate a cardinal principle of her religious faith effectively penalizes the free exercise of her constitutional liberties.

Significantly South Carolina expressly saves the Sunday worshipper from having to make the kind of choice which we here hold infringes the Sabbatarian's religious liberty. When in times of "national emergency" the textile plants are authorized by the State Commissioner of Labor to operate on Sunday, "no employee shall be required to work on Sunday . . . who is conscientiously opposed to Sunday work; and if any employee should refuse to work on Sunday on account of conscientious . . . objections he or she shall not jeopardize his or her seniority by such refusal or be discriminated against in any other manner." No question of the disqualification of a Sunday worshipper for benefits is likely to arise, since we cannot suppose that an employer will discharge him in violation of this statute. The unconstitutionality of the disqualification of the Sabbatarian is thus compounded by the religious discrimination which South Carolina's general statutory scheme necessarily effects.

III

We must next consider whether some compelling state interest enforced in the eligibility provisions of the South Carolina statute justifies the substantial infringement of appellant's First Amendment right. It is basic that no showing merely of a rational relationship to some colorable state interest would suffice; in this highly sensitive constitutional area, "[o]nly the gravest abuses, endangering paramount interests, give occasion for permissible limitation." No such abuse or danger has been advanced in the present case. The appellees suggest no more than a possibility that the filing of fraudulent claims by unscrupulous claimants feigning religious objections to Saturday work might not only dilute the unemployment compensation fund but also hinder the scheduling by employers of necessary Saturday work. But that possibility is not apposite here because no such objection appears to have been made before the South Carolina Supreme Court, and we are unwilling to assess the importance of an asserted state interest without the views of the state court. Nor, if the contention had been made below, would the record appear to sustain it; there is no proof whatever to warrant such fears of malingering or deceit as those which the respondents now advance. Even if consideration of such evidence is not foreclosed by the prohibition against judicial inquiry into the truth or falsity of religious beliefs—a question as to which we intimate no view since it is not before us—it is highly doubtful whether such evidence would be sufficient to warrant a substantial infringement of religious liberties. For even if the possibility of spurious claims did threaten to dilute the fund and disrupt the scheduling of work, it would plainly be incumbent upon the appellees to demonstrate that no alternative forms of regulation would combat such abuses without infringing First Amendment rights.

In these respects, then, the state interest asserted in the present case is wholly dissimilar to the interests which were found to justify the less direct burden upon religious practices in *Braunfeld.* The Court recognized that the Sunday closing law which that decision sustained undoubtedly served "to make the practice of [the Orthodox Jewish merchants'] . . . religious beliefs more expensive." But the statute was nevertheless saved by a countervailing factor which finds no equivalent in the instant case—a strong state interest in providing one uniform day of rest for all workers. That secular objective could be achieved, the Court found, only by declaring Sunday to be that day of rest. Requiring exemptions for Sabbatarians, while theoretically possible, appeared to present an administrative problem of such magnitude, or to afford the exempted class so great a competitive advantage, that such a requirement would have rendered the entire statutory scheme unworkable. In the present case no such justifications underlie the determination of the state court that appellant's religion makes her ineligible to receive benefits.

IV

In holding as we do, plainly we are not fostering the "establishment" of the Seventh-day Adventist religion in South Carolina, for the extension of unemployment benefits to Sabbatarians in common with Sunday worshippers reflects nothing more than the governmental obligation of neutrality in the face of religious differences, and does not represent that involvement of religious with secular institutions which it is the object of the Establishment Clause to forestall. Nor does the recognition of the appellant's right to unemployment benefits under the state statute serve to abridge any other person's religious liberties. Nor do we, by our decision today, declare the existence of a constitutional right to unemployment benefits on the part of all persons whose religious convictions are the cause of their unemployment. This is not a case in which an employee's religious convictions serve to make him a nonproductive member of society. Finally, nothing we say today constrains the States to adopt any particular form or scheme of unemployment compensation. Our holding today is only that South Carolina may not constitutionally apply the eligibility provisions so as to constrain a worker to abandon his religious convictions respecting the day of rest. This holding but reaffirms a principle that we announced a decade and a half ago, namely that no State may "exclude individual Catholics, Lutherans, Mohammedans, Baptists, Jews, Methodists, Non-believers, Presbyterians, or the members of any other faith, *because of their faith, or lack of it,* from receiving the benefits of public welfare legislation."

In view of the result we have reached under the First and Fourteenth Amendments' guarantee of free exercise of religion, we have no occasion to consider appellant's claim that the denial of benefits also deprived her of the equal protection of the laws in violation of the Fourteenth Amendment.

The judgment of the South Carolina Supreme Court is reversed and the case is remanded for further proceedings not inconsistent with this opinion.

It is so ordered.

MR. JUSTICE HARLAN, WHOM MR. JUSTICE WHITE JOINS, DISSENTING.

Today's decision is disturbing both in its rejection of existing precedent and in its implications for the future. The significance of the decision can best be understood after an examination of the state law applied in this case.

South Carolina's Unemployment Compensation Law was enacted in 1936 in response to the grave social and economic problems that arose during the depression of that period. As stated in the statute itself:

> Economic insecurity due to unemployment is a serious menace to health, morals and welfare of the people of this State; *involuntary unemployment* is therefore a subject of general interest and concern . . .; the achievement of social security requires protection against this greatest hazard of our economic life; this can be provided by encouraging the employers *to provide more stable employment and by the systematic accumulation of funds during periods of employment to provide benefits for periods of unemployment,* thus maintaining purchasing power and limiting the serious social consequences of poor relief assistance. (Emphasis added.)

Thus the purpose of the legislature was to tide people over, and to avoid social and economic chaos, during periods when *work was unavailable.* But at the same time there was clearly no intent to provide relief for those who for purely personal reasons were or became *unavailable for work.* In accordance with this design, the legislature provided that "[a]n unemployed insured worker shall be eligible to receive benefits with respect to any week *only* if the Commission finds that . . . [h]e is able to work and is available for work. . . . "

The South Carolina Supreme Court has uniformly applied this law in conformity with its clearly expressed purpose. It has consistently held that one is not "available for work" if his unemployment has resulted not from the inability of industry to provide a job but rather from personal circumstances, no matter how compelling. The reference to "involuntary unemployment" in the legislative statement of policy, whatever a sociologist, philosopher, or theologian might say, has been interpreted not to embrace such personal circumstances.

In the present case all that the state court has done is to apply these accepted principles. Since virtually all of the mills in the Spartanburg area were operating on a six-day week, the appellant was "unavailable for work," and thus ineligible for benefits, when personal considerations prevented her from accepting employment on a full-time basis in the industry and locality in which she had worked. The fact that these personal considerations sprang from her religious convictions was wholly without relevance to the state court's application of the law. Thus in no proper sense can it be said that the State discriminated against the appellant on the basis of her religious beliefs or that she was denied benefits *because* she was a Seventh-day Adventist. She was denied benefits just as any other claimant would be denied benefits who was not "available for work" for personal reasons.

With this background, this Court's decision comes into clearer focus. What the Court is holding is that if the State chooses to condition unemployment compensation on the applicant's availability for work, it is constitutionally compelled to *carve out an exception*—and to provide benefits—for those whose unavailability is due to their religious convictions. Such a holding has particular significance in two respects.

First, despite the Court's protestations to the contrary, the decision necessarily overrules *Braunfeld,* which held that it did not offend the "Free Exercise" Clause of the Constitution for a State to forbid a Sabbatarian to do business on Sunday. The secular purpose of the statute before us today is even clearer than that involved in *Braunfeld.* And just as in *Braunfeld*—where exceptions to the Sunday closing laws for Sabbatarians would have been inconsistent with the purpose to achieve a uniform day of rest and would have required case-by-case inquiry into religious beliefs—so here, an exception to the rules of eligibility based on religious convictions would necessitate judicial examination of those convictions and would be at odds with the limited purpose of the statute to smooth out the economy during periods of industrial instability. Finally, the indirect financial burden of the present law is far less than that involved in *Braunfeld.* Forcing a store owner to close his business on Sunday may well have the effect of depriving him of a satisfactory livelihood if his religious convictions require him to close on Saturday as well. Here we are dealing only with temporary benefits, amounting to a fraction of regular weekly wages and running for not more than 22 weeks. Clearly, any differences between this case and *Braunfeld* cut against the present appellant.

Second, the implications of the present decision are far more troublesome than its apparently narrow dimensions would indicate at first glance. The meaning of today's holding, as already noted, is that the State must furnish unemployment benefits to one who is unavailable for work if the unavailability stems from the exercise of religious convictions. The State, in other words, must *single out* for financial assistance those whose behavior is religiously motivated, even though it denies such assistance to others whose identical behavior (in this case, inability to work on Saturdays) is not religiously motivated.

It has been suggested that such singling out of religious conduct for special treatment may violate the constitutional limitations on state action. My own view, however, is that at least under the circumstances of this case it would be a permissible accommodation of religion for the State, if it *chose* to do so, to create an exception to its eligibility requirements for persons like the appellant. The constitutional obligation of "neutrality" is not so narrow a channel that the slightest deviation from an absolutely straight course leads to condemnation. There are too many instances in which no such course can be charted, too many areas in which the pervasive activities of the State justify some special provision for religion to prevent it from being submerged by an all-embracing secularism. The State violates its obligation of neutrality when, for example, it mandates a daily religious exercise in its public schools, with all the attendant pressures on the school children that such an exercise entails. But there is, I believe, enough flexibility in the Constitution to permit a legislative judgment accommodating an unemployment compensation law to the exercise of religious beliefs such as appellant's.

For very much the same reasons, however, I cannot subscribe to the conclusion that the State is constitutionally *compelled* to carve out an exception to its general rule of eligibility in the present case. Those situations in which the Constitution may require special treatment on account of religion are, in my view, few and far between, and this view is amply supported by the course of constitutional litigation in this area. Such compulsion in the present case is particularly inappropriate in light of the indirect, remote, and insubstantial effect of the decision below on the exercise of appellant's religion and in light of the direct financial assistance to religion that today's decision requires.

For these reasons I respectfully dissent from the opinion and judgment of the Court.

Wisconsin v. Yoder, 406 U.S. 205 (1972)

This case deals with the limitation of the state's power to compel children to attend school. Members of an Amish community in Wisconsin declined to send their children to public or private school after the eighth grade because they believed high school attendance to be contrary to their religion. Chief Justice Burger, in his opinion for the Court, affirmed that "only those interests of the highest order and those not otherwise served can overbalance legitimate claims to the free exercise of religion." Thus the Court found in favor of the Amish and determined that the compulsory attendance law violated rights under the Free Exercise Clause.

Since 1972 there has been little work for the Court in free exercise cases. Numerous opinions point to the fact that the Court does not insist upon theism as a basis for protection under the clause. In *United States v. Seeger* (1965). the Court held that any sincere belief that occupies in the life of the believer a place parallel to that held by God for orthodox believers qualifies the person for exemption under a conscientious objector law. Later, in *Torcaso,* the Court affirmed that the state cannot "aid those religions based on a belief in the existence of God as against those religions founded on different beliefs."

In the 1985–1986 Court term, two cases were decided that had free exercise implications. In *Goldman v. Weinberger* the Court rejected a challenge by an Air Force psychologist, an Orthodox Jew and ordained rabbi, to a service regulation that prohibited his wearing a yarmulke while performing his medical duties. In *Bowen v. Roy* the Court determined that free exercise is not offended by requiring a child to accept a Social Security number in order to receive food stamps, even though the parents believe the acceptance of such a number diminishes her religious spirit.

MR. CHIEF JUSTICE BURGER DELIVERED THE OPINION OF THE COURT.

On petition of the State of Wisconsin, we granted the writ of certiorari in this case to review a decision of the Wisconsin Supreme Court holding that respondents' convictions of violating the State's compulsory school-attendance law were invalid under the Free Exercise Clause of the First Amendment to the United States Constitution made applicable to the States by the Fourteenth Amendment. For the reasons hereafter stated we affirm the judgment of the Supreme Court of Wisconsin.

Respondents Jonas Yoder and Wallace Miller are members of the Old Order Amish religion, and respondent Adin Yutzy is a member of the Conservative Amish Mennonite Church. They and their families are residents of Green County, Wisconsin. Wisconsin's compulsory school-attendance law required them to cause their children to attend public or private school until reaching age 16 but the respondents declined to send their children, ages 14 and 15, to public school after they completed the eighth grade. The children were not enrolled in any private school, or within any recognized exception to the compulsory-attendance law, and they are conceded to be subject to the Wisconsin statute.

On complaint of the school district administrator for the public schools, respondents were charged, tried, and convicted of violating the compulsory-attendance law in Green County Court and were fined the sum of $5 each. Respondents defended on the ground that the application of the compulsory-attendance law violated their rights under the First and Fourteenth Amendments. The trial testimony showed that respondents believed, in accordance with the tenets of Old Order Amish communities generally, that their children's attendance at high school, public or private, was contrary to the Amish religion and way of life. They believed that by sending their children to high school, they would not only expose themselves to the danger of the censure of the church community, but, as found by the county court, also endanger their own salvation and that of their children. The State stipulated that respondents' religious beliefs were sincere.

In support of their position, respondents presented as expert witnesses scholars on religion and education whose testimony is uncontradicted. They expressed their opinions on the relationship of the Amish belief concerning school attendance to the more general tenets of their religion, and described the impact that compulsory high school attendance could have on the continued survival of Amish communities as they exist in the United States today. The history of the Amish sect was given in some detail, beginning with the Swiss Anabaptists of the 16th century who rejected institutionalized churches and sought to return to the early, simple, Christian life deemphasizing material success, rejecting the competitive spirit, and seeking to insulate themselves from the modern world. As a result of their common heritage, Old Order Amish communities today are characterized by a fundamental belief that salvation requires life in a church community separate and apart from the world and worldly influence. This concept of life, aloof from the world and its values is central to their faith.

A related feature of Old Order Amish communities is their devotion to a life in harmony with nature and the soil, as exemplified by the simple life of the early Christian era that continued in America during much of our early national life. Amish beliefs require members of the community to make their living by farming or closely related activities. Broadly speaking, the Old Order Amish religion pervades and determines the entire mode of life of its adherents. Their conduct is regulated in great detail by the *Ordnung,* or rules, of the church community. Adult baptism, which occurs in late adolescence, is the time at which Amish young people voluntarily undertake heavy obligations, not unlike the Bar Mitzvah of the Jews, to abide by the rules of the church community.

Amish objection to formal education beyond the eighth grade is firmly grounded in these central religious concepts. They object to the high school, and higher education generally, because the values they teach are in marked variance with Amish values and the Amish way of life; they view secondary school education as an impermissible exposure of their children to a "worldly" influence in conflict with their beliefs. The high school tends to emphasize intellectual and scientific accomplishments, self-distinction, competitiveness, worldly success, and social life with other students. Amish society emphasizes informal learning-through-doing; a life of "goodness" rather than a life of intellect; wisdom, rather than technical knowledge; community welfare, rather than competition; and separation from, rather than integration with, contemporary worldly society.

Formal high school education beyond the eighth grade is contrary to Amish beliefs, not only because it places Amish children in an environment hostile to Amish beliefs with increasing emphasis on competition in class work and sports and with pressure to conform to the styles, manners, and ways of the peer group, but also because it takes them away from their community, physically and emotionally, during the crucial and formative adolescent period of life. During this period, the children must acquire Amish attitudes favoring manual work and self-reliance and the specific skills needed to perform the adult role of an Amish farmer or housewife. They must learn to enjoy physical labor. Once a child has learned basic reading, writing, and elementary mathematics, these traits, skills, and attitudes admittedly fall within the category of those best learned through example and "doing" rather than in a classroom. And, at this time in life, the Amish child must also grow in his faith and his relationship to the Amish community if he is to be prepared to accept the heavy obligations imposed by adult baptism. In short, high school attendance with teachers who are not of the Amish faith—and may even be hostile to it—interposes a serious barrier to the integration of the Amish child into the Amish religious community. Dr. John Hostetler, one of the experts on Amish society, testified that the modern high school is not equipped, in curriculum or social environment, to impart the values promoted by Amish society.

The Amish do not object to elementary education through the first eight grades as a general proposition because they agree that their children must have basic skills in the "three R's" in order to read the Bible, to be good farmers and citizens, and to be able to deal with non-Amish people when necessary in the course of daily affairs. They view such a basic education as acceptable because it does not significantly expose their children to worldly values or interfere with their development in the Amish community during the crucial adolescent period. While Amish accept compulsory elementary education generally, wherever possible they have established their own elementary schools in many respects like the small local schools of the past. In the Amish belief higher learning tends to develop values they reject as influences that alienate man from God.

On the basis of such considerations, Dr. Hostetler testified that compulsory high school attendance could not only result in great psychological harm to Amish children, because of the conflicts it would produce, but would also, in his opinion, ultimately result in the destruction of the Old Order Amish church community as it exists in the United States today. The testimony of Dr. Donald A. Erickson, an expert witness on education, also showed that the Amish succeed in preparing their high school age children to be productive members of the Amish community. He described their system of learning through doing the skills directly relevant to their adult roles in the Amish community as "ideal" and perhaps superior to ordinary high school education. The evidence also showed that the Amish have an excellent record as law-abiding and generally self-sufficient members of society.

Although the trial court in its careful findings determined that the Wisconsin compulsory school-attendance law "does interfere with the freedom of the Defendants to act in accordance with their sincere religious belief" it also concluded that the requirement of high school attendance until age 16 was a "reasonable and constitutional" exercise of governmental power, and therefore denied the motion to dismiss the charges. The Wisconsin Circuit Court affirmed the convictions. The Wisconsin Supreme Court, however, sustained respondents' claim under the Free Exercise Clause of the First Amendment and reversed the convictions. A majority of the court was of the opinion that the State had failed to make an adequate showing that its interest in "establishing and maintaining an educational system overrides the defendants' right to the free exercise of their religion."

I

There is no doubt as to the power of a State, having a high responsibility for education of its citizens, to impose reasonable regulations for the control and duration of basic education. Providing public schools ranks at the very apex of the function of a State. Yet even this paramount responsibility was, in *Pierce,* made to yield to the right of parents to provide an equivalent education in a privately operated system. There the Court held that Oregon's statute compelling attendance in a public school from age eight to age 16 unreasonably interfered with the interest of parents in directing the rearing of their offspring, including their education in church-operated schools. As that case suggests, the values of parental direction of the religious upbringing and education of their children in their early and formative years have a high place in our society. Thus, a State's interest in universal education, however highly we rank it, is not totally free from a balancing process when it impinges on fundamental rights and interests, such as those specifically protected by the Free Exercise Clause of the First Amendment, and the traditional interest of parents with respect to the religious upbringing of their children so long as they, in the words of *Pierce,* "prepare [them] for additional obligations."

It follows that in order for Wisconsin to compel school attendance beyond the eighth grade against a claim that such attendance interferes with the practice of a legitimate religious belief, it must appear either that the State does not deny the free exercise of religious belief by its requirement, or that there is a state interest of sufficient magnitude to override the interest claiming protection under the Free Exercise Clause. Long before there was general acknowledgment of the need for universal formal education, the Religion Clauses had specifically and firmly fixed the right to free exercise of religious beliefs, and buttressing this fundamental right was an equally firm, even if less explicit, prohibition against the establishment of any religion by government. The values underlying these two provisions relating to religion have been zealously protected, sometimes even at the expense of other interests of admittedly high social importance. The invalidation of financial aid to parochial schools by government grants for a salary subsidy for teachers is but one example of the extent to which courts have gone in this regard, notwithstanding that such aid programs were legislatively determined to be in the public interest and the service of sound educational policy by States and by Congress.

The essence of all that has been said and written on the subject is that only those interests of the highest order and those not otherwise served can overbalance legitimate claims to the free exercise of religion. We can accept it as settled, therefore, that, however strong the

State's interest, in universal compulsory education, it is by no means absolute to the exclusion or subordination of all other interests.

II

We come then to the quality of the claims of the respondents concerning the alleged encroachment of Wisconsin's compulsory school-attendance statute on their rights and the rights of their children to the free exercise of the religious beliefs they and their forebears have adhered to for almost three centuries. In evaluating those claims we must be careful to determine whether the Amish religious faith and their mode of life are, as they claim, inseparable and interdependent. A way of life, however virtuous and admirable, may not be interposed as a barrier to reasonable state regulation of education if it is based on purely secular considerations; to have the protection of the Religion Clauses, the claims must be rooted in religious belief. Although a determination of what is a "religious" belief or practice entitled to constitutional protection may present a most delicate question, the very concept of ordered liberty precludes allowing every person to make his own standards on matters of conduct in which society as a whole has important interests. Thus, if the Amish asserted their claims because of their subjective evaluation and rejection of the contemporary secular values accepted by the majority, much as Thoreau rejected the social values of his time and isolated himself at Walden Pond, their claims would not rest on a religious basis. Thoreau's choice was philosophical and personal rather than religious, and such belief does not rise to the demands of the Religion Clauses.

Giving no weight to such secular considerations, however, we see that the record in this case abundantly supports the claim that the traditional way of life of the Amish is not merely a matter of personal preference, but one of deep religious conviction, shared by an organized group, and intimately related to daily living. That the Old Order Amish daily life and religious practice stem from their faith is shown by the fact that it is in response to their literal interpretation of the Biblical injunction from the Epistle of Paul to the Romans, "be not conformed to this world. . . . " This command is fundamental to the Amish faith. Moreover, for the Old Order Amish, religion is not simply a matter of theocratic belief. As the expert witnesses explained, the Old Order Amish religion pervades and determines virtually their entire way of life, regulating it with the detail of the Talmudic diet through the strictly enforced rules of the church community.

The record shows that the respondents' religious beliefs and attitude toward life, family, and home have remained constant—perhaps some would say static—in a period of unparalleled progress in human knowledge generally and great changes in education. The respondents freely concede, and indeed assert as an article of faith, that their religious beliefs and what we would today call "life style" have not altered in fundamentals for centuries. Their way of life in a church-oriented community, separated from the outside world and "worldly" influences, their attachment to nature and the soil is a way inherently simple and uncomplicated, albeit difficult to preserve against the pressure to conform. Their rejection of telephones, automobiles, radios, and television, their mode of dress, of speech, their habits of manual work do indeed set them apart from much of contemporary society; these customs are both symbolic and practical.

As the society around the Amish has become more populous, urban, industrialized, and complex, particularly in this century, government regulation of human affairs has correspondingly become more detailed and pervasive. The Amish mode of life has thus come into conflict increasingly with requirements of contemporary society exerting a hydraulic insistence on conformity to majoritarian standards. So long as compulsory education laws were confined to eight grades of elementary basic education imparted in a nearby rural schoolhouse, with a large proportion of students of the Amish faith, the Old Order Amish had little basis to fear that school attendance would expose their children to the worldly influence they reject. But modern compulsory secondary education in rural areas is now largely carried on in a consolidated school, often remote from the student's home and alien to his daily home life. As the record so strongly shows, the values and programs of the modern secondary school are in sharp conflict with the fundamental mode of life mandated by the Amish religion; modern laws requiring compulsory secondary education have accordingly engendered great concern and conflict. The conclusion is inescapable that secondary schooling, by exposing Amish children to worldly influences in terms of attitudes, goals, and values contrary to beliefs, and by substantially interfering with the religious development of the Amish child and his integration into the way of life of the Amish faith community at the crucial adolescent stage of development, contravenes the basic religious tenets and practice of the Amish faith, both as to the parent and the child.

The impact of the compulsory-attendance law on respondents' practice of the Amish religion is not only severe, but inescapable, for the Wisconsin law affirmatively compels them, under threat of criminal sanction, to perform acts undeniably at odds with fundamental tenets of their religious beliefs. Nor is the impact of the compulsory-attendance law confined to grave interference with important Amish religious tenets from a subjective point of view. It carries with it precisely the kind of objective danger to the free exercise of religion that the First Amendment was designed to prevent. As the record shows, compulsory school attendance to age 16 for Amish children carries with it a very real threat of undermining the Amish community and religious practice as they exist today; they must either abandon belief and be assimilated into society at large, or be forced to migrate to some other and more tolerant region.

In sum, the unchallenged testimony of acknowledged experts in education and religious history, almost 300 years of consistent practice, and strong evidence of a sustained faith pervading and regulating respondents' entire mode of life support the claim that enforcement of the State's requirement of compulsory formal education after the eighth grade would gravely endanger if not destroy the free exercise of respondents' religious beliefs.

III

Neither the findings of the trial court nor the Amish claims as to the nature of their faith are challenged in this Court by the State of Wisconsin. Its position is that the State's interest in universal compulsory formal secondary education to age 16 is so great that it is paramount to the undisputed claims of respondents that their mode of preparing their youth for Amish life, after the traditional elementary education, is an essential part of their religious belief and practice. Nor does the State undertake to meet the claim that the Amish mode of life and education is inseparable from and a part of the basic tenets of their religion—indeed, as much a part of their religious belief and practices as baptism, the confessional, or a sabbath may be for others.

Wisconsin concedes that under the Religion Clauses religious beliefs are absolutely free from the State's control, but it argues that "actions," even though religiously grounded, are outside the protection of the First Amendment. But our decisions have rejected the idea that religiously grounded conduct is always outside the protection of the Free Exercise Clause. It is true that activities of individuals, even when religiously based, are often subject to regulation by the States in the exercise of their undoubted power to promote the health, safety, and general welfare, or the Federal Government in the exercise of its delegated powers. But to agree that religiously grounded conduct must often be subject to the broad police power of the State is not to deny that there are areas of conduct protected by the Free Exercise Clause of the First Amendment and thus beyond the power of the State to control, even under regulations of general applicability. This case, therefore, does not become easier because respondents were convicted for their "actions" in refusing to send their children to the public high school; in this context belief and action cannot be neatly confined in logic-tight compartments.

Nor can this case be disposed of on the grounds that Wisconsin's requirement for school attendance to age 16 applied uniformly to all citizens of the State and does not, on its face, discriminate against religions or a particular religion, or that it is motivated by legitimate secular concerns. A regulation neutral on its face may, in its application, nonetheless offend the constitutional requirement for governmental neutrality if it unduly burdens the free exercise of religion. The Court must not ignore the danger that an exception from a general obligation of citizenship on religious grounds may run afoul of the Establishment Clause, but that danger cannot be allowed to prevent any exception no matter how vital it may be to the protection of values promoted by the right of free exercise. By preserving doctrinal flexibility and recognizing the need for a sensible and realistic application of the Religion Clauses

> we have been able to chart a course that preserved the autonomy and freedom of religious bodies while avoiding any semblance of established religion. This is a "tight rope" and one we have successfully traversed.

We turn, then, to the State's broader contention that its interest in its system of compulsory education is so compelling that even the established religious practices of the Amish must give away. Where fundamental claims of religious freedom are at stake, however, we cannot accept such a sweeping claim; despite its admitted validity in the generality of cases, we must searchingly examine the interests that the State seeks to promote by its requirement for compulsory education to age 16, and the impediment to those objectives that would flow from recognizing the claimed Amish exemption.

The State advances two primary arguments in support of its system of compulsory education. It notes, as Thomas Jefferson pointed out early in our history, that some degree of education is necessary to prepare citizens to participate effectively and intelligently in our open political system if we are to preserve freedom and independence. Further, education prepares individuals to be self-reliant and self-sufficient participants in society. We accept these propositions.

However, the evidence adduced by the Amish in this case is persuasively to the effect that an additional one or two years of formal high school for Amish children in place of their long-established program of informal vocational education would do little to serve those interests. Respondents' experts testified at trial, without challenge, that the value of all education must be assessed in terms of its capacity to prepare the child for life. It is one thing to say that compulsory education for a year or two beyond the eighth grade may be necessary when its goal is the preparation of the child for life in modern society as the majority live, but it is quite another if the goal of education be viewed as the preparation of the child for life in the separated agrarian community that is the keystone of the Amish faith.

The State attacks respondents' position as one fostering "ignorance" from which the child must be protected by the State. No one can question the State's duty to protect children from ignorance but this argument does not square with the facts disclosed in the record. Whatever their idiosyncrasies as seen by the majority, this record strongly shows that the Amish community has been a highly successful social unit within our society, even if apart from the conventional "mainstream." Its members are productive and very law-abiding members of society; they reject public welfare in any of its usual modern forms. The Congress itself recognized their self-sufficiency by authorizing exemption of such groups as the Amish from the obligation to pay social security taxes.

It is neither fair nor correct to suggest that the Amish are opposed to education beyond the eighth grade level. What this record shows is that they are opposed to conventional formal education of the type provided by a certified high school because it comes at the child's crucial adolescent period of religious development. Dr. Donald Erickson, for example, testified that their system of learning-by-doing was an "ideal system" of education in terms of preparing Amish children for life as adults in the Amish community, and that "I would be inclined to say they do a better job in this than most of the rest of us do." As he put it, "These people aren't purporting to be learned people, and it seems to me the self-sufficiency of the community is the best evidence I can point to—whatever is being done seems to function well."

We must not forget that in the Middle Ages important values of the civilization of the Western World were preserved by members of religious orders who isolated themselves from all worldly influences against great obstacles. There can be no assumption that today's majority is "right" and the Amish and others like them are "wrong." A way of life that is odd or even erratic but interferes with no rights or interests of others is not to be condemned because it is different.

The State, however, supports its interest in providing an additional one or two years of compulsory high school education to Amish children because of the possibiiity that some such children will choose to leave the Amish community, and that if this occurs they will be ill-equipped for life. The State argues that if Amish children leave their church they should not be in the position of making their way in the world without the education available in the one or two additional years the State requires. However, on this record, that argument is highly speculative. There is no specific evidence of the loss of Amish adherents by attrition, nor is there any showing that upon leaving the Amish community Amish children, with their practical agricultural training and habits of industry and self-reliance, would become burdens on society because of educational shortcoming. Indeed, this argument of the State appears to rest primarily on the State's mistaken assumption, already noted, that the Amish do not provide any education for their children beyond the eighth grade, but allow them to grow in "ignorance." To the contrary, not only do the Amish accept the necessity for formal schooling through the eighth grade level, but continue to provide what has been characterized by the undisputed testimony of expert educators as an "ideal" vocational education for their children in the adolescent years.

There is nothing in this record to suggest that the Amish qualities of reliability, self-reliance, and dedication to work would fail to find ready markets in today's society. Absent some contrary evidence supporting the State's position, we are unwilling to assume that persons possessing such valuable vocational skills and habits are doomed to become burdens on society should they determine to leave the Amish faith, nor is there any basis in the record to warrant a finding that an additional one or two years of formal school education beyond the eighth grade would serve to eliminate any such problem that might exist.

Insofar as the State's claim rests on the view that a brief additional period of formal education is imperative to enable the Amish to participate effectively and intelligently in our democratic process, it must fall. The Amish alternative to formal secondary school education has enabled them to function effectively in their day-to-day life under self-imposed limitations on relations with the world, and to survive and prosper in contemporary society as a separate, sharply identifiable and highly self-sufficient community for more than 200 years in this country. In itself this is strong evidence that they are capable of fulfilling the social and political responsibilities of citizenship without compelled attendance beyond the eighth grade at the price of jeopardizing their free exercise of religious belief. When Thomas Jefferson emphasized the need for education as a bulwark of a free people against tyranny, there is nothing to indicate he had in mind compulsory education through any fixed age beyond a basic education. Indeed, the Amish communities singularly parallel and reflect many of the virtues of Jefferson's ideal of the "sturdy yeoman" who would form the basis of what he considered as the ideal of a democratic society. Even their idiosyncratic separateness exemplifies the diversity we profess to admire and encourage.

The requirement for compulsory education beyond the eighth grade is a relatively recent development in our history. Less than 60 years ago, the educational requirements of almost all of the States were satisfied by completion of the elementary grades, at least where the child was regularly and lawfully employed. The independence and successful social functioning of the Amish community for a period approaching almost three centuries and more than 200 years in this country are strong evidence that there is at best a speculative gain, in terms of meeting the duties of citizenship, from an additional one or two years of compulsory formal education. Against this background it would require a more particularized showing from the State on this point to justify the severe interference with religious freedom such additional compulsory attendance would entail.

We should also note that compulsory education and child labor laws find their historical origin in common humanitarian instincts, and that the age limits of both laws have been coordinated to achieve their related objectives. In the context of this case, such considerations, if anything, support rather than detract from respondents' position. The origins of the requirement for school attendance to age 16, an age falling after the completion of elementary school but before completion of high school, are not entirely clear. But to some extent such laws reflected the movement to prohibit most child labor under age 16 that culminated in the provisions of the Federal Fair Labor Standards Act of 1938. It is true, then, that the 16-year child labor age limit may to some degree derive from a contemporary impression that children should be in school until that age. But at the same time, it cannot be denied that, conversely, the 16-year education limit reflects, in substantial measure, the concern that children under that age not be employed under conditions hazardous to their health, or in work that should be performed by adults.

The requirement of compulsory schooling to age 16 must therefore be viewed as aimed not merely at providing educational opportunities for children, but as an alternative to the equally undesirable consequence of unhealthful child labor displacing adult workers, or, on the other hand, forced idleness. The two kinds of statutes—compulsory school attendance and child labor laws—tend to keep children of certain ages off the labor market and in school; this regimen in turn provides opportunity to prepare for a livelihood of a higher order than that which children could pursue without education and protects their health in adolescence.

In these terms, Wisconsin's interest in compelling the school attendance of Amish children to age 16 emerges as somewhat less substantial than requiring such attendance for children generally. For, while agricultural employment is not totally outside the legitimate concerns of the child labor laws, employment of children under parental guidance and on the family farm from age 14 to age 16 is an ancient tradition that lies at the periphery of the objectives of such laws. There is no intimation that the Amish employment of their children on family farms is in any way deleterious to their health or that Amish parents exploit children at tender years. Any such inference would be contrary to the record before us. Moreover, employment of Amish children on the family farm does not present the undesirable economic aspects of eliminating jobs that might otherwise be held by adults.

IV

Finally, the State, on authority of *Prince* v. *Massachusetts,* argues that a decision exempting Amish children from the State's requirement fails to recognize the substantive right of the Amish child to a secondary education, and fails to give due regard to the power of the State as *parents patriae* to extend the benefit of secondary education to children regardless of the wishes of their parents. Taken at its broadest sweep, the Court's language in *Prince,* might be read to give support to the State's position. However, the Court was not confronted in *Prince* with a situation comparable to that of the Amish as revealed in this record; this is shown by the Court's severe characterization of the evils that it thought the legislature could legitimately associate with child labor, even when performed in the company of an adult. The Court later took great care to confine *Prince* to a narrow scope in *Sherbert* v. *Verner.*

This case, of course, is not one in which any harm to the physical or mental health of the child or to the public safety, peace, order, or welfare has been demonstrated or may be properly inferred. The record is to the contrary, and any reliance on that theory would find no support in the evidence.

Contrary to the suggestion of the dissenting opinion of Mr. Justice Douglas, our holding today in no degree depends on the assertion of the religious interest of the child as contrasted with that of the parents. It is the parents who are subject to prosecution here for failing to cause their children to attend school, and it is their right of free exercise, not that of their children, that must determine Wisconsin's power to impose criminal penalties on the parent. The dissent argues that a child who expresses a desire to attend public high school in conflict with the wishes of his parents should not be prevented from doing so. There is no reason for the Court to consider that point since it is not an issue in the case. The children are not parties to this litigation. The State has at no point tried this case on the theory that respondents were preventing their children from attending school against their expressed desires, and indeed the record is to the contrary. The State's position from the outset has been that it is empowered to apply its compulsory-attendance law to Amish parents in the same manner as to other parents—that is, without regard to the wishes of the child. That is the claim we reject today.

Our holding in no way determines the proper resolution of possible competing interests of parents, children, and the State in an appropriate state court proceeding in which the power of the State is asserted on the theory that Amish parents are preventing their minor children from attending high school despite their expressed desires to the contrary. Recognition of the claim of the State in such a proceeding would, of course, call into question traditional concepts of parental control over the religious upbringing and education of their minor children recognized in this Court's past decisions. It is clear that such an intrusion by a State into family decisions in the area of religious training would give rise to grave questions of religious freedom comparable to those raised here and those presented in *Pierce.* On this record we neither reach nor decide those issues.

The State's argument proceeds without reliance on any actual conflict between the wishes of parents and children. It appears to rest on the potential that exemption of Amish parents from the requirements of the compulsory-education law might allow some parents to act contrary to the best interests of their children by foreclosing their opportunity to make an intelligent choice between the Amish way of life and that of the outside world. The same argument could, of course, be made with respect to all church schools short of college. There is nothing in the record or in the ordinary course of human experience to suggest that non-Amish parents generally consult with children of ages 14–16 if they are placed in a church school of the parents' faith.

Indeed it seems clear that if the State is empowered, as *parens patriae,* to "save" a child from himself or his Amish parents by requiring an additional two years of compulsory formal high school education, the State will in large measure influence, if not determine, the religious future of the child. Even more markedly than in *Prince,* therefore, this case involves the fundamental interest of parents, as contrasted with that of the State, to guide the religious future and education of their children. The history and culture of Western civilization reflect a strong tradition of parental concern for the nurture and upbringing of their children. This primary role of the parents in the upbringing of their children is now established beyond debate as an enduring American tradition. If not the first, perhaps the most significant statements of the Court in this area are found in *Pierce.*

The duty to prepare the child for "additional obligations," referred to by the Court, must be read to include the inculcation of moral standards, religious beliefs, and elements of good citizenship. *Pierce,* of course, recognized that where nothing more than the general interest of the parent in the nurture and education of his children is involved, it is beyond dispute that the State acts "reasonably" and constitutionally in requiring education to age 16 in some public or private school meeting the standards prescribed by the State.

However read, the Court's holding in *Pierce* stands as a charter of the rights of parents to direct the religious upbringing of their children. And, when the interests of parenthood are combined with a free exercise claim of the nature revealed by this record, more than merely a "reasonable relation to some purpose within the competency of the State" is required to sustain the validity of the State's requirement under the First Amendment. To be sure, the power of the parent, even when linked to a free exercise claim, may be subject to limitation under *Prince* if it appears that parental decisions will jeopardize the health or safety of the child, or have a potential for significant social burdens. But in this case, the Amish have introduced persuasive evidence undermining the arguments the State has advanced to support its claims in terms of the welfare of the child and society as a whole. The record strongly indicates that accommodating the religious objections of the Amish by forgoing one, or at most two, additional years of compulsory education will not impair the physical or mental health of the child, or result in an inability to be self-supporting or to discharge the duties and responsibilities of citizenship, or in any other way materially detract from the welfare of society.

In the face of our consistent emphasis on the central values underlying the Religion Clauses in our constitutional scheme of government, we cannot accept a *parens patriae* claim of such all-encompassing scope and with such sweeping potential for broad and unforeseeable application as that urged by the State.

V

For the reasons stated we hold, with the Supreme Court of Wisconsin, that the First and Fourteenth Amendments prevent the State from compelling respondents to cause their children to attend formal high school to age 16. Our disposition of this case, however, in no way alters our recognition of the obvious fact that courts are not school boards or legislatures, and are ill-equipped to determine the "necessity" of discrete aspects of a State's program of compulsory education. This should suggest that courts must move with great circumspection in performing the sensitive and delicate task of weighing a State's legitimate social concern when faced with religious claims for exemption from generally applicable educational requirements. It cannot be overemphasized that we are not dealing with a way of life and mode of education by a group claiming to have recently discovered some "progressive" or more enlightened process for rearing children for modern life.

Aided by a history of three centuries as an identifiable religious sect and a long history as a successful and self-sufficient segment of American society, the Amish in this case have convincingly demonstrated the sincerity of their religious beliefs, the interrelationship of belief with their mode of life, the vital role that belief and daily conduct play in the continued survival of Old Order Amish communities and their religious organization, and the hazards presented by the State's enforcement of a statute generally valid as to others. Beyond this, they have carried the even more difficult burden of demonstrating the adequacy of their alternative mode of continuing informal vocational education in terms of precisely those overall interests that the State advances in support of its program of compulsory high school education. In light of this convincing showing, one that probably few other religious groups or sects could make, and weighing the minimal difference between what the State would require and what the Amish already accept, it was incumbent on the State to show with more particularity how its admittedly strong interest in compulsory education would be adversely affected by granting an exemption to the Amish.

Nothing we hold is intended to undermine the general applicability of the State's compulsory school-attendance statutes or to limit the power of the State to promulgate reasonable standards that, while not impairing the free exercise of religion, provide for continuing agricultural vocational education under parental and church guidance by the Old Order Amish or others similarly situated. The States have had a long history of amicable and effective relationships with church-sponsored schools, and there is no basis for assuming that, in this related context, reasonable standards cannot be established concerning the content of the continuing vocational education of Amish children under parental guidance, provided always that state regulations are not inconsistent with what we have said in this opinion.

Affirmed.

Mr. Justice Powell and Mr. Justice Rehnquist took no part in the consideration or decision of this case.

MR. JUSTICE DOUGLAS, DISSENTING IN PART.

I

I agree with the Court that the religious scruples of the Amish are opposed to the education of their children beyond the grade schools, yet I disagree with the Court's conclusion that the matter is within the dispensation of parents alone. The Court's analysis assumes that the only interests at stake in the case are those of the Amish parents on the one hand, and those of the State on the other. The difficulty with this approach is that, despite the Court's claim, the parents are seeking to vindicate not only their own free exercise claims, but also those of their high-school-age children.

It is argued that the right of the Amish children to religious freedom is not presented by the facts of the case, as the issue before the Court involves only the Amish parents' religious freedom to defy a state criminal statute imposing upon them an affirmative duty to cause their children to attend high school.

First, respondents' motion to dismiss in the trial court expressly asserts, not only the religious liberty of the adults, but also that of the children, as a defense to the prosecutions. It is, of course, beyond question that the parents have standing as defendants in a criminal prosecution to assert the religious interests of their children as a defense. Although the lower courts and a majority of this Court assume an identity of interest between parent and child, it is clear that they have treated the religious interest of the child as a factor in the analysis.

Second, it is essential to reach the question to decide the case, not only because the question was squarely raised in the motion to dismiss, but also because no analysis of religious-liberty claims can take place in a vacuum. If the parents in this case are allowed a religious exemption, the inevitable effect is to impose the parents' notions of religious duty upon their children. Where the child is mature enough to express potentially conflicting desires, it would be an invasion of the child's rights to permit such an imposition without canvassing his views. As in *Prince* v. *Massachusetts,* it is an imposition resulting from this very litigation. As the child has no other effective forum, it is in this litigation that his rights should be considered. And, if an Amish child desires to attend high school, and is mature enough to have that desire respected, the State may well be able to override the parents' religiously motivated objections.

Religion is an individual experience. It is not necessary, nor even appropriate, for every Amish child to express his views on the subject in a prosecution of a single adult. Crucial, however, are the views of the child whose parent is the subject of the suit. Frieda Yoder has in fact testified that her own religious views are opposed to high-school education. I therefore join the judgment of the Court as to respondent Jonas Yoder. But Frieda Yoder's views may not be those of Vernon Yutzy or Barbara Miller. I must dissent, therefore, as to respondents Adin Yutzy and Wallace Miller as their motion to dismiss also raised the question of their children's religious liberty.

II

The issue has never been squarely presented before today. Our opinions are full of talk about the power of the parents over the child's education. And we have in the past analyzed similar conflicts between parent and State with little regard for the views of the child. Recent cases, however, have clearly held that the children themselves have constitutionally protectible interests.

These children are "persons" within the meaning of the Bill of Rights. We have so held over and over again. In *Haley* v. *Ohio,* we extended the protection of the Fourteenth Amendment in a state trial of a 15-year-old boy. In *In re Gault,* we held that "neither the Fourteenth Amendment nor the Bill of Rights is for adults alone." In *In re Winship,* we held that a 12-year-old boy, when charged with an act which would be a crime if committed by an adult, was entitled to procedural safeguards contained in the Sixth Amendment.

In *Tinker* v. *Des Moines School District,* we dealt with 13-year-old, 15-year-old, and 16-year-old students who wore armbands to public schools and were disciplined for doing so. We gave them relief, saying that their First Amendment rights had been abridged.

> Students in school as well as out of school are "persons" under our Constitution. They are possessed of fundamental rights which the State must respect, just as they themselves must respect their obligations to the State.

In *Barnette,* we held that schoolchildren, whose religious beliefs collided with a school rule requiring them to salute the flag, could not be required to do so. While the sanction included expulsion of the students and prosecution of the parents, the vice of the regime was its interference with the child's free exercise of religion. We said: "Here . . . we are dealing with a compulsion of students to declare a belief." In emphasizing the important and delicate task of boards of education we said:

> That they are educating the young for citizenship is reason for scrupulous protection of Constitutional freedoms of the individual, if we are not to strangle the free mind at its source and teach youth to discount important principles of our government as mere platitudes.

On this important and vital matter of education, I think the children should be entitled to be heard. While the parents, absent dissent, normally speak for the entire family, the education of the child is a matter on which the child will often have decided views. He may want to be a pianist or an astronaut or an oceanographer. To do so he will have to break from the Amish tradition.

It is the future of the student, not the future of the parents, that is imperiled by today's decision. If a parent keeps his child out of school beyond the grade school, then the child will be forever barred from entry into the new and amazing world of diversity that we have today. The child may decide that that is the preferred course, or he may rebel. It is the student's judgment, not his parents', that is essential if we are to give full meaning to what we have said about the Bill of Rights and of the right of students to be masters of their own destiny. If he is harnessed to the Amish way of life by those in authority over him and if his education is truncated, his entire life may be stunted and deformed. The child, therefore, should be given an opportunity to be heard before the State gives the exemption which we honor today.

The views of the two children in question were not canvassed by the Wisconsin courts. The matter should be explicitly reserved so that new hearings can be held on remand of the case.

III

I think the emphasis of the Court on the "law and order" record of this Amish group of people is quite irrelevant. A religion is a religion irrespective of what the misdemeanor or felony records of its members might be. I am not at all sure how the Catholics, Episcopalians, the Baptists, Jehovah's Witnesses, the Unitarians, and my own Presbyterians would make out if subjected to such a test. It is, of course, true that if a group or society was organized to perpetuate crime and if that is its motive, we would have rather startling problems akin to those that were raised when some years back a particular sect was challenged here as operating on a fraudulent basis. But no such factors are present here, and the Amish, whether with a high or low criminal record, certainly qualify by all historic standards as a religion within the meaning of the First Amendment.

The Court rightly rejects the notion that actions, even though religiously grounded, are always outside the protection of the Free Exercise Clause of the First Amendment. In so ruling, the Court departs from the teaching of *Reynolds,* where it was said concerning the reach of the Free Exercise Clause of the First Amendment, "Congress was deprived of all legislative power over mere opinion, but was left free to reach actions which were in violation of social duties or subversive of good order." In that case it was conceded that polygamy was a part of the religion of the Mormons. Yet the Court said, "It matters not that his belief [in polygamy] was a part of his professed religion: it was still belief, and belief only."

Action, which the Court deemed to be antisocial, could be punished even though it was grounded on deeply held and sincere religious convictions. What we do today, at least in this respect, opens the way to give organized religion a broader base than it has ever enjoyed; and it even promises that in time *Reynolds* will be overruled.

In another way, however, the Court retreats when in reference to Henry Thoreau it says his "choice was philosophical and personal rather than religious, and such belief does not rise to the demands of the Religion Clauses." That is contrary to what we held in *United States* v. *Seeger,* where we were concerned with the meaning of the words "religious training and belief" in the Selective Service Act, which were the basis of many conscientious objector claims. We said:

> Within that phrase would come all sincere religious beliefs which are based upon a power or being, or upon a faith, to which

> all else is subordinate or upon which all else is ultimately dependent. The test might be stated in these words: A sincere and meaningful belief which occupies in the life of its possessor a place parallel to that filled by the God of those admittedly qualifying for the exemption comes within the statutory definition. This construction avoids imputing to Congress an intent to classify different religious beliefs, exempting some and excluding others, and is in accord with the well-established congressional policy of equal treatment for those whose opposition to service is grounded in their religious tenets.

Welsh v. *United States* was in the same vein, the Court saying:

> In this case, Welsh's conscientious objection to war was undeniably based in part on his perception of world politics. In a letter to his local board, he wrote:
>
> "I can only act according to what I am and what I see. And I see that the military complex wastes both human and material resources, that it fosters disregard for (what I consider a paramount concern) human needs and ends; I see that the means we employ to 'defend' our 'way of life' profoundly change that way of life. I see that in our failure to recognize the political, social, and economic realities of the world, we, *as a nation,* fail our responsibility *as a nation.*"

The essence of Welsh's philosophy, on the basis of which we held he was entitled to an exemption, was in these words:

> "I believe that human life is valuable in and of itself; in its living; therefore I will not injure or kill another human being. This belief (and the corresponding duty to abstain from violence toward another person) is not 'superior to those arising from any human relation.' On the contrary: *it is essential to every human relation.* I cannot, therefore, conscientiously comply with the Government's insistence that I assume duties which I feel are immoral and totally repugnant."

I adhere to these exalted views of "religion" and see no acceptable alternative to them now that we have become a Nation of many religions and sects, representing all of the diversities of the human race.